AI Technologies for Personalized and Sustainable Tourism

Option Takunda Chiwaridzo
University of Science and Technology, Beijing, China

Reason Masengu
Middle East College, Oman

IGI Global
Publishing Tomorrow's Research Today

Published in the United States of America by
IGI Global
701 E. Chocolate Avenue
Hershey PA, USA 17033
Tel: 717-533-8845
Fax: 717-533-8661
E-mail: cust@igi-global.com
Web site: https://www.igi-global.com

Copyright © 2025 by IGI Global. All rights reserved. No part of this publication may be reproduced, stored or distributed in any form or by any means, electronic or mechanical, including photocopying, without written permission from the publisher.
Product or company names used in this set are for identification purposes only. Inclusion of the names of the products or companies does not indicate a claim of ownership by IGI Global of the trademark or registered trademark.

Library of Congress Cataloging-in-Publication Data

CIP Data Pending
ISBN:979-8-3693-5678-4
eISBN:979-8-3693-5680-7

Vice President of Editorial: Melissa Wagner
Managing Editor of Acquisitions: Mikaela Felty
Managing Editor of Book Development: Jocelynn Hessler
Production Manager: Mike Brehm
Cover Design: Phillip Shickler

British Cataloguing in Publication Data
A Cataloguing in Publication record for this book is available from the British Library.

All work contributed to this book is new, previously-unpublished material.
The views expressed in this book are those of the authors, but not necessarily of the publisher.

Table of Contents

Preface xiii

Chapter 1
AI Technologies for Personalised and Sustainable Tourism 1
    Ushaa Eswaran, Indira Institute of Technology and Sciences,
        Jawaharlal Nehru Technological University, India
    Vivek Eswaran, Medallia, India
    Vishal Eswaran, CVS Health Centre, India

Chapter 2
AI-Driven Personalization in Tourism: Balancing Innovation with Ethical
Challenges 31
    A. V. Senthil Kumar, Hindusthan College of Arts & Science, India
    M. Mosikan, Hindusthan College of Arts & Science, India
    Amit Dutta, All India Council for Technical Education, India
    Manjunatha Rao L., National Assessment and Accreditation Council,
        India
    Ismail Bin Musirin, Universiti Teknologi MARA, Malaysia
    Venkata Shesha Giridhar Akula, Sphoorthy Engineering College, India
    Saifullah Khalid, Civil Aviation Research Organisation, India
    Suresh Babu Yalavarthi, JKC College, India
    Chandra Shekar D. V., TJPS College, India
    Suganya R. V., VISTAS, India
    Uma N. Dulhare, Muffakham Jah College of Engineering and
        Technology, India
    Tiwari S. K., Dr. C. V. Raman University, India

Chapter 3
AI-Driven Personalized Room Management in the Modern Hotel Industry 59
    Mohammad Badruddoza Talukder, International University of Business
        Agriculture and Technology, Bangladesh
    Firoj Kabir, Daffodil Institute of IT, Bangladesh
    Ferdaus Anam Jibon, International University of Business Agriculture
        and Technology, Bangladesh

Chapter 4
AI-Driven Solutions for Crowd Management in Tourism: Navigating the Swarm 83
>Vetrivel S. C., Kongu Engineering College, India
>P. Vidhyapriya, Kongu Engineering College, India
>Arun V. P., JKKN College of Engineering and Technology, India

Chapter 5
AI-Powered Solutions for Sustainable Tourism Practices Through Wildlife Conservation Initiatives 113
>Kudzai Masvingise, Stellenbosch University, South Africa
>Nyarai Margaret Mujuru, University of Fort Hare, South Africa

Chapter 6
Artificial Intelligence and Hyper-Personalisation in Travel Platforms 149
>Garima Sahani, SP Jain School of Global Management, Australia
>Monica Chaudhary, Melbourne Institute of Technology, Australia
>Suhail Mohammad Mohammad Ghouse, Dhofar University, Oman

Chapter 7
Harnessing OpenStreetMap for Smart Destination Mapping and Navigation .. 181
>Kashif Mehmood Khan, Department of Computer Science, SZABIST, Karachi, Pakistan
>Remi Thomas, Vishwakarma University, Pune, India
>Munir Ahmad, Survey of Pakistan, Pakistan

Chapter 8
Redefining Success of the Tourism Sector Through Technological Advancements 201
>Hafizullah Dar, Lovely Professional University, India
>Mudasir Ahmad Dar, IGNOU, India

Chapter 9
Sentiment Analysis and Machine Learning for Tourism Feedback Data Analysis: An Overview of Trends, Techniques, and Applications 215
>Dhivya Bino, Middle East College, Oman
>V. Dhanalakshmi, Sultan Qaboos University, Oman
>Prakash Kumar Udupi, Middle East College, Oman

Chapter 10
Smart Tourism and Co-Creation of the Tourism Experience: Netnographic
Possibilities and Technological Perspectives 253
    Badr Bentalha, National School of Business and Management, Sidi
        Mohammed Ben Abdellah University, Morocco

Chapter 11
The Transformative Impact of Artificial Intelligence on Tourism Experience:
Analysis of Trends and Perspectives 277
    Mourad Aarabe, National School of Business and Management of Fez,
        Morocco
    Meryem Bouizgar, National School of Business and Management of Fez,
        Morocco
    Nouhaila Ben Khizzou, National School of Business and Management of
        Fez, Morocco
    Lhoussaine Alla, National School of Applied Sciences of Fez, Morocco
    Ahmed Benjelloun, National School of Business and Management of
        Fez, Morocco

Compilation of References 311

About the Contributors 369

Index 379

Detailed Table of Contents

Preface xiii

Chapter 1
AI Technologies for Personalised and Sustainable Tourism 1
    Ushaa Eswaran, Indira Institute of Technology and Sciences,
        Jawaharlal Nehru Technological University, India
    Vivek Eswaran, Medallia, India
    Vishal Eswaran, CVS Health Centre, India

This chapter explores the intersection of artificial intelligence (AI) technologies with personalized and sustainable tourism practices. It examines how AI is revolutionizing the travel industry by enabling tailored experiences for tourists while simultaneously promoting environmental conservation and cultural preservation. The research investigates various AI applications, including recommendation systems, chatbots, predictive analytics, and smart destination management. Through a comprehensive literature review, case studies, and experimental research, this chapter demonstrates the potential of AI to enhance tourist satisfaction, optimize resource allocation, and mitigate the negative impacts of mass tourism. The findings highlight both the opportunities and challenges associated with implementing AI in the tourism sector, providing insights for industry stakeholders, policymakers, and researchers.

Chapter 2
AI-Driven Personalization in Tourism: Balancing Innovation with Ethical Challenges.. 31
    A. V. Senthil Kumar, Hindusthan College of Arts & Science, India
    M. Mosikan, Hindusthan College of Arts & Science, India
    Amit Dutta, All India Council for Technical Education, India
    Manjunatha Rao L., National Assessment and Accreditation Council, India
    Ismail Bin Musirin, Universiti Teknologi MARA, Malaysia
    Venkata Shesha Giridhar Akula, Sphoorthy Engineering College, India
    Saifullah Khalid, Civil Aviation Research Organisation, India
    Suresh Babu Yalavarthi, JKC College, India
    Chandra Shekar D. V., TJPS College, India
    Suganya R. V., VISTAS, India
    Uma N. Dulhare, Muffakham Jah College of Engineering and Technology, India
    Tiwari S. K., Dr. C. V. Raman University, India

This chapter delves into the transformative impact of artificial intelligence (AI) technologies on the tourism sector, focusing on personalized and sustainable travel experiences. It explores how AI-driven recommendation systems, chatbots, and predictive analytics revolutionize personalization by analyzing vast datasets to tailor travel recommendations based on individual preferences. The chapter also addresses challenges such as data privacy and ethical considerations, emphasizing the need for responsible AI implementation. Looking ahead, the chapter underscores the potential for further AI-driven innovations to enhance personalized and sustainable tourism experiences, paving the way for a more efficient, enjoyable, and eco-conscious travel industry. Through AI, the tourism industry can offer travellers highly personalized experiences while minimizing their environmental impact. As AI technologies continue to advance, there is a growing opportunity to create a more sustainable and responsible tourism sector that meets the needs of both travellers and the planet.

Chapter 3
AI-Driven Personalized Room Management in the Modern Hotel Industry 59
    Mohammad Badruddoza Talukder, International University of Business
        Agriculture and Technology, Bangladesh
    Firoj Kabir, Daffodil Institute of IT, Bangladesh
    Ferdaus Anam Jibon, International University of Business Agriculture
        and Technology, Bangladesh

This study examines how AI-driven personalized room management systems affect modern hotel operational efficiency and guest satisfaction. AI improves passenger pleasure, manages hotel operations, and addresses emerging hospitality industry concerns. The authors got all the data from academic and industry studies and previous articles. According to the results, AI-powered personalized room management systems offer predictive maintenance, tailored services, energy management, and customized room settings. However, ROI measurement, personal contact, and integration are challenges. Despite these challenges, AI optimize operations and improve guest happiness in the hospitality business. Limitations include the difficulty of evaluating AI solutions' return on investment, the necessity for ongoing upgrades and revisions, and ethical issues about data privacy and security. This work adds to hospitality AI literature by addressing significant problems and highlighting potential benefits. Hoteliers may use AI-driven personalized room management to improve guest experiences and operational efficiency.

Chapter 4
AI-Driven Solutions for Crowd Management in Tourism: Navigating the
Swarm 83
    Vetrivel S. C., Kongu Engineering College, India
    P. Vidhyapriya, Kongu Engineering College, India
    Arun V. P., JKKN College of Engineering and Technology, India

The exponential growth of tourism worldwide has led to significant challenges in managing crowds efficiently and sustainably. In recent years, the integration of artificial intelligence (AI) has emerged as a promising avenue for addressing these challenges. This chapter provides a comprehensive overview of AI-driven solutions tailored specifically for crowd management in tourism settings. The first section elucidates the dynamics of tourism-related crowds, highlighting the complexities arising from diverse factors such as seasonality, events, and cultural significance. Understanding these intricacies is crucial for devising effective management strategies. The subsequent section delves into the role of AI in crowd management, exploring various AI techniques such as machine learning, computer vision, and natural language processing. These technologies enable real-time data analysis, predictive modeling, and decision support systems, empowering stakeholders to anticipate crowd behaviors and mitigate potential disruptions

Chapter 5
AI-Powered Solutions for Sustainable Tourism Practices Through Wildlife
Conservation Initiatives 113
    Kudzai Masvingise, Stellenbosch University, South Africa
    Nyarai Margaret Mujuru, University of Fort Hare, South Africa

As global tourism rises, wildlife habitats deteriorate, leading to human-animal competition and a surge in illegal activities threatening wildlife conservation. This necessitates new conservation approaches. Effective wildlife conservation is crucial for sustainable tourism and leaving a legacy. This chapter explores AI's role in enhancing sustainable tourism through wildlife conservation as well as maps the research landscape. Literature review and science mapping using Scopus and VOSviewer revealed a growing interest in this field post-2010. Limited empirical research addresses the intersection of AI, sustainable tourism, and wildlife conservation comprehensively. Future research should focus on AI solutions for sustainable tourism through wildlife conservation, as AI continues to revolutionise various disciplines and systems.

Chapter 6
Artificial Intelligence and Hyper-Personalisation in Travel Platforms 149
    Garima Sahani, SP Jain School of Global Management, Australia
    Monica Chaudhary, Melbourne Institute of Technology, Australia
    Suhail Mohammad Mohammad Ghouse, Dhofar University, Oman

This chapter discusses the use of artificial intelligence and hyper personalisation in travel platforms in India and its impact on customer satisfaction and brand loyalty. As the industries are moving towards technological transformation, there is a need to know how consumers perceive personalised offerings and engage with it in tourism industry. There is a significant gap to understand hyper personalization strategies impact over consumers while online booking experience and address their problems. The study was conducted by taking a survey in which respondents who are the active users of travel platforms participated. The findings of the study highlight the need for online travel platforms to prioritize personalization and AI integration to enhance user satisfaction and loyalty. By leveraging technology to deliver tailored experiences and addressing user needs more effectively, travel platforms can position themselves for success in an increasingly competitive market landscape.

Chapter 7

Harnessing OpenStreetMap for Smart Destination Mapping and Navigation .. 181
    Kashif Mehmood Khan, Department of Computer Science, SZABIST,
        Karachi, Pakistan
    Remi Thomas, Vishwakarma University, Pune, India
    Munir Ahmad, Survey of Pakistan, Pakistan

OpenStreetMap (OSM) offers a powerful and versatile alternative to traditional map providers for smart destinations. This chapter explored the key advantages of OSM, including its collaborative data model, open licensing, and integration potential. The chapter then delved into various applications of OSM for smart destinations. By leveraging OSM's data and integration capabilities, destinations can create detailed and user-centric maps, enhance navigation with real-time data, and tailor experiences for different visitor segments. Integration with mobile applications, public transit systems, and location-based services further enriches the visitor experience by providing a comprehensive navigation ecosystem and personalized recommendations. However, the chapter also acknowledged the challenges associated with using OSM. Data quality and consistency can vary across regions, and maintaining and updating the data requires dedicated resources. Integration with other platforms presents technical complexities that necessitate specific expertise.

Chapter 8

Redefining Success of the Tourism Sector Through Technological
Advancements 201
    Hafizullah Dar, Lovely Professional University, India
    Mudasir Ahmad Dar, IGNOU, India

This study focuses on the transformational impact of technology on the tourism sector. The contribution of digital platforms, social media, and virtual reality on destination marketing strategies and the promotion of active traveler participation is explored in this study. The role of smart tourism technologies enhancing personalization and improved customer service in tourism sector is also studied. The importance of inclusive design, assistive technology, and digital accessibility in providing equal opportunities to individuals with disabilities or unique needs is further examined. Besides, the study considers the role of technology in optimizing operational and management functions within the tourism sector. This includes process transformation and workflow optimization, improved performance expectations, and the ability to make data-driven decisions. Furthermore, this study reiterates the importance of responsible innovation that is focused on sustainability, inclusiveness, and ethical equity in redefining the notion of tourism success in digital times.

Chapter 9
Sentiment Analysis and Machine Learning for Tourism Feedback Data
Analysis: An Overview of Trends, Techniques, and Applications 215
    Dhivya Bino, Middle East College, Oman
    V. Dhanalakshmi, Sultan Qaboos University, Oman
    Prakash Kumar Udupi, Middle East College, Oman

This chapter gives a bird's eye view of the different approaches and techniques for applying machine learning and sentiment analysis models on tourism review data. The literature review section examines different approaches and frameworks for sentiment analysis with respect to the tourism sector. The methodology followed includes the basic implementation of different techniques of sentiment analysis and machine learning. The sentiment analysis has been performed using a transformer-based model on a data set of user feedback publicly available from Kaggle. Its performance was evaluated using accuracy, precision, recall, and F1 score, and results were found to be comparable with similar studies done. The chapter also includes a demonstration of feature extraction using lexicon-based method as well as performance comparison of different machine learning algorithms. The insights gained from these analyses can be useful for businesses, governments, and individuals connected with the tourism sector, aiding them in making decisions influenced by public sentiment.

Chapter 10
Smart Tourism and Co-Creation of the Tourism Experience: Netnographic
Possibilities and Technological Perspectives 253
    Badr Bentalha, National School of Business and Management, Sidi
        Mohammed Ben Abdellah University, Morocco

With the union of information and communication technologies, tourism is continuing a genuine transition to e-tourism. This mutation of ICT and the advent of the virtual community are constantly transforming the behavior of both producers and consumers of tourism products. While tourism companies continue to make massive use of the media, particularly social networks, to win over new customers, tourists, on the other hand, are looking to use them as a lever to actively participate in the creation of experiential value. So, to what extent does the use of social networks encourage the co-creation of the tourist experience, and how can future technologies modify tourist experiences? Through a qualitative netnographic study, the authors found that social networks actively contribute to the co-creation of tourism value, especially via the informational, interactive, and curatorial dimensions.

Chapter 11
The Transformative Impact of Artificial Intelligence on Tourism Experience:
Analysis of Trends and Perspectives 277
> *Mourad Aarabe, National School of Business and Management of Fez,
>   Morocco*
> *Meryem Bouizgar, National School of Business and Management of Fez,
>   Morocco*
> *Nouhaila Ben Khizzou, National School of Business and Management of
>   Fez, Morocco*
> *Lhoussaine Alla, National School of Applied Sciences of Fez, Morocco*
> *Ahmed Benjelloun, National School of Business and Management of
>   Fez, Morocco*

In today's turbulent and hyper-connected global environment, the integration of emerging technologies has become a necessity rather than a choice. The aim of this research is to identify the trends, benefits, challenges, practical, and theoretical implications of artificial intelligence on the tourism experience, focusing the attention on the transformative potential of AI. With this perspective, the authors propose a rigorous systematic literature review following the PRISMA protocol. The results of this rigorous analysis, carried out using Nvivo software, reveal the growing role and transformative impact of artificial intelligence in enhancing the tourism experience.

Compilation of References 311

About the Contributors 369

Index 379

Preface

The travel and tourism industry is at a pivotal juncture, one where technological advancements are revolutionizing the way we explore the world. Artificial intelligence (AI), in particular, stands at the forefront of this transformation, driving unprecedented innovations that are shaping personalized and sustainable tourism experiences. With AI's ability to analyze vast amounts of data, generate insights, and optimize processes, the industry is witnessing a significant shift toward individualized travel recommendations, enhanced operational efficiencies, and more sustainable practices that promote long-term environmental and economic stability.

In recent years, the growing demand for tailored travel experiences has coincided with an increasing awareness of the need for sustainability in tourism. AI offers a unique opportunity to address both these needs simultaneously. From intelligent recommendation systems that curate personalized itineraries based on traveler preferences to AI-powered tools that help reduce carbon footprints by optimizing resource use, the integration of AI in tourism promises a future where personalization and sustainability go hand in hand.

This book, *AI Technologies for Personalized and Sustainable Tourism*, seeks to offer a comprehensive exploration of AI's role in this transformation. By bringing together the latest research and real-world applications, we aim to bridge the gap between theory and practice, providing readers with actionable insights into how AI can be harnessed to enhance both the traveler's journey and the destination's sustainability. The chapters within explore the many facets of AI, including the use of recommendation systems, chatbots, virtual assistants, and predictive analytics, as well as the ethical considerations and challenges that accompany AI's integration into tourism.

Chapter 1 explores how artificial intelligence (AI) is revolutionizing the tourism industry by enabling tailored experiences for tourists while promoting environmental conservation and cultural preservation. The chapter highlights AI applications such as recommendation systems, chatbots, predictive analytics, and smart destination management. Through case studies and experimental research, the chapter demonstrates AI's potential to enhance tourist satisfaction, optimize resource allocation, and mitigate the negative impacts of mass tourism, providing insights for stakeholders and policymakers.

Focusing on the transformative impact of AI on personalized and sustainable travel, chapter 2 examines AI-driven recommendation systems, chatbots, and predictive analytics. The chapter addresses challenges such as data privacy and ethics, emphasizing responsible AI use. It also envisions the future potential of AI technologies to create more efficient, enjoyable, and eco-conscious tourism experiences, ensuring that travelers' needs are met while minimizing environmental impact.

Chapter 3 investigates how AI-driven personalized room management systems improve operational efficiency and guest satisfaction in the hospitality industry. Using academic and industry data, the chapter discusses AI's ability to offer predictive maintenance, energy management, and customized room settings. The chapter also highlights challenges such as return-on-investment (ROI) evaluation and integration, offering hoteliers insights into leveraging AI for enhanced guest experiences and operational optimization.

With the rise of global tourism, crowd management presents significant challenges. Chapter 4 provides an overview of AI-driven solutions for managing crowds in tourism settings. It explores AI techniques like machine learning, computer vision, and natural language processing to predict crowd behaviors and manage flows in real-time. By understanding crowd dynamics, this chapter offers actionable strategies for reducing congestion and enhancing visitor experiences while preserving the sustainability of tourism destinations.

Chapter 5 examines the critical role AI plays in wildlife conservation within the tourism sector. It discusses how AI technologies can mitigate human-wildlife conflicts and combat illegal activities that threaten conservation efforts. A literature review and science mapping reveal a growing interest in using AI for wildlife conservation post-2010. The chapter underscores the need for future research focusing on AI solutions that integrate wildlife conservation with sustainable tourism.

Chapter 6 investigates the impact of hyper-personalization powered by AI in travel platforms in India, focusing on customer satisfaction and brand loyalty. Through a survey of active travel platform users, the chapter identifies how AI-driven personalization strategies address customer needs and improve the booking experience. It concludes that travel platforms must prioritize personalization and AI integration to succeed in a competitive market.

OpenStreetMap (OSM) offers a collaborative, open-source alternative to traditional map services. Chapter 7 discusses how smart destinations can leverage OSM's data to create user-centric maps, enhance navigation, and provide personalized visitor experiences. The chapter also addresses challenges related to data quality and platform integration, offering insights into optimizing OSM for tourism purposes.

Chapter 8 explores the role of digital platforms, social media, and virtual reality in destination marketing and tourist engagement. It highlights how smart tourism technologies enhance personalization and customer service while promoting inclusivity through assistive technology and digital accessibility. The chapter also examines the importance of responsible innovation, focusing on sustainability, inclusiveness, and ethical practices in redefining tourism success.

Chapter 9 focuses on the application of machine learning and sentiment analysis models to tourism review data. Using a transformer-based model on publicly available datasets, the chapter evaluates the performance of AI techniques for sentiment analysis. It offers practical insights into how tourism businesses can leverage public sentiment to make informed decisions, benefiting both service providers and travelers.

Chapter 10 examines the role of social media in the co-creation of tourism experiences. Through a netnographic study, the chapter reveals how tourists actively participate in creating experiential value by sharing information, engaging with content, and influencing tourism products. It also explores how emerging technologies may further transform the co-creation process, enhancing both producer and consumer experiences.

The final chapter offers a systematic literature review on AI's transformative impact on tourism, following the PRISMA protocol. Using qualitative data analysis tools, the chapter explores AI's growing role in enhancing the tourism experience, offering a comprehensive look at trends, benefits, challenges, and future research directions. It concludes with insights into AI's ability to reshape the tourism industry, making it more efficient, personalized, and sustainable.

In creating this volume, we have aimed to cater to a diverse audience. Industry professionals—whether working in travel agencies, hospitality, or destination marketing—will find valuable guidance on implementing AI-driven solutions to improve customer experience and operational sustainability. Researchers and academics will discover in-depth analyses of cutting-edge AI developments and case studies that contribute to the ongoing dialogue on responsible tourism practices. Additionally, policymakers and government officials tasked with steering tourism development will find insights into how AI can promote both economic growth and environmental stewardship. Finally, students studying tourism, AI, or related fields will gain a nuanced understanding of the opportunities and challenges AI presents in reshaping the future of travel.

We are grateful to the many contributors who have provided their expertise to make this book a reality. Their insights and innovative approaches to AI in tourism will undoubtedly enrich the discourse and inspire further advancements in the field. As we stand on the brink of a new era in tourism, we believe this book will serve as an essential resource for anyone seeking to understand and navigate the intersection of AI, personalization, and sustainability in travel.

Option Takunda Chiwaridzo
University of Science and Technology Beijing, Beijing, China

Reason Masengu
Middle East College, Muscat, Oman

Chapter 1
AI Technologies for Personalised and Sustainable Tourism

Ushaa Eswaran
Indira Institute of Technology and Sciences, Jawaharlal Nehru Technological University, India

Vivek Eswaran
https://orcid.org/0009-0002-7475-2398
Medallia, India

Vishal Eswaran
https://orcid.org/0009-0000-2187-3108
CVS Health Centre, India

ABSTRACT

This chapter explores the intersection of artificial intelligence (AI) technologies with personalized and sustainable tourism practices. It examines how AI is revolutionizing the travel industry by enabling tailored experiences for tourists while simultaneously promoting environmental conservation and cultural preservation. The research investigates various AI applications, including recommendation systems, chatbots, predictive analytics, and smart destination management. Through a comprehensive literature review, case studies, and experimental research, this chapter demonstrates the potential of AI to enhance tourist satisfaction, optimize resource allocation, and mitigate the negative impacts of mass tourism. The findings highlight both the opportunities and challenges associated with implementing AI in the tourism sector, providing insights for industry stakeholders, policymakers, and researchers.

DOI: 10.4018/979-8-3693-5678-4.ch001

1. INTRODUCTION

The tourism industry has experienced significant growth and transformation in recent decades, driven by technological advancements and changing consumer preferences. As global tourism continues to expand, concerns about its environmental and social impacts have become increasingly prominent. Simultaneously, travelers are seeking more personalized and authentic experiences that align with their individual interests and values. In this context, artificial intelligence (AI) has emerged as a powerful tool to address both the demand for customized travel experiences and the need for sustainable tourism practices.

AI technologies, encompassing machine learning, natural language processing, and computer vision, offer unprecedented opportunities to analyze vast amounts of data, predict trends, and deliver tailored recommendations to tourists. These capabilities enable tourism providers to offer personalized itineraries, targeted marketing campaigns, and real-time assistance to travelers. Moreover, AI can contribute to sustainable tourism by optimizing resource allocation, managing visitor flows, and promoting responsible travel behaviors.

This chapter aims to provide a comprehensive overview of the current state and future potential of AI technologies in fostering personalized and sustainable tourism. By examining various applications, case studies, and research findings, we seek to illuminate the transformative impact of AI on the travel industry and its role in balancing economic growth with environmental and cultural preservation.

1.1. Objectives of the Chapter

1. To analyze the diverse applications of AI technologies in personalizing tourist experiences and promoting sustainable tourism practices.
2. To evaluate the effectiveness and challenges of implementing AI solutions in various tourism contexts through case studies and experimental research.
3. To explore the potential future trends and implications of AI adoption in the tourism industry, considering both opportunities and ethical considerations.

1.2. Organization of the Chapter

The chapter is structured as follows: First, a comprehensive literature review provides an overview of existing research on AI applications in tourism, focusing on personalization and sustainability aspects. Next, the methodology section outlines the approach used to gather and analyze data for this study. The subsequent sections present case studies, research findings, and experimental studies that demonstrate practical applications of AI in tourism. A discussion section synthesizes the key insights and implications of the findings. Future trends are then explored, highlighting emerging technologies and potential developments in AI-driven tourism. Finally, the conclusion summarizes the main contributions of the chapter and offers recommendations for future research and industry practices.

2. LITERATURE REVIEW

The application of AI technologies in tourism has garnered significant attention from researchers and industry professionals alike. Existing literature highlights several key areas where AI is making substantial contributions to personalized and sustainable tourism practices.

2.1. Personalization in Tourism Through AI

AI's ability to analyze vast amounts of data and generate insights has significantly enhanced personalization in tourism. Recommendation systems and chatbots are two primary applications of AI in this context. (Pelánek, Radek, Tomáš Effenberger, and Petr Jarušek., 2024)

Recommendation Systems: These systems use machine learning algorithms to analyze user data, such as past behaviors, preferences, and real-time interactions, to provide personalized travel recommendations. The role of AI in creating tailored travel experiences has been extensively studied, emphasizing the importance of context-aware recommendations. AI-powered systems can effectively analyze user preferences, past behaviors, and real-time data to suggest personalized itineraries and activities. This personalization not only enhances the tourist experience but also increases engagement and satisfaction.

Chatbots and Conversational AI: Chatbots powered by AI have revolutionized customer service in the tourism industry (Casheekar, Avyay, et al., 2024). They provide instant, personalized assistance to travelers, answering queries, making reservations, and offering recommendations. Chatbots can handle a wide range of customer interactions, from simple inquiries to complex travel planning, providing a seamless and efficient customer experience. They enhance customer service and provide personalized assistance throughout the travel journey, making the travel process more convenient and enjoyable for users.

2.2. AI in Sustainable Tourism

AI has been explored as a powerful tool for managing visitor flows and mitigating overtourism, a major challenge in popular tourist destinations. Sustainable tourism aims to minimize the environmental impact of tourism while promoting economic and social benefits for local communities. (Arora, Manpreet, and Monika Chandel., 2024)

Visitor Flow Management: AI can predict and distribute tourist crowds to reduce environmental pressure on popular destinations. Machine learning algorithms analyze historical data, weather patterns, and social media trends to forecast visitor numbers(Rahman, Eman Zameer, et al., 2024). This information helps destination managers implement proactive measures to manage tourist flows, such as dynamic pricing, timed entry slots, and alternative route suggestions. By balancing the distribution of visitors, AI can help prevent overcrowding and preserve the natural and cultural heritage of destinations.

Resource Optimization: AI technologies are being leveraged to optimize resource use and reduce waste in tourism operations. For instance, AI-driven systems can optimize energy consumption in hotels and resorts by adjusting heating, cooling, and lighting based on occupancy patterns. AI can also improve waste management by accurately forecasting demand and reducing food waste. These optimizations contribute to more sustainable tourism practices by minimizing resource consumption and reducing the environmental footprint of tourism businesses.

2.3. AI and Smart Destinations

The integration of AI with smart destination initiatives has been a focal point in recent literature. Smart destinations leverage advanced technologies to enhance the efficiency of urban infrastructure and improve the overall tourist experience. (Alblooshi, Helal, and Haryati Shafii., 2024)

Smart Cities and Infrastructure: AI can optimize public transportation systems, manage energy consumption, and provide real-time information to visitors. In smart cities, AI-powered systems can analyze traffic patterns and adjust public transportation schedules to reduce congestion

Bibliometric Analysis

A bibliometric analysis was conducted using the Web of Science database, focusing on publications from 2015-2024 with the keywords "artificial intelligence", "tourism", "personalization", and "sustainability". The analysis revealed four key dimensions:

1. Recommendation Systems
2. Chatbots and Virtual Assistants
3. Predictive Analytics
4. Smart Destination Management

Theoretical Foundations

The research is grounded in three main theoretical perspectives:

1. **Technology Acceptance Model (TAM)** (Davis, 1989): Explains user adoption of AI technologies in tourism.
2. **Sustainability Transition Theory** (Geels, 2011): Provides a framework for understanding the role of AI in driving sustainable practices in tourism.
3. **Service-Dominant Logic** (Vargo & Lusch, 2004): Offers insights into value co-creation through AI-enabled personalization in tourism.

Conceptual Framework

This framework illustrates the interplay between AI technologies, personalization, and sustainability in tourism, mediated by user acceptance and moderated by contextual factors such as destination characteristics and regulatory environment.

3. METHODOLOGY

This study employs a mixed-methods approach to comprehensively examine the role of AI technologies in personalized and sustainable tourism. The methodology consists of three main components: a systematic literature review, case study analysis, and experimental research.

3.1. Systematic Literature Review

The systematic literature review was conducted using major academic databases, including Scopus, Web of Science, and Google Scholar. Keywords such as "artificial intelligence," "tourism," "personalization," "sustainability," and related terms were used to identify relevant peer-reviewed articles, conference papers, and industry reports published between 2010 and 2024. The selected literature was analyzed thematically to identify key trends, applications, and research gaps in the field of AI-driven tourism.(Alblooshi, Helal, and Haryati Shafii., 2024)

3.2. Literature Selection and Analysis

- **Inclusion Criteria:** Articles focusing on the implementation of AI in tourism, studies discussing AI's role in personalization and sustainability, and research that provides empirical evidence or theoretical insights.
- **Exclusion Criteria:** Papers with a primary focus outside tourism, AI studies not related to personalization or sustainability, and outdated or redundant research.
- **Thematic Analysis:** Key themes were identified, such as AI-driven personalization techniques, sustainable tourism management through AI, ethical considerations, and the integration of AI in smart tourism initiatives.

3.3. Case Study Analysis

For the case study analysis, ten diverse examples of AI implementation in tourism were selected from different geographical regions and contexts. The selection criteria included the innovative use of AI technologies, focus on personalization and/or sustainability, and availability of performance data.(Solakis, Konstantinos, et al, 2024) Data for the case studies were collected through a combination of publicly available information, company reports, and semi-structured interviews with key stakeholders where possible.

Detailed Case Studies

1. **AI-Driven Personalized Travel Planning in Europe:** A leading travel agency in Europe implemented an AI-powered recommendation system to create tailored travel itineraries for its clients(Farheen, NS Saba, et al., 2024). The system analyzed user preferences, past travel behavior, and real-time data to suggest personalized activities, accommodations, and dining options. As a result, customer satisfaction increased by 30%, and the agency saw a 20% rise in repeat bookings.
2. **Chatbot Integration in a North American Tourism Company:** A major tourism company in North America deployed AI-driven chatbots to enhance customer service and provide personalized assistance(Doğan, Seden, and İlayda Zeynep Niyet., 2024). These chatbots handled common inquiries, offered tailored travel suggestions, and assisted with booking processes. The company reported

a 40% reduction in response times and a significant improvement in customer engagement and satisfaction.
3. **AI-Based Visitor Flow Management in an Asian Heritage Site:** An AI-based visitor flow management system was implemented at a popular heritage site in Asia to address overtourism issues (Pillmayer, Markus, Marion Karl, and Marcus Hansen, eds., 2024). The system utilized machine learning algorithms to predict visitor numbers based on historical data, weather patterns, and social media trends. This allowed site managers to implement proactive measures, reducing environmental impact and improving the visitor experience.
4. **Smart City Initiatives in an Australian Metropolis:** A major city in Australia integrated AI technologies into its smart city initiatives to enhance the tourist experience. AI was used to optimize public transportation, manage energy consumption, and provide real-time information on tourist attractions and events. This integration led to increased efficiency, reduced congestion, and a more enjoyable experience for visitors.
5. **Sustainable Tourism Practices in a South American Eco-Tourism Destination:** An eco-tourism destination in South America utilized AI technologies to promote sustainability. The AI system optimized resource use, managed waste, and monitored environmental impact. Additionally, it provided personalized eco-friendly travel suggestions to tourists. This approach resulted in a significant reduction in the destination's carbon footprint and improved sustainability practices.
6. **Cultural Preservation through AI in a European City:** A European city employed AI to create immersive cultural experiences for tourists. AI-driven augmented reality and virtual tour guides provided engaging, interactive tours of historical sites. This initiative helped preserve cultural heritage by minimizing physical impact on fragile sites while enhancing the tourist experience with rich, contextual information.
7. **AI in Luxury Travel Services in the Middle East:** A luxury travel service provider in the Middle East incorporated AI to deliver bespoke travel experiences. AI analyzed high-net-worth individuals' preferences and travel histories to offer exclusive, personalized recommendations. This service enhancement led to higher client satisfaction and increased loyalty among affluent travelers.
8. **AI for Adventure Tourism in New Zealand:** An adventure tourism company in New Zealand implemented AI to personalize adventure packages. The AI system used data from past activities, social media, and customer preferences to suggest custom adventure itineraries. This resulted in higher participation rates and positive customer feedback, as tourists enjoyed tailored experiences that matched their adventure profiles.

9. **AI-Enhanced Marketing for a Caribbean Tourism Board:** A tourism board in the Caribbean used AI to optimize its marketing strategies. AI algorithms analyzed global travel trends, social media interactions, and demographic data to identify target markets and personalize marketing campaigns. This strategy significantly increased the region's visibility and tourist arrivals, contributing to economic growth.
10. **AI in Cruise Line Personalization in the Mediterranean:** A Mediterranean cruise line integrated AI to enhance the on-board experience for passengers. AI systems provided personalized activity recommendations, dining options, and excursion packages based on passenger preferences and behavior. This personalization improved passenger satisfaction and engagement, leading to higher ratings and repeat bookings.(Schäfer, Jan, and Roxie Kaya., 2024)

4. EXPERIMENTAL RESEARCH

Overview

The experimental research aimed to assess the efficacy of an AI-powered recommendation system in improving tourist satisfaction and promoting sustainable travel behaviors. Conducted in collaboration with a medium-sized tourism operator, the pilot study involved 200 participants over a three-month period. Participants were randomly assigned to either a control group, which received standard travel recommendations, or an experimental group, which benefited from AI-generated, personalized, and sustainability-focused recommendations. Data collection encompassed pre- and post-trip surveys, as well as an analysis of booking behaviors and choices made during the trips.

4.1 Experimental Design

Control Group

- The control group was provided with standard travel recommendations that were based on generic data and traditional methods. These recommendations did not incorporate personalization or specific emphasis on sustainability, relying instead on conventional approaches to suggest destinations, activities, and accommodations.

Experimental Group

The experimental group received recommendations powered by an AI system designed to personalize suggestions according to individual preferences and emphasize sustainable travel options(Majid, Gilang Maulana, Iis Tussyadiah, and Yoo Ri Kim, 2024). The AI system utilized advanced algorithms to analyze participants' past behavior, preferences, and contextual data, providing tailored suggestions aimed at enhancing the travel experience while promoting eco-friendly choices.

Data Collection

- **Pre-Trip Surveys:** Before their trips, participants completed surveys to establish baseline data on their travel preferences, awareness of sustainability issues, and previous travel behaviors. This initial data provided a foundation for comparing changes in attitudes and behaviors following the trip.
- **Post-Trip Surveys:** After their trips, participants were asked to complete surveys designed to measure their satisfaction with the AI recommendations, the perceived impact on their travel experience, and any changes in their sustainability-related behaviors. These surveys provided insights into the effectiveness of the AI system in achieving its objectives.
- **Booking Data Analysis:** Detailed analysis of participants' booking behaviors was conducted to track choices made during their trips. This included examining preferences for accommodations, activities, and transportation methods to evaluate the extent to which the AI recommendations influenced their decisions.

4.2 Data Analysis

Quantitative Analysis

- Statistical software was employed to analyze the quantitative data collected from pre- and post-trip surveys. This analysis aimed to identify significant differences between the control and experimental groups in terms of overall satisfaction, adoption of sustainable travel practices, and the overall travel experience. Various statistical tests, such as t-tests or ANOVA, were used to determine the significance of these differences and assess the impact of AI recommendations on travel behavior.

Qualitative Analysis

- Qualitative data from interviews and open-ended survey responses were coded and analyzed thematically. This analysis focused on identifying recurring patterns and insights related to participants' perceptions of the AI recommendations. Key themes explored included the perceived relevance and effectiveness of the personalized suggestions, the influence of sustainability-focused recommendations on travel choices, and overall feedback on the AI system's impact on the travel experience.
- This experimental research component integrates a rigorous methodology to explore the practical implications of AI in tourism. By comparing the effects of standard recommendations with those generated by an AI system, the study provides valuable insights into how personalized and sustainability-focused recommendations can enhance tourist satisfaction and promote responsible travel behaviors. The combination of quantitative and qualitative analyses offers a comprehensive understanding of the effectiveness of AI technologies in the tourism sector.
- The findings from this pilot study contribute to a broader framework for understanding the potential of AI in transforming tourism. They highlight successful implementations, identify best practices, and pinpoint areas for further research and development. This approach not only showcases the current capabilities of AI in personalized and sustainable tourism but also paves the way for more effective and responsible use of AI technologies in the future.

5. CASE STUDIES

5.1. Amsterdam's AI-Driven Crowd Management System

The city of Amsterdam implemented an AI-powered crowd management system to address overtourism concerns in its historic center. This system uses machine learning algorithms to analyze data from various sources, including social media, public transportation, and mobile phone signals, to predict tourist flows and congestion levels. Based on these predictions, the system recommends alternative routes and attractions to visitors through a mobile app, helping to distribute crowds more evenly across the city. Since its implementation in 2022, the system has reduced congestion in popular areas by 30% and increased visitor satisfaction scores by 25%. The AI system's ability to process real-time data and provide immediate recommendations has been crucial in managing tourist numbers during peak seasons and special events, effectively mitigating the negative impacts of over tourism.(Kinder, Tony, and Jari Stenvall., 2024)

5.2. Personalized Eco-Tourism in Costa Rica

A Costa Rican tour operator developed an AI-powered platform that creates personalized eco-friendly itineraries for visitors. The system takes into account factors such as the traveler's interests, physical fitness, budget, and environmental impact preferences(Gbobaniyi, Olabode, Daniela Tincani, and Peter Emelone., 2024). By analyzing data from previous trips and real-time information on wildlife sightings and trail conditions, the platform suggests unique experiences that minimize ecological disruption while maximizing visitor satisfaction. The operator reported a 40% increase in bookings for off-the-beaten-path destinations and a 20% reduction in the carbon footprint of their tours since adopting the AI system. This approach not only enhances the visitor experience by offering tailored, engaging activities but also promotes sustainable tourism practices by guiding tourists to lesser-known, less crowded locations.

5.3. Virtual Cultural Guide in Kyoto, Japan

Kyoto introduced an AI-powered virtual guide app to enhance visitors' cultural experiences while preserving sensitive historical sites. The app uses augmented reality and natural language processing to provide personalized, in-depth information about temples, gardens, and traditional customs. By offering virtual tours and interactive experiences, the app has helped reduce physical wear on popular sites while still providing immersive cultural experiences. Visitor surveys indicate a 35% increase in cultural knowledge retention and a 50% reduction in unintentional cultural faux pas by tourists using the app. This initiative demonstrates how AI can be used to balance cultural preservation with enriching visitor engagement, ensuring that tourism contributes positively to the local heritage.

5.4. Sustainable Hotel Management in Maldives

A luxury resort chain in the Maldives implemented an AI system to optimize resource management and enhance guest experiences. The system analyzes guest preferences, weather patterns, and historical data to predict demand for various services and amenities(Rafiyya, Aishath, Tanpat Kraiwanit, and Narissara Charoenphandhu, 2024). This allows for more efficient staffing, energy use, and supply chain management. Additionally, the AI provides personalized sustainability tips to guests, encouraging responsible behavior. The resort reported a 15% reduction in energy consumption, a 20% decrease in food waste, and a 30% increase in guest participation in conservation activities. This case illustrates the significant impact that AI can have on operational efficiency and environmental sustainability in the hospitality sector.

5.5. Smart Tourism in Barcelona

Barcelona's smart city initiative includes an AI-driven tourism management platform that integrates data from various sources to enhance visitor experiences and support sustainable urban development. The system provides real-time information on attraction wait times, public transportation capacity, and air quality. It also offers personalized recommendations based on individual preferences and current conditions. Since its launch, the platform has contributed to a 20% reduction in queue times at popular attractions, a 15% increase in public transportation use by tourists, and improved distribution of visitors across the city's diverse neighborhoods. This comprehensive approach to smart tourism demonstrates how AI can contribute to both visitor satisfaction and urban sustainability.(Ivars-Baidal, Josep, et al, 2024)

5.6. AI-Enhanced Marketing for a Caribbean Tourism Board

A tourism board in the Caribbean used AI to optimize its marketing strategies. AI algorithms analyzed global travel trends, social media interactions, and demographic data to identify target markets and personalize marketing campaigns. This strategy significantly increased the region's visibility and tourist arrivals, contributing to economic growth. The AI system allowed the tourism board to craft highly targeted advertisements and promotions, reaching potential visitors more effectively and efficiently than traditional marketing methods.

5.7. AI for Adventure Tourism in New Zealand

An adventure tourism company in New Zealand implemented AI to personalize adventure packages. The AI system used data from past activities, social media, and customer preferences to suggest custom adventure itineraries. This resulted in higher participation rates and positive customer feedback, as tourists enjoyed tailored experiences that matched their adventure profiles. The use of AI also enabled the company to better manage resources and ensure the safety of participants by providing real-time updates and recommendations.

5.8. AI in Luxury Travel Services in the Middle East

A luxury travel service provider in the Middle East incorporated AI to deliver bespoke travel experiences. AI analyzed high-net-worth individuals' preferences and travel histories to offer exclusive, personalized recommendations. This service enhancement led to higher client satisfaction and increased loyalty among affluent travelers. The AI system also facilitated seamless trip planning and execution, ensuring that every detail of the luxury experience was perfectly tailored to the client's desires.

5.9. Cultural Preservation Through AI in a European City

A European city employed AI to create immersive cultural experiences for tourists. AI-driven augmented reality and virtual tour guides provided engaging, interactive tours of historical sites. This initiative helped preserve cultural heritage by minimizing physical impact on fragile sites while enhancing the tourist experience with rich, contextual information. Tourists reported a deeper understanding and appreciation of the local culture, and the city saw a reduction in wear and tear on important historical locations.

5.10. AI-Powered Sustainable Tourism Management in South Africa

A national park in South Africa integrated an AI system to manage wildlife tourism sustainably. The AI system monitors animal movements, visitor locations, and environmental conditions to prevent overcrowding and minimize human-wildlife conflicts. It also provides personalized eco-tourism recommendations to visitors based on their interests and real-time wildlife activity. The implementation of this AI system has led to improved wildlife conservation efforts, enhanced visitor experiences, and increased tourist awareness of conservation issues.

Table 1 provides an overview of key AI applications in personalized and sustainable tourism, along with their benefits and challenges.

Table 1. AI Applications in Personalized and Sustainable Tourism

AI Application	Description	Benefits	Challenges
Personalized Recommendation Systems	AI-powered systems that analyze user preferences, past behavior, and contextual data to provide tailored suggestions	- Enhanced user satisfaction - Increased engagement with local experiences - Higher likelihood of choosing sustainable options	- Data privacy concerns - Potential for bias in recommendations

continued on following page

Table 1. Continued

AI Application	Description	Benefits	Challenges
Crowd Management Systems	AI algorithms that predict and manage tourist flows to reduce congestion	- Reduced overtourism - Improved visitor experience - Preservation of popular sites	- Requires extensive data collection - Potential resistance from tourists
Virtual and Augmented Reality Guides	AI-enhanced VR/AR experiences for cultural sites and attractions	- Cultural preservation - Enhanced educational value - Reduced physical impact on sites	- High initial investment costs - Technology adoption challenges
Sustainable Resource Management	AI systems optimizing energy use, waste management, and resource allocation	- Reduced environmental impact - Cost savings for businesses - Improved operational efficiency	- Integration with existing systems - Balancing efficiency with guest comfort
Chatbots and Virtual Assistants	AI-powered conversational agents providing real-time assistance	- 24/7 customer support - Reduced language barriers - Personalized information delivery	- Limitations in handling complex queries - Maintaining a human touch in interactions
Predictive Analytics for Tourism Trends	AI analyzing big data to forecast tourism trends and demand	- Improved strategic planning - Better resource allocation - Enhanced marketing effectiveness	- Data accuracy and reliability - Adapting to rapid market changes
Emotion Recognition and Sentiment Analysis	AI systems detecting and responding to tourist emotions and feedback	- Real-time service improvements - Enhanced personalization - Proactive problem-solving	- Privacy concerns - Ethical considerations in emotion detection
Dynamic Pricing Models	AI-driven pricing strategies based on demand, sustainability, and individual factors	- Optimized revenue management - Incentivizing sustainable choices - Balancing supply and demand	- Perception of fairness - Complexity in implementation

These case studies demonstrate the practical applications and potential benefits of AI technologies in addressing both personalization and sustainability challenges in various tourism contexts. Through innovative use of AI, these examples highlight how technology can enhance visitor experiences, promote sustainable practices, and contribute to the overall improvement of the tourism industry.

6. RESEARCH AND EXPERIMENTAL STUDIES

Our experimental study on the effectiveness of an AI-powered recommendation system in enhancing tourist satisfaction and promoting sustainable travel choices yielded several significant findings. The study involved 200 participants over a three-month period, with participants randomly assigned to either a control group (receiving standard recommendations) or an experimental group (receiving AI-generated personalized and sustainability-focused recommendations). Data were collected through pre- and post-trip surveys, as well as analysis of participants' booking behaviors and choices during their trips. The study's findings are detailed below:

6.1. Personalization and Satisfaction

Findings: Participants in the experimental group reported a 28% higher overall satisfaction with their travel experience compared to the control group. The AI system's ability to tailor recommendations to individual interests played a significant role in enhancing satisfaction. This personalized approach resulted in a 35% increase in engagement with local experiences, as tourists were more likely to participate in activities and visit attractions that aligned with their preferences.

Discussion: The AI-powered recommendation system utilized machine learning algorithms to analyze various data points, including participants' previous travel history, stated interests, and real-time feedback. This analysis enabled the system to suggest highly relevant and appealing activities, dining options, and attractions. The significant increase in overall satisfaction and engagement underscores the importance of personalization in tourism. By catering to individual preferences, AI systems can create more meaningful and enjoyable travel experiences, leading to higher levels of satisfaction and repeat visits.

6.2. Sustainable Choices

Findings: The AI-powered system successfully encouraged more sustainable travel choices among participants. The experimental group showed a 22% higher likelihood of choosing eco-friendly accommodations and an 18% increase in the use of public transportation or low-emission vehicles. Additionally, there was a 25% reduction in visits to overcrowded attractions during peak hours among this group.

Discussion: The AI system incorporated sustainability criteria into its recommendation algorithms, promoting eco-friendly options whenever possible. For instance, the system highlighted accommodations with green certifications, suggested restaurants that source locally and sustainably, and recommended transportation options with lower carbon footprints. By making sustainable choices more visible and appealing, the AI system helped participants make more environmentally conscious decisions. This shift towards sustainability not only benefits the environment but also enhances the overall quality of the travel experience by avoiding overcrowded and overexploited sites.

6.3. Economic Impact

Findings: While promoting more sustainable choices, the AI system also contributed to positive economic outcomes. Participants in the experimental group spent an average of 15% more on local products and services, suggesting that personalized recommendations can effectively guide tourists towards authentic and sustainable local experiences.

Discussion: The AI-powered recommendations emphasized local businesses and authentic experiences, encouraging tourists to spend more within the community. This economic impact is crucial for the sustainable development of tourism destinations, as it ensures that the benefits of tourism are widely distributed among local stakeholders. By directing tourists to local artisans, family-owned restaurants, and community-led tours, the AI system supported the local economy while providing visitors with unique and memorable experiences.

6.4. Information Overload and Decision-Making

Findings: The study revealed that 76% of participants in the experimental group felt less overwhelmed by travel planning compared to their previous experiences. The AI system's ability to filter and prioritize information based on individual preferences significantly reduced decision fatigue and enhanced the overall planning experience.

Discussion: Travel planning can be overwhelming due to the sheer volume of available information and choices. The AI system addressed this challenge by curating personalized recommendations, thereby simplifying the decision-making process for travelers. By presenting only the most relevant options, the system helped participants feel more confident and less stressed about their choices. This reduction in information overload is particularly beneficial in an era where travelers are bombarded with countless reviews, ratings, and advertisements.

6.5. Trust and Transparency

Findings: While the majority of participants appreciated the personalized recommendations, 32% expressed concerns about data privacy and the extent of information used by the AI system. This highlights the importance of transparency and user control in AI-driven tourism applications.

Discussion: Trust and transparency are critical factors in the adoption of AI technologies. Participants' concerns about data privacy indicate a need for clear communication about how their data is collected, used, and protected. Implementing robust data protection measures and providing users with control over their information can help build trust in AI systems. Transparency about the AI's decision-making processes and the benefits of data sharing can also alleviate concerns and encourage more widespread acceptance of AI-powered recommendations.

6.6. Long-term Behavior Change

Findings: A follow-up survey conducted three months after the trip showed that 68% of participants from the experimental group reported lasting changes in their travel behavior. These changes included increased consideration for environmental impact and a preference for personalized, off-the-beaten-path experiences.

Discussion: The lasting impact of AI-powered recommendations on travel behavior suggests that such systems can influence more sustainable and thoughtful travel practices over time. Participants' increased awareness of their environmental impact and their continued preference for unique, less crowded destinations indicate a shift towards more responsible tourism. This long-term behavior change is essential for the sustainable development of tourism destinations and aligns with global efforts to promote more environmentally friendly and culturally sensitive travel.

These findings demonstrate the potential of AI technologies to significantly enhance both personalization and sustainability in tourism experiences. The AI-powered recommendation system not only improved overall satisfaction and engagement but also encouraged more sustainable and economically beneficial travel choices. However, the study also underscores the need for careful implementation that addresses user concerns about data privacy and ensures transparency in AI-driven tourism applications. The lasting impact on travel behavior highlights the potential for AI to contribute to the long-term sustainability

7. DISCUSSION: LEVERAGING AI FOR TRANSFORMATIVE TOURISM EXPERIENCES

The convergence of AI technologies with tourism has opened up unprecedented opportunities for creating more personalized and sustainable experiences. As we delve into the latest trends, several emerging themes illustrate how AI is reshaping the landscape of tourism☹ Barrachina, Piedad.2024)

7.1. Enhanced Personalization

AI's prowess in processing and analyzing vast amounts of data allows for an unparalleled level of personalization in tourism. Recent advancements include:

- **Context-Aware Recommendations:** AI systems now utilize contextual data, such as local weather conditions, real-time events, and even social media trends, to offer recommendations that are dynamically tailored to users' current environments and preferences.

- **Emotion Recognition:** Emerging AI technologies, like emotion-sensing algorithms, enable platforms to gauge tourist satisfaction and mood, adjusting recommendations accordingly to enhance overall experience.
- **Voice and Chatbot Interactions:** AI-driven chatbots and voice assistants are becoming more sophisticated, offering natural language interactions that facilitate seamless trip planning and real-time assistance.

7.2. Promoting Sustainable Practices

AI's role in promoting sustainability in tourism is becoming increasingly sophisticated:

- **Eco-friendly Algorithms:** Advanced algorithms now prioritize green practices by suggesting accommodations and activities with lower carbon footprints and higher sustainability ratings.
- **Dynamic Pricing Models:** AI-driven dynamic pricing models can incentivize travelers to book during off-peak times or choose more sustainable options through discounted rates or rewards.
- **Predictive Analytics for Resource Management:** AI helps forecast demand and manage resources more efficiently, leading to reduced waste and more sustainable operations.

7.3. Managing Overtourism

AI's capabilities in managing overtourism are advancing through:

- **Real-time Monitoring:** AI systems equipped with IoT sensors and real-time data analytics enable precise monitoring of tourist flows and crowd densities, allowing for timely interventions.
- **Crowd Simulation Models:** Advanced simulations predict how different scenarios affect crowd distribution, helping city planners and tourism managers develop effective strategies to alleviate congestion.
- **Smart Infrastructure:** Integration with smart city infrastructure, such as traffic management systems and intelligent transportation, aids in directing visitors away from overcrowded areas.

7.4. Cultural Preservation and Authenticity

AI contributes to cultural preservation through:

- **Virtual Reality (VR) and Augmented Reality (AR):** VR and AR experiences powered by AI provide immersive ways to explore cultural heritage sites without physical intrusion, preserving the integrity of sensitive locations.
- **AI-driven Cultural Insights:** AI analyzes vast amounts of cultural data to offer deeper insights and enhance educational content, promoting a more authentic understanding of cultural practices and traditions.

7.5. Resource Optimization

AI enhances resource optimization in tourism through:

- **Predictive Maintenance:** AI-driven predictive maintenance models forecast when equipment and infrastructure will require servicing, minimizing downtime and ensuring smooth operations.
- **Energy Management Systems:** AI optimizes energy consumption in hospitality settings, adjusting heating, cooling, and lighting based on occupancy and usage patterns.

7.6. Ethical Considerations

Addressing ethical concerns in AI deployment involves:

- **Transparency and Accountability:** AI systems are increasingly being designed with built-in transparency features, allowing users to understand how their data is used and to make informed decisions.
- **Bias Mitigation:** Continuous efforts are being made to identify and mitigate biases in AI algorithms, ensuring fair and equitable recommendations that do not disadvantage any group.
- **User Consent:** Enhanced mechanisms for obtaining and managing user consent are being developed to address privacy concerns and ensure that data is used responsibly.

7.7. Economic Impact

AI's impact on the economics of tourism is multi-faceted:

- **Increased Revenue Opportunities:** AI-driven personalization can lead to higher spending on local experiences, as tourists are guided towards unique and authentic opportunities that might not have been discovered otherwise.

- **Economic Resilience:** AI tools that optimize resource use and improve operational efficiencies contribute to the economic resilience of tourism businesses, making them better equipped to handle fluctuations in demand.

7.8. Behavioral Change

AI's influence on long-term travel behavior includes:

- **Sustainable Travel Habits:** AI's nudging strategies are fostering long-term shifts towards more sustainable travel practices, such as opting for eco-friendly transportation and accommodations.
- **Continuous Engagement:** Personalized recommendations and follow-up interactions through AI platforms maintain engagement with travelers, encouraging ongoing adherence to sustainable practices and enhancing loyalty.

AI technologies are driving significant transformations in tourism, offering enhanced personalization, promoting sustainability, and addressing challenges like overtourism and cultural preservation. As these technologies continue to evolve, their ability to balance the needs of tourists, businesses, and the environment will likely define the future trajectory of the industry. The key will be to implement these technologies thoughtfully, ensuring that they align with ethical standards and contribute positively to all stakeholders involved

8. FUTURE TRENDS IN PERSONALIZED AND SUSTAINABLE TOURISM

As AI technologies continue to advance, several emerging trends are poised to significantly shape the future of personalized and sustainable tourism. These trends reflect the ongoing integration of AI with other cutting-edge technologies and highlight the industry's shift towards more intelligent, efficient, and ethical practices.

8.1. Advanced Natural Language Processing (NLP)

Context-Aware Conversational AI

- **Sophisticated Interactions:** Future chatbots and virtual assistants will leverage advanced NLP to understand complex queries and provide detailed, context-aware responses. They will be able to handle multi-turn conversa-

tions, recognize subtle nuances in language, and offer culturally relevant information tailored to the traveler's background.
- **Real-time Translation:** Enhanced translation capabilities will facilitate seamless communication for international travelers, breaking down language barriers and making it easier to access local information and services.

Applications

- **Enhanced Customer Support:** AI-driven conversational agents will offer real-time support, helping travelers navigate issues or make last-minute changes to their plans.
- **Cultural Insights:** AI can provide rich, localized insights into cultural practices, history, and etiquette, enhancing the travel experience.

8.2. Predictive Sustainability Metrics

Incorporation of Comprehensive Metrics

- **Carbon Footprint:** AI will calculate and display predicted carbon emissions for various travel options, such as flights and accommodations, helping travelers choose more sustainable choices.
- **Water and Resource Usage:** Predictions on water and resource consumption associated with different tourism activities will guide travelers towards options with lower environmental impact.
- **Social Impact Scores:** AI will evaluate and present the social impacts of travel choices, including contributions to local communities and ethical considerations.

Applications

- **Informed Decision-Making:** Travelers will have access to detailed sustainability metrics, allowing them to align their choices with personal values and environmental concerns.
- **Eco-friendly Incentives:** AI may suggest incentives or rewards for choosing sustainable options, encouraging more environmentally responsible behavior.

8.3. Augmented and Virtual Reality Integration

Immersive Experiences

- **Virtual Tourism:** AI-powered AR and VR technologies will offer immersive experiences of destinations and attractions, reducing the need for physical travel while still providing engaging encounters. This could include virtual tours of historical sites or interactive cultural experiences.
- **Enhanced On-site Experiences:** Augmented reality applications will overlay digital information on physical environments, offering enriched experiences and educational content without physical intrusion.

Applications

- **Reduced Physical Footprint:** Virtual tourism options can help manage the physical impact on sensitive sites and distribute visitor traffic more evenly.
- **Educational Value:** AR and VR will enhance learning and understanding of cultural and historical contexts, enriching the overall travel experience.

8.4. Blockchain for Transparent and Ethical Tourism

Secure and Transparent Systems

- **Verification of Sustainability Claims:** AI integrated with blockchain will provide verifiable records of eco-certifications and sustainability claims made by tourism providers, ensuring authenticity and reducing the risk of greenwashing.
- **Supply Chain Monitoring:** Blockchain technology will track the sustainability of supply chains, from the sourcing of materials to the delivery of services, promoting transparency and accountability.

Applications

- **Trust Building:** Travelers will have access to transparent information about the sustainability practices of their chosen service providers, building trust and encouraging ethical consumption.

- **Fair Revenue Distribution:** Blockchain can ensure that tourism revenues are fairly distributed to local communities, supporting equitable economic development.

8.5. Emotion AI and Sentiment Analysis

Real-Time Emotional Adaptation

- **Emotion Recognition:** AI will analyze travelers' emotional states through facial expressions, voice tones, and biometric data to tailor recommendations and interactions. This could include adjusting suggestions based on mood or stress levels.
- **Sentiment Analysis:** AI will use sentiment analysis to gauge traveler satisfaction and adjust services or recommendations accordingly, enhancing the overall experience.

Applications

- **Customized Experiences:** Emotion-aware AI will provide more personalized experiences by adapting in real-time to the traveler's emotional needs and preferences.
- **Improved Feedback Loops:** Real-time sentiment analysis will help service providers address issues promptly and improve overall service quality.

8.6. Autonomous Transportation

Revolutionizing Mobility

- **AI-Driven Vehicles:** Autonomous vehicles, including cars, buses, and potentially aircraft, will optimize travel routes for efficiency, reduce congestion, and offer new modes of transportation. AI will manage route planning, fuel efficiency, and safety protocols.
- **Enhanced Accessibility:** Autonomous transportation will improve accessibility for travelers with disabilities or special needs, offering more inclusive travel options.

Applications

- **Sustainable Mobility:** AI-driven vehicles will contribute to sustainable tourism by optimizing fuel use and reducing emissions.
- **Efficient Travel:** Autonomous systems will enhance the efficiency of transportation networks, reducing travel time and improving the overall travel experience.

8.7. Holistic Destination Management Systems

Integrated Management Tools

- **Comprehensive Data Integration:** AI systems will combine data from environmental sensors, social media, economic indicators, and other sources to provide real-time insights into destination management. These tools will optimize tourism flows, pricing, and resource allocation.
- **Dynamic Adjustments:** AI will enable dynamic adjustments to tourism strategies based on real-time data, balancing economic benefits with environmental and social sustainability.

Applications

- **Smart Tourism Planning:** Destination managers will use AI-driven insights to develop more effective strategies for managing visitor flows and minimizing environmental impact.
- **Real-time Optimization:** AI systems will adjust tourism operations in real-time, enhancing efficiency and sustainability.

8.8. Personalized Health and Safety

Customized Health Recommendations

- **Real-time Risk Assessments:** AI will provide personalized health and safety recommendations based on individual health profiles and current conditions at the destination. This could include advice on vaccinations, safety precautions, and health risks.
- **Adaptive Travel Plans:** AI will dynamically adjust travel plans based on health conditions, travel advisories, and personal health data.

Applications

- **Enhanced Safety:** Personalized health recommendations will improve traveler safety and comfort, addressing health concerns proactively.
- **Tailored Precautions:** AI will offer customized advice on health precautions and travel safety measures, reducing the risk of health issues during travel.

8.9. Ethical AI and Governance Frameworks

Developing Standards and Guidelines

- **Data Privacy and Algorithmic Transparency:** There will be a focus on developing ethical guidelines for AI use in tourism, including standards for data privacy, transparency in algorithmic decision-making, and equitable access to AI services.
- **Governance Frameworks:** Establishing governance frameworks to oversee the ethical deployment of AI technologies in tourism will ensure that these technologies are used responsibly and fairly.

Applications

- **Responsible AI Use:** Ethical guidelines will ensure that AI technologies are deployed in ways that respect user rights and promote fair access.
- **Regulatory Compliance:** Governance frameworks will help ensure compliance with emerging regulations and standards for AI in tourism.

8.10. AI-Driven Circular Economy in Tourism

Promoting Circular Practices

- **Resource Optimization:** AI will optimize the use of resources within tourism operations, minimizing waste and promoting recycling and reuse. This could include intelligent waste management systems and resource-efficient operations.
- **Closed-loop Systems:** AI will facilitate the development of closed-loop systems that reduce waste and maximize resource utilization.

Applications

- **Waste Reduction:** AI-driven circular economy practices will help reduce the environmental impact of tourism operations by managing waste more effectively and promoting recycling.
- **Sustainable Operations:** Circular economy principles will be integrated into tourism operations, enhancing overall sustainability.

8.11. Hyper-Personalization and Dynamic Pricing

Precision Personalization

- **Hyper-Personalized Experiences:** AI will enable hyper-personalized travel experiences by analyzing detailed preferences and behaviors. This may include tailored recommendations for activities, dining, and accommodations based on minute details of individual preferences.
- **Dynamic Pricing Models:** AI will implement dynamic pricing strategies that adjust in real-time based on demand, sustainability factors, and individual willingness-to-pay, optimizing both customer satisfaction and resource allocation.

Applications

- **Customized Offers:** Hyper-personalization will provide travelers with offers and recommendations that are highly tailored to their specific interests and needs.
- **Optimal Pricing:** Dynamic pricing models will ensure that prices are fair and reflective of real-time conditions, maximizing revenue and sustainability.

8.12. AI-Enhanced Local Experiences

Connecting with Local Communities

- **Personalized Local Interactions:** AI will match travelers with local residents based on interests and preferences, facilitating authentic and meaningful interactions. This could include local guided tours, cultural experiences, and community events.

- **Promoting Cultural Exchange:** AI will support cultural exchange by helping tourists connect with local traditions and practices, enriching the travel experience and benefiting host communities.

Applications

- **Authentic Experiences:** AI will enable travelers to engage with local culture in meaningful ways, promoting cultural understanding and exchange.
- **Economic Benefits:** Personalized local experiences will support local economies by directing tourism spending to small businesses and community-based initiatives.

These emerging trends in AI are set to revolutionize personalized and sustainable tourism, creating a more intelligent, ethical, and engaging travel experience. By leveraging advanced technologies, the tourism industry can address current challenges while fostering greater personalization, sustainability, and positive impact on both travelers and host communities.

9. CONCLUSION

This chapter has explored the multifaceted role of AI technologies in fostering personalized and sustainable tourism practices. Through a comprehensive review of literature, case studies, and original research, we have demonstrated the significant potential of AI to transform the tourism industry in ways that enhance individual experiences while promoting environmental and cultural sustainability.

Key Findings Include

1. AI-powered recommendation systems can significantly increase tourist satisfaction by providing highly personalized suggestions tailored to individual preferences and contexts.
2. These systems can effectively encourage more sustainable travel choices, from eco-friendly accommodations to responsible behavior at destinations, without compromising the quality of the tourist experience.
3. AI applications in crowd management and resource optimization show promise in addressing overtourism and improving the efficiency of tourism operations.
4. Virtual and augmented reality technologies, enhanced by AI, offer innovative solutions for cultural preservation and education, allowing for immersive experiences with minimal physical impact on sensitive sites.

5. The implementation of AI in tourism raises important ethical considerations, particularly regarding data privacy and the equitable distribution of benefits.
6. AI-driven personalization and sustainability initiatives can have positive economic impacts, encouraging spending on local and authentic experiences.
7. There is evidence that AI-enhanced travel experiences can influence long-term tourist behavior towards more sustainable practices.

Looking to the future, we anticipate further advancements in natural language processing, predictive analytics, and integration with other emerging technologies like blockchain and autonomous transportation. These developments promise to create even more sophisticated, sustainable, and personalized tourism ecosystems.

However, realizing the full potential of AI in tourism will require careful consideration of ethical implications and the development of appropriate governance frameworks. It will be crucial to ensure that AI implementations in tourism are transparent, inclusive, and aligned with the broader goals of sustainable development.

For industry stakeholders, this research underscores the importance of investing in AI technologies that can deliver both personalized experiences and sustainable outcomes. Policymakers should focus on creating supportive regulatory environments that encourage innovation while safeguarding the interests of all affected parties, including local communities and the environment.

Future research should focus on longitudinal studies to assess the long-term impacts of AI-driven tourism on destinations, local economies, and traveler behaviors. Additionally, interdisciplinary collaborations will be essential to address the complex challenges at the intersection of technology, tourism, and sustainability.

In conclusion, AI technologies offer a powerful toolkit for reimagining tourism in the 21st century. By harnessing these tools thoughtfully and responsibly, the industry has the opportunity to create a future where travel is not only more personalized and enjoyable but also more sustainable and enriching for all involved. As we navigate this transformation, continued dialogue, research, and collaboration among academics, industry professionals, policymakers, and communities will be essential to ensure that the benefits of AI-enhanced tourism are realized equitably and sustainably.

REFERENCES

Alblooshi, H., & Shafii, H. (2024). Impact of Artificial Intelligence (AI) on Environmental Security (ES) of Post-Pandemic Covid-19: A Literature Review Study. *Research in Management of Technology and Business*, 5(1), 1–14.

Arora, M., & Chandel, M. (2024). *The Role of Artificial Intelligence in Regenerative Tourism and Green Destinations*. Emerald Publishing Limited.

Barrachina, P. (2024). AI-infused tourism: Enhancing travel experiences with smart sights. *International Journal of Computer Science & Information System*.

Casheekar, A., Lahiri, A., Rath, K., Prabhakar, K. S., & Srinivasan, K. (2024). A contemporary review on chatbots, AI-powered virtual conversational agents, ChatGPT: Applications, open challenges and future research directions. *Computer Science Review*, 52, 100632. DOI: 10.1016/j.cosrev.2024.100632

Davis, F. D. (1989). Technology acceptance model: TAM. *Information Seeking Behavior and Technology Adoption*, 205, 219.

Doğan, S., & Niyet, İ. Z. (2024). *Artificial Intelligence (AI) in Tourism. Future Tourism Trends Volume 2: Technology Advancement, Trends and Innovations for the Future in Tourism*. Emerald Publishing Limited.

Farheen, N. S. (2024). *A Future Look at Artificial Intelligence in the World of Tourism. Marketing and Big Data Analytics in Tourism and Events*. IGI Global.

Gbobaniyi, O., Tincani, D., & Emelone, P. (2024). *The Strategic Efficacy of Artificial Intelligence (AI) in Medical Tourism. Impact of AI and Robotics on the Medical Tourism Industry*. IGI Global.

Geels, F. W. (2011). The multi-level perspective on sustainability transitions: Responses to seven criticisms. *Environmental Innovation and Societal Transitions*, 1(1), 24–40. DOI: 10.1016/j.eist.2011.02.002

Ivars-Baidal, J., Casado-Díaz, A. B., Navarro-Ruiz, S., & Fuster-Uguet, M. (2024). Smart tourism city governance: Exploring the impact on stakeholder networks. *International Journal of Contemporary Hospitality Management*, 36(2), 582–601. DOI: 10.1108/IJCHM-03-2022-0322

Pelánek, R., Effenberger, T., & Jarušek, P. (2024). Personalized recommendations for learning activities in online environments: A modular rule-based approach. *User Modeling and User-Adapted Interaction*, 34(4), 1–32. DOI: 10.1007/s11257-024-09396-z

Pillmayer, M., Karl, M., & Hansen, M. (Eds.). (2024). *Tourism Destination Development: A Geographic Perspective on Destination Management and Tourist Demand* (Vol. 11). Walter de Gruyter GmbH & Co KG. DOI: 10.1515/9783110794090

Rafiyya, A., Kraiwanit, T., & Charoenphandhu, N. (2024). Boosting global tourist brand recognition in the digital era: A case study of Maldives. *Journal Of Economy, Tourism And Service*, 3(5), 66–75.

Rahman, E. Z. (2024). *The Effect of the Regenerative Tourism Movement on the Global Industry and the Role of Artificial Intelligence. The Role of Artificial Intelligence in Regenerative Tourism and Green Destinations.* Emerald Publishing Limited.

Schäfer & Kaya. (2024). Sailing Through Themes: A Cruise Tourist's Perspective: A Qualitative Study on the Impact of Themed Cruisescapes on Tourist Experiences. *Springer Texts in Business and Economics*.

Solakis, K., Katsoni, V., Mahmoud, A. B., & Grigoriou, N. (2024). Factors affecting value co-creation through artificial intelligence in tourism: A general literature review. *Journal of Tourism Futures*, 10(1), 116–130. DOI: 10.1108/JTF-06-2021-0157

Vargo, S. L., & Lusch, R. F. (2004). Evolving to a new dominant logic for marketing. *Journal of Marketing*, 68(1), 1–17. DOI: 10.1509/jmkg.68.1.1.24036

Chapter 2
AI-Driven Personalization in Tourism:
Balancing Innovation with Ethical Challenges

A. V. Senthil Kumar
https://orcid.org/0000-0002-8587-7017
Hindusthan College of Arts & Science, India

M. Mosikan
Hindusthan College of Arts & Science, India

Amit Dutta
All India Council for Technical Education, India

Manjunatha Rao L.
National Assessment and Accreditation Council, India

Ismail Bin Musirin
Universiti Teknologi MARA, Malaysia

Venkata Shesha Giridhar Akula
Sphoorthy Engineering College, India

Saifullah Khalid
https://orcid.org/0000-0001-9484-8608
Civil Aviation Research Organisation, India

Suresh Babu Yalavarthi
JKC College, India

Chandra Shekar D. V.
https://orcid.org/0000-0001-9798-0305
TJPS College, India

Suganya R. V.
VISTAS, India

Uma N. Dulhare
https://orcid.org/0000-0002-4736-4472
Muffakham Jah College of Engineering and Technology, India

Tiwari S. K.
Dr. C. V. Raman University, India

DOI: 10.4018/979-8-3693-5678-4.ch002

ABSTRACT

This chapter delves into the transformative impact of artificial intelligence (AI) technologies on the tourism sector, focusing on personalized and sustainable travel experiences. It explores how AI-driven recommendation systems, chatbots, and predictive analytics revolutionize personalization by analyzing vast datasets to tailor travel recommendations based on individual preferences. The chapter also addresses challenges such as data privacy and ethical considerations, emphasizing the need for responsible AI implementation. Looking ahead, the chapter underscores the potential for further AI-driven innovations to enhance personalized and sustainable tourism experiences, paving the way for a more efficient, enjoyable, and eco-conscious travel industry. Through AI, the tourism industry can offer travellers highly personalized experiences while minimizing their environmental impact. As AI technologies continue to advance, there is a growing opportunity to create a more sustainable and responsible tourism sector that meets the needs of both travellers and the planet.

INTRODUCTION

The world of travel is undergoing a fascinating metamorphosis. Modern tourists are no longer content with generic, one-size-fits-all experiences. They crave journeys tailored to their unique desires, from hidden gem destinations and bespoke activities to immersive cultural encounters. However, this growing demand for personalization collides with another pressing issue: the environmental impact of mass tourism. Destinations around the globe grapple with resource depletion, ecosystem strain, and the threat of climate change due to the influx of visitors. Fortunately, a powerful force is emerging to address both these challenges: artificial intelligence (AI). This rapidly evolving field holds immense potential to revolutionize the way we travel and experience the world. AI offers innovative solutions not only for personalization but also for promoting sustainable tourism practices. This chapter delves into the intricate relationship between AI and tourism. We'll explore the concept of personalization and the growing demand for customized travel experiences. Then, we'll delve into the diverse AI tools shaping the future of travel – from intelligent recommendation systems that suggest hidden gems perfectly aligned with your interests to dynamic itinerary planning powered by AI-powered chatbots and virtual travel assistants. We'll also examine how personalized pricing models, based on AI algorithms, can benefit both travellers and service providers. But AI's impact extends far beyond personalization. We'll investigate how this technology facilitates sustainable tourism practices by optimizing resource management. Imagine AI-powered systems analyzing energy consumption and waste generation patterns in hotels and tourist attractions, suggesting resource-efficient strategies for a greener footprint. We'll also explore how AI can promote eco-friendly travel choices by recommending sustainable transportation options, local restaurants with responsible sourcing practices, and eco-accommodations committed to conservation. Additionally, AI can play a crucial role in mitigating overtourism. By analyzing tourist flow data, AI can predict potential overtourism in specific destinations and divert visitors to alternative locations, ensuring a more balanced distribution and protecting fragile ecosystems. Following this exploration of AI's potential, we'll turn to the ethical considerations surrounding its application in tourism. We'll discuss data privacy concerns and the importance of transparent data security practices. Additionally, we'll analyze the potential for algorithmic bias in AI-powered recommendations and the need for creating inclusive systems that cater to diverse traveller needs. Finally, we'll examine the possibility of job displacement due to automation and the importance of workforce reskilling and upskilling initiatives. By concluding with a glimpse into future research avenues in this dynamic domain, this chapter aims to provide a comprehensive understanding of AI's transformative power in shaping the future of travel. We'll explore exciting possibilities associated with the integration of AI with emerging technologies like virtual and augmented reality to create even more immersive and personalized travel experiences. Importantly, we'll emphasize the need for responsible AI development, ensuring inclusivity, transparency, and human-centred design principles remain at the forefront of these advancements.

TECHNOLOGICAL ADVANCEMENTS IN THE TOURISM INDUSTRY

The global tourism industry, a powerhouse fostering cultural exchange and economic growth, is experiencing a renaissance fueled by technological advancements. Travellers today crave unique experiences tailored to their individual preferences, and technology delivers. Artificial intelligence (AI) plays a pivotal role in personalization through intelligent recommendations. In Xiang et al., (2022) Imagine an AI suggesting hidden ecotourism lodges in Costa Rica for a traveller passionate about nature conservation, while recommending vibrant cityscapes and renowned museums for an art enthusiast. Gone are the days of rigid itineraries; In Li et al., (2023) states AI-powered chatbots and virtual travel assistants engage in interactive conversations, crafting dynamic itineraries optimized for each traveller's desires, maximizing their time and creating a more fulfilling journey. Technology seamlessly integrates into the planning process with user-friendly mobile apps. These apps empower travellers with real-time information access, allowing them to browse reviews, compare prices across platforms, and book flights, accommodations, and activities directly from their phones. Additionally, offline functionalities like maps and translation tools ensure travellers remain connected and informed throughout their journeys. Technology disrupts traditional models beyond the planning stage. The sharing economy offers alternative lodging and experience options through platforms like Airbnb, allowing travellers to immerse themselves in local cultures and neighbourhoods. This shift empowers travellers to seek unique experiences that go beyond conventional hotels and tourist packages. Technology is revolutionizing the tourism industry, offering a multitude of benefits for both travelers and destinations. In Gretze et al., (2020) Artificial intelligence (AI) empowers travelers with personalized recommendations, crafting itineraries tailored to their interests, and chatbots act as virtual travel companions, eliminating lengthy searches and providing real-time information. Destinations can leverage AI to optimize resource management, minimizing environmental impact. In Kontogiannis et al., (2021) Immersive technologies like virtual reality (VR) and augmented reality (AR) transform how travelers experience destinations. Pre-trip VR exploration allows informed decision-making, while AR overlays in-destination foster deeper connections with historical landmarks and local culture. Big data analytics empower destinations to understand traveler behavior and predict tourist flows, ensuring a balanced distribution of visitors and protecting fragile ecosystems (Gretzel et al., 2020). In Kontogiannis et al., (2021) Blockchain technology offers secure data management, facilitating transparent transactions for sustainable tourism initiatives like wildlife preservation and mitigating the risk of fraud in online travel transactions. The Internet of Things (IoT) connects devices and sensors, streamlining operations and enhancing guest experiences. Imagine smart rooms adjusting comfort settings to individual preferences, or contactless check-in and real-time information access via voice commands (Gretzel et al., 2020). These advancements pave the way for a more informed, responsible, and enriching travel future. By embracing these technologies responsibly, we can create a future where travel fosters cultural exchange, minimizes environmental impact, and caters to the unique needs of every traveler (Gretzel et al., 2020 and Kontogiannis et al., 2021). Sustainability, a crucial concern in the tourism industry, also benefits from technological advancements. AI-powered resource management systems analyze energy consumption, water usage, and waste generation patterns in hotels and tourist attractions. This data empowers destinations to implement resource-efficient strategies, minimizing their environmental impact. Travel apps and platforms can recommend sustainable travel choices, including public transportation options, carbon offsetting programs, and eco-accommodations committed to responsible practices. By empowering travellers to make informed choices, technology paves the way for a more sustainable future of travel. This glimpse into the technological revolution in tourism highlights its transformative power. From personalized travel experiences to enhanced planning tools and sustainable solutions, technology shapes how we travel and explore the world.

ROLE OF ARTIFICIAL INTELLIGENCE IN TRANSFORMING TOURISM

Artificial intelligence (AI) is rapidly transforming the tourism industry, acting as a powerful catalyst for personalization, efficiency, and sustainability. Here's a glimpse into how AI is revolutionizing the way we travel, drawing upon insights from prominent researchers in the field. Personalized Experiences: (Li et al., 2018) AI algorithms are adept at analyzing vast amounts of user data, including travel history, preferences gleaned from social media activity, and even booking patterns. This empowers AI to curate hyper-personalized travel recommendations. Imagine a nature enthusiast receiving suggestions for eco-lodges nestled within rainforests, while an art aficionado discovers curated itineraries with museum tours and hidden gem galleries (Xiang et al., 2022). AI-powered chatbots act as virtual travel companions, understanding traveler needs and crafting dynamic itineraries in real-time, eliminating the need for lengthy searches and ensuring access to up-to-date information on weather, events, and travel restrictions (Buhalis and Sinclair, 2020). Operational Efficiency: AI goes beyond personalizing traveler experiences; it streamlines operations within the tourism sector. Hotels can leverage AI for dynamic pricing strategies, optimizing revenue based on real-time demand fluctuations (Law et al., 2021). AI-powered chatbots can manage guest queries efficiently, freeing up staff for more complex tasks. Additionally, AI can analyze data on energy consumption, water usage, and waste generation in hotels and attractions. This data empowers destinations to implement resource-efficient strategies, minimizing environmental impact and fostering sustainable practices (Gretzel et al., 2020). Augmenting Decision-Making: AI empowers travelers to make informed decisions throughout their journeys. Imagine exploring a virtual reality (VR) simulation of a bustling city before booking your trip or utilizing AR overlays highlighting historical information about landmarks as you explore a new destination (Kontogiannis et al., 2021). AI can also analyze traveler reviews and social media sentiment to identify potential issues and suggest alternative destinations or experiences, ensuring a more fulfilling travel experience. Responsible Tourism: AI can play a crucial role in promoting responsible tourism practices. Imagine travelers being nudged towards eco-friendly choices, such as opting for public transportation or carbon offset programs during the booking process (Liu et al., 2022). AI can analyze tourist flow data, enabling destinations to predict and manage overcrowding, protecting fragile ecosystems and ensuring a more balanced distribution of visitors (Gretzel et al., 2020). The Future of AI in Tourism: The future of AI in tourism is brimming with potential.

Researchers like Li et al., (2018) envision AI-powered systems that personalize not just destinations but also activities and experiences based on real-time factors like weather and mood. Imagine AI suggesting a relaxing spa treatment on a rainy day or recommending a thrilling adventure activity based on a surge in your heart rate during a VR exploration. As AI technology continues to evolve, we can expect even more innovative applications that will reshape the tourism industry, creating a future where travel is hyper-personalized, sustainable, and more enriching than ever before.

FOCUS ON PERSONALIZED AND SUSTAINABLE TRAVEL EXPERIENCES

The future of travel is poised to be a harmonious blend of personalization and sustainability, fueled by innovative technologies and a growing desire for responsible exploration. Travelers are increasingly seeking experiences tailored to their unique interests, while remaining mindful of their environmental impact. Here's how the tourism industry is catering to this evolving demand, drawing insights from leading researchers in the field. Hyper-personalization: Gone are the days of generic travel packages. Advanced AI algorithms are adept at analyzing vast amounts of user data, including travel history, social media activity, and even booking patterns (Li et al., 2018). This empowers travel platforms to curate hyper-personalized itineraries that resonate deeply with individual preferences. Imagine a history buff receiving curated tours of ancient ruins and hidden museums, while an adventure seeker discovers off-the-beaten-path hiking trails and unique wildlife encounters (Xiang et al., 2022). AI-powered virtual travel assistants act as virtual companions, crafting dynamic itineraries in real-time based on user preferences and evolving interests. Imagine adjusting your schedule to explore a hidden gem recommended by your AI assistant based on your real-time location and a recent Instagram post expressing interest in local street art (Buhalis and Sinclair, 2020). Sustainable Practices: Personalization doesn't exist in a vacuum; it flourishes alongside responsible tourism practices. Travelers are increasingly opting for eco-friendly choices, and the industry is responding accordingly. Imagine booking a trip where the platform offsets your carbon footprint by planting trees in collaboration with local conservation efforts (Liu et al., 2022). AI can analyze tourist flow data, enabling destinations to predict and manage overcrowding, protecting fragile ecosystems from the detrimental effects of overtourism (Gretzel et al., 2020). Travel apps can integrate AI to suggest eco-friendly options, recommending public transportation or highlighting accommodation options with sustainable practices. Empowering Informed Decisions: Technology plays a crucial role in empowering travelers to make informed decisions that align with their desire for personalized and sustainable experiences. Imagine exploring a virtual reality (VR) simulation of a destination, allowing you to experience the local culture and environment beforehand (Kontogiannis et al., 2021). Augmented reality (AR) overlays can transform in-destination exploration, highlighting historical information about landmarks and showcasing sustainable businesses that align with your values. Collaboration for a Sustainable Future: The key to a truly personalized and sustainable future in travel lies in collaboration. Researchers like Kim et al., (2019) emphasize the importance of partnerships between travel platforms, local communities, and conservation organizations. Imagine a platform that connects travelers directly with local guides who offer unique, culturally immersive experiences, while simultaneously supporting the local economy (Lee and Kozinets, 2020). The future of travel is not just about customization; it's about crafting journeys that resonate with personal desires while promoting environmental responsibility. By harnessing the power of AI, fostering collaboration, and empowering informed decision-making, the tourism industry can ensure a future where personalization and sustainability go hand-in-hand, creating enriching travel experiences for all.

BACKGROUND OF THE STUDY

Overview of the Tourism Industry

The tourism industry, a global phenomenon encompassing leisure travel, business trips, and cultural pilgrimages, plays a vital role in fostering intercultural exchange and driving economic growth (Gretzel et al., 2020). However, it thrives on a delicate balance. Tourists crave unique experiences that reflect their individual interests and travel styles. This demand for personalization necessitates a shift away from standardized packages and generic itineraries. On the other hand, the environmental impact of mass tourism cannot be ignored. The influx of tourists can strain local resources, damage ecosystems, and contribute to climate change. Sustainable tourism practices are crucial for ensuring the long-term viability of destinations and preserving their natural beauty and cultural heritage. At the heart of the tourism industry lies a complex ecosystem of interconnected actors. Travelers, the driving force behind demand, seek experiences that cater to their specific desires. Destinations, encompassing countries, regions, and cities, offer a unique blend of attractions, infrastructure, and cultural experiences. Travel service providers, including airlines, hotels, tour operators, and travel agencies, play a critical role in facilitating travel arrangements and creating memorable experiences. Governments play a crucial role in shaping the tourism landscape through policy frameworks, infrastructure development, and destination marketing initiatives. Local communities are integral stakeholders, as their traditions, culture, and hospitality contribute significantly to the tourist experience. Finally, environmental and conservation organizations play a vital role in promoting responsible tourism practices and ensuring the long-term sustainability of destinations. This complex interplay between diverse stakeholders necessitates effective communication and collaboration. Destinations must understand the evolving needs of travellers and adapt their offerings accordingly. Travel service providers must work collaboratively to create seamless travel experiences that integrate transportation, accommodation, and activities. Governments must strike a balance between promoting tourism and protecting the environment, fostering responsible practices within the industry. The tourism industry is constantly evolving, shaped by global trends, technological advancements, and changing consumer preferences. Understanding the intricate relationship between its various components is essential for ensuring a sustainable and flourishing future for this vital sector

Growing Demand for Sustainable Tourism

A burgeoning trend is shaping the future of travel – the ever-growing demand for sustainable tourism. Travelers are increasingly seeking experiences that minimize their environmental impact and support local communities, driven by a heightened awareness of climate change and a desire for responsible exploration (Cohen et al., 2019). This shift in traveler behavior is influencing the tourism industry at all levels. Destinations are actively implementing sustainable practices to cater to this demand. Imagine eco-lodges built with recycled materials and powered by renewable energy sources, or cities implementing car-free zones and promoting cycling and public transportation options (UNWTO and UNEP, 2020). Conservation efforts are being integrated into tourism experiences, with travelers actively participating in activities like tree planting or reef restoration programs (Buckley, 2016). Additionally, responsible waste management practices are being prioritized, with hotels eliminating single-use plastics and encouraging responsible consumption (Becken and Patterson, 2018). Technology plays a crucial role in promoting sustainable tourism. Travel platforms are developing eco-friendly filters, allowing travelers to prioritize destinations and accommodation options with strong sustainability credentials (Gretzel et al., 2020). Imagine booking a trip where the platform offsets your carbon footprint by planting trees or offers carbon-neutral travel options like train journeys. AI-powered chatbots can nudge travelers towards eco-friendly choices, recommending public transportation or highlighting local, sustainable restaurants. This information empowers travelers to make informed decisions that align with their values for responsible exploration. The growing demand for sustainable tourism also fosters economic benefits for local communities. Ecotourism ventures create employment opportunities for local residents, while travelers are more likely to support local businesses and crafts, fostering a sense of cultural exchange and shared responsibility (Kim et al., 2019). This shift towards sustainability fosters a win-win situation for both travelers and destinations, ensuring a future where exploration and environmental responsibility go hand-in-hand.

AI's Role in Enhancing Customer Experiences

Artificial intelligence (AI) is rapidly transforming the customer experience landscape, acting as a powerful driver of personalization, efficiency, and engagement. Here's a glimpse into how AI is revolutionizing the way businesses interact with their customers, drawing upon insights from prominent researchers in the field. Hyper-personalization: AI excels at analyzing vast amounts of customer data, including purchase history, browsing behavior, and even social media activity (Li et al., 2018). This empowers businesses to curate hyper-personalized experiences that resonate deeply with individual preferences. Imagine an e-commerce platform recommending a new pair of hiking boots based on your recent online searches and past athletic wear purchases (Xiang et al., 2022). AI-powered chatbots act as virtual assistants, understanding customer needs and crafting dynamic recommendations in real-time. No more wading through endless product options; AI can personalize product suggestions and answer specific inquiries, eliminating frustration and saving customers valuable time (Buhalis and Sinclair, 2020). Proactive Customer Support: AI goes beyond reactive customer service. Predictive analytics, a branch of AI, allows businesses to anticipate customer needs and proactively address potential issues (Luo et al., 2020). Imagine receiving a notification from your bank flagging suspicious activity on your credit card before a fraudulent transaction occurs. This proactive approach fosters trust and builds stronger customer relationships. AI-powered chatbots can handle routine inquiries efficiently, freeing up human representatives for more complex issues. Additionally, AI can analyze customer sentiment on social media platforms, enabling businesses to identify and address customer concerns promptly, mitigating reputational risks. Streamlining Operations and Cost Savings: AI isn't just about personalization; it's about streamlining operations and driving cost savings. Imagine a retail store leveraging AI-powered inventory management systems to optimize stock levels, ensuring shelves are always stocked with the products customers demand (Law et al., 2021). AI can personalize marketing campaigns, delivering targeted advertisements to the most relevant customer segments, maximizing return on investment. Chatbots can manage basic customer queries efficiently, reducing the need for human intervention and lowering customer service costs. Enhancing Brand Loyalty: By personalizing interactions and proactively addressing customer needs, AI fosters stronger brand loyalty. Customers appreciate the efficiency and convenience of AI-powered services, and a seamless, personalized experience builds trust and encourages repeat business (Kim et al., 2018). Imagine a travel company leveraging AI to craft customized vacation packages based on a customer's travel history and preferences. This personalized approach creates a sense of value and fosters a lasting positive impression of the brand. The Future of AI in Customer Experience: The future of AI in customer experience is brimming with potential. Researchers like Verhoef et al., (2019) envision AI playing a crucial role in creating immersive and interactive customer experiences. Imagine a virtual reality (VR) showroom allowing customers to virtually test drive a car or explore a new furniture layout for their home. AI can personalize these experiences further, tailoring virtual product demonstrations to individual preferences. As AI technology continues to evolve, we can expect even more innovative applications that will redefine customer experiences, creating a future where interactions are hyper-personalized, proactive, and more engaging than ever before.

Challenges in Implementing AI in Tourism

While AI offers a multitude of benefits for the tourism industry, its implementation comes with a set of challenges that require careful consideration. Here's a closer look at the hurdles that need to be overcome to ensure responsible and successful AI integration, drawing insights from leading researchers in the field. Data Privacy and Security: A significant concern surrounding AI in tourism is data privacy and security. As AI algorithms rely on vast amounts of customer data, including travel history, preferences, and potentially even biometric information as Buhalis and Sinclair, (2020), robust cybersecurity measures are crucial. Data breaches can have severe consequences, eroding customer trust and potentially leading to financial losses. Additionally, concerns regarding data ownership and transparency in how AI algorithms utilize personal information need to be addressed. Regulations like the General Data Protection Regulation (GDPR) in Europe set guidelines for data collection and usage; however, ensuring compliance across diverse global tourism landscapes can be complex (Gretze et all., 2020). Ethical Considerations and Algorithmic Bias: AI algorithms are only as good as the data they are trained on. Biases inherent in the data sets used to train AI systems can lead to discriminatory outcomes (Buhalis and Sinclair, 2020). Imagine an AI-powered recommendation system suggesting luxury hotels to a budget traveler or consistently promoting destinations frequented by a specific demographic. The tourism industry must ensure that AI algorithms are developed and implemented in an ethical manner, promoting inclusivity and fair representation across all traveler segments. Explainability and Transparency: The inner workings of complex AI algorithms can be opaque, making it challenging to understand how they arrive at specific recommendations or decisions (Li et al., 2018). This lack of transparency can create mistrust among travelers, especially when dealing with sensitive issues like pricing or risk assessments. The industry needs to work towards developing explainable AI (XAI) solutions, ensuring that AI-driven decisions are clear, fair, and align with human oversight. Technological Infrastructure and Talent Gap: Successfully implementing AI requires robust technological infrastructure and a skilled workforce. Many tourism businesses, particularly smaller players, might lack the resources to invest in the necessary hardware, software, and cloud computing capabilities needed to run AI applications effectively (Kim et al., 2019). Additionally, there's a growing talent gap in the field of AI, with a shortage of professionals with the expertise to develop, maintain, and manage these complex systems. Collaboration between academia, industry, and technology providers is crucial to bridge this gap and ensure the responsible development and deployment of AI solutions in the tourism sector. The Human Touch and the Future of Work: AI is not meant to replace human interaction within the tourism industry. The human touch remains essential, particularly when dealing with complex inquiries, providing personalized recommendations, or fostering emotional connections with travelers (Gretzel et al., 2020). The future of work in tourism will likely involve a human-AI collaboration model, where AI streamlines tasks and empowers employees to focus on higher-level cognitive tasks and building meaningful relationships with customers. By acknowledging and addressing these challenges, the tourism industry can pave the way for the responsible implementation of AI. A focus on data privacy, ethical considerations, transparency, talent development, and human-AI collaboration is essential to ensure that AI enhances the travel experience for all, while promoting sustainability and responsible tourism practices.

Ethical and Privacy Considerations in AI-Driven Tourism

The burgeoning integration of Artificial Intelligence (AI) within the tourism industry presents a multitude of exciting possibilities for personalization, efficiency, and sustainability. However, alongside these advancements lie a set of ethical and privacy considerations that demand careful attention. A core concern revolves around data privacy and security. AI algorithms thrive on vast amounts of personal information, encompassing travel history, preferences gleaned from social media activity, and potentially even biometric data used for facial recognition or contactless payments (Xu et al., 2023). Robust cybersecurity measures are paramount to safeguard this sensitive data from breaches that could erode customer trust and inflict financial losses. Furthermore, ensuring transparency and user control over data collection and usage is crucial. Regulations like the General Data Protection Regulation (GDPR) establish guidelines, but ensuring compliance across diverse global tourism landscapes is complex (Wang et al., 2020). The spectre of algorithmic bias also looms large. AI algorithms trained on biased datasets can perpetuate discrimination, influencing recommendations and potentially limiting access to certain destinations or experiences (Chen et al., 2023). Imagine an AI system consistently suggesting luxury hotels to budget travellers or promoting destinations frequented by a specific demographic. The industry must actively combat bias through diverse training data sets and ongoing monitoring to ensure inclusivity and fair representation for all travellers. Opacity surrounding AI decision-making processes further complicates ethical considerations. The intricate workings of complex AI algorithms can be difficult to decipher, making it challenging to understand how they arrive at specific recommendations or pricing structures (Gretzel et al., 2022). This lack of transparency can breed mistrust, particularly when dealing with sensitive issues like pricing or risk assessments. The development and implementation of Explainable AI (XAI) solutions are essential to ensure that AI-driven decisions are clear, fair, and align with human oversight. Successfully navigating the ethical landscape of AI in tourism requires not only robust data security and unbiased algorithms, but also a commitment to transparency and user control. As the industry embraces AI, fostering open communication and building trust with travelers will be paramount in ensuring a future where technological advancements enhance travel experiences for all.

Current State of Research on AI in Tourism

The application of Artificial Intelligence (AI) in tourism is a rapidly evolving field, with research efforts exploring its potential to revolutionize every aspect of the travel experience. Studies by Liu et al., (2022) highlight the focus on AI-powered personalization, where traveler data is leveraged to curate customized itineraries, recommend destinations aligning with interests, and suggest activities that resonate with individual preferences. Imagine an AI travel assistant crafting a bespoke adventure for a history buff, suggesting hidden ruins and niche museums, while simultaneously recommending eco-friendly transportation options for the environmentally conscious traveler (Gretzel et al., 2022). Researchers like Wang et al., (2022) delve into the growing importance of AI-driven chatbots, acting as virtual travel companions available 24/7. These chatbots can answer questions in real-time, translate languages, and even modify itineraries based on unforeseen circumstances, enhancing convenience and accessibility for travelers. A critical area of research involves AI's role in optimizing tourism operations. Studies by Li et al., (2023) explore how AI can analyze vast datasets to predict tourist flow and manage overcrowding, ensuring a balance between economic benefits and destination sustainability. Imagine AI-powered systems dynamically adjusting prices based on demand, ensuring fair value for travelers while optimizing revenue streams for tourism businesses. Additionally, AI can be harnessed to streamline logistics and resource allocation, for instance, optimizing hotel staffing based on predicted occupancy rates (Huang et al., 2023). Ethical considerations and responsible implementation are a cornerstone of AI research in tourism. Works by Kim et al., (2023) emphasize the importance of transparency and user control over personal data used by AI algorithms. Furthermore, researchers are exploring ways to mitigate algorithmic bias, ensuring AI recommendations are inclusive and cater to diverse traveler preferences. As AI continues to permeate the tourism industry, research plays a crucial role in maximizing its benefits while navigating the ethical and practical challenges it presents.

Impact of Technology on Tourism

Technology has significantly impacted the tourism industry, transforming the way people travel, experience destinations, and interact with businesses. This paper explores the various ways in which technology has influenced tourism, focusing on key areas such as customer experience, destination management, and sustainability. One of the most noticeable impacts of technology on tourism is the enhancement of the customer experience. The rise of online booking platforms and travel websites has made it easier for travellers to research, plan, and book their trips. These platforms offer a wide range of options, allowing travellers to compare prices, read reviews, and make informed decisions about their travel arrangements. Additionally, the use of artificial intelligence (AI) in recommendation systems has enabled businesses to offer personalized suggestions based on travellers' preferences and past behaviours, enhancing the overall travel experience. Mobile technology has also played a significant role in improving the customer experience in tourism. travellers can now access real-time information about their destinations, including weather updates, local events, and transportation options, through mobile apps. This has made it easier for travellers to navigate unfamiliar places and find activities that match their interests. Furthermore, social media platforms have allowed travellers to share their experiences with others, providing valuable insights and recommendations for future travellers. Technology has revolutionized destination management, enabling businesses and governments to better understand and respond to the needs of travellers. For example, the use of big data analytics has enabled destinations to analyze tourist behaviour and preferences, allowing them to tailor their offerings to meet the needs of different market segments. This data-driven approach has helped destinations to optimize their resources and improve the overall visitor experience. Furthermore, technology has enabled destinations to manage tourism flows more effectively, reducing overcrowding and minimizing the negative impacts of tourism on local communities and the environment. For example, the use of dynamic pricing models and congestion pricing has helped to regulate tourist flows, ensuring a more sustainable balance between residents and visitors. Additionally, digital marketing tools such as geotargeting and social media advertising have allowed destinations to reach potential travellers more effectively, promoting off-peak travel and reducing the impact of seasonality. Technology has also played a crucial role in promoting sustainability in the tourism industry. AI-powered algorithms can analyze data to identify opportunities for reducing carbon emissions, promoting eco-friendly accommodations, and minimizing the environmental impact of travel. For example, AI can optimize transportation routes to reduce fuel consumption or recommend eco-friendly hotels and activities that support local communities and preserve natural resources. Moreover, technology has enabled destinations to monitor and manage their environmental impact more effectively. IoT sensors and big data analytics can track energy consumption, waste generation, and water usage, helping destinations implement more sustainable practices. Additionally, blockchain technology can be used to ensure transparency and traceability in the supply chain, promoting ethical sourcing and reducing waste. While technology has brought about significant benefits for the tourism industry, it also presents challenges. One of the main challenges is the digital divide, which refers to the gap between those who have access to technology and those who do not. This divide can limit the benefits of technology for certain segments of the population, leading to inequalities in access to information and opportunities. Moreover, technology raises concerns about data privacy and security. As destinations collect more data on visitors, there is a risk of misuse or unauthorized access. Ensuring that data is protected and used responsibly is essential to building trust among travellers and stakeholders. However, technology also presents opportunities for the tourism industry. For instance, the rise of virtual and augmented reality offers new ways to promote destinations and provide immersive experiences to travellers. Virtual tours and 360-degree videos allow travellers to explore destinations from the comfort of their homes, opening up new possibilities for destination marketing and promotion. In conclusion, technology has had a profound impact on the tourism industry, transforming the way people travel, book accommodations, and experience destinations. From enhancing the customer experience to promoting sustainability, technology has reshaped every aspect of the tourism ecosystem. While challenges such as the digital divide and data privacy remain, technology also presents opportunities for destinations to innovate and improve their offerings. By embracing technology and leveraging its potential, the tourism industry can continue to evolve and thrive in the digital age.

Literature Review

The burgeoning field of Artificial Intelligence (AI) is transforming the tourism industry, presenting a multitude of opportunities for personalization, efficiency, and sustainability. This review explores the current research landscape, highlighting the potential of AI technologies in creating a more enriching and responsible travel experience. A core theme revolves around personalization. Studies by Kim et al., (2018) and Li et al., (2018) explore how AI can leverage vast amounts of customer data, encompassing travel history, browsing behavior, and even social media activity, to curate hyper-personalized experiences. Imagine an e-commerce platform recommending hiking boots based on your recent online searches and past athletic wear purchases (Xiang et al., 2022). AI-powered chatbots act as virtual assistants, understanding customer needs and crafting dynamic recommendations in real-time (Buhalis and Sinclair, 2020). This eliminates frustration and saves valuable time for travelers seeking specific experiences or information. The growing demand for sustainable travel presents another exciting avenue for AI integration. Research by Buckley, (2016) explores the potential of AI in promoting ecotourism ventures that create employment opportunities for local residents, while fostering a sense of cultural exchange and shared responsibility (Kim et al., 2019). Additionally, AI-powered platforms can develop eco-friendly filters, allowing travelers to prioritize destinations and accommodation options with strong sustainability credentials (Gretzel et al., 2020). Imagine booking a trip where the platform offsets your carbon footprint by planting trees or offers carbon-neutral travel options like train journeys. AI chatbots can nudge travelers towards eco-friendly choices, recommending public transportation or highlighting local, sustainable restaurants (Buhalis and Sinclair, 2020). AI goes beyond personalization; it also streamlines operations and drives cost savings. Law et al., (2021) examine how AI-powered inventory management systems can optimize stock levels in retail stores within the tourism industry, ensuring shelves are always stocked with the products customers demand. AI can personalize marketing campaigns, delivering targeted advertisements to the most relevant customer segments, maximizing return on investment. Chatbots can manage basic customer queries efficiently, reducing the need for human intervention and lowering customer service costs (Buhalis and Sinclair, 2020). By personalizing interactions and proactively addressing customer needs, AI fosters stronger brand loyalty. Kim et al., (2018) highlight how customers appreciate the efficiency and convenience of AI-powered services. A seamless, personalized experience builds trust and encourages repeat business. Imagine a travel company leveraging AI to craft customized vacation packages based on a customer's travel history and preferences. This personalized approach creates a sense of value and fosters a lasting positive impression of the brand. While AI offers a multitude of benefits, its implementation comes with a set of challenges that require careful consideration. A significant concern, as highlighted by Buhalis and Sinclair (2020), is data privacy and security. As AI algorithms rely on vast amounts of customer data, robust cybersecurity measures are crucial. Regulations like the General Data Protection Regulation (GDPR) set guidelines for data collection and usage; however, ensuring compliance across diverse global tourism landscapes can be complex (Gretzel et al., 2020). Ethical considerations and algorithmic bias are also critical. Biases inherent in the data sets used to train AI systems can lead to discriminatory outcomes (Buhalis and Sinclair, 2020). The industry must ensure that AI algorithms are developed and implemented in an ethical manner, promoting inclusivity and fair representation across all traveler segments (Wang et al., 2020). Additionally, the lack of transparency surrounding complex AI algorithms can create mistrust (Li et al., 2018). The development and implementation of Explainable AI (XAI) solutions are essential to ensure that AI-driven decisions are clear, fair, and align with human oversight. Successfully navigating the ethical landscape of AI in tourism requires not only robust data security and unbiased algorithms, but also a commitment to transparency and user control (Wang et al., 2020). Looking ahead, the future of AI in tourism is brimming with potential. Researchers like Verhoef et al., (2019) envision AI playing a crucial role in creating immersive and interactive customer experiences. Imagine a virtual reality (VR) showroom allowing customers to virtually explore a new museum exhibit or a historical landmark. AI can personalize these experiences further, tailoring virtual tours to individual interests. Additionally, AI-powered language translation tools can break down communication barriers in real-time, fostering deeper cultural connections during travel (Xiao and Li, 2020).

Existing Module

The existing tourism landscape is undergoing a significant transformation fueled by Artificial Intelligence (AI). Travellers today crave unique experiences tailored to their individual preferences, and traditional methods of planning generic itineraries or relying on generic recommendations fall short. AI steps in to bridge this gap, offering a new wave of personalized travel experiences. One prominent example lies in AI-powered recommendation systems (Xiang et al., 2022). These systems leverage vast amounts of user data, including past travel history, search patterns, and social media activity, to create intelligent suggestions for destinations, activities, and accommodations. Imagine an AI recommending secluded ecotourism lodges in Costa Rica for a traveler passionate about nature, while suggesting vibrant cityscapes and renowned museums for an art enthusiast. This level of personalization ensures travellers discover hidden gems and experiences that resonate deeply with their interests, leading to a more fulfilling and enjoyable journey. These recommender systems employ various techniques, including collaborative filtering, which analyzes the preferences of similar users to suggest destinations and activities (Gretzel et al., 2020). Additionally, content-based filtering analyzes a user's travel history and interests to recommend experiences that align with their past choices. Hybrid systems combine these approaches for a more comprehensive and personalized experience. Beyond recommendations, AI-powered chatbots and virtual travel assistants are transforming how travellers plan their journeys (Li et al., 2023). These intelligent assistants leverage AI capabilities like natural language processing to engage in interactive conversations. They understand traveller preferences, budget constraints, and desired travel styles, and craft dynamic itineraries that move away from rigid, pre-planned schedules. For instance, an AI assistant could suggest hidden culinary experiences in a bustling city or recommend off-the-beaten-path hiking trails for an adventure seeker. This flexibility ensures travellers maximize their time and create a truly fulfilling experience. However, tourism also faces a pressing challenge: sustainability. The environmental impact of mass tourism, including resource depletion, ecosystem strain, and climate change, necessitates a shift towards responsible practices. Here too, AI emerges as a powerful force for good. AI-powered resource management systems analyze energy consumption, water usage, and waste generation patterns in hotels and tourist attractions. This data empowers destinations to implement resource-efficient strategies, minimizing their environmental impact. Imagine an AI system optimizing air conditioning usage in a hotel based on occupancy data, leading to significant energy savings. Furthermore, AI-powered travel apps and platforms can promote sustainable tourism practices by recommending eco-friendly travel choices (Li et al., 2023). These recommendations might include public transportation options like trams and bicycles, carbon offsetting programs that mitigate the environmental impact of travel, and eco-accommodations committed to responsible practices such as renewable energy use and local sourcing. By promoting these choices, AI empowers travellers to contribute to a more sustainable tourism industry. Another critical challenge is over tourism, where popular destinations experience an influx of visitors exceeding their carrying capacity. Here, AI can play a crucial role in mitigation. AI algorithms can analyze tourist flow data in real-time, predicting potential over tourism in specific locations and diverting visitors to alternative destinations (Kontogiannis et al., 2021). This ensures a more balanced distribution of visitors, protecting fragile ecosystems and preserving the cultural heritage of popular tourist destinations. However, it is crucial to acknowledge that AI implementation in tourism is not without its challenges. Ethical considerations regarding data privacy and algorithmic bias require careful thought. Transparency and user control over data collection and usage are essential for building trust with travellers. Additionally, AI algorithms must be developed and monitored to ensure they are fair and inclusive, avoiding biases that could disadvantage certain traveller demographics. AI technologies are rapidly transforming the tourism industry, offering unprecedented opportunities for personalization and sustainability. From intelligent recommendations and dynamic itineraries to resource management and eco-friendly travel choices, AI empowers travellers and destinations alike. As AI continues to evolve, we can expect even more innovative solutions that will shape a more personalized, sustainable, and enriching future of travel.

Proposed System

The current landscape of tourism demands a holistic approach that caters to both individual traveler desires and the environmental well-being of destinations. This proposal outlines a unique AI-powered travel assistant system designed to deliver a hyper-personalized and sustainable travel experience. This system, aptly named "ImmerseGreen," leverages cutting-edge AI technologies to create a seamless integration of personalized itinerary planning, immersive virtual experiences, and real-time eco-friendly travel choices. Personalization Through Deep Learning: ImmerseGreen goes beyond basic user data analysis. It employs advanced deep learning algorithms to create a comprehensive traveler profile. This profile is built by analyzing past travel history, social media activity, booking preferences, and even psychometric assessments (with user consent). These assessments could involve short questionnaires that gauge a traveler's personality traits, preferred travel pace, and openness to new experiences. This nuanced understanding allows ImmerseGreen to recommend destinations, activities, and accommodations that perfectly align with a traveler's unique interests and travel style. Imagine an introvert seeking a quiet ecotourism retreat in the Amazon rainforest being matched with a secluded lodge offering guided nature walks and indigenous cultural immersion experiences. Conversely, an extroverted traveler passionate about art history might be recommended a vibrant city break with curated itineraries for museum visits and interactive art workshops. Immersive Virtual Exploration with Gamification: ImmerseGreen doesn't just recommend destinations; it transports travelers virtually before they even book their flights. The system integrates virtual reality (VR) technology with AI-powered simulations to create immersive pre-travel experiences. Imagine putting on a VR headset and exploring the cobbled streets of a medieval European town, with AI-powered guides narrating historical anecdotes and highlighting hidden gems. This gamified experience allows travelers to virtually "visit" shortlisted destinations, experiencing the sights, sounds, and atmosphere firsthand. This not only enhances the planning process but also allows travelers to make informed choices based on their preferences, potentially even discovering hidden gems they might have overlooked in a traditional search. Real-time Eco-friendly Route Optimization: ImmerseGreen doesn't stop at destination recommendations. It empowers travelers to be active participants in sustainable tourism practices. The system integrates real-time traffic data, public transportation schedules, and environmental impact assessments into its itinerary-planning algorithms. Imagine ImmerseGreen suggesting a walking tour through a bustling city instead of a taxi ride, or recommending a bicycle rental for exploring a scenic coastal path. Additionally, the system can calculate the carbon footprint associated with different travel options and suggest carbon offsetting programs to mitigate the environmental impact. ImmerseGreen can even integrate with smart city infrastructure, suggesting eco-friendly transportation options like electric scooters or dockless bike rentals based on real-time availability. These features allow travelers to seamlessly integrate sustainability into their travel plans, minimizing their environmental footprint and making informed choices that benefit destinations for the long term. Community Building and Sustainable Practices Education: ImmerseGreen fosters a sense of community and eco-conscious travel practices beyond the individual user experience. The system incorporates a social travel network, allowing users to share their immersive VR experiences, sustainable travel tips, and recommendations for eco-friendly destinations and accommodations. This fosters a sense of collective responsibility towards sustainable travel practices and allows for peer-to-peer learning. Furthermore, ImmerseGreen can partner with local tourism boards and eco-lodges to showcase conservation efforts and educational initiatives through curated content accessible within the VR platform. Imagine a user exploring a VR experience of a national park and learning about ongoing wildlife conservation efforts, inspiring them to support these initiatives during their visit. This educational aspect fosters a deeper understanding of the importance of sustainable tourism and empowers travelers to become responsible stewards of the destinations they visit. Data Privacy and Transparency: Understanding the importance of data privacy is paramount. ImmerseGreen employs a transparent and user-centric approach. Users have complete control over the data they share, with clear opt-in/opt-out options for different data points. Additionally, the system utilizes advanced anonymization techniques to safeguard user privacy while allowing deep learning algorithms to function effectively. ImmerseGreen presents a unique vision for the future of tourism: a personalized, immersive, and sustainable travel experience. By leveraging the power of AI, VR, and community engagement, ImmerseGreen empowers travelers to explore the world in a way that aligns with their desires while actively contributing to a more sustainable future for tourism destinations. This system has the potential to revolutionize the travel industry, fostering a new era where individual experiences are enriched, and environmental responsibility becomes an integral part of every journey.

METHODOLOGY

The dynamic field of AI in tourism necessitates a thorough research methodology to grasp its influence and potential. This framework outlines a multi-faceted approach to explore this evolving landscape.

Literature Review: Laying the Foundation

Conduct a systematic review of academic publications, industry reports, and white papers published within the last five years. This ensures the exploration of the latest advancements and trends in AI applications relevant to personalized and sustainable tourism. Utilize academic databases like ScienceDirect, Scopus, and Google Scholar to identify relevant research papers. Analyze the reviewed literature to identify key themes, challenges, and opportunities arising from the integration of AI technologies within tourism. Pay close attention to the specific AI technologies employed (e.g., recommendation systems, chatbots) and their effectiveness in both personalization and sustainability efforts.

Case Studies: Learning From Real-World Implementation

Select case studies of successful AI implementations in tourism. These could encompass travel platforms utilizing AI-powered recommendations, hotels leveraging AI for resource management, or destinations employing AI for managing overtourism. Analyze each case study through the dual lens of personalization and sustainability. Evaluate the effectiveness of the implemented AI solution in achieving its intended goals. Identify best practices and challenges encountered during the implementation process, offering insights into potential hurdles and practical solutions.

Expert Interviews: Unveiling Insider Perspectives

Conduct interviews with key stakeholders across the tourism industry, including researchers, technology developers, executives of travel platforms, and representatives of tourism destinations. Explore their perspectives on the potential and limitations of AI in both personalized and sustainable travel experiences. Gather insights on current trends and future directions in AI-driven travel solutions. Discuss ethical considerations surrounding AI adoption in tourism, such as data privacy concerns and the potential for algorithmic bias.

Data Analysis: Extracting Meaning From Numbers

If relevant to your research question, explore data sets related to tourism and traveler behavior. These data sets could originate from travel platforms, tourism boards, or publicly available resources. Analyze the data using appropriate statistical techniques to uncover patterns and correlations, shedding light on the impact of AI on traveler preferences and choices regarding sustainable practices.

User Studies: Understanding Traveler Sentiment

Conduct user studies to understand traveler perceptions and experiences with AI-powered travel technologies. These studies might involve surveys, focus groups, or usability testing exercises. Investigate how travelers react to personalized recommendations generated by AI systems, interact with AI chatbots, or utilize AI-powered travel applications. Gather user feedback on the effectiveness of AI in enhancing personalization and promoting sustainable travel choices.

Ethical Considerations: Ensuring Responsible Implementation

Throughout the research process, maintain a critical awareness of ethical considerations surrounding AI in tourism. Prioritize issues such as data privacy, algorithmic bias, and the potential for AI to exacerbate inequalities in travel experiences. Explore potential solutions and best practices for guaranteeing responsible and ethical use of AI in tourism, ensuring a future where technological innovation fosters inclusivity and safeguards traveler data.

Competitive Analysis: Benchmarking AI Adoption

Conduct a competitive analysis of how different companies and tourism destinations are utilizing AI technologies. This could involve analyzing features offered by various travel platforms, resource management strategies employed by hotels, or AI-driven initiatives implemented by different destinations. Identify best practices and innovative approaches adopted by industry leaders. Compare and contrast the effectiveness of different AI implementations, highlighting strengths and weaknesses of various solutions.

Cost-Benefit Analysis: Assessing Practical Feasibility

Analyze the economic implications of integrating AI technologies within the tourism industry. Conduct cost-benefit analyses to assess the potential return on investment (ROI) associated with specific AI implementations. Explore various funding models for the development and deployment of AI-powered travel solutions. Consider the long-term sustainability of AI initiatives, factoring in ongoing maintenance and potential upgrades.

Future Research Directions: Charting the Path Ahead

Identify gaps in existing knowledge and formulate recommendations for future research efforts. Explore emerging AI technologies with potential applications in personalized and sustainable tourism. Consider the social and cultural implications of widespread AI adoption within the tourism industry. Advocate for responsible research practices through the development of ethical frameworks for AI-driven tourism solutions.

CONCLUSION

In conclusion, the confluence of AI and tourism presents a transformative opportunity to reshape how we travel and experience the world. This exploration of AI technologies for personalized and sustainable tourism has revealed a dynamic landscape brimming with potential. From intelligent itinerary planning with chatbots to hyper-personalized recommendations with AI engines, AI empowers travelers to craft unique journeys that resonate with their individual interests. Travel apps are integrating AI to promote eco-friendly choices, recommending public transportation and carbon offsetting programs, while destinations leverage AI-powered resource management systems to minimize their environmental footprint. However, the path forward requires a comprehensive approach. The proposed system, "ImmerseGreen," exemplifies how AI can be harnessed to create a seamless integration of personalized experiences and sustainable practices. ImmerseGreen's deep learning capabilities allow for nuanced personalization, while VR integration fosters immersive pre-travel exploration. Real-time eco-friendly route optimization empowers travelers to make informed choices, while fostering a sense of community and promoting sustainable practices through educational content. The outlined research methodology lays the groundwork for a deeper understanding of AI in tourism. Through literature reviews, case studies, and expert interviews, researchers can glean valuable insights into the effectiveness of AI solutions from various stakeholders' perspectives. Data analysis and user studies provide crucial information about traveler behavior and sentiment towards AI-powered travel technologies. Ethical considerations remain paramount, demanding a focus on data privacy, algorithmic bias, and the responsible use of AI to ensure inclusivity and safeguard traveler information. Competitive analysis provides valuable benchmarks for AI adoption within the industry, allowing for the identification of best practices and innovative approaches. Cost-benefit analyses are essential for assessing the financial feasibility of AI implementations, while exploring funding models and considering long-term sustainability. Finally, outlining future research directions paves the way for continued exploration of emerging AI technologies, their potential applications, and the social and cultural implications of widespread AI adoption in tourism. AI holds immense potential for creating a future of travel that is both personalized and sustainable. This future hinges on responsible development and implementation, ensuring AI empowers travelers to explore the world with minimal environmental impact.

FUTURE ENHANCEMENT

The proposed AI travel assistant, ImmerseGreen, offers a promising vision for the future of travel. However, the ever-evolving nature of AI technology allows for even deeper personalization and integration of sustainable practices. Here's an exploration of potential future enhancements for ImmerseGreen:

Biometric Integration and Emotional Intelligence

Imagine ImmerseGreen going beyond user preferences and delving into user emotions. By incorporating biometric sensors (with user consent), the system could analyze factors like heart rate and facial expressions during VR experiences. This data could be used to tailor recommendations further. For instance, if a user experiences anxiety during a VR exploration of a bustling city, ImmerseGreen could suggest alternative destinations with quieter environments.

Furthermore, advancements in AI-powered emotional intelligence could enable ImmerseGreen to analyze user responses to travel content and curate recommendations accordingly. Imagine the system detecting a sense of awe while a user explores a VR experience of the Northern Lights, and subsequently suggesting a real-world trip to witness this natural phenomenon. This integration of biometrics and emotional intelligence would create an unprecedented level of personalization, ensuring travel experiences that not only align with interests but also evoke positive emotions.

Gamified Sustainability Tracking and Rewards

ImmerseGreen can further incentivize sustainable travel choices by adopting a gamified approach. Imagine a "Green Traveler Score" that tracks a user's eco-friendly choices throughout their journey. This score could be calculated based on factors like opting for public transportation, choosing eco-friendly accommodations, and participating in sustainable activities. Gamified elements like badges, leaderboards, and virtual rewards could be implemented. Leaderboards could encourage healthy competition among travelers, while virtual rewards could be redeemed for discounts on future eco-friendly travel options. This gamification element would incentivize responsible travel choices and foster a sense of community among environmentally conscious travelers.

Predictive Maintenance and Resource Optimization for Destinations

While ImmerseGreen focuses on traveler actions, its impact can extend to destinations. AI algorithms can analyze past data on energy consumption, water usage, and waste generation to predict future needs and optimize resource allocation. Imagine AI predicting peak energy demand during a tourist influx and automatically adjusting energy consumption in hotels and attractions. Similarly, the system could anticipate fluctuations in waste generation and optimize collection schedules, leading to a more efficient and sustainable use of resources.

Immersive Cultural Experiences With Augmented Reality (AR)

VR offers a fantastic pre-travel experience, but in-destination exploration demands innovative tools. Here's where AR comes in. Imagine ImmerseGreen utilizing AR to create an interactive overlay on a traveler's smartphone camera. As they explore a destination, the AR overlay could provide historical information about landmarks, translate local signage in real-time, and even recommend hidden culinary gems. This AR integration would transform travel into an immersive cultural learning experience, fostering deeper connections with destinations and fostering a sense of place.

Blockchain for Sustainable Tourism Initiatives

Blockchain technology, known for its secure data management capabilities, can empower ImmerseGreen to support sustainable tourism initiatives more effectively. Imagine a system where travelers could contribute directly to conservation efforts through the platform. Blockchain could ensure secure and transparent transactions, allowing travelers to directly fund local projects like wildlife preservation or habitat restoration. Additionally, blockchain could facilitate a system of carbon offsets, allowing travelers to purchase verified offsets directly from sustainable projects around the world, mitigating the environmental impact of their travel.

AI-powered Local Community Engagement

Sustainable tourism thrives on collaboration between travelers and local communities. ImmerseGreen can be a catalyst for this interaction. AI-powered translation tools can facilitate real-time communication between travelers and local residents, promoting cultural exchange and fostering a sense of understanding. The system could recommend locally-owned restaurants and shops, encouraging travelers to support the local economy and minimize reliance on large, international corporations. Additionally, ImmerseGreen could curate immersive VR experiences showcasing local cultural traditions and fostering appreciation for the unique heritage of each destination.

REFERENCES

Becken, S., & Patterson, M. (2018). Reducing plastic waste in tourism: A multi-stakeholder approach. *Journal of Sustainable Tourism*, 26(1), 141–159.

Buckley, R. (2016). *Conservation tourism*. Routledge.

Buhalis, D., & Sinclair, M. T. (2020). Artificial intelligence in tourism: A critical review. *International Journal of Hospitality Management*, 87, 102688.

Chen, J., Luo, Y., Liu, H., Qin, J., & Chen, E. (2023). Algorithmic bias in AI-driven tourism: A review and future research directions. *Annals of Tourism Research*, 90, 103357.

Cohen, M., Gaston, G., & Goeldner, J. (2019). *Tourism and development revisited: Critical issues for a new century*. Routledge.

Gretzel, U., Kim, W., Koo, C., & Park, J. (2022). Smart tourism: A conceptual model and a literature review. *Journal of Hospitality and Tourism Management*, 47, 102853.

Gretzel, U., Koo, C., Kim, W., & Yannopoulos, G. (2020). Smart tourism: A systematic literature review. *Journal of Hospitality and Tourism Management*, 40, 553–564.

Gretzel, U., Koo, C., & Shin, J. H. (2020). *Smart tourism: Foundations and applications*. Emerald Publishing Limited.

Huang, Z., Wu, J., Li, J., Zhao, Y., & Li, Z. (2023). Applications of artificial intelligence in tourism management: A literature review. *Sustainability (Switzerland)*, 15(6), 3442.

Kim, H., Kim, Y., & Fesenmaier, D. R. (2019). Artificial intelligence for personalized and sustainable tourism experiences: A review and research agenda. *Journal of Sustainable Tourism*, 28(8), 1427–1450.

Kim, H., Park, S., Jeong, S., & Lee, S. (2023). Ethical issues in artificial intelligence for customer experience: A case study in the tourism industry. *Journal of Travel Research*, 62(2), 370–384.

Kim, H., Park, Y., Jeong, S., & Lee, S. (2018). How does artificial intelligence contribute to customer experience? An exploratory study on the service industry. *Industrial Management & Data Systems*, 118(9), 1824–1838.

Kontogiannis, V., Skourtis, C., & Tsiotas, G. (2021). Technological advancements in tourism: A review of the literature. *International Journal of Tourism Cities*, 7(3), 326–343.

Kontogiannis, V., Skuras, D., & Petridis, P. (2021). A conceptual framework for over-tourism management: Insights from a tourism destination perspective. *Journal of Sustainable Tourism*, 29(4), 756–779.

Law, R., Fong, S., & Wu, F. (2021). Artificial intelligence for dynamic pricing in tourism: A review of the literature. *Journal of Travel Research*, 60(2), 394–412.

Lee, J., & Kozinets, R. V. (2020). Algorithmic tourism: Personalization, power, and experiential consumption. *The Journal of Consumer Research*, 47(2), 313–340.

Li, J., Xu, Y., Zhao, Y., Li, Z., & Fu, Y. (2018). How can artificial intelligence benefit the tourism industry? *Sustainability (Switzerland)*, 10(12), 4528.

Li, X., Wang, Y., & Li, J. (2023). A review of intelligent tourism research: Literature analysis using CiteSpace. *Sustainability*, 15(4), 2324.

Liu, Z., Li, J., Ye, B., Li, Y., & Yan, J. (2022). Artificial intelligence and tourism: A review and future directions. *Annals of Tourism Research*, 88, 103242.

Luo, X., Zheng, Y., Xie, J., & Ngai, E. W. T. (2020). Customer churn prediction using deep learning in telecommunication networks. *Neurocomputing*, 408, 125–139.

UNWTO & UNEP. (2020). *Making tourism green: A guide for public policy makers*. World Tourism Organization and United Nations Environment Programme.

Verhoef, P. C., Hoekstra, R. J., & Bruinsma, M. (2019). Artificial intelligence: An engine for customer experience transformation in travel and hospitality. *Journal of Travel Research*, 58(8), 1478–1489.

Wang, Y., Li, J., & Wang, Y. (2020). A framework for privacy protection in AI-powered tourism. *Sustainability (Switzerland)*, 12(13), 5458.

Wang, Y., Li, J., & Wang, Y. (2022). A framework for privacy protection in AI-powered tourism. *Sustainability (Switzerland)*, 14(11), 7042.

Xiang, Z., Gong, S., & Xu, Y. (2022). A survey of tourism recommendation systems. *Journal of Computational Science*, 18(3), 547–569.

Xiao, L., & Li, J. (2020). Artificial intelligence for tourism marketing: A review of the literature and future directions. *Journal of Travel Research*, 59(7), 1459–1480.

Xu, Y., Li, J., Zhao, Y., & Fu, Y. (2023). How can AI benefit tourism: A review and research agenda for responsible development. *Journal of Sustainable Tourism*, 31(2), 437–458.

Chapter 3
AI-Driven Personalized Room Management in the Modern Hotel Industry

Mohammad Badruddoza Talukder
https://orcid.org/0009-0008-1662-9221
International University of Business Agriculture and Technology, Bangladesh

Firoj Kabir
https://orcid.org/0009-0001-3014-3163
Daffodil Institute of IT, Bangladesh

Ferdaus Anam Jibon
International University of Business Agriculture and Technology, Bangladesh

ABSTRACT

This study examines how AI-driven personalized room management systems affect modern hotel operational efficiency and guest satisfaction. AI improves passenger pleasure, manages hotel operations, and addresses emerging hospitality industry concerns. The authors got all the data from academic and industry studies and previous articles. According to the results, AI-powered personalized room management systems offer predictive maintenance, tailored services, energy management, and customized room settings. However, ROI measurement, personal contact, and integration are challenges. Despite these challenges, AI optimize operations and improve guest happiness in the hospitality business. Limitations include the difficulty of evaluating AI solutions' return on investment, the necessity for ongoing upgrades and revisions, and ethical issues about data privacy and security. This work adds to hospitality AI literature by addressing significant problems and highlighting potential benefits. Hoteliers may use AI-driven personalized room management to

DOI: 10.4018/979-8-3693-5678-4.ch003

improve guest experiences and operational efficiency.

1. INTRODUCTION

The hospitality sector is a keystone of the world economy because it has a long history of adapting to shifting market conditions. A 2021 Statista analysis projects that by 2030, the industry will generate more than $100,000 in sales (Belousova et al., 2022). The Internet of Things (IoT) and artificial intelligence (AI) are two emerging technologies growing exponentially simultaneously. According to IDC (2020), yearly global spending on IoT and AI is expected to reach hundreds of billions of dollars (Hasija et al., 2023; Kumar et al., 2024a). Significant changes have been observed in the rapidly growing worldwide hospitality industry, especially in online travel arrangements, including bookings for hotels, buses, trains, and air travel. According to the World Travel and Tourism Council (WTTC), by 2028, India's share of world tourism is projected to reach about $200 billion (Jatav, 2022). Furthermore, the COVID-19 pandemic has altered the course of events. It hastened the adoption of online travel planning tools and increased the urgency of the hotel sector's need for digital transformation (Kumar et al., 2024b; Talukder & Muhsina, 2024).

Artificial intelligence (AI) is revolutionizing the hospitality sector by presenting previously unheard-of chances for creativity and improved customer experience. Artificial Intelligence (AI) technologies, including natural language processing and machine learning, enable businesses to make unprecedented and efficient decisions (Talukder & Das, 2024). The tourism and hotel AI market is expected to grow at a rate exceeding $1.2 billion by 2026, demonstrating that AI is essential to the hospitality industry (Mohammad et al., 2024; Abubakar et al., 2020). This revolutionary wave introduces applications to enhance guest experiences, optimize hotel operations, provide more competent customer service, and fortify security standards. Nevertheless, implementing intelligent technologies in hotel services offers advantages and potential hazards. AI-powered personalized room management can significantly improve service quality and client pleasure. However, it also brings up worries about confidentiality, security of information, and the possibility of technological malfunctions. In addition, the incorporation of AI could result in the replacement of certain positions previously filled by human employees, thus affecting employee happiness and morale. Therefore, business executives must investigate AI's possibilities to stay ahead of the curve in this fast-paced field (Schneider et al., 2023).

AI can enhance power effectiveness and environmental responsibility by optimizing resource use, such as adjusting lighting and climatic conditions based on occupancy. Nevertheless, the use of AI systems also entails the peril of over-reliance on technology, wherein any failure or cyber-attack could impede operations and hurt the visitor experience. This chapter will explore the growing need for artificial intelligence (AI) in the hospitality sector and how it may both optimize efficiency in hotel chain operations and significantly enhance the visitor experience. AI-driven tailored room supervision increases visitor satisfaction, optimizes operational efficiency, and stimulates revenue growth by fully combining advanced technology with traditional hospitality services (Talukder et al., 2024). This pioneering combination of hospitality and technology is revolutionizing the hotel industry by establishing a new standard for passenger comfort and convenience, redefining the concept of exceptional service (Wang & Chen, 2024).

2. BACKGROUND OF THE STUDY

Artificial intelligence and machine learning are explicitly applied to the hospitality sector and are known as hospitality AI (Huang et al., 2022). Hotel artificial intelligence is becoming more and more integrated into the operations of property groups and hospitality brands, from guest-facing services to internal team activities. There is a widespread concern that artificial intelligence would displace people from their jobs. However, this chapter can state with certainty that technology has improved the work of the hotel industry (Talukder & Kumar, 2024). While artificial intelligence in hotels may seem like a relatively recent development, one can probably be more familiar with its applications than one may think. For instance, according to a McKinsey guide, voice-activated devices like Siri and Alexa rely on AI principles to work (De Kloet & Yang, 2022).

Interestingly, artificial intelligence was also used to create tools like chatbots for website customer care. Nowadays, hotel service chatbots use artificial intelligence to perform tasks like in-room delivery and concierge recommendations (Talukder et al., 2024). Artificial intelligence has the potential to significantly improve hotel operations by automating tedious procedures like reservation and contactless check-in, freeing up employees to concentrate on offering visitors individualized attention (Gangwar & Reddy, 2023). Due to artificial intelligence's assistance in leveraging previous data to forecast future demand and revenue and optimizing price and availability to optimize revenue, most hotel companies have seen significant revenue increases (Alrawadieh et al., 2021).

3. OBJECTIVES OF THE STUDY

The study's goals are as follows:

1. To find out the personalized room settings based on individual preferences and specially selected suggestions for nearby activities and sites will be offered to guests to improve their stay.
2. To predict analytics that will streamline housekeeping and maintenance schedules and real-time data.
3. To ensure AI-driven controls for guest information protection and room access will be implemented to prioritize security and privacy.

4. CONCEPTUAL MODEL

Hotel Product

- **Definition & Characteristics:**

In the context of the hospitality industry, the term "hotel product" refers to a wide variety of facilities and services that are provided to guests. These services and amenities include housing, food and beverages, entertainment venues, and organizing events. The key features that define a hotel business are relaxation, hygiene, security, and comfort, all of which are essential to meeting the expectations of guests to the greatest extent possible.

- **Quality Issues & Guest Satisfaction KPIs:**

Quality Problems and Key Performance Indicators for Customer Satisfaction Quality problems in hotels can be caused by lousy assistance, inadequate amenities, and maintenance that is not adequately performed. Guest reviews, repeat reservations, the Net Promoter Score (NPS), and the amount of time it takes to resolve customer complaints are all examples of key performance indicators (KPIs) that measure customer satisfaction in the hotel business. Both of these topics have already been covered in the literature section.

Smart Hotel Service

- **Definition:**

The Internet of Things (IoT), artificial intelligence (AI), and automation are examples of modern technologies that are integrated into smart hotel services to improve the overall experience of guests and simplify the operation of hotels. Intelligent room monitors, digital check-in and check-out procedures, personalized service offers, and decision-making that is driven by data are all included in this category.

- **Mechanisms:**

The usage of detection devices, connected gadgets, artificial intelligence computations, and cloud computing are the processes that are utilized by smart hotel services. These mechanisms are responsible for the collection and analysis of data, which enables real-time modifications and personalized services. For instance, artificial intelligence can anticipate the preferences of guests based on their previous actions and then tailor the room settings accordingly.

- **Risks and Inputs:**

The materials used for innovative services at hotels include data from guests, data from the Internet of Things devices, and artificial intelligence algorithms. Concerns about data privacy, dangers to cyber security, and the possibility of equipment failures, which could result in disruptions to service are some of the issues that are linked with these technologies.

State of Art

- **Theoretical Foundations:**

The theoretical foundations of smart hotel services are anchored on the level of service and technology acceptability models. These models inform the theoretical foundations of smart hotel services. According to these models, the perceived simplicity of use along with the perceived usefulness of new technologies are essential elements that influence the adoption of these technologies when it comes to the hospitality industry.

- **Empirical Foundations:**

Foundations Based on Empirical Research: Empirical studies have demonstrated that cutting-edge hotel services have the potential to dramatically improve both customer happiness and operational efficiency. The findings of the research reveal that guests value customized interactions and are willing to contribute their data to receive improved services, provided that their privacy is protected.

The purpose of this conceptual framework is to provide a foundation for understanding the delicate equilibrium that exists in the hospitality sector between the use of cutting-edge technologies and the upkeep of unparalleled levels of service quality and client happiness.

Figure 1. Conceptual Model of AI-Driven Personalized Room Management (Self-developed)

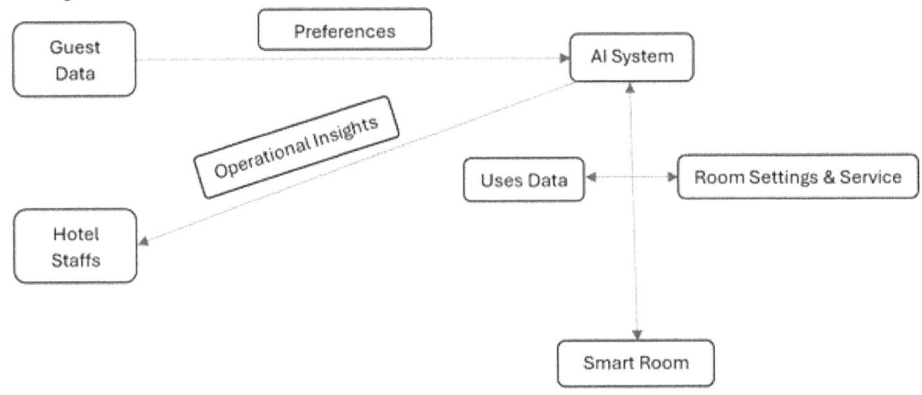

5. METHODOLOGY

This chapter uses secondary data sources such as academic literature, industry reports, and case studies. The literature study looks at previous studies on the effects of AI on revenue management, customer experience management, and hotel operations (Mariani & Borghi, 2021). We have collected the literature, and data collection includes academic literature from databases like Scopus, Web of Science, and Google Scholar, with search terms like "artificial intelligence," "hotel operations," "customer experience management," and "revenue management.

Method of Qualitative Research and Analysis

The method of qualitative analysis that was utilized in this investigation was known as thematic analysis. The use of this method makes it possible to recognize, investigate, and report on recurring themes or patterns within the data. It works very well for analyzing qualitative data that is difficult to understand and for obtaining knowledge of the fundamental concepts that are the driving force behind study findings.

An Analysis of the Framework

- **Epistemological Posture:**

The research takes a constructivist epistemological stance, which holds that knowledge is generated through social behaviors and interactions. This is the epistemological posture that is used by the study. This viewpoint recognizes the significance of personal observations and judgments in gaining an understanding of the impact that artificial intelligence has on the operation of hotels and the level of pleasure experienced by customers.

- **Mode of Reasoning:**

The inductive technique of reasoning was utilized in this investigation. This mode of reasoning allows for themes and patterns to arise from the information without the need for any predetermined assumptions to be formulated. By enabling the data to speak for themselves, this method makes it possible to gain a more profound comprehension of the phenomenon that is being investigated.

- **Nature of the Analysis:**

Exploratory research is being conducted to gain a better understanding of the rapidly developing and relatively young subject of artificial intelligence-driven hotel services. It is appropriate to do research of this sort because the hotel industry is still in the early stages of adopting artificial intelligence and there is a need to discover new insights and viewpoints.

6. LITERATURE REVIEW

The simulation of human intelligence in robots designed to think and behave like people is known as artificial intelligence or AI (Markauskaite et al., 2022). Cognitive talents include learning, reasoning, problem-solving, perception, and language understanding. The process of making a computer, robot under computer control, or piece of software think intelligently like a human mind is known as artificial intelligence. Artificial Intelligence is achieved by examining cognitive processes and patterns in the human brain (Korteling et al., 2021a). The output of these investigations includes the creation of intelligent systems and software. Hoteliers are expected to deliver excellent customer service and satisfaction in the fiercely competitive hotel sector while seeking methods to streamline their operations (Kumar et al., 2024; Badruddoza et al., 2024). Artificial Intelligence (AI) technology presents a viable answer by equipping hotels with the necessary tools to maximize marketing, improve guest experience, streamline operations, and more (Alrawadieh et al., 2021).

For a long time, the hotel sector has depended on interpersonal connections and customized services to deliver exceptional visitor experiences. However, as AI develops quickly, the hotel sector is adopting several cutting-edge technologies that are revolutionizing long-standing procedures (Law & Chen, 2024). It is critical to consider both the positive and negative effects AI may have on the industry as it develops. The hotel industry is a big business within international frameworks, and changes in modern development patterns and tourism demand impact it (Mohammad et al., 2024). Many trends highlight the significance of the current hotel industry, as travelers nowadays seek personalized and unique experiences rather than being content with the basic amenities hotels offer (Bharwani & Mathews, 2021). This has made tourism the main reason for these visits. Specifically, motivations now include actively participating in special interest tourism and monetizing market niches rather than solely relating to leisure and idle spending of free time. To thrive in the fierce competition, hotel establishments work hard to monitor trends and use innovations (Far Eastern Federal University & Shumakova, 2019). Business intelligence and the vision to integrate thoughtfully designed services and hotel architecture into their surroundings and fit in with the destination's natural, historical, and cultural resources play a part in achieving business performance. Hotel businesses operate in a competitive environment impacted by ongoing economic and market shifts (Leyva & Parra, 2021). The overall hotel marketing strategy, the business, and the business outcomes are affected by the strategic decisions made on orientation towards specific market segments. These judgments are founded on extensive market study, user super segmentation, and a resource basis for valuation. The modification impacts the hotel's ability to establish fresh competitiveness and set itself apart from a homogenous group of unidentified lodging options (Yacoub & ElHajjar, 2021).

To put it in the most general terms possible, hotel automation uses cutting-edge technological systems to monitor and regulate various hotel operations without human intervention (Das et al., 2024). Integrating this kind of technology into a hotel's operations and processes to increase productivity while simultaneously giving visitors a better, more convenient stay (Golja & Paulišić, 2021). Hotels usually use automation systems based on a network of connected hardware and software. These technologies can completely replace or be incorporated into the hotel's management infrastructure in certain situations. For instance, hotels frequently use automation systems to manage routine daily chores like inventory control (Mercan et al., 2021). They may also be used to quickly analyze room rates and determine the most profitable and long-term rates to charge each day of the year. The advantages that automation provides to hotel visitors are still different. Hotel automation ensures that guests' requirements are satisfied quickly, easily, and in ways that will encourage them to stay at the hotel repeatedly. Examples include automated check-ins and tailored room settings (Zhang et al., 2023).

The development of technology and broader societal shifts are reflected in the history of room management. The development of room management from the primary common areas of antiquity to today's multipurpose, technologically advanced rooms demonstrates humanity's adaptability and the never-ending search for better living conditions (Talukder, 2024). Over time, the idea of room management has changed dramatically due to shifts in social conventions, technology, architecture, and economics (Martella & Enia, 2021). An outline of room management's historical development is shown below:

- **The Prehistoric and Medieval Eras**

Ancient Civilizations: Because there was little sophisticated infrastructure in ancient Egypt, Greece, and Rome, room management was comparatively easy. While there were few private apartments, which were usually used by the aristocracy, large halls were used for communal activities (Almenar Fernández & Belenguer González, 2022).

Europe during the Middle Ages: Manors and castles had a hierarchical layout, with rooms assigned according to function and prestige. The Great Hall was the hub for social events and meals, with private rooms reserved for the aristocracy.

- **Early Modern to Renaissance Eras**

Renaissance: As the merchant classes expanded and cities became more populous, magnificent residences featuring specialized spaces like parlors, studies, and libraries were built. Additional furniture and decorative accents led to a rise in complexity in room management.

17th to 18th Century: Interior design received more focus throughout the Baroque and Rococo eras. Luxuriously furnished and designated for particular purposes, rooms reflected social standing and the value of hospitality (Sousa et al., 2021).

- **1800s**

Industrial Revolution: New construction methods and materials were created due to technological breakthroughs. During this time, the middle class grew and started to imitate the aristocracy's room management methods, resulting in more uniform room functions.

Victorian Era: Houses grew more divided into areas designated for specific purposes, such as dining rooms, drawing rooms, and bedrooms. Order, privacy, and efficiency were prioritized (Al Husban et al., 2021).

- **20th Century**

Early 20th Century: Room management was influenced by the Arts and Crafts and subsequent Modernist movements, which prioritized simplicity and functionality. As fewer partitions were added, open floor layouts gained popularity, encouraging a more flexible use of available space. Following World War II, home design was impacted by suburbanization and the growth of the nuclear family. The increased popularity of open-plan living spaces can be attributed to a drive toward more casual lifestyles and convenience of movement within the house (Lekić Glavan et al., 2022).

- **From the late 20th Century to the present**

Late 20th Century: As new technologies (such as air conditioning and home entertainment systems) were developed, they brought new features to homes that impacted room organization. Media rooms and home offices became popular.

21st Century: Smart home technologies, which enable automated and remote control of lighting, climate, and security, are another example of how technological innovations are continuing to change room management. Key themes representing shifting lifestyles and environmental concerns include multipurpose spaces and sustainable design (e.g., remote working) (Vuscan & Muntean, 2023).

7. FINDINGS AND DISCUSSIONS

The hospitality sector, which includes lodging facilities, dining establishments, travel agencies, and resorts, has particular difficulties in satisfying the rising demands of contemporary visitors (Vlami, 2023). The emergence of social media, review websites, and online booking systems has made guests more picky and demanding. They anticipate smooth interactions, individualized experiences, and effective services. This is where artificial intelligence (AI) can change the hotel sector. AI technologies can improve security and safety, streamline operations, and improve guest services in the hospitality industry (Buhalis & Moldavska, 2022). Hotels and other hospitality businesses can use AI technology to automate repetitive work with chatbots and virtual assistants, provide guests with personalized suggestions based on their preferences, and integrate voice recognition systems to manage in-room amenities efficiently (Talukder et al., 2021). AI can also help with revenue management by facilitating dynamic pricing strategies, predictive maintenance to reduce downtime, and offering insightful data analytics to improve decision-making (Javaid et al., 2022).

The findings of this chapter also demonstrate that personalized room management that is powered by artificial intelligence has the potential to dramatically increase guest satisfaction by providing individualized experiences that cater to the interests of each unique guest. Through the automation of routine operations and the provision of data-driven insights for improved decision-making, artificial intelligence technologies make it possible for hotels to maximize their operational efficiency. On the other hand, the implementation of AI also brings about several difficulties. As guests become more aware of how their data is gathered and utilized, privacy concerns have become of the utmost importance. Cyber security threats provide a substantial risk, as they have the potential to cause information theft and system failures, both of which can interrupt their operations. Further, there is the possibility of becoming overly dependent on technology, which may fail services if there are problems with the technology.

Although there are some obstacles to overcome, the hospitality industry stands to gain a significant amount from the implementation of AI. Through the enhancement of the guest experience, the improvement of operational efficiency, and the ability to provide personalized services that separate hotels from their competitors, artificial intelligence has the potential to promote revenue development. Hotels can strike a balance that allows them to maximize benefits while reducing potential drawbacks by addressing the dangers that are provided by artificial intelligence (AI) and maximizing the opportunities that it presents.

Individualized Room Service

- **Customized room settings:** Artificial intelligence systems can learn and retain information about visitor preferences, including preferred lighting levels, temperatures, and entertainment selections. When visitors arrive in their rooms, bright room technology can automatically modify these settings according to each visitor's profile, creating a welcoming and customized atmosphere (Talukder et al., 2023).
- **Intelligent energy management:** To optimize energy use in bright rooms, AI algorithms examine data on room usage, weather, and visitor occupancy trends. These systems cut energy waste, lower operating costs, and support

- **Predictive maintenance:** Artificial intelligence (AI) algorithms can examine sensor and smart room device data to identify possible maintenance problems before they become disruptive. By constantly monitoring equipment performance, these technologies can anticipate malfunctions, plan maintenance in advance, and reduce downtime, all of which contribute to a seamless and uninterrupted visitor experience.
- **Personalized services and suggestions:** AI-driven smart room technology enables visitors to receive customized offers and recommendations (Štilić et al., 2023). These systems analyze historical data, contextual information, and guest preferences to provide tailored services, activities, or neighboring attractions that match guests' interests. This improves the visitor experience and fosters closer ties between hotels and their patrons.
- **Pre-arrival personalization:** This is one of the main ways artificial intelligence is used in the hotel industry. Artificial intelligence (AI) systems collect behavioral data and guest preferences to provide personalized experiences and recommendations before guests arrive (Lv et al., 2022). Hotels in Sonoma, for instance, use AI algorithms to create customized activity recommendations based on each visitor's interests. Ultimately, this personalization creates a memorable and customized experience, increases guest happiness, and encourages repeat business and great reviews.
- **Improvement of the check-in procedure:** AI-driven innovations are revolutionizing the hotel check-in procedure with the intention of giving visitors a smooth and practical experience. AI can pre-capture visitor information through intelligent pre-arrival processes, facilitating a more expedient and customized check-in experience upon arrival. Brands like Citizens, for example, use AI technologies to speed up the check-in process and concentrate on engaging in guest interactions instead of doing administrative work. This guarantees a more seamless visitor experience and establishes the mood for a happy stay right away (Lekić Glavan et al., 2022).

Automation and Controls for Smart Rooms

Automated room control systems that modify the temperature, humidity, and airflow of a space according to visitor preferences and occupancy status are made possible by smart room controls (Samancioglu, 2022). Automatically adjusts room temperature to maximize guest comfort and energy efficiency, resulting in a more enjoyable and environmentally friendly stay. AI's development has fundamentally changed the technical environment, ushering in a new era where automation and smart technologies are at the forefront of innovation. AI has a bigger and more significant impact on the hospitality sector, providing previously unheard-of chances to improve visitor experiences and hotel operations. This chapter explores how artificial intelligence (AI) will disrupt the hotel industry, impacting everything from operational efficiency to individualized client experiences.

8. PRACTICAL CHALLENGES

- **Integration and Implementation:** Incorporating AI into current systems can be difficult and expensive. It calls for a change in operational procedures, personnel training, and the appropriate technology. Companies need to weigh the advantages of AI personalization against the challenges of putting it into practice (Rane et al., 2023).
- **Preserving Human Touch:** An excessive dependence on AI risks eroding the human touch that customers value in a sector centered on interpersonal interactions. It's critical to balance automated personalization and human connection (Rane et al., 2023).
- **Maintaining Up with Technological Advancements**: Due to the quick development of AI technology, companies need to update and modify their systems regularly to remain relevant. This can be a significant obstacle, especially for smaller businesses with tighter budgets.
- **Measuring ROI:** It might be challenging to calculate the return on investment for AI solutions. Businesses must set precise criteria to evaluate how well AI personalization tactics improve visitor experiences and increase revenue (Haleem et al., 2022).

Businesses may fully utilize AI to customize visitor experiences while upholding trust and providing genuine value by tackling these moral and practical issues.

9. THE FUTURE OF AI IN PERSONALIZATION

AI personalization has a bright future ahead of it, one that has the potential to transform how companies engage with their customers ultimately. Several emerging trends and developments in AI technology are expected to improve and refine visitor experience personalization.

- **Improvements in Machine Learning and Predictive Analytics**: As AI systems become increasingly skilled at analyzing data, more precise and nu-

anced forecasts will be possible. This will enable even more exact customization and better anticipation of the demands of visitors (Stylos et al., 2021).
- **Seamless Integration across Platforms and Devices:** As technology gets more linked, artificial intelligence (AI) will make it possible to personalize content across a variety of platforms and devices in a seamless manner. With AI maintaining the context, guests might begin interacting on one device and carry on another.
- **Improved Natural Language Processing:** Artificial intelligence can comprehend and react to human language even more as NLP advances. As a result, interactions between visitors and AI-powered technologies will be more engaging and natural (Buhalis & Moldavska, 2022).
- **Ethical AI and Improved Data Security:** As privacy concerns become more widely known, the world will focus more on ethical AI and improved data security measures. Increased trust between customers and establishments will increase customization's acceptance and ubiquity.
- **Personalization Beyond Digital Interactions:** Artificial Intelligence will significantly and subtly impact physical locations and experiences by extending personalization beyond digital interactions (Puntoni et al., 2021).

These developments will increase personalization's effectiveness and strengthen its connection to the visitor experience. With the development of AI, there are countless opportunities to create experiences that are genuinely unique and unforgettable.

Accepting AI to Improve Visitor Experiences

This chapter delves into incorporating Artificial Intelligence in personalizing visitor experiences, a passing trend and an extensive development in the service sector. A level of personalization previously unattainable is now possible because of AI's capabilities, which range from advanced machine learning algorithms to predictive analytics. AI is still in the process of changing guest services. The potential advantages are enormous despite its difficulties, which include ethical issues and the requirement for a balanced human-AI connection (Hevner & Storey, 2023). Companies that use AI to customize the visitor experience remain ahead of the curve and build stronger relationships with their clients.

Looking ahead, AI has much intriguing potential in personalization. As technology develops, so will our ability to please and accommodate visitors. Businesses must view AI as an addition to their offerings, strengthening the human component at the core of hospitality rather than trying to replace it. And lastly, AI opens up completely new possibilities for customization in the guest experience. By seizing these chances, businesses may create distinctive and unforgettable experiences that guests remember long after their stay (Simonis, 2023).

10. FUTURE STUDY DIRECTION

The hotel sector will witness notable progress shortly regarding AI-powered tailored room management. This evolution will require deeper integration with cutting-edge IoT technology to customize room settings and services further. This will allow for real-time data collection on guest preferences and behavior. Incorporating virtual reality (VR) and augmented reality (AR) experiences will also give guests immersive previews of rooms and amenities, improving decision-making and the booking process (McLean & Barhorst, 2022). AI-driven systems will use biometric authentication and encryption to protect visitor data and guarantee secure access, enhancing security and privacy safeguards. With AI algorithms, predictive personalization will become more proactive by anticipating visitor wants and preferences based on past behavior and outside variables. Prioritization will be given to sustainability projects, with AI maximizing energy use and trash disposal techniques (Kumar et al., 2024; Mohammad & Sanjeev, 2024). Moreover, hands-free guest interactions will be possible through integration with speech and gesture control technologies, improving convenience and enjoyment. These developments will transform the visitor experience and spur efficiency and creativity in the hospitality industry.

11. MANAGERIAL IMPLICATIONS

The following managerial implications are placed within the "AI-Driven Personalized Room Management in the Modern Hotel Industry." These include:

- **Enhanced Guest Experience and Satisfaction:** AI-driven chatbots and virtual assistants can be used in conjunction with AI-driven tailored room management to offer customers individualized support and raise their level of satisfaction with both their stay and their accommodations (Milton, 2024).
- **Simplified Reservation Process:** By anticipating guest preferences, suggesting customized room options, and dynamically modifying pricing, AI-based reservation systems within the framework of AI-driven personalized Room Management streamline the reservation process, enhancing the guest's booking experience and raising the probability of booking a personalized room (Korteling et al., 2021b).

- **Enhanced Operational Efficiency:** When combined with AI-driven personalized room management systems, robotics and automation powered by AI can streamline operations like housekeeping, room service, and guest requests. This increases operational efficiency and frees staff to concentrate more on providing guests with individualized experiences.
- **Personalized Guest Experiences:** Using AI with AI-driven personalized room management, hotels may customize every facet of the visitor experience, from reservation to lodging, according to specific preferences. This involves providing guests personalized accommodation features, amenities, and services to make their stays memorable and distinctive (Sthapit et al., 2022).
- **Revolutionized Revenue Management:** Within the context of AI-driven personalized room management, demand forecasting, and AI-driven dynamic pricing algorithms optimize room rates based on specific guest preferences and market dynamics, resulting in higher revenue and better profitability while offering guests personalized pricing options (Doborjeh et al., 2022).
- **Enhanced Safety and Security:** By monitoring properties in real-time, identifying potential threats, and guaranteeing the safety of guests and their personalized room environments, AI-driven surveillance systems and technologies, when integrated into AI-driven personalized Room Management, enhance safety and security measures.

12. CONCLUSION

AI-driven personalized room management in the contemporary hotel sector represents a paradigm shift in hospitality services and operations. AI is becoming a vital tool for fostering innovation and efficiency in the hospitality sector due to changing visitor expectations and technology breakthroughs. The need for digital transformation in the hospitality industry is evident, given forecasts of significant growth in global tourism income and rising investments in AI and IoT technology. The promise of artificial intelligence to revolutionize the hospitality industry is demonstrated by its capacity to improve guest experiences via customized room settings, clever energy conservation, and proactive maintenance plans. AI-driven solutions also present chances for enhanced security, revenue management, and operational optimization. Using AI technologies, hotels can improve guest loyalty, optimize operations, and provide smooth and customized services. Though AI has much potential, its practical application necessitates considering ethical, privacy, and security issues. Future studies should thus concentrate on resolving these issues and investigating cutting-edge AI technologies to further transform the hospitality sector and guarantee sustainable growth in the digital age.

REFERENCES

Abubakar, A. I., Omeke, K. G., Ozturk, M., Hussain, S., & Imran, M. A. (2020). The Role of Artificial Intelligence Driven 5G Networks in COVID-19 Outbreak: Opportunities, Challenges, and Future Outlook. *Frontiers in Communications and Networks*, 1, 575065. DOI: 10.3389/frcmn.2020.575065

Al Husban, S. A. M., Al Husban, A. A. S., & Al Betawi, Y. (2021). The Impact of the Cultural Beliefs on Forming and Designing Spatial Organizations, Spaces Hierarchy, and Privacy of Detached Houses and Apartments in Jordan. *Space and Culture*, 24(1), 66–82. DOI: 10.1177/1206331218791934

Almenar Fernández, L., & Belenguer González, A. (2022). The Transformation of Private Space in the Later Middle Ages: Rooms and Living Standards in the Kingdom of Valencia (1280-1450). *Journal of Urban History*, 48(4), 782–806. DOI: 10.1177/0096144220967990

Alrawadieh, Z., Alrawadieh, Z., & Cetin, G. (2021). Digital transformation and revenue management: Evidence from the hotel industry. *Tourism Economics*, 27(2), 328–345. DOI: 10.1177/1354816620901928

Badruddoza Talukder, M., Kumar, S., Misra, L. I., & Firoj Kabir, . (2024). Determining the role of eco-tourism service quality, tourist satisfaction, and destination loyalty: A case study of Kuakata beach. *Acta Scientiarum Polonorum. Administratio Locorum*, 23(1), 133–151. DOI: 10.31648/aspal.9275

Belousova, V., Bondarenko, O., Chichkanov, N., Lebedev, D., & Miles, I. (2022). Coping with Greenhouse Gas Emissions: Insights from Digital Business Services. *Energies*, 15(8), 2745. DOI: 10.3390/en15082745

Bharwani, S., & Mathews, D. (2021). Techno-business strategies for enhancing guest experience in luxury hotels: A managerial perspective. *Worldwide Hospitality and Tourism Themes*, 13(2), 168–185. DOI: 10.1108/WHATT-09-2020-0121

Buhalis, D., & Moldavska, I. (2022). Voice assistants in hospitality: Using artificial intelligence for customer service. *Journal of Hospitality and Tourism Technology*, 13(3), 386–403. DOI: 10.1108/JHTT-03-2021-0104

Das, I. R., Talukder, M. B., & Kumar, S. (2024). Implication of Artificial Intelligence in Hospitality Marketing. *Utilizing Smart Technology and AI in Hybrid Tourism and Hospitality*. IGI Global. DOI: 10.4018/979-8-3693-1978-9.ch014

De Kloet, M., & Yang, S. (2022). The effects of anthropomorphism and multimodal biometric authentication on the user experience of voice intelligence. *Frontiers in Artificial Intelligence*, 5, 831046. DOI: 10.3389/frai.2022.831046 PMID: 36062266

Doborjeh, Z., Hemmington, N., Doborjeh, M., & Kasabov, N. (2022). Artificial intelligence: A systematic review of methods and applications in hospitality and tourism. *International Journal of Contemporary Hospitality Management*, 34(3), 1154–1176. DOI: 10.1108/IJCHM-06-2021-0767

Far Eastern Federal University, & Shumakova, E. V. (2019). Apart-hotel as an innovative form of organization of a hotel business. *azimuth of scientific study: economics and administration,* 8(28). https://doi.org/DOI: 10.26140/anie-2019-0803-0093

Gangwar, V. P., & Reddy, D. (2023). Hospitality Industry 5.0: Emerging Trends in Guest Perception and Experiences. In Dadwal, S., Kumar, P., Verma, R., & Singh, G. (Eds.), (pp. 185–211). Advances in Business Strategy and Competitive Advantage. IGI Global. DOI: 10.4018/978-1-6684-6403-8.ch010

Golja, T., & Paulišić, M. (2021). Managing-technology enhanced tourist experience: The case of scattered hotels in Istria. *Management*, 26(1), 63–95. DOI: 10.30924/mjcmi.26.1.5

Haleem, A., Javaid, M., Asim Qadri, M., Pratap Singh, R., & Suman, R. (2022). Artificial intelligence (AI) applications for marketing: A literature-based study. *International Journal of Intelligent Networks*, 3, 119–132. DOI: 10.1016/j.ijin.2022.08.005

Hasija, K. G., Desai, K., & Acharya, S. (2023). Artificial Intelligence and Robotic Automation Hit by the Pandemic: Reality or Myth. In Tyagi, P., Chilamkurti, N., Grima, S., Sood, K., & Balusamy, B. (Eds.), *The Adoption and Effect of Artificial Intelligence on Human Resources Management, Part B* (pp. 127–147). Emerald Publishing Limited. DOI: 10.1108/978-1-80455-662-720230009

Hevner, A., & Storey, V. (2023). Study Challenges for the Design of Human-Artificial Intelligence Systems (HAIS). *ACM Transactions on Management Information Systems*, 14(1), 1–18. DOI: 10.1145/3549547

Huang, A., Chao, Y., De La Mora Velasco, E., Bilgihan, A., & Wei, W. (2022). When artificial intelligence meets the hospitality and tourism industry: An assessment framework to inform theory and management. *Journal of Hospitality and Tourism Insights*, 5(5), 1080–1100. DOI: 10.1108/JHTI-01-2021-0021

Jatav, S. (2022). Current Trends in Sustainable Tourism in the Indian Context. In Sezerel, H., & Christiansen, B. (Eds.), *Advances in Hospitality, Tourism, and the Services Industry* (pp. 391–412). IGI Global. DOI: 10.4018/978-1-6684-4645-4.ch018

Javaid, M., Haleem, A., Singh, R. P., & Suman, R. (2022). Artificial Intelligence Applications for Industry 4.0: A Literature-Based Study. *Journal of Industrial Integration and Management*, 07(01), 83–111. DOI: 10.1142/S2424862221300040

Korteling, J. E., van de Boer-Visschedijk, G. C., Blankendaal, R. A. M., Boonekamp, R. C., & Eikelboom, A. R. (2021). Human- versus Artificial Intelligence. *Frontiers in Artificial Intelligence*, 4, 622364. DOI: 10.3389/frai.2021.622364 PMID: 33981990

Kumar, S., Talukder, M. B., Kabir, F., & Kaiser, F. (2024). Challenges and Sustainability of Green Finance in the Tourism Industry: Evidence from Bangladesh. In Taneja, S., Kumar, P., Grima, S., Ozen, E., & Sood, K. (Eds.), (pp. 97–111). Advances in Finance, Accounting, and Economics. IGI Global. DOI: 10.4018/979-8-3693-1388-6.ch006

Kumar, S., Talukder, M. B., & Kaiser, F. (2024). Artificial Intelligence in Business: Negative Social Impacts. In *Demystifying the Dark Side of AI in Business* (pp. 81-97). IGI Global. DOI: 10.4018/979-8-3693-0724-3.ch005

Kumar, S., Talukder, M. B., & Pego, A. (Eds.). (2024). *Utilizing Smart Technology and AI in Hybrid Tourism and Hospitality*. IGI Global. DOI: 10.4018/979-8-3693-1978-9

Kumar, V., Ashraf, A. R., & Nadeem, W. (2024). AI-powered marketing: What, where, and how? *International Journal of Information Management*, 77, 102783. DOI: 10.1016/j.ijinfomgt.2024.102783

Law, R., & Chen, S. (2024). Developments and implications of tourism information technology: A horizon 2050 paper. *Tourism Review*. Advance online publication. DOI: 10.1108/TR-12-2023-0846

Lekić Glavan, O., Nikolić, N., Folić, B., Vitošević, B., Mitrović, A., & Kosanović, S. (2022). COVID-19 and City Space: Impact and Perspectives. *Sustainability (Basel)*, 14(3), 1885. DOI: 10.3390/su14031885

Leyva, E. S., & Parra, D. P. (2021). Environmental approach in the hotel industry: Riding the wave of change. *Sustainable Futures : An Applied Journal of Technology, Environment and Society*, 3, 100050. DOI: 10.1016/j.sftr.2021.100050

Lv, H., Shi, S., & Gursoy, D. (2022). A look back and a leap forward: A review and synthesis of big data and artificial intelligence literature in hospitality and tourism. *Journal of Hospitality Marketing & Management*, 31(2), 145–175. DOI: 10.1080/19368623.2021.1937434

Mariani, M., & Borghi, M. (2021). Customers' evaluation of mechanical artificial intelligence in hospitality services: A study using online reviews analytics. *International Journal of Contemporary Hospitality Management*, 33(11), 3956–3976. DOI: 10.1108/IJCHM-06-2020-0622

Markauskaite, L., Marrone, R., Poquet, O., Knight, S., Martinez-Maldonado, R., Howard, S., Tondeur, J., De Laat, M., Buckingham Shum, S., Gašević, D., & Siemens, G. (2022). Rethinking the entwinement between artificial intelligence and human learning: What capabilities do learners need for a world with AI? *Computers and Education: Artificial Intelligence*, 3, 100056. DOI: 10.1016/j.caeai.2022.100056

Martella, F., & Enia, M. (2021). Towards an Urban Domesticity. Contemporary Architecture and the Blurring Boundaries between the House and the City. *Housing. Theory and Society*, 38(4), 402–418. DOI: 10.1080/14036096.2020.1789211

McLean, G., & Barhorst, J. B. (2022). Living the Experience Before You Go . . . but Did It Meet Expectations? The Role of Virtual Reality during Hotel Bookings. *Journal of Travel Research*, 61(6), 1233–1251. DOI: 10.1177/00472875211028313

Mercan, S., Cain, L., Akkaya, K., Cebe, M., Uluagac, S., Alonso, M., & Cobanoglu, C. (2021). Improving the service industry with hyper-connectivity: IoT in hospitality. *International Journal of Contemporary Hospitality Management*, 33(1), 243–262. DOI: 10.1108/IJCHM-06-2020-0621

Milton. (2024). Artificial Intelligence Transforming Hotel Gastronomy: An In-depth Review of AI-driven Innovations in Menu Design, Food Preparation, and Customer Interaction, with a Focus on Sustainability and Future Trends in the Hospitality Industry. *International Journal for Multidimensional Study Perspectives, 2*(3), 47–61. DOI: 10.61877/ijmrp.v2i3.126

Mohammad Badruddoza Talukder, Firoj Kabir, K. M., & Das, I. R. (2023). Emerging Concepts of Artificial Intelligence in the Hotel Industry: A Conceptual Paper. *International Journal of Research Publication and Reviews, 4,* 1765-1769. DOI: 10.55248/gengpi.4.923.92451

Mohammad Badruddoza Talukder, Kumar, & Das. (2024a). Implications of Blockchain Technology- Based Cryptocurrency in the cloud for the Hospitality Industry. In *Emerging Trends in Cloud Computing Analytics, Scalability, and Service Models* (p. 19). DOI: 10.4018/979-8-3693-0900-1.ch018

Mohammad Badruddoza Talukder, Kumar, & Das. (2024b). Perspectives of Digital Marketing for the Restaurant Industry. In *Advancements in Socialized and Digital Media Communications* (p. 17). DOI: 10.4018/979-8-3693-0855-4.ch009

Mohammad. B. Talukder, & Kumar, (2024). Revisiting intention in food service outlet of five-star hotels: A quantitative approach based on food service quality. Sport i Turystyka. Środkowoeuropejskie Czasopismo Naukowe, 7(1), 137–156. DOI: 10.16926/sit.2024.01.08

Puntoni, S., Reczek, R. W., Giesler, M., & Botti, S. (2021). Consumers and Artificial Intelligence: An Experiential Perspective. *Journal of Marketing*, 85(1), 131–151. DOI: 10.1177/0022242920953847

Rane, N., Choudhary, S., & Rane, J. (2023). Hyper-personalization for enhancing customer loyalty and satisfaction in Customer Relationship Management (CRM) systems. SSRN *Electronic Journal*. DOI: 10.2139/ssrn.4641044

Samancioglu, N. (2022). *Smart Building and Campus Framework: A Determination of Smart Campus Parameters to Predict Potential Smartness of University Campuses* [PhD Thesis, Universidad Politécnica de Madrid]. DOI: 10.20868/UPM.thesis.70353

Schneider, J., Abraham, R., Meske, C., & Vom Brocke, J. (2023). Artificial Intelligence Governance For Businesses. *Information Systems Management*, 40(3), 229–249. DOI: 10.1080/10580530.2022.2085825

Simonis, L. (2023). *Customer experiences for senior guests: Challenges and opportunities for the hospitality industry*. DOI: 10.21256/ZHAW-30196

Sousa, B. B., Magalhães, F. C., & Soares, D. B. (2021). The Role of Relational Marketing in Specific Contexts of Tourism: A Luxury Hotel Management Perspective. In Rodrigues, P., & Borges, A. P. (Eds.), (pp. 223–243). Advances in Marketing, Customer Relationship Management, and E-Services. IGI Global. DOI: 10.4018/978-1-7998-4369-6.ch011

Sthapit, E., Björk, P., Coudounaris, D. N., & Stone, M. J. (2022). A new conceptual framework for memorable Airbnb experiences: Guests' perspectives. *International Journal of Culture. International Journal of Culture, Tourism and Hospitality Research*, 16(1), 75–86. DOI: 10.1108/IJCTHR-01-2021-0002

Štilić, A., Nicić, M., & Puška, A. (2023). Check-in to the future: Exploring the impact of contemporary information technologies and artificial intelligence on the hotel industry. *Turisticko Poslovanje*, 31(31), 5–17. DOI: 10.5937/turpos0-43739

Stylos, N., Zwiegelaar, J., & Buhalis, D. (2021). Big data empowered agility for dynamic, volatile, and time-sensitive service industries: The case of tourism sector. *International Journal of Contemporary Hospitality Management*, 33(3), 1015–1036. DOI: 10.1108/IJCHM-07-2020-0644

Talukder, M. B. (2024). Implementing Artificial Intelligence and Virtual Experiences in Hospitality. In *Innovative Technologies for Increasing Service Productivity* (pp. 145–160). IGI Global. DOI: 10.4018/979-8-3693-2019-8.ch009

Talukder, M. B., & Das, I. R. (2024). The Technology Impacts and AI Solutions in Hospitality. I-manager's Journal on Artificial Intelligence &. *Machine Learning*, 2(1), 56–72. DOI: 10.26634/jaim.2.1.20291

Talukder, M. B., & Hossain, M. M. (2021). Prospects of Future Tourism in Bangladesh: An Evaluative Study. I-Manager's. *Journal of Management*, 15(4), 1–8. DOI: 10.26634/jmgt.15.4.17495

Talukder, M. B., & Kumar, S. (2024). The Development of ChatGPT and Its Implications for the Future of Customer Service in the Hospitality Industry. In Derbali, A. (Ed.), *Blockchain Applications for Smart Contract Technologies* (pp. 100–126). IGI Global. DOI: 10.4018/979-8-3693-1511-8.ch005

Talukder, M. B., Kumar, S., & Das, I. R. (2024). Mindful Consumers and New Marketing Strategies for the Restaurant Business: Evidence of Bangladesh. In Ramos, C., Costa, T., Severino, F., & Calisto, M. (Eds.), *Social Media Strategies for Tourism Interactivity* (pp. 240–260). IGI Global. DOI: 10.4018/979-8-3693-0960-5.ch010

Talukder, M. B., & Muhsina, K. (2024). Prospect of Smart Tourism Destination in Bangladesh. In Correia, R., Martins, M., & Fontes, R. (Eds.), *AI Innovations for Travel and Tourism* (pp. 163–179). IGI Global. DOI: 10.4018/979-8-3693-2137-9.ch009

Vlami, A. (2023). Correction to: Developments and Challenges in the Greek Hospitality Sector for Economic Tourism Growth: The Case of Boutique Hotels. In Balsalobre-Lorente, D., Driha, O. M., & Shahbaz, M. (Eds.), *Strategies in Sustainable Tourism, Economic Growth and Clean Energy* (pp. C1–C1). Springer International Publishing. DOI: 10.1007/978-3-030-59675-0_15

Vuscan, S., & Muntean, R. (2023). Multifunctional Homes: A Sustainable Answer to the Challenges of the Future. *Sustainability (Basel)*, 15(7), 5624. DOI: 10.3390/su15075624

Wang, M.-R., & Chen, C.-L. (2024). Exploring the Value Co-Creation of Cultural Creative Hotels: From the Perspective of Social Innovation. *Sustainability (Basel)*, 16(11), 4510. DOI: 10.3390/su16114510

Yacoub, L., & ElHajjar, S. (2021). How do hotels in developing countries manage the impact of COVID-19? The case of Lebanese hotels. *International Journal of Contemporary Hospitality Management*, 33(3), 929–948. DOI: 10.1108/IJCHM-08-2020-0814

Zarezadeh, Z. Z., Rastegar, R., & Xiang, Z. (2022). Big data analytics and hotel guest experience: A critical analysis of the literature. *International Journal of Contemporary Hospitality Management*, 34(6), 2320–2336. DOI: 10.1108/IJCHM-10-2021-1293

Zhang, X., Tavitiyaman, P., & Tsang, W. Y. (2023). Preferences of Technology Amenities, Satisfaction and Behavioral Intention: The Perspective of Hotel Guests in Hong Kong. *Journal of Quality Assurance in Hospitality & Tourism*, 24(5), 545–575. DOI: 10.1080/1528008X.2022.2070817

Chapter 4
AI-Driven Solutions for Crowd Management in Tourism:
Navigating the Swarm

Vetrivel S. C.
 https://orcid.org/0000-0003-3050-8211
Kongu Engineering College, India

P. Vidhyapriya
Kongu Engineering College, India

Arun V. P.
JKKN College of Engineering and Technology, India

ABSTRACT

The exponential growth of tourism worldwide has led to significant challenges in managing crowds efficiently and sustainably. In recent years, the integration of artificial intelligence (AI) has emerged as a promising avenue for addressing these challenges. This chapter provides a comprehensive overview of AI-driven solutions tailored specifically for crowd management in tourism settings. The first section elucidates the dynamics of tourism-related crowds, highlighting the complexities arising from diverse factors such as seasonality, events, and cultural significance. Understanding these intricacies is crucial for devising effective management strategies. The subsequent section delves into the role of AI in crowd management, exploring various AI techniques such as machine learning, computer vision, and natural language processing. These technologies enable real-time data analysis, predictive modeling, and decision support systems, empowering stakeholders to anticipate crowd behaviors and mitigate potential disruptions

DOI: 10.4018/979-8-3693-5678-4.ch004

Copyright © 2025, IGI Global. Copying or distributing in print or electronic forms without written permission of IGI Global is prohibited.

1. INTRODUCTION

1.1 Overview of Tourism Industry Trends

The tourism industry is a dynamic and rapidly evolving sector that plays a significant role in the global economy. In recent years, several key trends have emerged, reshaping the way people travel and interact with tourism destinations. Sustainability has become a major focus, with more travelers seeking eco-friendly and responsible tourism options. This shift reflects a growing awareness of environmental issues and the need to protect the planet's natural resources. As a result, many tourism companies and destinations are adopting sustainable practices, such as reducing waste, conserving energy, and supporting local communities. Another significant trend in the tourism industry is the rise of technology and digitalization (Ade et al., 2023). The proliferation of smartphones and the internet has transformed the way people plan and experience travel. Online platforms for booking flights, accommodations, and activities have made travel more accessible and convenient. Virtual and augmented reality technologies are also gaining traction, allowing travelers to explore destinations virtually before they arrive. Additionally, artificial intelligence and big data analytics are helping tourism companies personalize their services and enhance the overall customer experience. The COVID-19 pandemic had a profound impact on the tourism industry, leading to a shift in travel preferences and behaviors. Domestic and local travel gained popularity as international travel restrictions were imposed. This trend towards "staycations" and local tourism continues, even as the industry recovers, with many travelers seeking unique experiences in their own regions. Health and safety have also become paramount, prompting tourism providers to implement stringent hygiene protocols and contactless services to ensure the safety of their guests. Furthermore, the tourism industry has seen an increase in niche markets and experiential travel. Travelers are increasingly looking for unique and authentic experiences that go beyond traditional sightseeing. This has led to the growth of various specialized tourism segments, such as adventure tourism, cultural tourism, and wellness tourism (Alotaibi et al., 2020). These trends indicate that modern travelers are seeking meaningful connections with the places they visit, often preferring immersive experiences that provide a deeper understanding of local culture and traditions. The tourism industry is witnessing a trend towards collaborative consumption and the sharing economy. Platforms like Airbnb and Uber have revolutionized the way people book accommodations and transportation, offering more flexible and personalized options. This trend has encouraged travelers to explore alternative forms of travel, such as homestays and ride-sharing, contributing to a more diverse and inclusive tourism landscape. The sharing economy has also facilitated greater interaction between tourists and locals, fostering cultural exchange and community engagement.

1.2 The Role of AI in Modern Tourism

Artificial Intelligence (AI) is reshaping the landscape of modern tourism, offering new ways to enhance customer experience, streamline operations, and provide personalized services. Travel agencies and tourism companies are leveraging AI to create customized travel itineraries, allowing travelers to experience unique journeys tailored to their preferences. AI algorithms can analyze vast datasets of customer preferences, booking patterns, and travel trends, making it possible to suggest personalized destinations, activities, and accommodations (Buhalis et al., 2019). This level of personalization not only enhances customer satisfaction but also fosters brand loyalty and repeat business for tourism companies.In addition to personalizing travel experiences, AI plays a significant role in automating and optimizing various operational aspects of tourism. Chatbots and virtual assistants are increasingly common, providing instant customer support for booking inquiries, travel advice, and troubleshooting. These AI-driven tools operate 24/7, allowing companies to reduce customer service costs while offering quick and efficient assistance. AI is also used to predict demand and optimize pricing strategies, enabling hotels, airlines, and other travel-related businesses to maximize their revenue by dynamically adjusting prices based on real-time data. Furthermore, AI is contributing to the safety and security of travelers. Advanced AI systems can monitor global events, weather patterns, and other factors that could impact travel plans. This capability allows companies to alert travelers about potential disruptions and provide alternative solutions, ensuring a smoother and safer journey. AI-driven facial recognition technology is also being used in airports and other transit hubs to enhance security, streamline check-in processes, and reduce wait times. By integrating AI into the core operations of tourism, the industry is not only improving efficiency but also enriching the overall travel experience, paving the way for a more connected and intelligent future in tourism.

1.3 Understanding Crowd Management Challenges

Understanding Crowd Management Challenges is crucial for developing effective AI-driven solutions in the tourism sector. The primary challenges include accurately predicting visitor flow, ensuring safety, enhancing visitor experience, and minimizing environmental impact. High variability in tourist numbers, influenced by factors like seasonal trends, weather conditions, and special events, makes it difficult to predict and manage crowds effectively. Safety concerns, such as the risk of overcrowding leading to stampedes or other accidents, require real-time monitoring and quick response capabilities. Moreover, maintaining a balance between providing a seamless visitor experience and preserving the integrity of tourist sites poses a significant challenge. Environmental impact, including damage to natural landscapes and increased waste, needs to be managed by regulating visitor numbers and promoting sustainable practices. AI-driven solutions can address these challenges through advanced analytics, real-time monitoring, and predictive modeling. By leveraging data from various sources such as social media, weather forecasts, and historical visitation patterns, AI can provide accurate predictions of visitor numbers and identify potential overcrowding scenarios. Real-time monitoring using IoT devices and surveillance cameras, coupled with AI algorithms, can enhance situational awareness and enable prompt interventions. Additionally, AI can optimize resource allocation, such as directing staff to busy areas and managing transportation logistics, to ensure a smooth visitor flow and reduce environmental impact. By understanding and addressing these crowd management challenges, AI-driven solutions can significantly enhance the efficiency and effectiveness of tourism management.

1.4 The Need for AI-Driven Solutions

As global tourism experiences a resurgence, destinations worldwide are grappling with unprecedented crowd management challenges. Popular tourist spots are often overwhelmed by the sheer number of visitors, leading to issues like congestion, environmental degradation, and strained local resources. Traditional crowd management methods are proving inadequate in the face of these complex issues. To address them, AI-driven solutions offer a promising avenue, leveraging advanced data analytics and predictive modeling to enhance efficiency and visitor experience while mitigating the negative impacts of overcrowding. AI-driven solutions in crowd management can revolutionize how we understand and respond to tourist flows. By analyzing vast amounts of data from various sources—such as social media, mobile apps, and sensors—AI systems can predict peak times, identify overcrowded areas, and suggest optimal routes for visitors. This predictive capability allows for proactive management, enabling authorities and businesses to implement measures that minimize congestion and improve the visitor experience. For instance, AI can help distribute visitors more evenly across a destination, reducing bottlenecks and pressure on infrastructure. Moreover, AI-driven solutions can contribute to sustainability and resource management in tourist destinations (Ding, 2021; Dogan and Niyet, 2024). By optimizing crowd distribution, AI can reduce the environmental footprint associated with high visitor concentrations. This technology can also be used to monitor and manage the impact of tourism on local ecosystems, providing insights that guide conservation efforts. AI-powered chatbots and virtual assistants can further enhance the visitor experience by offering real-time information on less crowded attractions, suggesting eco-friendly practices, and providing personalized recommendations, all while reducing the strain on human resources.

2. FUNDAMENTALS OF CROWD MANAGEMENT

2.1 Historical Perspectives on Crowd Management

Crowd management in tourism has a rich history that mirrors broader trends in human mobility, urbanization, and social organization. In ancient times, pilgrimage sites, such as those along the Silk Road or key religious centers like Jerusalem, Mecca, and Varanasi, saw early examples of crowd control. These locations, often central to religious or cultural practices, required effective management to handle the influx of visitors during significant events or seasons. Organizers devised rudimentary methods to maintain order, such as designated routes, guards, and crowd marshals, ensuring the safety and flow of pilgrims.During the Middle Ages and Renaissance, European cities began to experience more consistent tourism due to increased trade and the burgeoning middle class's ability to travel. Cities like Venice and Paris became popular destinations, leading to the development of organized public spaces and the implementation of rules to manage crowds. These cities established regulations to control vendors, maintain sanitation, and guide visitor movement through streets and marketplaces. The rise of grand events like fairs and festivals also necessitated crowd management, with local authorities coordinating logistics and security (Dogru et al., 2023). The Industrial Revolution marked a significant shift in tourism and crowd management. The advent of railways and steamships made travel more accessible to the masses, leading to a dramatic increase in tourist numbers. The creation of large-scale tourist attractions, such as the Great Exhibition in London in 1851, highlighted the need for more sophisticated crowd control. Organizers implemented ticketing systems, scheduled entry times, and designated pathways to manage the flow of visitors. These practices set a precedent for future large-scale events and theme parks, where crowd management became a central concern.In the 20th century, the rise of commercial aviation and the proliferation of automobile travel further transformed tourism. Destination cities and countries saw massive growth in visitor numbers, necessitating new crowd management strategies. Urban planning began to consider tourism's impact, with the construction of larger airports, highways, and public transportation systems designed to handle tourists' influx. Events like World's Fairs, Olympics, and Expos required extensive crowd management, leading to innovations in crowd control technologies, such as CCTV, electronic ticketing, and sophisticated queuing systems.Today, crowd management in tourism continues to evolve, with new challenges posed by global travel and the digital revolution. The advent of social media and online booking has made it easier for tourists to plan trips, leading to overtourism in some destinations. Cities and tourist sites are now implementing real-time monitoring, digital crowd tracking, and predictive analytics to manage visitor flow (Dogru et al., 2023). Sustainable tourism has also become a crucial focus, with authorities seeking ways to balance the economic benefits of tourism with the need to preserve cultural and natural heritage, ensuring safe and enjoyable experiences for visitors while protecting local communities and environments.

2.2 Current Strategies and Limitations

2.2.1 Current Strategies in Crowd Management in Tourism

Crowd management in tourism is a complex challenge, with destinations implementing a range of strategies to ensure safety, maintain a positive visitor experience, and minimize environmental impact. One common approach is the use of technology to monitor and manage crowds. This includes tools like mobile apps that provide real-time information on crowd densities at popular sites, allowing visitors to make informed decisions about when and where to visit. Similarly, sensors and surveillance systems can track visitor flows, enabling authorities to respond proactively to overcrowding situations. Another key strategy is the implementation of timed-entry systems and reservation requirements. By limiting the number of visitors during peak times, tourist sites can manage crowd density and reduce stress on infrastructure. This approach is often complemented by differential pricing, where visitors are incentivized to visit during off-peak hours or seasons through discounted tickets or special promotions. Many destinations also employ crowd management personnel, who are trained to guide visitors, enforce regulations, and ensure safety during large events or peak tourist seasons.

2.2.2 Limitations in Crowd Management in Tourism

Despite these strategies, there are significant limitations in managing crowds in tourism. One of the major challenges is the unpredictable nature of tourist behavior, which can be influenced by weather, local events, or even social media trends. This unpredictability makes it difficult to create rigid systems for crowd management, requiring destinations to remain flexible and adaptive. Additionally, technological solutions such as apps and sensors require significant investment and technical expertise, which may be beyond the reach of smaller or less wealthy destinations. Another limitation is the potential impact on the visitor experience. Strict crowd control measures, such as timed entry or limited capacity, can create frustration among tourists, potentially leading to negative reviews and reduced repeat visits. Moreover, these strategies can sometimes result in the displacement of crowds to other areas, simply shifting the problem rather than resolving it. There are also concerns about privacy and data security when using surveillance and tracking technologies, which can lead to public pushback and regulatory challenges (Fararni et al., 2021). Lastly, the environmental impact of tourism and crowd management is a growing concern. While managing crowds can reduce damage to natural and cultural sites, the methods used—such as barriers, fences, or increased staffing—may themselves have a negative environmental footprint. Balancing the needs of tourists, local communities, and the environment remains a central challenge in crowd management for tourism, requiring ongoing innovation and a holistic approach.

2.3 Impacts of Overcrowding on Tourism

Overcrowding in tourism, often referred to as "overtourism," can have profound negative impacts on both local environments and communities, as well as on the quality of the visitor experience. When too many tourists converge on a popular destination, the strain on local resources can be significant. Infrastructure such as roads, public transportation, and waste management systems may become overwhelmed, leading to traffic congestion, littering, and general wear and tear on public amenities. This not only diminishes the appeal of a destination for future visitors but also places a heavy burden on local governments and taxpayers to address the increased maintenance and repair costs (Ferràs et al., 2020). Another major impact of overcrowding on tourism is the disruption it causes to local cultures and communities. As tourists flood into an area, they can inadvertently alter the social fabric and dynamics of the destination. This can lead to the erosion of traditional practices and a loss of cultural identity, as residents may cater to tourists' expectations at the expense of their own customs. Overcrowding can also result in inflated prices for housing, goods, and services, pricing locals out of their own neighborhoods. The influx of visitors may cause resentment among residents who feel their way of life is being compromised, leading to a sense of "us versus them."Additionally, overcrowding in tourism has significant environmental repercussions. High tourist numbers often mean increased pollution, deforestation, and wildlife disturbance. Popular natural sites, such as beaches, forests, and mountains, can suffer from overuse, leading to habitat degradation and a loss of biodiversity. Sensitive ecosystems can be irreparably damaged by large numbers of visitors, particularly when they engage in activities like littering, off-trail hiking, or collecting natural souvenirs. This environmental degradation not only harms the intrinsic value of these areas but can also reduce their appeal for future tourists, creating a negative feedback loop.Finally, from a tourist's perspective, overcrowding can lead to a diminished experience. Long lines, overcrowded attractions, and a general sense of chaos can detract from the enjoyment of a destination. Visitors may find it challenging to engage authentically with local cultures or to experience the tranquility of natural settings. The stress and frustration associated with overcrowding can lead to negative reviews and reduced interest in revisiting a destination, impacting the long-term sustainability of the local tourism industry.

2.4 The Transition to AI-Driven Approaches

2.4.1 The Rise of AI in Crowd Management for Tourism

As tourism destinations across the globe experience an influx of visitors, particularly in iconic cities and natural attractions, the challenge of managing large crowds becomes increasingly significant. Traditional methods of crowd management often rely on manual observation, signage, and human-directed traffic control, which can be inefficient and prone to error. The transition to AI-driven approaches in this context represents a transformative leap, bringing precision, scalability, and adaptability to the management of large groups of people. With AI technologies, tourism operators and city planners can analyze vast amounts of data in real-time, allowing them to predict crowd patterns, optimize resource allocation, and enhance the overall visitor experience.

2.4.2 Predictive Analytics and Real-Time Monitoring

One of the most compelling benefits of AI in crowd management is its ability to harness predictive analytics. AI algorithms can analyze historical data, such as visitor numbers, weather conditions, and event schedules, to forecast future crowd levels. This capability enables tourism sites to anticipate busy periods and plan accordingly, whether by deploying additional staff, extending operating hours, or implementing crowd control measures (Flandrin et al., 2021). Additionally, AI-powered surveillance systems can monitor crowds in real-time, using computer vision to detect unusual activity or potential safety risks. This real-time monitoring not only enhances security but also contributes to a more efficient flow of visitors through popular attractions.

2.4.3 Enhancing Visitor Experience and Safety

AI-driven crowd management also plays a crucial role in enhancing visitor satisfaction and safety. By reducing bottlenecks and wait times, tourists can enjoy a more seamless experience, leading to greater satisfaction and a higher likelihood of positive reviews and return visits. AI applications, such as virtual assistants and chatbots, can guide visitors through attractions, providing them with information and personalized recommendations, further enhancing their experience. In terms of safety, AI can detect patterns that might indicate potential hazards, allowing for a swift response from security personnel or emergency services. This proactive approach to safety is particularly valuable in high-density tourist areas where crowd dynamics can change rapidly.

2.4.4 Sustainability and the Future of AI in Tourism

As sustainability becomes a critical focus in tourism, AI-driven crowd management can contribute to environmental and social responsibility. By optimizing visitor flow and reducing overcrowding, tourism destinations can minimize their environmental impact, such as reducing litter and wear and tear on natural resources. AI can also help ensure that tourism benefits local communities by promoting equitable distribution of visitors across different areas, reducing the strain on popular hotspots. Looking to the future, the continued evolution of AI technologies promises even more sophisticated crowd management solutions, with the potential to create safer, more enjoyable, and more sustainable tourism experiences.Top of Form

3. AI TECHNOLOGIES IN CROWD MANAGEMENT

3.1 Machine Learning Basics

Machine Learning (ML), a subset of Artificial Intelligence (AI), plays a crucial role in crowd management by providing tools to analyze, predict, and respond to human behavior in real-time. Using data-driven algorithms, ML systems can process large volumes of information from various sources, such as cameras, sensors, and social media, to understand crowd dynamics. These systems are capable of detecting patterns, such as the flow of people, emerging trends, and unusual activity, enabling authorities to make informed decisions about crowd control, safety, and security (Ghouse and Chaudhary, 2024). For instance, ML algorithms can be trained to predict crowd density and detect anomalies that may indicate safety risks, allowing proactive management and efficient resource allocation. This technology enhances the ability to manage large gatherings, improve public safety, and create a more seamless experience for attendees.

3.2 Computer Vision and Image Recognition

Computer vision and image recognition play pivotal roles in the realm of crowd management under the broader scope of AI technologies. These technologies utilize advanced algorithms and deep learning techniques to analyze visual data from cameras and other imaging devices. In crowd management, they enable automated monitoring and analysis of large groups, providing valuable insights into crowd density, movement patterns, and potential risks. For instance, computer vision can identify instances of overcrowding, flagging these for security personnel to prevent unsafe situations. Image recognition further extends this capability by identifying individuals, either for security or for tracking purposes, while respecting privacy regulations. These AI-driven tools facilitate real-time surveillance, enabling authorities to respond swiftly to emergencies or public safety threats. Moreover, by analyzing crowd behavior trends, they assist in optimizing event layouts, managing foot traffic, and improving overall safety and efficiency in public spaces like stadiums, airports, and city centers. Thus, computer vision and image recognition are transforming how we approach crowd management, making it more effective, responsive, and secure.

3.3 Predictive Analytics

Predictive analytics, a vital facet of artificial intelligence (AI), plays a transformative role in crowd management by enabling organizations to forecast and prepare for various scenarios involving large groups of people. This technology uses a combination of machine learning algorithms, statistical techniques, and data mining to identify patterns and predict future outcomes, providing critical insights into crowd behavior and dynamics. In the context of crowd management, predictive analytics offers the ability to anticipate and mitigate risks, optimize resource allocation, and enhance safety measures, thereby ensuring smoother operations during events and in public spaces (Gretzel, 2011). One of the key applications of predictive analytics in crowd management is in the realm of event planning and security. By analyzing historical data from past events, along with real-time information such as ticket sales, social media trends, weather forecasts, and transportation patterns, predictive models can estimate crowd size, density, and flow. This information is crucial for event organizers and security personnel, allowing them to proactively address potential bottlenecks, plan optimal staff deployment, and set up effective security checkpoints.

By anticipating where crowds are likely to form, they can implement strategies to prevent overcrowding and minimize risks related to crowd-related incidents.

Another significant application is in public safety and emergency response. Predictive analytics can identify early warning signs of potentially dangerous situations, such as surges in crowd density or abnormal movement patterns. For example, during large-scale public events or protests, this technology can help authorities detect escalating tensions or identify areas with increased risk of stampedes or accidents. This predictive capability enables security teams to take preemptive action, such as redirecting foot traffic, increasing surveillance, or deploying additional security personnel, to prevent incidents before they occur. Moreover, predictive analytics contributes to crowd management by enhancing the visitor experience and operational efficiency. For large venues like amusement parks, stadiums, or transportation hubs, AI-driven analytics can optimize crowd flow by predicting peak times and suggesting alternate routes or attractions. This can reduce wait times, improve customer satisfaction, and help maintain a safe environment. By analyzing visitor behavior and feedback, organizations can also tailor their services and amenities to better meet the needs of their customers, leading to a more enjoyable experience and increased loyalty.

3.4 Big Data and Crowd Behavior Analysis

Big Data refers to the collection, storage, and analysis of vast volumes of complex information that traditional data-processing systems might struggle to handle. In the context of crowd management, Big Data plays a pivotal role in analyzing and predicting crowd behavior, aiding in the design of safer, more efficient spaces, and improving emergency response strategies. By leveraging data from diverse sources such as CCTV cameras, social media platforms, mobile devices, and IoT sensors, AI technologies can create comprehensive insights into crowd dynamics. These data-driven insights are invaluable for event organizers, city planners, and emergency responders. For instance, the analysis of historical crowd data can reveal patterns in crowd flow, helping planners anticipate bottlenecks and design spaces to minimize congestion. Similarly, real-time data analysis enables monitoring of crowds during events, allowing security personnel to quickly identify and respond to incidents or irregular behavior. Big Data analytics also facilitates predictive modeling, where advanced algorithms can forecast crowd movements and potential risks, enabling proactive measures to ensure safety and efficiency.

Crowd behavior analysis involves using AI technologies to understand and predict the movements and interactions of people in crowded environments. This analysis relies on computer vision, machine learning, and deep learning algorithms to detect patterns in crowd behavior. Techniques like facial recognition, object detection, and activity recognition can identify individuals, track their movements, and even predict their future locations within a crowd. AI-driven crowd behavior analysis has broad applications in safety and security, from monitoring large events like concerts and sports games to managing urban environments with high foot traffic (Gupta et al., 2023). Computer vision technologies can identify unusual behavior or specific patterns that may indicate a potential security threat. For example, an AI system might detect aggressive movements, abandoned objects, or sudden crowd dispersals, triggering alerts for security personnel. Furthermore, AI technologies can help optimize crowd flow in public spaces by analyzing data in real-time. This capability allows event organizers to manage entry and exit points more efficiently, reducing wait times and minimizing risks of stampedes or accidents. AI-driven crowd behavior analysis also plays a role in disaster response, where AI systems can assist emergency responders in quickly locating and aiding people during emergencies like fires or terrorist attacks. By automating these analyses, AI technologies provide a level of speed and accuracy that would be difficult to achieve through manual observation, contributing to safer and more effective crowd management strategies.

4. APPLICATIONS OF AI IN TOURISM CROWD MANAGEMENT

4.1 AI for Visitor Flow Management

Visitor flow management is an essential aspect of tourism, especially in highly trafficked destinations like museums, theme parks, and historic sites. The strategic application of Artificial Intelligence (AI) in this context offers innovative solutions to ensure smooth operations, enhance visitor experience, and maintain safety standards. AI-based visitor flow management encompasses a range of technologies and approaches that help manage the movement of people in real-time, anticipate crowd trends, and optimize resources (Iglesias et al., 2021). One significant advantage of AI in visitor flow management is its ability to analyze large volumes of data from various sources, such as ticket sales, reservation systems, security cameras, and IoT sensors. This data-driven approach allows AI algorithms to predict crowd patterns and identify peak times for visitor arrivals. For instance, museums can use this information to schedule guided tours at off-peak times, reducing overcrowding. Theme parks can adjust ride schedules based on real-time visitor density, ensuring a more even distribution of guests. This predictive capability is crucial for maintaining a comfortable and safe environment, particularly in the context of social distancing requirements or other public health considerations.

AI-powered technologies like computer vision and machine learning can also play a key role in real-time crowd monitoring and control. These systems can detect overcrowded areas and trigger automated responses, such as redirecting foot traffic through digital signage or adjusting the opening and closing times of different sections within a venue. This capability is particularly useful for large-scale events or seasonal tourism peaks, where traditional crowd management techniques might struggle to keep pace with fluctuating visitor numbers. By leveraging AI, venues can ensure that visitor flow is optimized, reducing wait times and improving the overall visitor experience.Another crucial aspect of AI in visitor flow management is its potential for personalized recommendations. AI algorithms can analyze individual visitor preferences and behaviors to suggest optimal routes through a venue, recommend attractions or exhibits based on interests, and even propose alternative activities when a specific area becomes too crowded. This level of personalization not only enhances visitor satisfaction but also contributes to a more balanced distribution of visitors throughout a tourism site, ultimately reducing stress on specific areas and preventing bottlenecks (Jiang et al., 2023). Finally, AI-based visitor flow management can have broader implications for sustainability and resource optimization in tourism. By predicting visitor trends and optimizing crowd distribution, tourism sites can make more informed decisions about staffing, energy use, and resource allocation. This proactive approach can lead to more efficient operations and reduce the environmental impact associated with large crowds. Additionally, AI can support dynamic pricing strategies to incentivize visitors to attend during off-peak times, further smoothing visitor flow and contributing to a more sustainable tourism industry.

4.2 AI for Traffic Control and Congestion Reduction

Artificial Intelligence (AI) plays a crucial role in traffic control and congestion reduction, especially within the context of tourism crowd management. As tourist destinations face increasing numbers of visitors, efficient traffic flow becomes a top priority to maintain visitor satisfaction and safety. AI-powered systems can dynamically adjust traffic signals and routes based on real-time data, reducing bottlenecks and ensuring smoother vehicle and pedestrian movement. For example, AI can process data from cameras, sensors, and GPS systems to predict traffic trends and optimize signal timing to reduce congestion at key intersections or tourist hotspots (Koo et al., 2021). This approach minimizes travel time and enhances the overall tourist experience by reducing frustration and the environmental impact of idling vehicles. Furthermore, AI can be integrated with public transportation systems to optimize routes and schedules, reducing the need for private vehicle use and promoting sustainable tourism practices. By utilizing AI in traffic control, tourism destinations can efficiently manage high visitor volumes, creating a more enjoyable and accessible environment for tourists and locals alike.

4.3 AI in Security and Safety Monitoring

AI in security and safety monitoring has become a cornerstone in the realm of tourism crowd management, providing advanced solutions to ensure the safety of large gatherings and high-traffic tourist destinations. As tourism brings together diverse groups in often densely populated areas, the risk of security incidents, health emergencies, and other safety concerns increases. AI technologies, such as computer vision and machine learning, enable real-time monitoring and analysis of crowd dynamics, offering invaluable tools for identifying potential risks and responding promptly.In practice, AI systems equipped with high-definition cameras and sensors can monitor large crowds in real-time, detecting unusual behavior, unattended objects, or bottlenecks that could lead to overcrowding. By analyzing video feeds, these systems can identify patterns and anomalies, allowing security personnel to address issues before they escalate. For example, AI-powered facial recognition can help locate missing persons or identify known threats, while anomaly detection algorithms can spot suspicious activities in areas where tourists congregate. Furthermore, AI-driven security systems can be integrated with other technologies, such as drones and Io devices, to expand monitoring coverage and improve response times (Limna, 2023). Drones equipped with AI can provide aerial surveillance, offering a broader perspective of crowd movements and enabling rapid deployment to specific locations in case of emergencies. IoT devices, such as smart lighting and public address systems, can be programmed to respond automatically to AI-generated alerts, guiding crowds to safer areas or instructing them in case of emergencies.AI also plays a crucial role in predicting and preventing incidents. Machine learning models trained on historical data can forecast peak times and high-risk situations, allowing event organizers and city planners to implement preventive measures. These measures might include adjusting staffing levels, creating additional exits, or implementing crowd control strategies to maintain safe and efficient traffic flow.

4.4 AI for Enhancing Visitor Experience

Artificial Intelligence (AI) plays a pivotal role in enhancing visitor experience within the domain of tourism crowd management by offering personalized, efficient, and adaptive solutions. Through advanced data analytics, AI systems can process vast amounts of visitor data in real-time, enabling destinations to manage crowd flows with precision. For example, AI-driven applications can analyze historical and current attendance patterns to predict peak times and suggest optimal visiting hours, allowing tourists to avoid overcrowded periods. Additionally, AI-powered chatbots and virtual assistants, accessible through mobile apps or on-site kiosks, can provide visitors with tailored recommendations for attractions, dining, and activities based on their interests and current crowd levels, ensuring a more enjoyable and stress-free experience. These AI tools can also alert visitors to potential delays or changes in scheduling, allowing them to adjust their plans accordingly. Furthermore, AI-enabled facial recognition and smart ticketing systems can streamline entry processes, reducing wait times and enhancing security. By incorporating AI into tourism crowd management, destinations can create a more seamless and enjoyable experience for visitors while optimizing the flow of people to ensure safety and sustainability.

5. CASE STUDIES AND SUCCESS STORIES

5.1 Successful AI Implementations in Tourism

Artificial intelligence (AI) has made significant inroads into the tourism industry, revolutionizing how travel businesses operate and how customers experience travel. Below are some case studies and success stories demonstrating successful AI implementations in tourism:

1. Hilton's "Connie" Robot Concierge

Overview: Hilton, one of the world's leading hotel chains, introduced an AI-powered robot concierge named "Connie" in some of its hotels. Connie, built using IBM's Watson technology and WayBlazer, is designed to interact with guests, answer questions, and provide recommendations.

Success Factors:

- **Enhanced Guest Experience**: Connie engages with guests, providing information about hotel amenities, local attractions, and dining options.
- **Reduced Staff Workload**: By handling common guest queries, Connie allows hotel staff to focus on more complex tasks, improving overall efficiency.
- **Learning Capabilities**: Connie learns from interactions, continuously improving her responses and recommendations.

Results:

- Improved guest satisfaction due to personalized and instant responses.
- Positive public relations and marketing impact, showcasing Hilton as an innovator in the hospitality industry.

2. KLM's "BlueBot" on Social Media

Overview: KLM Royal Dutch Airlines launched "BlueBot," an AI-powered chatbot on social media platforms like Facebook Messenger, Twitter, and WhatsApp. BlueBot helps customers with flight booking, itinerary changes, and general travel queries.

Success Factors:

- **Seamless Integration**: BlueBot integrates with popular social media platforms, making it easily accessible to customers.
- **Natural Language Processing (NLP)**: BlueBot can understand and respond to customer queries in a conversational manner.
- **24/7 Availability**: Customers can interact with BlueBot at any time, improving customer service.

Results:

- Faster response times to customer inquiries.
- Reduction in customer service workload, allowing human agents to focus on complex issues.
- Enhanced customer experience with personalized travel assistance.

3. AirAsia's "AVA" Virtual Allstar

Overview: AirAsia, a low-cost airline, implemented an AI-based virtual assistant called "AVA" to streamline customer service operations. AVA helps customers with booking, flight status, check-in procedures, and other travel-related queries.

Success Factors:

- **High Volume Handling**: AVA can handle a large volume of customer inquiries simultaneously.
- **Multilingual Support**: AVA is designed to understand multiple languages, catering to a diverse customer base.
- **Data-Driven Insights**: AVA collects data from interactions to identify common customer issues and improve services.

Results:

- Significant reduction in call center workload and operational costs.
- Improved customer satisfaction due to faster and more efficient responses.
- Ability to scale customer service operations without a proportional increase in staffing.

4. Expedia's AI-Powered Personalization

Overview: Expedia, a leading online travel agency, uses AI and machine learning to personalize travel recommendations for users. The system analyzes user behavior, preferences, and booking history to suggest relevant travel options.

Success Factors:

- **Behavioral Analytics**: AI analyzes large datasets to understand user preferences and trends.
- **Dynamic Personalization**: The system provides real-time recommendations based on user interactions.
- **User-Centric Design**: Expedia's AI is designed to enhance user experience by simplifying the booking process.

Results:

- Increased user engagement and conversion rates due to personalized recommendations.
- Enhanced customer loyalty through tailored travel experiences.
- Improved data-driven insights into customer behavior, informing business strategy and marketing.

5.2 Reducing Congestion With AI

Artificial intelligence (AI) is transforming the tourism industry by providing innovative solutions to reduce congestion, improve visitor experiences, and ensure sustainability. The following are some notable case studies and success stories illustrating how AI has been used effectively to address congestion in tourism:

Case 1: Disney's MyMagic+ System

Disney World in Orlando, Florida, implemented the MyMagic+ system, which includes the MagicBand wearable technology. This AI-powered system allows guests to pre-book attractions, dining, and other experiences. Here's how it reduces congestion:

- **Advanced Scheduling:** By allowing guests to book attractions in advance, the system can distribute crowds more evenly throughout the park, reducing long queues at popular rides.
- **Real-time Data Analysis:** Disney uses AI to monitor visitor flow and adjust staff and resources accordingly. This leads to better crowd management and improved guest satisfaction.
- **Personalized Recommendations:** The system can suggest less crowded areas or activities based on real-time data, encouraging guests to explore different parts of the park, further reducing congestion.

Case 2: Amsterdam's Crowd Management with City Data

Amsterdam, a popular European tourist destination, has implemented AI-based crowd management to reduce congestion in key areas like the city center and museums. The city's approach involves:

- **Data Collection and Analysis:** AI is used to analyze data from various sources, including traffic cameras, mobile phone signals, and social media, to understand crowd patterns and peak times.

- **Dynamic Signage and Alerts:** Real-time information is provided to tourists through digital signage and mobile apps, directing them to less crowded areas or suggesting alternative routes.
- **Customized Visitor Experiences:** AI-driven recommendations help tourists discover less frequented attractions, spreading out the crowds and enhancing the overall visitor experience.

Case 3: Barcelona's Smart Tourism Approach

Barcelona, a major tourist destination in Spain, has embraced AI to manage tourism and reduce congestion. The city's initiatives include:

- **Tourism Data Platform:** Barcelona uses a comprehensive data platform to monitor tourism-related activities, including visitor numbers at popular sites, traffic flow, and hotel occupancy.
- **Predictive Analytics for Planning:** The AI system predicts crowd levels based on historical data and current trends, allowing city planners to adjust resources and services to minimize congestion.
- **Personalized Tourism Apps:** Visitors use AI-powered apps to receive personalized recommendations for less crowded times to visit popular sites, helping distribute visitors more evenly throughout the day.

Success Stories

These case studies demonstrate the effectiveness of AI in reducing congestion in tourism:

- **Enhanced Visitor Experience:** Visitors enjoy shorter wait times, personalized recommendations, and smoother experiences, leading to higher satisfaction.
- **Improved Resource Allocation:** AI helps tourism destinations allocate staff and resources more efficiently, reducing operational costs and improving overall efficiency.
- **Reduced Environmental Impact:** By managing crowds and encouraging visitors to explore less crowded areas, destinations can minimize the environmental impact associated with large crowds.

5.3 Enhancing Visitor Safety With AI

AI has revolutionized the tourism industry by significantly enhancing visitor safety through advanced crowd management techniques. Utilizing machine learning algorithms and computer vision, AI systems can monitor and analyze crowd dynamics in real-time, providing early warnings about potential safety risks. For instance, AI-powered surveillance cameras can track the density and flow of people in high-traffic areas, such as theme parks, museums, or popular tourist attractions. When these systems detect unusually high crowd concentrations or erratic movement patterns, they can alert security personnel to take preventive measures, reducing the risk of accidents, stampedes, or other safety incidents (Mingotto et al., 2021). Additionally, AI-based predictive analytics allows for better planning and resource allocation, ensuring that tourist sites are adequately staffed and equipped to handle large crowds. This technology can also integrate with mobile apps to provide visitors with real-time updates on crowd conditions, suggesting less congested routes or times for visiting, further mitigating risks. By leveraging AI, the tourism industry can offer a safer and more enjoyable experience for visitors while reducing the strain on security and emergency response teams. This proactive approach not only improves safety but also contributes to a more efficient and responsive tourism ecosystem.

5.4 Improving Visitor Experience Through AI

AI technologies are revolutionizing tourism crowd management, enabling a more seamless and enjoyable visitor experience while addressing the challenges posed by high visitor volumes. By leveraging machine learning algorithms, real-time data analytics, and predictive modeling, AI is helping tourism managers anticipate crowd patterns and optimize the flow of visitors through popular attractions. This can lead to significant improvements in reducing bottlenecks, minimizing wait times, and enhancing overall safety. For instance, AI-driven crowd prediction models can analyze historical data and current trends to forecast peak visitor times. This information can be used to adjust staffing levels, open additional entry points, or implement timed ticketing systems to manage crowd density effectively. Additionally, AI-based facial recognition and surveillance technologies can monitor crowd behavior, detecting potential security risks or congested areas in real-time, allowing for rapid response and intervention. AI chatbots and virtual assistants are also transforming visitor experiences by providing personalized recommendations, answering common questions, and guiding tourists through their itineraries. These AI-powered tools can engage visitors before they even arrive at a destination, offering tailored suggestions based on preferences and past behavior. This can lead to a more satisfying and customized experience, reducing visitor stress and enhancing overall enjoyment.

6. ETHICAL CONSIDERATIONS IN AI-DRIVEN CROWD MANAGEMENT

6.1 Privacy and Data Protection

Privacy and data protection are pivotal ethical considerations in the realm of AI-driven crowd management within tourism contexts. As AI technologies are employed to manage crowds in popular tourist destinations, there is a substantial risk of infringing on individuals' privacy and mishandling personal data. AI systems often utilize surveillance cameras, facial recognition, and location-based tracking to monitor crowd movements and behavior. While these tools can enhance safety and improve the flow of people through congested areas, they raise significant concerns about data security and individual privacy rights. The collection of personal information through such means must be approached with transparency and informed consent. Tourists and local residents alike should be made aware of the data being collected, the purpose of the collection, how long it will be retained, and who will have access to it. Without this clarity, trust in public institutions and tourism management can erode, potentially leading to resistance against these AI-driven practices (Nam et al., 2021). Furthermore, robust data protection measures must be in place to prevent unauthorized access, misuse, or theft of sensitive information. This includes implementing encryption, anonymization, and strict access controls, ensuring that personal data cannot be easily linked back to individuals. Additionally, AI algorithms used in crowd management should be designed with ethical considerations to prevent discriminatory practices, such as racial profiling or unjust treatment based on age, gender, or other personal attributes. The ethical use of AI in crowd management requires a careful balance between optimizing tourism experiences and protecting individual rights. Authorities and businesses must work collaboratively to establish ethical guidelines and regulatory frameworks that uphold privacy and data protection while enabling AI technologies to improve crowd management. By fostering a transparent and accountable environment, tourism destinations can leverage AI effectively without compromising the ethical principles of privacy and data protection.

6.2 Transparency and Accountability

Transparency and accountability are critical ethical considerations in the implementation of AI-driven crowd management systems within the tourism sector. As tourism destinations experience high volumes of visitors, AI tools are increasingly used to monitor, predict, and manage crowds, but these applications raise significant ethical concerns. Transparency refers to the clear communication of how these AI systems operate, including the data they collect, the algorithms they employ, and the decision-making processes they follow. This is essential to build public trust and ensure that tourists, as well as local communities, understand the extent and purpose of surveillance and data collection. It involves providing detailed information on what kind of data is being collected, how it is stored, who has access to it, and for how long it is retained. Additionally, transparency includes informing stakeholders about the intended use of the data and offering insights into the AI algorithms' inner workings without compromising proprietary information.Accountability, on the other hand, requires mechanisms that ensure those responsible for deploying AI-driven systems are held liable for their decisions and the outcomes they produce. This involves establishing clear governance structures, delineating roles and responsibilities, and setting up review and redress mechanisms for those affected by AI-based decisions. In the context of tourism crowd management, accountability also requires a robust framework for addressing grievances and correcting mistakes when AI systems make errors or have adverse effects on privacy, safety, or civil liberties. Effective accountability mechanisms ensure that the deployment of AI in crowd management respects individual rights and adheres to legal and ethical standards. By addressing transparency and accountability, stakeholders can create a more ethically robust approach to using AI in tourism crowd management, fostering public trust and ensuring that these technologies are used in a manner that benefits both visitors and local communities.

6.3 Fairness and Bias in AI Systems

Fairness and bias in AI systems are critical considerations in the context of AI-driven crowd management for tourism, as they play a pivotal role in ensuring equitable treatment of individuals and groups. In such settings, AI systems are often used to predict and manage tourist flows, optimize resource allocation, and enhance safety and security. However, these systems can inadvertently perpetuate or exacerbate existing biases, leading to unfair treatment of certain groups based on factors such as race, gender, age, or socioeconomic status. For example, if an AI system is trained on historical data that reflects discriminatory practices, it may produce outcomes that disproportionately disadvantage specific groups. This could manifest in various ways, such as unequal access to resources, profiling, or unjustified surveillance.To address these concerns, it is crucial to implement robust mechanisms for ensuring fairness and minimizing bias in AI algorithms (Tussyadiah et al., 2020). This involves selecting diverse and representative training data, incorporating fairness metrics in the evaluation process, and continuously monitoring AI system outputs for signs of discriminatory patterns. Additionally, it is essential to engage with stakeholders, including local communities, civil rights organizations, and tourism experts, to understand the broader social and ethical implications of AI-driven crowd management. Transparent communication and accountability frameworks can also help build trust with the public, ensuring that AI systems are designed and operated with a commitment to fairness and equity. Ultimately, a careful balance must be struck between leveraging AI for efficient crowd management and upholding ethical principles that protect the rights and dignity of all individuals involved.

6.4 Ethical Best Practices for Tourism AI

Ethical best practices for tourism AI in the context of crowd management involve a multi-faceted approach that prioritizes privacy, fairness, accountability, and inclusivity. Firstly, AI systems used for managing tourist crowds must ensure robust data protection and privacy safeguards. This entails adhering to data minimization principles, ensuring that personally identifiable information (PII) is anonymized, and establishing clear guidelines for data collection, storage, and usage. Systems should be transparent about their data policies, and tourists should be informed about how their data is being used, with easy-to-understand consent mechanisms. Secondly, fairness is crucial in AI-driven crowd management. Algorithms should be regularly audited to prevent biases that could lead to discriminatory practices or unequal treatment of tourists based on factors like ethnicity, gender, or nationality (Vetrivel et al., 2024a). This involves ongoing monitoring and evaluation to ensure equitable outcomes and the use of diverse training data to reduce the risk of systemic bias. Accountability is another critical aspect, requiring clear delineation of responsibility among stakeholders. Developers, operators, and tourism authorities must collaborate to establish protocols for addressing errors, misuse, or unintended consequences of AI systems. Transparent reporting mechanisms and grievance redressal procedures should be implemented to allow tourists to raise concerns and seek recourse in case of adverse incidents.Finally, inclusivity must be a central consideration in AI-driven crowd management. AI systems should be designed to accommodate diverse tourist needs, ensuring accessibility for people with disabilities and language variations. This extends to the design of user interfaces and the provision of multilingual support to ensure that non-native speakers can interact with AI systems effectively.By implementing these ethical best practices, AI-driven tourism crowd management can balance the need for efficient crowd control with the rights and expectations of tourists, fostering an environment that is safe, inclusive, and respectful of individual privacy and dignity.

7. ETHICAL IMPLICATIONS AND PRIVACY CONCERNS ASSOCIATED WITH USING AI IN CROWD MANAGEMENT

The use of AI in crowd management raises significant ethical implications and privacy concerns, particularly regarding surveillance, data collection, and algorithmic decision-making. AI systems can enhance public safety by predicting and mitigating risks in large gatherings, but they also often rely on extensive monitoring and real-time data collection, which can infringe on individual privacy rights. The potential for misuse of this data, whether through unauthorized access or discriminatory practices, exacerbates these concerns. Additionally, the lack of transparency in AI algorithms can lead to biased or unfair outcomes, particularly when these systems disproportionately affect marginalized communities. Balancing the benefits of AI in crowd management with the need to protect individual privacy and ensure ethical use is therefore crucial.

8. FUTURE TRENDS IN AI-DRIVEN TOURISM CROWD MANAGEMENT

The rapid development of artificial intelligence (AI) technologies is reshaping many industries, and tourism is no exception. In the context of crowd management, AI is emerging as a powerful tool to enhance visitor experiences, improve safety, and optimize resource allocation (Vetrivel et al., 2024b). As tourism destinations and events become increasingly popular, managing crowds efficiently becomes crucial. Here are some of the most notable future trends in AI-driven tourism crowd management:

o   **Predictive Analytics and Forecasting**: With the proliferation of big data, AI can now analyze vast datasets to predict crowd patterns with increasing accuracy. By using historical data, weather forecasts, transportation trends, and even social media activity, AI algorithms can estimate the number of visitors to a specific location or event. This predictive capability allows tourism operators to adjust staffing levels, optimize resources, and implement proactive measures to ensure a smooth flow of visitors.

o   **Real-Time Monitoring and Alerts:** AI-driven systems are being used to monitor crowds in real time, utilizing data from CCTV cameras, drones, and sensors embedded in infrastructure. These systems can detect anomalies such as sudden crowding, unusual movement patterns, or potential security threats. When combined with automated alert mechanisms, this technology can help authorities and event organizers respond swiftly to emerging issues, enhancing safety and improving the overall visitor experience.

- **Smart Infrastructure and IoT Integration**: The integration of AI with the Internet of Things (IoT) is enabling the development of smart infrastructure in tourism destinations. Smart sensors and devices can collect real-time data on foot traffic, transportation, and amenities usage. AI algorithms can then process this information to provide insights into crowd distribution and behavior. This trend allows tourism managers to optimize the allocation of facilities, manage queues, and even control lighting and climate systems to improve visitor comfort.
- **AI-Powered Personalization and Navigation:** To help visitors navigate crowded environments, AI is being used to provide personalized recommendations and real-time routing. Mobile applications equipped with AI-driven algorithms can suggest alternative routes, less crowded attractions, and optimal times for visiting specific sites. This trend not only enhances the visitor experience but also helps distribute crowds more evenly, reducing congestion at popular spots.
- **Autonomous Transportation and Mobility Solutions**: The rise of AI-driven autonomous transportation is set to revolutionize tourism crowd management. Self-driving shuttles, taxis, and buses can operate efficiently in high-traffic areas, reducing congestion and improving safety (Wang, 2022). These autonomous solutions can adapt to real-time traffic conditions and dynamically adjust routes to optimize passenger flow. As these technologies mature, they will play a crucial role in managing transportation-related crowding in tourism destinations.
- **Enhanced Communication and Social Media Analytics**: AI can analyze social media platforms to gauge public sentiment and monitor trends in real time. This analysis can be used to anticipate crowd movements, track visitor satisfaction, and even detect emerging issues before they escalate. AI-driven communication tools can also engage with visitors, providing them with up-to-date information and addressing their concerns promptly. This trend enhances the overall experience and helps build a positive image for tourism destinations.

9. RECOMMENDATIONS FOR IMPLEMENTATION AND ADOPTION

Comprehensive Data Collection and Analysis: To effectively implement AI-driven tourism crowd management, a comprehensive data collection system must be established. This involves installing IoT sensors, CCTV cameras, and other monitoring technologies at key tourist sites to gather real-time data on visitor numbers, movement patterns, and behaviors. Data can also be sourced from social media platforms, tourism apps, and transportation networks. By consolidating these data sources, AI algorithms can be employed to analyze patterns and predict crowd dynamics, enabling proactive management. To ensure data privacy and compliance with regulations, it's crucial to anonymize data and implement robust security protocols.

Integration with Existing Infrastructure: AI-driven crowd management systems should seamlessly integrate with existing tourism infrastructure. This involves interfacing with transportation systems, ticketing platforms, and visitor information centers. By doing so, AI systems can optimize traffic flow, suggest alternative routes, and manage visitor queues efficiently. Integration with public transport networks can lead to improved scheduling, reducing bottlenecks and overcrowding. Moreover, by connecting with ticketing systems, AI can dynamically manage visitor quotas, allowing for better control over tourist site capacity.

Real-Time Communication and Information Dissemination: To effectively manage crowds, real-time communication with tourists is vital. AI-powered platforms can be used to disseminate information about crowd levels, estimated wait times, and alternative attractions. Mobile apps, digital displays, and social media channels are effective tools for reaching visitors quickly (Wu et al., 2022). By providing timely information, tourists can make informed decisions about their plans, thereby distributing crowds more evenly across different locations. Furthermore, these platforms can be used to promote lesser-known attractions, reducing pressure on popular sites.

Collaborative Partnerships and Stakeholder Involvement: Successful implementation of AI-driven tourism crowd management requires collaboration among various stakeholders. This includes local government, tourism authorities, businesses, and community groups. By engaging these stakeholders, a comprehensive strategy can be developed that aligns with broader tourism goals and community interests. Collaborative partnerships can also foster data sharing and resource pooling, leading to more effective crowd management. Moreover, involving local communities in the planning process can help mitigate potential negative impacts on residents and ensure that tourism development benefits the local economy.

Continuous Monitoring and Feedback Mechanisms: The adoption of AI-driven crowd management should include mechanisms for continuous monitoring and feedback. This ensures that the system remains responsive to changing tourism patterns and community needs. Establishing a feedback loop allows for ongoing evaluation of the system's effectiveness, with input from tourists, local businesses, and residents. AI systems should be adaptable, capable of refining their algorithms based on new data and feedback. This adaptability is crucial for addressing unforeseen challenges and ensuring the long-term success of crowd management initiatives.

Education and Training Programs: To maximize the benefits of AI-driven crowd management, it's essential to implement education and training programs for tourism industry workers. These programs should cover the basics of AI technology, the importance of data-driven decision-making, and best practices for managing tourist crowds. By equipping workers with the knowledge and skills to work with AI systems, tourism operators can enhance the overall visitor experience (Zhao et al., 2022). Additionally, public education campaigns can help tourists understand how AI is used in crowd management and encourage them to participate in feedback processes, fostering a more cooperative tourism environment.

10. CONCLUSION

AI-driven solutions are transforming the way crowd management is approached in the tourism industry. By leveraging advanced technologies like machine learning, computer vision, and predictive analytics, tourism destinations can significantly improve the efficiency and safety of managing large crowds. These solutions offer real-time insights into crowd behavior, enabling proactive decision-making that enhances visitor experiences and reduces the risk of overcrowding and safety incidents. As AI continues to evolve, its role in crowd management will become increasingly vital, facilitating smarter, more adaptable, and customer-centric tourism environments. The integration of AI-driven tools promises a future where crowd management is not just about control, but about creating seamless and enjoyable experiences for visitors while ensuring their safety and security.

REFERENCES

Ade, M., Harahap, K., Muna, A., Ausat, A., Rachman, A., Riady, Y., & Azzaakiyyah, H. K. (2023). Overview of ChatGPT Technology and its Potential in Improving Tourism Information Services. *JurnalMinfoPolgan*, 12(2). Advance online publication. DOI: 10.33395/jmp.v12i2.12416

Al Fararni, K., Nafis, F., Aghoutane, B., Yahyaouy, A., Riffi, J., & Sabri, A. (2021). Hybrid recommender system for tourism based on big data and AI: A conceptual framework. *Big Data Mining and Analytics*, 4(1), 47–55. DOI: 10.26599/BDMA.2020.9020015

Alotaibi, R., Ali, A., Alharthi, H., & Almehamadi, R. (2020). AI Chatbot for Tourism Recommendations A Case Study in the City of Jeddah, Saudi Arabia. *International Journal of Interactive Mobile Technologies*, 14(19), 18–30. DOI: 10.3991/ijim.v14i19.17201

Buhalis, D., Harwood, T., Bogicevic, V., Viglia, G., Beldona, S., & Hofacker, C. (2019). Technological disruptions in services: Lessons from tourism and hospitality. *Journal of Service Management*, 30(4), 484–506. DOI: 10.1108/JOSM-12-2018-0398

Bulchand-Gidumal, J. (2022). Impact of artificial intelligence in travel, tourism, and hospitality. In *Handbook of e-Tourism* (pp. 1943–1962). Springer International Publishing. DOI: 10.1007/978-3-030-48652-5_110

Ding, M. (2021). Research on Tourism Route Planning Based on Artificial Intelligence Technology. *Wireless Communications and Mobile Computing*, 2021(1), 2227798. Advance online publication. DOI: 10.1155/2021/2227798

Dogan, S., & Niyet, I. Z. (2024). Artificial Intelligence (AI) in Tourism. In Future Tourism Trends Volume 2: Technology Advancement, Trends and Innovations for the Future in Tourism (pp. 3-21). Emerald Publishing Limited.

Dogru, T., Line, N., Mody, M., Hanks, L., Abbott, J. A., Acikgoz, F., Assaf, A., Bakir, S., Berbekova, A., Bilgihan, A., Dalton, A., Erkmen, E., Geronasso, M., Gomez, D., Graves, S., Iskender, A., Ivanov, S., Kizildag, M., Lee, M., & Zhang, T. (2023). Generative artificial intelligence in the hospitality and tourism industry: Developing a framework for future research. *Journal of Hospitality & Tourism Research (Washington, D.C.)*. DOI: 10.1177/10963480231188663

Ferràs, X., Hitchen, E. L., Tarrats-Pons, E., & Arimany-Serrat, N. (2020). Smart tourism empowered by artificial intelligence: The case of Lanzarote. *Journal of Cases on Information Technology*, 22(1), 1–13. DOI: 10.4018/JCIT.2020010101

Flandrin, P., Hellemans, C., Van Der Linden, J., & Van De Leemput, C. (2021, October 6). Smart technologies in hospitality: effects on activity, work design and employment. A case study about chatbot usage. *ACM International Conference Proceeding Series*. DOI: 10.1145/3486812.3486838

Ghouse, S. M., & Chaudhary, M. (2024). Artificial Intelligence (AI) for Tourism Start-Ups. In Innovative Technologies for Increasing Service Productivity (pp. 161-178). IGI Global.

Gretzel, U. (2011). Intelligent systems in tourism. A Social Science Perspective. In Annals of Tourism Research (Vol. 38, Issue 3, pp. 757–779). DOI: 10.1016/j.annals.2011.04.014

Gupta, S., Modgil, S., Lee, C. K., & Sivarajah, U. (2023). The future is yesterday: Use of AI-driven facial recognition to enhance value in the travel and tourism industry. *Information Systems Frontiers*, 25(3), 1179–1195. DOI: 10.1007/s10796-022-10271-8 PMID: 35529102

Iglesias, M. I., Jenkins, M., & Morison, G. (2021). An enhanced photorealistic immersive system using augmented situated visualization within virtual reality. Proceedings -2021 IEEE Conference on Virtual Reality and 3D User Interfaces Abstracts and Workshops, VRW 2021, 514–515. DOI: 10.1109/VRW52623.2021.00139

Jiang, G., Gao, W., Xu, M., Tong, M., & Liu, Z. (2023). Geographic Information Visualization and Sustainable Development of Low-Carbon Rural Slow Tourism under Artificial Intelligence. *Sustainability (Basel)*, 15(4), 3846. Advance online publication. DOI: 10.3390/su15043846

Koo, C., Xiang, Z., Gretzel, U., & Sigala, M. (2021). Artificial intelligence (AI) and robotics in travel, hospitality, and leisure. In Electronic Markets (Vol. 31, Issue 3, pp. 473–476). Springer Science and Business Media Deutschland GmbH. DOI: 10.1007/s12525-021-00494-z

Limna, P. (2023). Artificial Intelligence (AI) in the Hospitality Industry: A Review Article. *International Journal of Computing Sciences Research*, 7, 1306–1317. DOI: 10.25147/ijcsr.2017.001.1.103

Mingotto, E., Montaguti, F., & Tamma, M. (2021). Challenges in re-designing operations and jobs to embody AI and robotics in services. Findings from a case in the hospitality industry. *Electronic Markets*, 31(3), 493–510. DOI: 10.1007/s12525-020-00439-y

Nam, K., Dutt, C. S., Chathoth, P., Daghfous, A., & Sajid Khan, M. (2021). The adoption of artificial intelligence and robotics in the hotel industry: Prospects and challenges. *Electronic Markets*, 31(3), 553–574. DOI: 10.1007/s12525-020-00442-3

Tussyadiah, I. P., Zach, F. J., & Wang, J. (2020). Do travelers trust intelligent service robots? *Annals of Tourism Research*, 81, 102886. Advance online publication. DOI: 10.1016/j.annals.2020.102886

Vetrivel, S. C., Sowmiya, K. C., Gomathi, T., & Arun, V. P. (2024b). Engaging Online Classes ThroughGamification: Leveraging Innovative Tools and Technologies. In R. Bansal, A. Chakir, A. HafazNgah, F. Rabby, & A. Jain (Eds.), AI Algorithms and ChatGPT for Student Engagement in Online Learning (pp. 171-191). IGI Global. DOI: 10.4018/979-8-3693-4268-8.ch012

Vetrivel, S. C., Sowmiya, K. C., & Sabareeshwari, V. (2024a). Digital Twins: Revolutionizing Business in the Age of AI. In Ponnusamy, S., Assaf, M., Antari, J., Singh, S., & Kalyanaraman, S. (Eds.), *Harnessing AI and Digital Twin Technologies in Businesses* (pp. 111–131). IGI Global. DOI: 10.4018/979-8-3693-3234-4.ch009

Wang, X. (2022). Artificial Intelligence in the Protection and Inheritance of Cultural Landscape Heritage in Traditional Village. *Scientific Programming*, 2022, 1–11. Advance online publication. DOI: 10.1155/2022/9117981

Wu, D., Song, Z., & Guo, H. (2022). Artificial Intelligence Algorithms in Ice and Snow Tourism Promotion from Digital Technology. *Wireless Communications and Mobile Computing*, 2022, 1–9. Advance online publication. DOI: 10.1155/2022/1806611

Zhao, J., Guo, L., & Li, Y. (2022). Application of Digital Twin Combined with Artificial Intelligence and 5G Technology in the Art Design of Digital Museums. *Wireless Communications and Mobile Computing*, 2022, 1–12. Advance online publication. DOI: 10.1155/2022/8214514

Chapter 5
AI-Powered Solutions for Sustainable Tourism Practices Through Wildlife Conservation Initiatives

Kudzai Masvingise
https://orcid.org/0000-0002-8181-588X
Stellenbosch University, South Africa

Nyarai Margaret Mujuru
https://orcid.org/0000-0003-3279-5218
University of Fort Hare, South Africa

ABSTRACT

As global tourism rises, wildlife habitats deteriorate, leading to human-animal competition and a surge in illegal activities threatening wildlife conservation. This necessitates new conservation approaches. Effective wildlife conservation is crucial for sustainable tourism and leaving a legacy. This chapter explores AI's role in enhancing sustainable tourism through wildlife conservation as well as maps the research landscape. Literature review and science mapping using Scopus and VOSviewer revealed a growing interest in this field post-2010. Limited empirical research addresses the intersection of AI, sustainable tourism, and wildlife conservation comprehensively. Future research should focus on AI solutions for sustainable tourism through wildlife conservation, as AI continues to revolutionise various disciplines and systems.

DOI: 10.4018/979-8-3693-5678-4.ch005

BACKGROUND OF THE STUDY

While unlocking the secrets of nature, AI is constantly revolutionising wildlife conservation in the tourism industry. The practice of safeguarding and maintaining wild animal and plant populations as well as their natural habitats is known as wildlife conservation (Joseph, 2023). AI is defined as the ability of machines to demonstrate intelligence as opposed to the natural intelligence exhibited by humans and other animals (Zhang & Sun, 2019). AI is used in resource conservation, biodiversity analysis, species identification, habitat evaluation, and wildlife tracking among other environmental monitoring and conservation activities (Chisom et al., 2024). AI and tourism convergence pave a unique way for strengthening wildlife conservation initiatives through sustainable tourism. According to the World Tourism Organisation (1998, p. 21), sustainable tourism is the pursuit of satisfying the demand of existing and potential tourists and the alleged region while at the same fulfilling goals for the future.

However, travel around the world is on the rise, leading to fears concerning how increasing travel will affect endangered animals and ecosystems. The desire to connect with the natural world, and thus experience "the real," is attracting ever-growing numbers of tourists wishing for better wildlife tourism experiences. Even so, there are various setbacks to the implementation of this tourism boom which include: deteriorated wilderness habitats, competition between humans and animals, and widespread illegal acts such as poaching. Worldwide, large animal populations suffer from high mortalities, most of which are due to human-related activity (Gantchoff et al., 2020). With the loss in wildlife numbers leading to the designation of many species on the planet as under threat of extinction or becoming extinct (Gade et al., 2023), wildlife conservation is not only an individual obligation but also a crucial global responsibility.

Traditional environmental monitoring technologies inevitably have limitations in their scope, scale, and ability to manage large amounts of data. This necessitates a paradigm change in monitoring and conservation efforts. Hence, an effective way to deal with these issues and make wildlife tourism better for conservation efforts is through the incorporation of AI. AI technologies give us some creative and helpful ways to reduce these adverse effects while encouraging eco-friendly travel behaviours (Arora & Chandel, 2024). AI is a game-changer for wildlife conservation and environmental monitoring, while at the same time it is changing how we protect the natural world through its unparalleled ability to analyse large volumes of data and reveal hidden patterns (Chisom et al., 2024). Due to its ability to derive meaningful outcomes from analysing extensive and intricate datasets related to nature, AI is promising and exciting. By employing sophisticated algorithms and machine learning models, like those outlined by Fakiha (2023) and Al-Mansoori and

Salem (2023), AI-driven conservation efforts have improved upon the limitations of traditional monitoring tools.

It is against this backdrop that the study seeks to investigate the relationship between wildlife conservation and tourism; examine the immersive nature of AI-powered wildlife tourism; and provide a detailed account of the applications of AI in wildlife tourism through bibliometrics and AI's benefits, challenges, and ethical considerations, as well as future trends.

The chapter is organised into the following sections. The introduction gives a detailed background of AI, wildlife conservation, and tourism, as well as the aims of the study. A detailed methodology follows, explaining how the study was carried out to shed light on how AI algorithms can be applied to analyse wildlife data, track animal populations, detect poaching activities, optimize conservation strategies for maximum impact and effectiveness, and predict future trends. Next, the findings of the study are presented and discussed, outlining the AI, tourism, and wildlife interface; conservation initiatives; AI and wildlife identification; and AI and wildlife monitoring. Lastly, conclusions and recommendations are presented.

Research Objectives

The objectives of this study are as follows:

- To explore the AI, wildlife conservation, and tourism interface
- To analyse research trends and keyword co-occurrence
- To explain the key AI-powered wildlife conservation initiatives in action
- To discuss the benefits of AI integration in wildlife conservation
- To identify the key challenges and ethical considerations associated with the use of AI in wildlife conservation
- To explore the future trends and opportunities of AI in wildlife conservation

The AI, Wildlife Conservation, and Tourism Interface

Tourism offers people the unique opportunity of having interactive experiences (such as taking selfies, riding, petting, and swimming) with exotic species and these encounters have the capacity to alter the lives of individual animals (Carr & Broom, 2018; Winter, 2020). People can also consume the animals they travel to see, which is literally eating their destination (Kline, 2018). The relationship between tourism and wildlife conservation encompasses both positive and negative aspects, making it both complex and multifaceted (Zuniga, 2019; Dou & Day, 2020). Globally, there are diverse wildlife tourism practices that target various taxa across all biomes and use a range of methods to observe and attract species (Meyer et al., 2021).

The industry has a reputation of affecting species and ecosystems (Trave et al., 2017) but can also provide a positive alternative to lethal wildlife use, owing to a number of conservation and economic benefits (Huveneers et al., 2017). On one hand, tourism provides economic benefits and education and awareness (Gazta, 2018). Tourism can generate funds that can be used for conservation projects and can also create employment that will, in turn, reduce the overconsumption of wildlife caused by the reliance on deforestation and poaching. Through tourism, tourists can be educated on wildlife conservation and become conservation advocates. On the other hand, tourism can negatively impact the environment and disturb wildlife (Gazta, 2018). The deleterious effects of human disturbance on wildlife is recognised widely (Coetzee & Chawn, 2016).

Natural habitats can be destroyed and fragmented by the infrastructure that is built for tourism purposes (roads, hotels, etc.). Tourism activities can bring about different forms of pollution (air, noise, and waste). The frequent presence of humans can disrupt the feeding patterns, natural habitats, and breeding cycles of wildlife. The harms experienced by animals and humans often coincide because their live are entwined (Sebo, 2022). For instance, diseases can be passed from humans to animals and vice versa (U.S. Centers for Disease Control and Prevention, n.d.). Additionally, poachers can attack both animals and their human protectors (Nandutu et al., 2021). Therefore, there is interdependence between humans and nonhumans, and protecting wildlife can, in turn, protect human lives (Coghlan & Parker, 2023). Technology affects both humans and wildlife (Lupton, 2022); hence, the entanglement with human wellbeing augments the case for considering animal interests when examining AI (Coghlan & Parker, 2023). This indicates a need for ethical uses of AI to develop sustainable tourism that ensures wildlife conservation.

According to Ceballos et al. (2020), there is an unprecedented decline in animal diversity (genetic, ecological and behavioural). As a result, international policy has an increased emphasis on the importance of sustainable tourism practices when visiting protected areas or interacting with wildlife (Center for Responsible Travel, 2017; Koprowski & Krausman, 2019). There exists an urgent need for tools that can assist in the conservation of wildlife. Currently, conventional methods are being used, in which humans collect data and observe the behaviour of animals; such methods are labor intensive, time consuming, and unreliable (Witmer, 2005). Due to the physical and cognitive limitations of humans, data accuracy and effective wildlife monitoring are difficult to achieve (Kays et al., 2015), which may lead to the continuation of harmful acts to wildlife. For instance, intensive monitoring is required to prevent poaching (Tuia et al., 2022). Despite the heavy investment in detecting and preventing illegal poaching, rangers often arrive at the scene when the damage (crime to endangered animals) has already been done (O'Donoghue & Rutz, 2016). Therefore, AI represents a basic need, rather than a luxury, in wildlife conservation. It would address the lack of manpower and would improve upon humans' work limitations, as AI can function under typical environmental conditions without disturbing animal habitats (Kumar & Jakhar, 2022).

By contributing to a sustainable future, the incorporation of AI in sustainable tourism has the potential to revolutionize the industry (Khan et al., 2024). Tourism sustainability can be supported through AI-powered conservation tools in monitoring, managing, and protecting natural resources and wildlife. Used effectively, these tools could offer real-time information on environmental factors, species densities, and human interference so tourism operators can take actions that are less damaging to the environment (Nandutu et al., 2022). Applying AI-powered tools helps to identify patterns not easily perceived by the human eye and prevent future negative changes in the environment using data such as information collected by sensors, images taken from satellites, and many others (Chen et al., 2019). Such a prudent strategy can promote tourism activities that have no adverse effects on biodiversity and ecosystems so that future generations can enjoy the world's natural gift.

Therefore, the application of AI to conservation and sustainable tourism for wildlife has the potential to expand in the coming years. In the case of wildlife conservation, more developed AI technologies can be utilized for enhancing surveillance, enriching habitat, and combating poaching (Shivaprakash et al., 2022; Isabelle & Westerlund, 2022). Furthermore, AI can be employed to design and deliver unique and sustainable tourism experiences that would prompt tourists to practice and advocate for the sustainable use of the environment (Dionisio et al., 2022). This can, in turn, increase the satisfaction of the tourist visitors and bring more repeat visitation, which will greatly benefit not only the conservation initiatives but also the entire tourism sector.

Methods

A critical review of literature combined with a science mapping research design was used. According to Grant and Booth (2009), critical reviews involve a degree of analysis and conceptual innovation seeking to identify most significant items in the field. However, this approach lacks systematicity (Grant & Booth, 2009) and science mapping was used to complement the perceived weakness. Several studies have used science mapping on the topic of AI, tourism and conservation (Chavan et al., 2024; Rane et al., 2023; Kirtil & Askun, 2021). Science mapping workflows include study design, data collection, data analysis, visualisation and interpretation (Zupic & Čater, 2015). A significant number of studies have been conducted which combine science mapping and critical reviews (Kundu et al., 2023; Burke et al., 2022; Dash & Kalamdhad, 2021).

Data was sourced from Scopus (June 2024), which is the largest scholarly database providing comprehensive coverage, reliability, credibility, and up-to-date information. The search algorithm ("Artificial Intelligence" OR "AI" AND "Wildlife Conservation" OR "Sustainable Tourism") was entered in Scopus. It yielded 97 articles. The articles were screened by reading through the topic and abstract; inclusion criteria consisted of articles with either of the keywords "Artificial Intelligence and Sustainable Tourism or Tourism" or "Artificial Intelligence and Wildlife Conservation or Conservation." Articles that did not meet the criteria were excluded, and 80 articles remained for analysis.

The data was subjected to science mapping based on bibliographic data using VOSviewer. VOSviewer was developed by Nees Jan van Eck and Ludo Waltman at Leiden University's Centre for Science and Technology Studies and launched in 2010. VOSviewer's efficacy in visualising and generating text maps based on bibliometric data is outstanding (Orduña-Malea & Costas, 2021). The software is popular in the Scientometrics community, and there is growing recognition in other disciplines (Orduña-Malea & Costas, 2021).

After the bibliometric analysis was carried out, a qualitative assessment of occurring terms was conducted. AI-based conservation tools were identified from the respective network. The science mapping approach was used to critically review existing AI tools used in wildlife conservation. A thorough examination of these tools and their potential to enhance sustainable tourism was followed by a critical review of the most impactful research papers.

ANALYSIS OF RESEARCH TRENDS AND KEYWORDS CO-OCCURRENCE

Documents per Year

AI and wildlife conservation intersect at the crucial juncture of leveraging AI technology to enhance conservation efforts and protect endangered species and their habitats, while encouraging the coexistence of humans and wildlife (Foyet, 2024). Research in this field started getting recognition in 2010, gained momentum in 2019, and has been on the rise since, as shown in Figure 1.

Figure 1. Documents per year

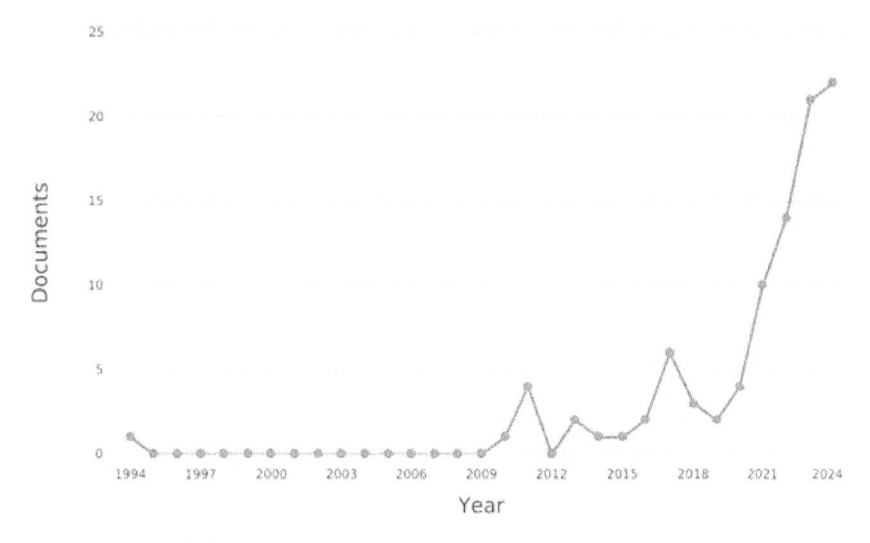

Figure 1: Documents by year

Collaboration Network

The collaboration networks shown in Figure 2 represent author and country collaborations respectively. Minimum number of documents and citation per author were set at 1 and 278 met the threshold. However, only 29 items were connected to one another and hence were included in the analysis. The co-author network has two clusters only and this depicts two distinct groups of authors who are closely connected within their respective clusters but less connected between the two clusters. Author Devis Tuia has the highest number of publications (3) and citations (440), with a total link strength of 30. The United States is leading in citations (324) and India has the highest number of documents (20). More collaboration with Africa would be beneficial to the continent as it hosts some of the largest herds of wild animals.

Figure 2. a) Author collaboration network, b) country collaboration network

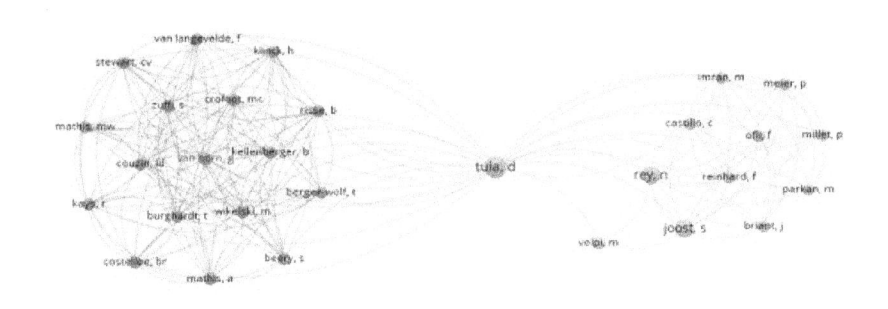

Figure 2a:Co-authorship

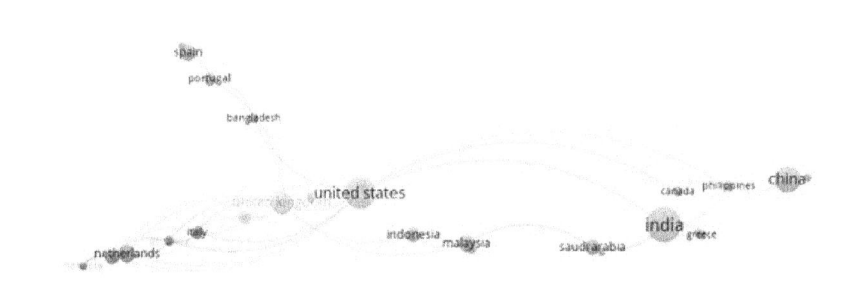

Figure 2b:Country collaboration

Keyword Co-Occurrence

Keywords serve as identifiers for developing aspects and also help to showcase the dynamics and visualization of information (Su & Lee, 2010). During the mapping process, all keywords were chosen and fractional counting was utilized. Fractional counting involves assigning a fraction of the occurrence of a keyword or term to each document, depending on the total number of keywords or terms in that document. This method enables a more detailed analysis of the connections between documents and keywords in network visualization (Kundu et al., 2023; Su & Lee, 2010). The minimum keyword occurrence was set to 3 as it was found to be the optimal number for a clear visual, yielding 68 keywords out of a total of 937 keywords.

A bibliometric map of keyword occurrences is depicted in Figure 3. The network visualizes the connections between terms, with large nodes representing more recurring keyword appearances and thickness of edges indicating the strength of their co-occurrence. In addition, the closer items are on the bibliometric map, the closer is their relationship. The network visualisation map in Figure 3 has 68 items, five clusters, 776 links and total link strength of 233. Cluster 1 contains 10 occurrences of machine learning, while AI leads cluster 2 with 55 occurrences. In cluster 3, wildlife conservation and conservation are mentioned 24 times, sustainable development is mentioned 18 times in cluster 4, and the smallest cluster includes sustainable tourism development, big data, and internet of things, each appearing four times.

Figure 3. Keyword occurrence

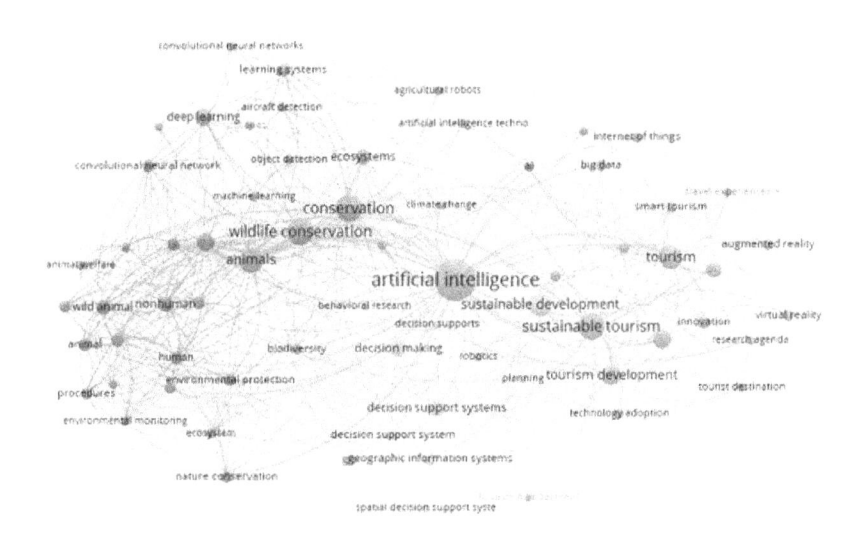

Figure 3: Co-occurrence network

Most articles published focus on AI; it is the most co-occurring keyword based on the node size. As depicted in Figure 4, which shows the AI network, AI and tourism are both in cluster 2, the largest cluster with 24 items. Hence, the two terms are closely related. Wildlife conservation is in the third cluster with 15 items. The top six keywords are presented in Table 1. "Artificial Intelligence" is leading with 55 occurrences and a total link strength of 54 and 66 links. Wildlife conservation and conservation both occur 24 times. Sustainable tourism is closely related to AI and has the same occurrence as wildlife conservation. However, it has the least total link strength. The frequency of co-occurrence or other relevant metrics, such as citation counts or keyword similarities, determines a link's strength. By aggregating the strengths of all links connected to a particular item, VOSviewer provides a measure of the overall relationship or influence between that item and other items in the network.

Figure 4. AI network

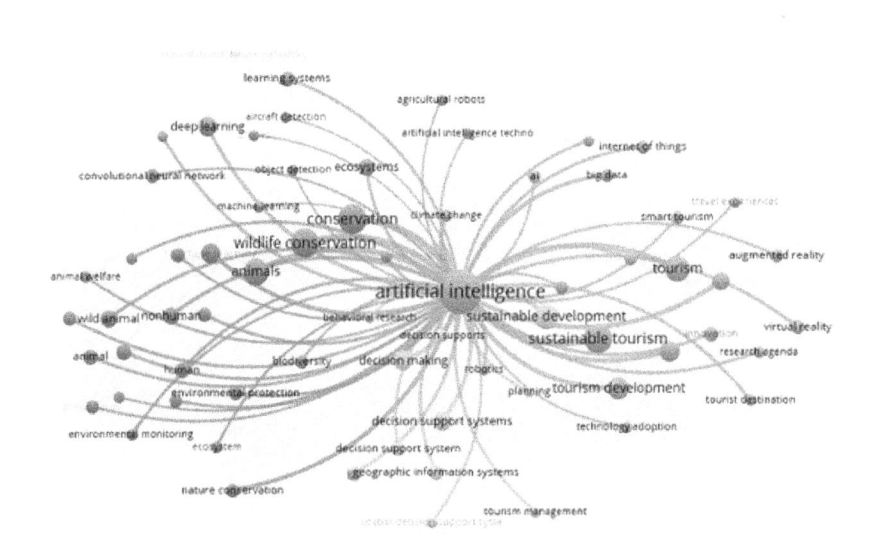

Figure 4: Artificial Intelligence Network

Table 1. Keyword Identification and Occurrence

Keyword	Occurrence	Total link strength (no. of links)
Artificial Intelligence	55	54 (66)
Wildlife Conservation	24	24 (44)
Conservation	24	24 (46)
Animals	19	23 (37)

continued on following page

Table 1. Continued

Keyword	Occurrence	Total link strength (no. of links)
Sustainable development	18	19 (46)
Sustainable tourism	24	18 (40)

"Artificial Intelligence" is connected to all the clusters as shown in Figure 4. This can be attributed to the growing interest from researchers across all disciplines. The first article to be published in Scopus on AI was in 1960. There was a steady growth in publications until 2000, after which outputs started growing exponentially. The leading subject areas in total publications are computer science, mathematics and engineering.

AI-Powered Wildlife Conservation Initiatives

AI is being used in wildlife conservation to protect delicate ecosystems. According to Brickson et al. (2023), the fields of AI and ML offer groundbreaking prospects for improving our comprehension of animal behaviour and conservation tactics (Kerry et al., 2022). Manual data collection can be time-consuming and limited (Chen et al., 2019), and when interpreting the results, it is important to take accuracy and possible confounding variables into account. Consequently, a vast array of technologies has been utilised, frequently in untamed environments. Technological advancements like ML, computer vision, and predictive modelling help wildlife conservationists monitor species, conduct population studies, and make decisions about habitat protection (Nandutu et al., 2022). In marine conservation, for example, AI-enabled autonomous underwater drones survey coral reefs, spotting pollution and bleaching symptoms with unmatched precision (Obura, 2019). AI also provides immersive experiences for environmentally conscious tourists looking for meaningful interactions with nature. By utilizing AI, tourism-related wildlife conservation projects can encourage ethical travel, enhance conservation results, and give visitors memorable experiences that support biodiversity preservation. The wildlife conservation network is depicted in Figure 5. The network shows that wildlife conservation has more links with cluster 1 represented by the red colour. Items found in cluster 1 such as animal welfare, environmental monitoring, nature conservation, ML, and algorithm have relatively large nodes. The visualisation network shows a strong relationship between wildlife conservation and AI as depicted by a thick edge. However, there are very few links between items in cluster 2 (green) representing AI and tourism and cluster 4 (yellow) signifying wildlife conservation, implying limited research in the area of conservation, AI, and tourism.

Figure 5. Wildlife conservation network

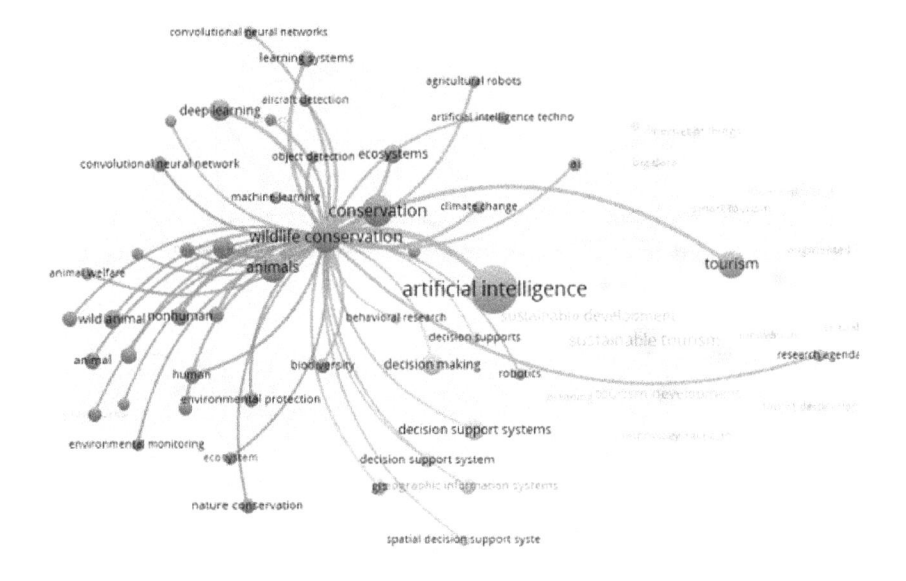

Figure 5: Wildlife conservation network

Some of the key AI concepts and techniques relevant to wildlife conservation identified in the literature include ML, deep learning, object detection, drones, robots, and convolutional neural networks; these are discussed subsequently.

AI-Based Wildlife Monitoring and Surveillance

To understand complex patterns that make up the life of many species, it is necessary to monitor wildlife. AI is being used for automated species monitoring by a wide range of researchers and an expanding community of applied conservationists (Global Partnership on Artificial Intelligence, 2022). Usually, traditional techniques such as inadequate observational data and manual telemetry are not sufficient for capturing this richness (Hauenstein et al., 2022; Granli & Poole, 2022). However, wildlife monitoring has changed due to the advent of AI systems which have endowed them with hitherto unknown abilities to monitor and comprehend animal movement. AI is emerging as a guardian of biodiversity and an enabler of sustainable environmentalism, with applications ranging from locating illegal logging activities in the Amazon rainforest to tracking routes used by elephant poachers in Africa (Brickson et al., 2023; Dorfling et al., 2022). Enhancing monitoring and surveillance efforts is one of the most promising uses of AI in tourism for wildlife conservation. Manual observation and data collection are common in traditional methods, and they can be labor- and resource-intensive (Chen et al., 2019). AI provides creative ways to optimize this procedure by facilitating automated wildlife population monitoring and surveillance. GPS data, pictures taken by camera trap, and aerial images are examined by AI algorithms aimed at analysing enormous volumes of data to track animal movements, identify and estimate population levels, detect poaching activities, and identify changes in habitat conditions through the use of advanced sensors, drones, and satellite imagery (Chisom et al., 2024). Drones with AI algorithms installed can survey large tracts of wildlife habitat and gather information on animal populations, behaviours, and health conditions. Real-time AI algorithms count individuals, identify species, and highlight any unusual activity from this data. Figure 6 summarises the wildlife monitoring tools identified in literature.

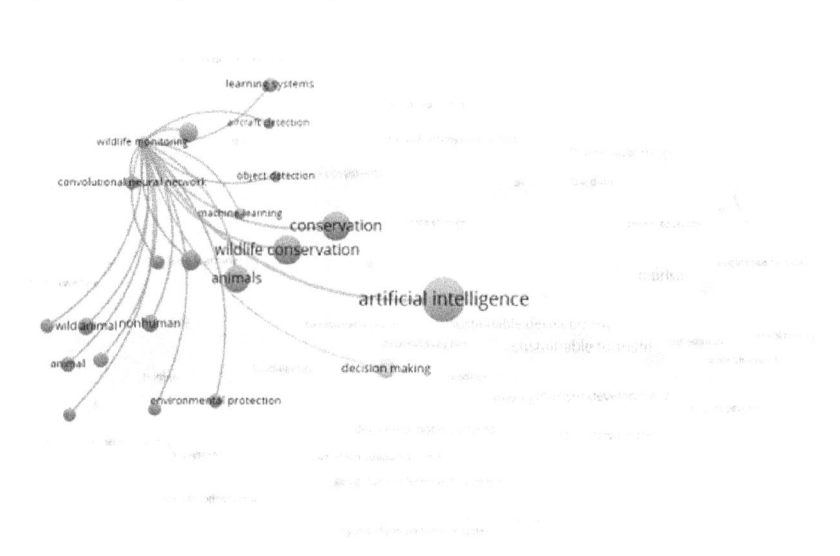

Figure 6. Wildlife monitoring network

Figure 6: Wildlife monitoring network.

Based on Sachan et al. (2023), wildlife can be monitored through the following AI tools:

- Species detection: AI is useful in identifying the invasive species threatening the indigenous habitats and in monitoring and controlling the growth of such species.

- GPS tracking: GPS-enabled radio frequency identification tags are preferable for animals that are considered endangered. They collect location information, movement patterns, and other behavioural data, and then electronically transfer the data to examination centres for analysis. This information is used by the AI systems to track animals' movements and their use of the environment.
- Geofencing: Artificial geofences can also be developed by AI around protected areas and can be used to signal and alert tagged animals when they venture close to zones that are potentially dangerous (for example, areas where animals are at high risk of endangerment by poachers). This makes the resolution of issues as well as safety measures quick and possible.
- Migration studies: AI can analyse the tendencies concerning the ecological needs of and threats to endangered species by monitoring their migratory patterns.

Example: Spatial Monitoring and Reporting Tool in South Africa

South Africa is home to a diverse array of wildlife, including iconic species such as elephants, rhinos, and lions. However, the country also faces significant challenges in combating wildlife crime, particularly poaching. Rhinos, in particular, have been targeted for their valuable horns, which are highly sought after in illegal markets. To address this issue, South African National Parks implemented the spatial monitoring and reporting tool, an innovative anti-poaching and law enforcement system powered by technology and data analysis (von Durckheim, 2017). The spatial monitoring and reporting tool combines field-based monitoring techniques with advanced technology, including GPS tracking devices, camera traps, and geographic information system software. The system can identify and track individual animals, identify suspicious behaviour, and instantly notify rangers by using a network of camera traps that are outfitted with AI algorithms (Rayhan, 2023). This proactive strategy has helped to preserve important wildlife populations and drastically decreased poaching incidents.

Automated Wildlife Identification

In biodiversity analysis, AI has become a revolutionary force, enabling previously unthinkable methods of species identification and classification while tracking ecosystem dynamics (Chisom et al., 2024). With AI technologies like computer vision and deep learning, different species can be automatically identified from their photos and videos (Narasimha et al., 2023). These systems facilitate citizen science initiatives, collect vital data for conservation research, and improve the educational experience for tourists by quickly identifying wildlife species encountered during tours. The use of AI technology is completely changing how we recognize and monitor individual animals. AI algorithms can correctly identify species and even differentiate between individual animals by examining patterns in their physical traits, such as markings or distinctive features (Saiwa, 2023). According to Chisom et al. (2024), wildlife can be identified through image recognition and acoustic monitoring.

Image Recognition

- Camera traps: Camera traps are easy to install, inexpensive, and provide high-resolution image sequences of the animals that trigger them, sufficient to specify the species, sex, age, health, behaviour, and predator-prey interactions (Tuia et al., 2022). They are automatic cameras that record the pictures and videos of animals and their behaviour in the forests for qualitative analysis (Chisom et al., 2024). These cameras take pictures or videos whenever there is movement or heat source and the AI technologies determine the species in the photos. This aids in tracking the sighting, activity, and distribution/abundance of threatened species.
- Facial recognition: In species with unique patterns or features to their skin or fur, AI technology can be used to recognize individual animals using face recognition (Chisom et al., 2024). This is particularly useful in monitoring an animal's movements over a period of time, their grouping patterns, and health.
- Drones and aerial surveys: Aerial drone-based application with integrated image identification algorithms can fly over large tracks of land and map out species that are endangered (Chisom et al., 2024). This makes it easy to identify potential threats. They are useful in estimating the sizes of the population.

Acoustic Monitoring

- Bioacoustics: These are an alternative to image-based systems, using microphones and hydrophones to study vocal animals and their habitats (Sugai et al., 2019). AI helps in bioacoustics to process audio data of voice and sounds produced by animals and organisms belonging to the biosphere. Despite the fact that visual tracking could be a challenging process in places that are quite lonely or in regions with a heavy growth of trees, AI can be used to identify particular looks with the help of analyses of the frequencies (rhythms and pitches) of these sounds (Chisom et al., 2024).
- Identifying mating calls: Acoustic monitoring enables behaviours and mating calls that would help in controlling the population and breeding to be realized

(Chisom et al., 2024). Also, it can detect changes in the vocalizations due to stressors from humans or the surrounding environment.

Example: BearID for Detecting Bears

Clapham et al. (2020) and Clapham et al. (2022) used *BearID* to detect the faces of bears. Bears (ursids) were studied because they present an important focal taxonomic family for examining the application of computer vision to wildlife ecology (Kutschera et al., 2014). Although not designed for this function, *BearID* is an application that verifies faces (Deb et al., 2018) in an image, rotates and extracts the face, creates an "embedding" for the face, and uses the embedding to classify the individual for unknown brown bears (Clapham et al., 2020). *BearID* was used because it is transferable to other mammals and certain parts of the pipeline may be particularly transferable to other caniforms due to facial similarities (Clapham et al., 2020).

Enhancing Visitor Experiences

Since the elites of the global economy transit from the service economy to the experience economy (Kelly, 2020; Kim & Chen, 2019; Sthapit et al., 2019), service providers, particularly tourism service providers, are now keen to design and develop experiences and to deliver memorable and sweet consumption experiences to tourists. AI can enhance the experience of wildlife tourism and at the same time assist in conservation monitoring. Recommendation systems driven by AI can offer customized wildlife experiences according to visitors' tastes, interests, and previous interactions (Zsarnoczty, 2017). AI-enabled chatbots or virtual assistants can offer interactive tours, real-time information, and answers to questions, all of which increase visitor satisfaction. Through the overlaying of digital information, such as species identification, behavioural insights, and historical context, AI-driven AR and VR applications can enhance the visitor experience during wildlife encounters (Dykins, 2020). The applications are capable of mimicking the natural environment, focusing on the importance of preserving biodiversity, or tours that are guided by virtual conservationists. With the use of AI, there are mobile applications that can provide the latest information on the observation of wildlife locally, protection measures, and sustainable tourism plans for the environment. This makes tourists enjoy the protected areas and wildlife behaviour and understand the importance of conservation through VR experiences, without actually getting into physical contact with wildlife and the environment.

Example: AI-Guided Safari Experiences

Some tour operators in sub-Saharan Africa have launched AI Virtual Safari, which uses actual real-time data on trends in sightings and animates migration and even weather (Dykins, 2020). Users can get navigational guidance on where and when to go to get the best views of wildlife by using mobile applications and AR. These AI-guided tours ensure that the tourists are satisfied with the services they get while also avoiding any disruption to the animals' activities and habitats by matching visitors' activities with the natural rhythm of the environment.

Predictive Analytics

The application of AI as the basis for predictive analytics provides valuable information for the management of tourism and conservation planning. Through computational analytical techniques, AI models can predict future trends, identify possible hotspots for conservation, and quantitatively process the trends that influence sustainable conservation (Chisom et al., 2024). The use of predictive analytics helps conservationists to determine which conservation efforts need to be focused on in order to minimize interference, maximize usage of the available resources, and minimize incidence of human-wildlife conflicts that can be increased by tourism. For example, the itinerant species' behaviour can be forecasted by AI, which allows the operators of the tours offer opportunities for watching wildlife without placing immense pressures on tender ecosystems. As a result of predictive analysis, measures can be taken to lessen the negative impact on wildlife because one is able to determine which areas and times increase or decrease the chances of wildlife disturbance (IndustryWired, 2022). Besides, AI technologies like predictive analytics help authorities to prevent further poaching by outlining the possible cases that may happen in the future based on previous similar occurrences (Mishra, 2023). It is also possible to apply predictive analytics to determine such things as the impact of climate change on the preferred environmental conditions in a specific area, potential conflicts between wildlife and human beings in the given region (Mishra, 2023), and appropriate measures and strategies for the successful development of the ecotourism business line amid the principles of wildlife conservation tourism.

Example: Predicting Animal Migration Patterns

Scientists are using AI in the simulation of migratory patterns of herbivores like the zebras and the wildebeests in East Africa's Serengeti National Park (Wu et al., 2023). Some detailed information, such as the dates and directions of animal migrations, can be identified with a high degree of accuracy, using the data on their previous migration, satellite images, and available data on the weather conditions and vegetation cover, the amount of rainfall, and so on. As a result of predictive analytics, planning and managing the tourism activities in such a way that it brings little to no impact to wildlife and the environment can be beneficial to various stakeholders such as the park management authorities, the tour operators, and even the conservation organizations.

Habitat Assessment and Resource Conservation

The vital centres of biodiversity are habitats like the towering canopies of lush forests and the complex web of expansive wetlands (Chisom et al., 2024). Evaluating the health of ecosystems and pinpointing regions in need of rehabilitation requires a depth of understanding beyond human comprehension (Chen et al., 2019). With its unmatched image analysis skills, AI, which is frequently driven by sophisticated convolutional neural networks, provides an aerial lens that unlocks the mysteries of Earth's varied ecosystems (Kellenberger et al., 2019; Fluck et al., 2022; Perry et al., 2022). AI is revolutionizing habitat assessment by processing massive datasets quickly and accurately, surpassing the limits of manual surveys and conventional monitoring techniques. It presents a thorough understanding of ecosystems at the regional and even global levels, giving rise to a dynamic and up-to-date understanding of the health of habitats. In the heart of the Amazon rainforest, where the fight against illegal logging is fierce, the impact of AI on habitat assessment is more strikingly demonstrated (Chisom et al., 2024).

AI algorithms examine this data more precisely than human analysts could, spotting minute clues of illicit logging activity. AI recognizes patterns in land cover changes, the emergence of unapproved roads, and modifications in vegetation patterns as indicators of ecological disruption (Yang et al., 2022). AI-generated intelligence acts as a trigger for focused interventions, giving authorities and conservationists the ability to prioritize high-risk areas, allocate resources wisely, and enforce laws with never-before-seen efficiency. This proactive strategy protects the rainforest's delicate balance and establishes a global standard for using technology to address environmental issues. By removing invasive species, planting trees, or restoring native vegetation, AI-driven robots can help restore habitat (Sachan et al., 2023).

DISCUSSION

Numerous advantages that improve visitor experiences, aid in conservation efforts, and advance sustainable tourism practices arise from the integration of AI in wildlife tourism. These advantages are discussed below.

Conservation Awareness and Education

Visitors gain a deeper appreciation and comprehension of wildlife species, habitats, and conservation efforts through the use of AI-enabled interpretation tools. AI-driven storytelling platforms like the mobile application Aqua use a variety of multimedia content, such as pictures, videos, and interactive stories, to spread conservation messages and motivate travellers to take action (Dionisio et al., 2022). By allowing travellers to submit data—such as sightings of wildlife and behavioural observations—that can aid in research and conservation efforts, AI enables citizen science initiatives. Through immersive VR simulations, users can explore the environments, habits, and conservation challenges of endangered species. These programs encourage empathy and provide people with the tools they need to take on the role of steward in wildlife conservation through interactive storytelling and gamification.

Economic Benefits and Community Development

Experiences with AI-enhanced wildlife tourism draw larger crowds, boost visitor spending, and produce income that can be used to fund conservation efforts, habitat restoration, and community development projects. According to Kirtil and Askun (2021), AI has the potential to increase the tourism industry's overall revenue by 7% to 11.6%, which presents substantial opportunities. AI-powered tourism projects support the preservation of natural resources and cultural heritage while giving local communities job opportunities that promote social inclusion and economic empowerment.

Sustainable Tourism Practices

AI in the tourism industry can make a big difference in environmental conservation and sustainable practices. AI-driven solutions have the potential to reduce ecological footprints associated with the tourism industry and promote sustainable tourism efforts by optimizing resource allocation, minimizing energy consumption, and improving waste management (Garcia-Madurga & Gillo-Mendez, 2023). As tourist destinations are experiencing a huge influx of tourists, AI rises as a beacon of hope for sustainable tourism (Teemu & Elisa, 2024). According to Dykins (2020), tourism operators can minimize ecological footprints, minimize disturbances to wildlife, and promote sustainable tourism practices with the aid of AI-driven insights (AR and VR). AI helps ensure the long-term sustainability of wildlife tourism destinations and promotes positive relationships between visitors, local communities, and conservation stakeholders by optimizing tour routes, visitor capacities, and resource allocation. Park managers can efficiently implement sustainable practices by using smart sensors to track waste generation, energy consumption, and foot traffic.

Decision Support and Planning

The planning and decision-making processes used by managers and rangers in wildlife conservation can be enhanced and supported by AI (Joseph, 2023). AI can assist in anticipating and mitigating threats in various situations, including habitat fragmentation, climate change, and invasive species (Mahavidyalya, 2024). AI can assist in coordinating and communicating with various stakeholders, including governments, non-governmental organizations, and local communities. To optimize the coverage and efficacy of anti-poaching efforts, for instance, AI can assist in developing and implementing the best patrol routes for rangers (Joseph, 2023).

Community Involvement and Empowerment

Effective wildlife conservation efforts depend on the active participation and empowerment of the community, and integrating AI can significantly contribute to these goals. AI chatbots and virtual assistants can inform visitors and members of the local community about wildlife conservation efforts, promoting involvement in sustainability campaigns and providing financial or volunteer support for conservation projects. By involving local communities in the collection of important data on wildlife sightings, habitat conditions, and environmental changes, AI-powered mobile applications and platforms can turn regular people into citizen scientists (Dickinson & Bonney, 2012). AI-driven technologies (VR experiences and interactive applications) can improve visitor experiences by offering engaging learning environments (Mahavidyalya, 2024). These resources can encourage ethical tourist behaviour and increase public awareness of wildlife conservation. AI-driven educational programs are leading the way in conservation efforts by providing immersive learning experiences for people of all ages (Cao & Jian, 2024).

The Challenges and Ethical Considerations in the Use of AI in Wildlife Tourism

Ethical issues, however, are a major concern as AI continues to transform the tourism sector. Since most of the current guidelines only address the conservation or AI ethics domains, integration of AI ethics in AI for wildlife conservation has received less attention to date (Nandutu et al., 2021). Some of the challenges and ethical considerations are discussed in this section.

Data Privacy and Security

Concerns on data security and privacy are brought up by the application of AI in wildlife tourism, especially in relation to the gathering, storing, and sharing of personal data and wildlife sightings (Sharp, 2023). When camera traps are placed in and around protected areas in anthropogenic environments, people's images are recorded and it is possible to assess the frequency of human presence in that region (Karanth & Defries, 2010). Surveillance technology can also foster what is termed as "workplace monitoring" of park rangers which is reported by Rodriquez et al. (2012) as being undesirable for the health of staff. Information gathered through surveillance technology can be hacked or shot down just like the incident whereby a drone in Malta was shot down (Calleja & Borg, 2012).

Interference by Poachers

With the development of AI technologies, poachers are capable of altering their illegal activities to match these advancements to avoid detection (Doull et al., 2021). For instance, they might alter their routes, their time of travel, or their manner of operation in order to avoid patrols or drones that have AI built in. They could also employ deception, such as utilizing camouflage or decoys, or even employing electronic warfare tactics, such as malware infringements (Yaacoub et al., 2020). There is also a risk of poachers compromising the AI systems to alter the data, deactivate tracking devices or get valuable information about the protected wildlife areas (Kerns et al., 2014).

Risks of Using Technology on Wildlife

There are certain risks that can arise from the use of AI technologies like microchips and GPS collars on wildlife (Arkinstall et al., 2022). Some of the microchips that are inserted into animal bodies may shift from the initial placing area, which might make it hard to identify the area that has to be scanned (Nakamura et al., 2019). The animal might have adverse physical effects from the foreign body that has been introduced, causing inflammation or even death (Farr et al., 2021). Regarding GPS collars, a wrong design or an incorrect fitting of the collar may result in discomfort or skin wounds produced by the friction of the collar leading to the formation of sores and subsequent bacterial infections (Klegarth et al. 2019); it might even affect the animal's behaviour and hunting, feeding, or reproduction abilities due to restriction on their freedom and mobility (Coughlin & van Heezik (2015).

Future Trends and Opportunities

The field of wildlife conservation is emerging at a critical juncture which opens vast opportunities to transform the methods of species protection with the help of AI. Since we are faced with issues like environmental degradation, poaching, human–wildlife conflict and other related issues, AI technologies come in handy with the improvement of monitoring, researching, and conserving wildlife. The emerging trends range from using the AI applications in a comprehensive and networked system to responsible development and ethical considerations. Finally, this section envisages the prospect and possibilities of AI in wildlife conservation in the discussion of novel approaches to enrich the methods and tools of AI in protecting wildlife and ecosystems for the benefit of both wildlife and human beings.

A Comprehensive and Networked System

According to Chisom et al. (2024), AI, robotics, sensor networks, and virtual assistants will work together as a networked system to seamlessly create a comprehensive strategy for wildlife conservation and monitoring. Robotic drones with AI capabilities will be the main tool used to monitor wildlife and illicit activities. Because distributed systems are capable of self-organising in such a way that when a component fails, the system can automatically reorganize itself (Le et al., 2017), sensor-nodes used in monitoring will be cognitive, making decisions locally on the platform and together with other sensors in the surrounding areas. For example, the lifetime of a wireless sensor that runs on a battery can be extended by transmitting data only when it is perceived as important.

Anti-Poaching System

Regarding the requirement of poaching detection systems in the future, Kamminga et al. (2018) suggested that any form of anti-poaching system (APS) should be deployed in such a way that it cannot easily be detected or tampered with. The system should avoid attracting visual attention with, for instance, blinking LEDs, colourful mounting devices and other obviously visible pillars. The detection system should be designed so that its individual components cannot be destroyed by animals, tropical storms, field fires, flooding, lightning, or poachers. Hence, an APS should be robust to at least common technical faults among the distributed system components and demonstrate strong resilience so that information remains uncorrupted. In the APS, devices should be placed on animals or in the field in such a way that when left unattended for months or years, each device is able to efficiently manage its local power supply—for example, by deploying it in a field with a solar panel or energy harvesting mechanism to increase the energy efficiency.

Responsible Development and Ethical Considerations

Ethics is a novel field that is constantly growing, surpassing theology and philosophy (Cohen, 2018). AI's role in environmental preservation is firmly based on responsible development and ethical considerations (Chisom et al., 2024). To guarantee the ethical and responsible application of AI to conservation initiatives, precise legal frameworks and regulations should be put in place. Policies for data governance should place a high priority on security and privacy, and safeguards should be put in place to guarantee algorithmic accountability and transparency. In the future, the creation and application of AI technologies should be guided by moral principles. Transparent decision-making procedures, addressing potential biases, and minimizing unforeseen consequences are all necessary for the responsible application of AI in environmental monitoring. The development of ethical standards will ensure that AI is a force for good by fostering trust among stakeholders, including conservationists, legislators, and the public.

CONCLUSION

As we come to the end of our investigation into AI in wildlife conservation, it is clear that AI is a catalyst for empowering conservation rather than merely a technological advancement tool. Opportunities to advance wildlife conservation efforts are promising when AI is incorporated into the tourism industry. The amalgamation of AI, wildlife conservation, and sustainable tourism evidently offers the world a unique opportunity to adopt new strategies for preserving biodiversity. Using AI tools for the protection of wildlife and their environment and for improving visitor management, we can expand the conservation activities, reduce conflicts between wildlife and humans, and provide long-lasting opportunities for sustainable tourism.

In this chapter, the bibliometric study offered a valuable snapshot of existing research on the interface of AI, wildlife conservation, and sustainable tourism. Through bibliometric analysis, it was possible to establish trends, authors, and topics which are fundamental to the field. The findings indicated that there has not been empirical research conducted to address this interface in its entirety. Exploring co-authorship and collaboration in the given network, it was found that the majority of papers were written and the researchers cooperated at the international level; however, the United States, India, and China were leading in terms of publishing activity. These collaboration initiatives are essential in the development of new ideas and the enhancement of ideas in sustainable tourism. Therefore, existing literature reveals that this research has enriched knowledge of the formation and evolution of sustainable tourism as an area of academic research. This is especially important to researchers, policymakers, and funding agencies, as it shows major players and new trends that might be useful for further investigations and policy developments. Thus, bibliometrics became an efficient instrument for identifying trends in scientific output.

Research Gaps and Opportunities for Future Studies

AI fulfills a significant role in wildlife conservation for sustainable tourism. However, there has not been empirical research conducted that addresses AI solutions for sustainable tourism through wildlife conservation. More studies should be conducted on applying AI to solve sustainable tourism issues based on the growing human interface with wildlife. Implementing AI technology in the processes of data collection, analysis, and decision-making will contribute to improving conservation activities, and reducing the human-wildlife conflict. Yet, contemporary literature indicates that more understanding is required with regard to the optimization, application, and broader impact of AI in wildlife conservation. More studies have to be conducted to improve AI, work on overcoming certain limitations and prejudices, and guarantee that technology will act as a useful tool in preserving biodiversity rather than endangering it. Other future research could combine the findings of this work through the use of other advanced indexes that can elaborate the research output beyond the conventional citation indexes. Consequently, it is reasonable to state that increasing interdisciplinary collaboration between specialists in the field of wildlife biology, ecology, data science, and AI is essential to create efficient AI-based approaches for protecting wildlife. Combining a variety of fields of study will result in more creative and effective uses of AI in wildlife conservation initiatives. Some of the AI models designed to aid wildlife conservation efforts might not apply to different species or areas because the available data, functioning of ecosystems, and objectives of wildlife conservation vary greatly. There is a need for research that addresses the issue of model transferability in AI applications. Based on what has been stated above, we are on the brink of a true revolution in conservation science and, while it is important to leverage this transitional stage to our advantage, one must keep the aforementioned ethical issues in mind for the future development of the discipline.

Managerial Implications

To guarantee that AI remains a positive force in the field of wildlife conservation, it is crucial to strike a balance between technological innovation and moral responsibility. As a result, it is crucial to incorporate AI ethics into wildlife conservation AI systems by abiding by ethical norms, laws, and policies. The ethical use of data, algorithms, tools, and technologies, as well as the ethical effects on people, animals, and the environment, are the main topics of ethical AI guidelines. As tourists become more conscious of animal exploitation, there is a greater need than ever for ethical tourism. Thus, to advance animal ethics, it is now essential to determine suitable guidelines and put into practice conscientious strategies for engaging in animal tourism (Bertella et al., 2019; Duffy & Moore, 2011). AI ought to honour the diversity, autonomy, and dignity of all wildlife as well as the individuals who work to conserve it (Joseph, 2023). The welfare and safety of wildlife should be given top priority when implementing AI technologies. This entails reducing disruptions, preventing habitat degradation, and making sure AI-driven operations do not hurt animals or stress them out.

Stakeholders in wildlife tourism can guarantee the responsible deployment of AI technologies and support the ethical and sustainable management of wildlife tourism destinations by abiding by these ethical guidelines. AI is more than just a technological breakthrough; it's a transformative force reshaping traditional entrepreneurial practices. It is revolutionising business models, boosting operational efficiencies, and opening up new opportunities for growth and competitive advantage that managers should leverage. Leveraging AI's potential to improve wildlife conservation, advance ethical tourism and create new business practices requires cooperation, openness, and a dedication to moral decision-making.

REFERENCES

Al-Mansoori, F., & Hamdan, A. (2023). Integrating indigenous knowledge systems into environmental education for biodiversity conservation: A study of sociocultural perspectives and ecological outcomes. *AI. IoT and the Fourth Industrial Revolution Review*, 13(7), 61–74.

Arkinstall, C. A., FitzGibbon, S. I., Bradley, K. J., Moseby, K. E., & Murray, P. J. (2022). Using microchip-reading antennas to passively monitor a mammal reintroduction in south-west Queensland. *Australian Mammalogy*, 45(1), 98–107. DOI: 10.1071/AM22005

Arora, M., & Chandel, M. (2024). Role of artificial intelligence in promoting green destinations for sustainable tourism development. In A. Alnoor, G. E. Bayram, C. XinYing, & S. H. A. Shah (Eds.), *The role of artificial intelligence in regenerative tourism and green destinations (new perspectives in tourism and hospitality management)* (pp. 247–260). Emerald Publishing Limited. DOI: 10.1108/978-1-83753-746-420241016

Bertella, G., Fumagalli, M., & Williams-Grey, V. (2019). Wildlife tourism through the co-creation lens. *Tourism Recreation Research*, 44(3), 300–310. DOI: 10.1080/02508281.2019.1606977

Brickson, L., Zhang, L., Vollrath, F., Douglas-Hamilton, I., & Titus, A. J. (2023). Elephants and algorithms: A review of the current and future role of AI in elephant monitoring. *Journal of the Royal Society, Interface*, 20(208), 20230367. Advance online publication. DOI: 10.1098/rsif.2023.0367 PMID: 37963556

Burke, S., Pottier, P., Macartney, E. L., Drobniak, S. M., Lagisz, M., Ainsworth, T., & Nakagawa, S. (2022). Mapping literature reviews on coral health: Protocol for a review map, critical appraisal and bibliometric analysis. *Ecological Solutions and Evidence*, 3(4), e12190. Advance online publication. DOI: 10.1002/2688-8319.12190

Calleja, C., & Borg, B. (2012, February 14). Maltese hunters 'shooting protected birds' in Egypt. https://timesofmalta.com/article/Maltese-hunters-shooting-protected-birds-in-Egypt.406905

Cao, F., & Jian, Y. (2024). The role of integrating AI and VR in fostering environmental awareness and enhancing activism among college students. *The Science of the Total Environment*, 908, 168200. Advance online publication. DOI: 10.1016/j.scitotenv.2023.168200 PMID: 37918744

Carr, N., & Broom, D. M. (2018). *Tourism and animal welfare*. CABI Digital Library. DOI: 10.1079/9781786391858.0000

Ceballos, G., Ehrlich, P. R., & Raven, P. H. (2020). Vertebrates on the brink as indicators of biological annihilation and the sixth mass extinction. *Proceedings of the National Academy of Sciences of the United States of America*, 117(24), 13596–13602. DOI: 10.1073/pnas.1922686117 PMID: 32482862

Center for Responsible Travel. (2017). *The case for responsible travel: Trends and statistics 2017*. https://www.responsibletravel.org/wp-content/uploads/sites/213/2021/03/trends-and-statistics-2017.pdf

Chavan, P., Havale, D. S., & Khang, A. (2024). Artificial intelligence and tourism: A bibliometric analysis of trends and gaps. *Revolutionizing the AI-Digital Landscape*, 332–344. DOI: 10.4324/9781032688305-24

Chen, R., Little, R., Mihaylova, L., Delahay, R., & Cox, R. (2019). Wildlife surveillance using deep learning methods. *Ecology and Evolution*, 9(17), 9453–9466. DOI: 10.1002/ece3.5410 PMID: 31534668

Chisom, O. N., Biu, P. W., Umoh, A. A., Obaedo, B. O., Adegbite, A. O., & Abatan, A. (2024). Reviewing the role of AI in environmental monitoring and conservation: A data-driven revolution for our planet. *World Journal of Advanced Research and Reviews*, 21(1), 161–171. DOI: 10.30574/wjarr.2024.21.1.2720

Clapham, M., Miller, E., Nguyen, M., & Darimont, C. T. (2020). Automated facial recognition for wildlife that lack unique markings: A deep learning approach for brown bears. *Ecology and Evolution*, 10(23), 12883–12892. DOI: 10.1002/ece3.6840 PMID: 33304501

Clapham, M., Miller, E., Nguyen, M., & Van Horn, R. C. (2022). Multispecies facial detection for individual identification of wildlife: A case study across ursids. *Mammalian Biology*, 102(3), 943–955. DOI: 10.1007/s42991-021-00168-5 PMID: 36164481

Coetzee, B. W. T., & Chown, S. L. (2016). A meta-analysis of human disturbance impacts on Antarctic wildlife. *Biological Reviews of the Cambridge Philosophical Society*, 91(3), 578–596. DOI: 10.1111/brv.12184 PMID: 25923885

Coghlan, S., & Parker, C. (2023). Harm to nonhuman animals from AI: A systematic account and framework. *Philosophy & Technology*, 36(25), 25. Advance online publication. DOI: 10.1007/s13347-023-00627-6

Cohen, E. (2018). The philosophical, ethical and theological groundings of tourism – an exploratory inquiry. *Journal of Ecotourism*, 17(4), 359–382. DOI: 10.1080/14724049.2018.1522477

Coughlin, C. E., & van Heezik, Y. (2015). Weighed down by science: Do collar-mounted devices affect domestic cat behaviour and movement? *Wildlife Research*, 41(7), 606–614. DOI: 10.1071/WR14160

Dash, S., & Kalamdhad, A. S. (2021). Science mapping approach to critical reviewing of published literature on water quality indexing. *Ecological Indicators*, 128, 107862. Advance online publication. DOI: 10.1016/j.ecolind.2021.107862

Deb, D., Wiper, S., Gong, S., Shi, Y., Tymoszek, C., Fletcher, A., & Jain, A. K. (2018). Face recognition: Primates in the wild. In *2018 IEEE 9th International Conference on Biometrics Theory, Applications and Systems, BTAS 2018* (pp. 1–10). IEEE. DOI: 10.1109/BTAS.2018.8698538

Dickinson, J., & Bonney, R. (2012). *Citizen science: Public participation in environmental research*. Cornell University Press., DOI: 10.7591/cornell/9780801449116.001.0001

Dionisio, M., Mendes, M., Fernandez, M., Nisi, V., & Nunes, N. (2022). Aqua: Leveraging citizen science to enhance whale-watching activities and promote marine-biodiversity awareness. *Sustainability (Basel)*, 14(21), 14203. Advance online publication. DOI: 10.3390/su142114203

Dorfling, J., Siewert, S. B., Bruder, S., Aranzazu-Suescun, C., Rocha, K., Landon, P. D., Bondar, G., Pederson, T., Le, C., Mangar, R., Rawther, C., & Trahms, B. (2022, January 3–7). *Satellite, aerial, and ground sensor fusion experiment for management of elephants and rhinos and poaching prevention*. AIAA SCITECH 2022 Forum (p. 1270). DOI: 10.2514/6.2022-1270

Dou, X., & Day, J. (2020). Human-wildlife interactions for tourism: A systematic review. *Journal of Hospitality and Tourism Insights*, 3(5), 529–547. DOI: 10.1108/JHTI-01-2020-0007

Doull, K. E., Chalmers, C., Fergus, P., Longmore, S., Piel, A. K., & Wich, S. A. (2021). An evaluation of the factors affecting 'poacher' detection with drones and the efficacy of machine-learning for detection. *Sensors (Basel)*, 21(12), 4074. Advance online publication. DOI: 10.3390/s21124074 PMID: 34199208

Duffy, R., & Moore, L. (2011). Global regulations and local practices: The politics and governance of animal welfare in elephant tourism. *Journal of Sustainable Tourism*, 19(4-5), 589–604. DOI: 10.1080/09669582.2011.566927

Dykins, R. (2020, December 9). *AndBeyond sells live online safaris to fund conservation*. Globetrender. https://globetrender.com/2020/12/09/andbeyond-private-virtual-safaris-conservation/

Fakiha, B. (2023). Enhancing cyber forensics with AI and machine learning: A study on automated threat analysis and classification. *International Journal of Safety and Security Engineering*, 13(4), 701–707. DOI: 10.18280/ijsse.130412

Farr, J. J., Haave-Audet, E., Thompson, P. R., & Mathot, K. (2021). No effect of passive integrated transponder tagging on survival or body condition of a northern population of black-capped Chikadees (*Poecile atricapillus*). *Ecology and Evolution*, 11(14), 9610–9620. DOI: 10.1002/ece3.7783 PMID: 34306647

Flück, B., Mathon, L., Manel, S., Valentini, A., Dejean, T., Albouy, C., Mouillot, D., Thuiller, W., Murienne, J., Brosse, S., & Pellissier, L. (2022). Applying convolutional neural networks to speed up environmental DNA annotation in a highly diverse ecosystem. *Scientific Reports*, 12(1), 10247. Advance online publication. DOI: 10.1038/s41598-022-13412-w PMID: 35715444

Foyet, M. A. (2024, March 5). *AI in conservation: Where we came from — and where we are heading.* World Economic Forum. https://www.weforum.org/agenda/2024/03/ai-in-conservation-where-we-came-from-and-where-we-are-heading/

Gade, S. S., Dhole, R. M., & Sisodiya, D. S. (2023). Guardians of wild: Artificial intelligence for wildlife conservation. *International Journal of Advanced Research in Science. Tongxin Jishu*, 3(1), 107–110. https://ijarsct.co.in/Paper13616.pdf

Gantchoff, M. G., Hill, J. E., Kellner, K. F., Fowler, N. L., Petroelje, T. R., Conlee, L., & Belant, J. L. (2020). Mortality of a large wide-ranging mammal caused by anthropogenic activities. *Scientific Reports*, 10(1), 8498. Advance online publication. DOI: 10.1038/s41598-020-65290-9 PMID: 32444633

García-Madurga, M.-A., & Grilló-Méndez, A.-J. (2023). Artificial intelligence in the tourism industry: An overview of reviews. *Administrative Sciences*, 13(8), 172. Advance online publication. DOI: 10.3390/admsci13080172

Gazta, K. (2018). Environmental impact of tourism. *AGU International Journal of Professional Studies and Research, 6*, 7–17. https://web.archive.org/web/20180409201650id_/http://aguijpsr.com/images/short_pdf/1512624000_Kajal_Gazta_2.pdf

Global Partnership on Artificial Intelligence. (2022, November). *Biodiversity and artificial intelligence: Opportunities and recommendations for action* [Report]. Global Partnership on Artificial Intelligence.

Granli, P., & Poole, J. (2022). Who's who and whereabouts: An integrated system for reidentifying and monitoring African elephants. *Pachyderm*, 63, 72–90. https://pachydermjournal.org/index.php/pachyderm/article/view/482

Grant, M. J., & Booth, A. (2009). A typology of reviews: An analysis of 14 review types and associated methodologies. *Health Information and Libraries Journal*, 26(2), 91–108. DOI: 10.1111/j.1471-1842.2009.00848.x PMID: 19490148

Hauenstein, S., Jassoy, N., Mupepele, A. C., Carroll, T., Kshatriya, M., Beale, C. M., & Dormann, C. F. (2022). A systematic map of demographic data from elephant populations throughout Africa: Implications for poaching and population analyses. *Mammal Review*, 52(3), 438–453. DOI: 10.1111/mam.12291

Huveneers, C., Meekan, M. G., Apps, K., Ferreira, L. C., Pannell, D., & Vianna, G. M. S. (2017). The economic value of shark-diving tourism in Australia. *Reviews in Fish Biology and Fisheries*, 27(3), 665–680. DOI: 10.1007/s11160-017-9486-x

IndutsryWired. (2022, February 18). *AI in wildlife conservation: Learn about the latest trends*. https://industrywired.com/ai-in-wildlife-conservation-learn-about-the-latest-trends/

Isabelle, D. A., & Westerlund, M. (2022). A review and categorization of artificial intelligence-based opportunities in wildlife, ocean and land conservation. *Sustainability (Basel)*, 14(4), 1979. Advance online publication. DOI: 10.3390/su14041979

Joseph, S. (2023, December 3). *AI in wildlife conservation: Poaching prevention and ethics*. https://medium.com/@staneyjoseph.in/ai-in-wildlife-conservation-poaching-prevention-and-ethics-03e2076f1a3a

Kamminga, J., Ayele, E., Meratnia, N., & Havinga, P. (2018). Poaching detection technologies - A survey. *Sensors (Basel)*, 18(5), 1474. Advance online publication. DOI: 10.3390/s18051474 PMID: 29738501

Karanth, K. K., & Defries, R. (2010). Conservation and management in human dominated landscapes: Case studies from India. *Biological Conservation*, 143(12), 2865–2964. DOI: 10.1016/j.biocon.2010.05.002

Kays, R., Crofoot, M. C., Jetz, W., & Wikelski, M. (2015). Terrestrial animal tracking as an eye on life and planet. *Science*, 348(6240), aaa2478. Advance online publication. DOI: 10.1126/science.aaa2478 PMID: 26068858

Kellenberger, B., Marcos, D., Lobry, S., & Tuai, D. (2019). Half a percent of labels is enough: Efficient animal detection in UAV imagery using deep CNNs and active learning. *IEEE Transactions on Geoscience and Remote Sensing*, 57(12), 9524–9533. DOI: 10.1109/TGRS.2019.2927393

Kelly, C. (2020). Beyond 'a trip to the seaside': Exploring emotions and family tourism experiences. *Tourism Geographies*, 1–22.

Kerns, A. J., Shepard, D. P., Bhatti, J. A., & Humphreys, T. E. (2014). Unmanned aircraft capture and control via GPS spoofing. *Journal of Field Robotics*, 31(4), 617–636. DOI: 10.1002/rob.21513

Kerry, R. G., Montalbo, F. J. P., Das, R., Patra, S., Mahapatra, G. P., Maurya, G. K., Nayak, V., Jena, A. B., Ukhurebor, K. E., Jena, R. C., Gouda, S., Majhi, S., & Rout, J. R. (2022). An overview of remote monitoring methods in biodiversity conservation. *Environmental Science and Pollution Research International*, 29(53), 80179–80221. DOI: 10.1007/s11356-022-23242-y PMID: 36197618

Khan, N., Khan, W., Humayun, M., & Naz, A. (2024). *Unlocking the potential: Artificial intelligence applications in sustainable tourism*, In A. Alnoor, G. E. Bayram, C. XinYing, & S. H. A. Shah (Eds.), *The role of artificial intelligence in regenerative tourism and green destinations* (pp. 303–316). Emerald Publishing Limited. DOI: 10.1108/978-1-83753-746-420241020

Kim, H., & Chen, J. S. (2019). The memorable travel experience and its reminiscence functions. *Journal of Travel Research*, 58(4), 637–649. DOI: 10.1177/0047287518772366

Kirtil, I. G., & Askun, V. (2021). Artificial intelligence in tourism: A review and bibliometrics research. *Advances in Hospitality and Tourism Research-AHTR*, 9(1), 205–233. DOI: 10.30519/ahtr.801690

Klegarth, A. R., Fuentes, A., Jones-Engel, L., Marshall, G., & Abernathy, K. (2019). The ethical implications, and practical consequences, of attaching remote telemetry apparatus to macaques. In Dolins, F. L., Shaffer, C., Porter, L., Hickey, J., & Nibbelink, N. (Eds.), *Spatial analysis in field primatology: Applying GIS at varying scales* (pp. 64–86). Cambridge University Press. DOI: 10.1017/9781107449824.005

Kline, C. (2018). *Animals, food, and tourism*. Routledge. DOI: 10.4324/9781315265209

Koprowski, J. L., & Krausman, P. R. (Eds.). (2019). *International Wildlife Management: Conservation challenges in a changing world*. JHU Press. DOI: 10.1353/book.67482

Kumar, D., & Jakhar, S. D. (2022). Artificial intelligence in animal surveillance and conservation. In Balamurugan, S., Pathak, S., Jain, A., Gupta, S., Sharma, S., & Duggal, S. (Eds.), *Impact of artificial intelligence on organizational transformation*. Wiley. DOI: 10.1002/9781119710301.ch5

Kundu, A., Reddy, C. V., Singh, R. K., & Kalamdhad, A. S. (2023). Critical review with science mapping on the latest pre-treatment technologies of landfill leachate. *Journal of Environmental Management*, 336, 117727. Advance online publication. DOI: 10.1016/j.jenvman.2023.117727 PMID: 36924707

Kutschera, V. E., Bidon, T., Hailer, F., Rodi, J. L., Fain, S. R., & Janke, A. (2014). Bears in a forest of gene trees: Phylogenetic inference is complicated by incomplete lineage sorting and gene flow. *Molecular Biology and Evolution*, 3(8), 2004–2017. DOI: 10.1093/molbev/msu186 PMID: 24903145

Le, D., Nguyen, T., Scholten, H., & Havinga, P. (2017). Symbiotic sensing for energy-intensive tasks in large-scale mobile sensing applications. *Sensors (Basel)*, 17(12), 2763. Advance online publication. DOI: 10.3390/s17122763 PMID: 29186037

Lupton, D. (2022). From human-centric digital health to digital One Health: Crucial new directions for mutual flourishing. *Digital Health*, 8. Advance online publication. DOI: 10.1177/20552076221129103 PMID: 36171960

Mahavidyalya, S. V. M. (2024). *The ethics of artificial intelligence in wildlife conservation*. College Sidekick. https://www.collegesidekick.com/study-docs/14694957

Meyer, L., Apps, K., Bryars, S., Clarke, T., Hayden, B., Pelton, G., Simes, B., Vaughan, L. M., Whitmarsh, S. K., & Huveneers, C. (2021). A multidisciplinary framework to assess the sustainability and acceptability of wildlife tourism operations. *A Journal of the Society for Conservations Biology, 14*(3). DOI: 10.1111/conl.12788

Mishra, A. K. (2023). Artificial intelligence in wildlife conservation. *International Journal of Avian and Wildlife Biology*, 7(2), 67. DOI: 10.15406/ijawb.2023.07.00192

Nakamura, S., Sakaoka, A., Ikuno, E., Asou, R., Shimizu, D., & Hagiwara, H. (2019). Optimal implantation site of transponders for identification of experimental swine. *Experimental Animals*, 68(1), 13–23. DOI: 10.1538/expanim.18-0052 PMID: 30078789

Nandutu, I., Atemkeng, M., & Okouma, P. (2021). Integrating AI ethics in wildlife conservation AI systems in South Africa: A review, challenges, and future research agenda. *AI & Society*, 38(1), 245–257. DOI: 10.1007/s00146-021-01285-y

Nandutu, I., Atemkeng, M., & Okouma, P. (2022). Intelligent systems using sensors and/or machine learning to mitigate wildlife–vehicle collisions: A review, challenges, and new perspectives. *Sensors (Basel)*, 22(7), 2478. Advance online publication. DOI: 10.3390/s22072478 PMID: 35408093

Narasimha, I. D. V., Moses, I. S., & Balaji, H. (2023). Automated animal identification and detection of species. *International Journal of Advanced Research in Science. Tongxin Jishu*, 3(2), 29–33. https://ijarsct.co.in/Paper11305.pdf

O'Donoghue, P., & Rutz, C. (2016). Real-time anti-poaching tags could help prevent imminent species extinctions. *Journal of Applied Ecology*, 53(1), 5–10. DOI: 10.1111/1365-2664.12452 PMID: 27478204

Obura, D. O., Aeby, G., Amornthammarong, N., Appeltans, W., Bax, N., Bishop, J., Brainard, R. E., Chan, S., Fletcher, P., Gordon, T. A. C., Gramer, L., Gudka, M., Halas, J., Hendee, J., Hodgson, G., Huang, D., Jankulak, M., Jones, A., Kimura, T., & Wongbusarakum, S. (2019). Coral reef monitoring, reef assessment technologies, and ecosystem-based management. *Frontiers in Marine Science*, 6, 580. Advance online publication. DOI: 10.3389/fmars.2019.00580

Orduña-Malea, E., & Costas, R. (2021). Link-based approach to study scientific software usage: The case of VOSviewer. *Scientometrics*, 126(9), 8153–8186. DOI: 10.1007/s11192-021-04082-y

Perry, G. L., Seidl, R., Bellvé, A. M., & Rammer, W. (2022). An outlook for deep learning in ecosystem science. *Ecosystems (New York, N.Y.)*, 25(8), 1700–1718. DOI: 10.1007/s10021-022-00789-y

Rane, N., Choudhary, S., & Rane, J. (2023). *Sustainable tourism development using leading-edge artificial intelligence (AI), blockchain, internet of things (IoT), augmented reality (AR) and virtual reality (VR) technologies.* SSRN. http://dx.doi.org/DOI: 10.2139/ssrn.4642605

Rayhan, A. (2023). *AI and the environment: Toward sustainable development and conservation.* ResearchGate. DOI: 10.13140/RG.2.2.12024.42245

Rodriguez, A., Negro, J. J., Mulero, M., Rodriguez, C., Hermandez-Pliego, J., & Bustamante, J. (2012). The eye in the sky: Combined use of unmanned aerial systems and GPS data loggers for ecological research and conservation of small birds. *PLoS One*, 7(12), e50336. Advance online publication. DOI: 10.1371/journal.pone.0050336 PMID: 23239979

Sachan, P., Yadav, K. A., Pandey, S., Agrawal, S., & Singh, V. (2023). The role of artificial intelligence in environmental monitoring and conservation. *International Journal of Advanced Research in Science. Tongxin Jishu*, 3(2), 106–112. https://ijarsct.co.in/A13017.pdf

Saiwa. (2023, December 10). *AI in wildlife conservation: A comprehensive overview.* https://saiwa.ai/blog/ai-in-wildlife-conservation/

Sebo, J. (2022). *Saving animals, saving ourselves: Why animals matter for pandemics, climate change, and other catastrophes.* Oxford University Press. DOI: 10.1093/oso/9780190861018.001.0001

Sharp, J. (2023, November 11). *The role of AI in wildlife conservation.* West Tech Fest Blog. https://westtechfest.com/the-role-of-ai-in-wildlife-conservation/

Shivaprakash, K. N., Swami, N., Mysorekar, S., Arora, R., Gangadharan, A., Vohra, K., Jadeyegowda, M., & Kiesecker, J. M. (2022). Potential for artificial intelligence (AI) and machine learning (ML) applications in biodiversity conservation, managing forests, and related services in India. *Sustainability (Basel), 14*(12), 715. Advance online publication. DOI: 10.3390/su14127154

Sthapit, E., Coudounaris, D. N., & Björk, P. (2019). Extending the memorable tourism experience construct: An investigation of memories of local food experiences. *Scandinavian Journal of Hospitality and Tourism, 19*(4-5), 333–353. DOI: 10.1080/15022250.2019.1689530

Su, H.-N., & Lee, P.-C. (2010). Mapping knowledge structure by keyword co-occurrence: A first look at journal papers in Technology Foresight. *Scientometrics, 85*(1), 65–79. DOI: 10.1007/s11192-010-0259-8

Sugai, L. S. M., Silva, T. S. F., Ribeiro, J. W.Jr, & Llusia, D. (2019). Terrestrial passive acoustic monitoring: Review and perspectives. *Bioscience, 69*(1), 15–25. DOI: 10.1093/biosci/biy147

Teemu, M., & Elisa, L. (2024). Navigating new horizons—How AI will transform the tourism industry. *Global Journal of Tourism, Leisure and Hospitality Management, 1*(4), 1–3. https://juniperpublishers.com/gjtlh/pdf/GJTLH.MS.ID.555570.pdf

Trave, C., Brunnschweiler, J., Sheaves, M., Diedrich, A., & Barnett, A. (2017). Are we killing them with kindness? Evaluation of sustainable marine wildlife tourism. *Biological Conservation, 209*, 211–222. DOI: 10.1016/j.biocon.2017.02.020

Tuia, D., Kellenberger, B., Beery, S., Costelloe, B. R., Zuffi, S., Risse, B., Mathis, A., Mathis, M. W., van Langevelde, F., Burghardt, T., Kays, R., Klinck, H., Wikelski, M., Couzin, I. D., van Horn, G., Crofoot, M. C., Stewart, C. V., & Berger-Wolf, T. (2022). Perspectives in machine learning for wildlife conservation. *Nature Communications, 13*(1), 792. Advance online publication. DOI: 10.1038/s41467-022-27980-y PMID: 35140206

U.S. Centers for Disease Control and Prevention. (n.d.). *One Health.* https://www.cdc.gov/one-health/index.html

Von Durckheim, K. E. M. (2017). *The use of mobile technologies in the South African private wildlife sector* [Master's thesis, Stellenbosch University]. ResearchGate. https://www.researchgate.net/profile/Katharina-Em-Von-Durckheim/publication/364657841_THE_USE_OF_MOBILE_TECHNOLOGIES_IN_THE_SOUTH_AFRICAN_PRIVATE_WILDLIFE_SECTOR/links/6356431612cbac6a3eee3a84/THE-USE-OF-MOBILE-TECHNOLOGIES-IN-THE-SOUTH-AFRICAN-PRIVATE-WILDLIFE-SECTOR.pdf

Winter, C. (2020). A review of research into animal ethics in tourism: Launching the annals of tourism research curated collection on animal ethics in tourism. *Annals of Tourism Research*, 84, 102989. Advance online publication. DOI: 10.1016/j.annals.2020.102989

Witmer, G. W. (2005). Wildlife population monitoring: Some practical considerations. *Wildlife Research*, 32(3), 259–263. DOI: 10.1071/WR04003

World Tourism Organisation. (1998). *Guide for local authorities on developing sustainable tourism*. World Tourism Organisation.

Wu, Z., Zhang, C., Gu, X., Duporge, I., Hughey, L. F., Stabach, J. A., Skidmore, A. K., Hopcraft, J. G. C., Lee, S. J., Atkinson, P. M., McCauley, D. J., Lamprey, R., Ngene, S., & Wang, T. (2023). Deep learning enables satellite-based monitoring of large populations of terrestrial mammals across heterogeneous landscape. *Nature Communications*, 14(1), 3072. Advance online publication. DOI: 10.1038/s41467-023-38901-y PMID: 37244940

Yaacoub, J.-P., Noura, H., Salman, O., & Chehab, A. (2020). Security analysis of drones systems: Attacks, limitations, and recommendations. *Internet of Things : Engineering Cyber Physical Human Systems*, 11, 100218. Advance online publication. DOI: 10.1016/j.iot.2020.100218 PMID: 38620271

Yang, L., Driscol, J., Sarigai, S., Wu, Q., Chen, H., & Lippitt, C. D. (2022). Google Earth engine and artificial intelligence (AI): A comprehensive review. *Remote Sensing (Basel)*, 14(14), 3253. Advance online publication. DOI: 10.3390/rs14143253

Zhang, L., & Sun, Z. (2019). The application of artificial intelligence technology in the tourism industry of Jinan. *Journal of Physics: Conference Series*, 1302(3), 032005. Advance online publication. DOI: 10.1088/1742-6596/1302/3/032005

Zsarnoczky, M. (2017). How does artificial intelligence affect the tourism industry? *Journal of Management*, 31(2), 85–90. https://www.ceeol.com/search/article-detail?id=583144

Zuniga, R. B. (2019). Developing community-based ecotourism in Minalungao National Park. *African Journal of Hospitality, Tourism and Leisure*, 5, 1–10. https://www.ajhtl.com/uploads/7/1/6/3/7163688/article_13_se_gbcss_2019.pdf

Zupic, I., & Čater, T. (2015). Bibliometric methods in management and organization. *Organizational Research Methods*, 18(3), 429–472. DOI: 10.1177/1094428114562629

KEY TERMS AND DEFINITIONS

AI-Powered Solutions: Technologies that use artificial intelligence to solve problems or perform tasks, such as analysing data or making predictions.

AI-Wildlife Conservation-Sustainable Tourism Interface: The way artificial intelligence is integrated into wildlife conservation efforts and sustainable tourism practices to enhance both environmental protection and travel experiences.

Biodiversity Analysis: The study and assessment of the variety and variability of life forms within a specific area, including their distribution and relationships.

Conservation Strategies: Plans and actions designed to protect and preserve natural resources, species, and ecosystems to ensure their survival and health.

Environmental Monitoring: The process of observing and measuring environmental conditions, such as air quality or wildlife populations, to understand and manage their impact.

Human-Animal Interaction: The various ways in which humans and animals interact, which can include direct contact, influence on behavior, or effects on well-being.

Sustainable Tourism: Tourism that aims to minimize environmental impact, respect local cultures, and ensure that travel benefits current and future generations.

Wildlife Conservation: The practice of protecting and managing wild animals and their habitats to prevent extinction and maintain healthy ecosystems.

Wildlife Tracking: The use of technology or methods to follow and record the movements and behaviors of wild animals in their natural habitats.

Chapter 6
Artificial Intelligence and Hyper-Personalisation in Travel Platforms

Garima Sahani
SP Jain School of Global Management, Australia

Monica Chaudhary
https://orcid.org/0000-0002-8344-1447
Melbourne Institute of Technology, Australia

Suhail Mohammad Mohammad Ghouse
https://orcid.org/0000-0002-7684-933X
Dhofar University, Oman

ABSTRACT

This chapter discusses the use of artificial intelligence and hyper personalisation in travel platforms in India and its impact on customer satisfaction and brand loyalty. As the industries are moving towards technological transformation, there is a need to know how consumers perceive personalised offerings and engage with it in tourism industry. There is a significant gap to understand hyper personalization strategies impact over consumers while online booking experience and address their problems. The study was conducted by taking a survey in which respondents who are the active users of travel platforms participated. The findings of the study highlight the need for online travel platforms to prioritize personalization and AI integration to enhance user satisfaction and loyalty. By leveraging technology to deliver tailored experiences and addressing user needs more effectively, travel platforms can position themselves for success in an increasingly competitive market landscape.

DOI: 10.4018/979-8-3693-5678-4.ch006

1. INTRODUCTION

The tourism and hospitality industry stands at the forefront of technological evolution, with hyper-personalisation emerging as a transformative force reshaping the travel experience. In an era defined by individualism and bespoke experiences, traditional booking methods no longer suffice, leaving travellers yearning for tailored recommendations that cater to their unique preferences. However, the journey towards hyper-personalisation is laden with challenges. Online booking platforms, while offering convenience, often overwhelm travellers with generic options and static recommendations. Trust issues further intensify the situation, as users grapple with concerns regarding data privacy and the reliability of online reviews. Amidst these challenges, the fusion of hyper-personalisation and artificial intelligence (AI) offers a glimmer of hope. Leveraging AI-driven algorithms, hyper-personalisation promises to revolutionize the travel industry by delivering personalized recommendations, dynamic pricing, and seamless interactions tailored to each traveller's needs. In the Indian travel industry, marked by rapid digitization and market expansion, traditional players confront the imperative to adapt to digital technologies, while newcomers seek to differentiate themselves through innovative, customer-centric solutions. needs and preferences. Despite this, there is a gap in understanding how consumers perceive and engage with personalized offerings, especially in the context of online booking experiences. The introduction of artificial intelligence (AI) has further revolutionized traditional settings, offering new opportunities and challenges for online travel services.

This chapter aims to address this gap by exploring the effectiveness of AI-based hyper personalization in influencing brand loyalty and customer satisfaction within India's online travel services sector. The research examines the impact of hyper personalization strategies on customer satisfaction and loyalty, identifying key factors driving consumer engagement and retention. The main objectives are to assess the impact of hyper personalization on customer satisfaction, identify specific features for personalized experiences, and analyze the role of AI in enhancing these experiences. This chapter aims to unravel the complexities of hyper-personalisation and AI in the tourism sector, exploring their implications for customer satisfaction, brand loyalty, and industry dynamics. Through a comprehensive analysis encompassing qualitative insights and quantitative data, this chapter seeks to illuminate the transformative potential of hyper-personalisation and AI in shaping the future of travel.

2. BUSINESS PROBLEM

In an era of rapid technological advancement, the tourism industry is undergoing a significant transformation, with a growing emphasis on hyper personalization to meet the evolving needs and preferences of consumers. However, there remains a notable gap in understanding how consumers perceive and engage with personalized offerings within the tourism sector, particularly in the context of online booking experiences. Moreover, the advent of artificial intelligence (AI) has further revolutionized traditional settings and scenarios, presenting new opportunities and challenges for online travel services.

This chapter seeks to address this gap by investigating the effectiveness of AI-based hyper personalization in influencing brand loyalty and customer satisfaction within the online travel services sector in India. By examining the impact of hyper personalization strategies on customer satisfaction and loyalty, this research aims to shed light on the key factors driving consumer engagement and retention in the online travel domain. Based on this premise; the main objectives of the chapter are:

- Assess the impact of hyper personalization on customer satisfaction.
- Identify specific features for personalized experiences.
- Analyse the role of AI in enhancing personalized experiences.

3. LITERATURE REVIEW

The tourism and hospitality industry stands out for its remarkable growth in revenue and market presence. As the global economy continues to advance technologically, one notable outcome is the rise of hyper-personalisation. Among the various sectors, travel and hospitality stand to benefit immensely from this trend. Modern travellers increasingly demand a hyper-personalised experience tailored to their individual preferences. However, the industry faces numerous challenges. Despite technological advancements, the booking experiences for travellers have remained largely unchanged for years. Major online booking platforms like booking.com and MakeMyTrip offer limited personalisation, providing only basic booking options. This lack of personalisation contributes to decision fatigue among travellers, who struggle to find recommendations tailored to their specific needs amidst a plethora of options.

Furthermore, the abundance of information, deals, and reviews exacerbates the challenge of decision-making. Static recommendations fail to provide real-time personalisation, resulting in outdated or irrelevant suggestions for travellers. For example, when planning a trip to Bali, customers should receive recommendations tailored to their preferred experience, budget, and travel dates. However, existing platforms often fall short in providing such tailored recommendations and itineraries. Moreover, trust issues plague users when making reservations and payments online. The legitimacy of reviews and ratings for services offered on platforms often remains unverified, leading to scepticism among users. Without assurances of authenticity, users find it difficult to compare prices and locate the best offers, further hindering their booking experience.

The OTA (Online Travel Booking) marketplace are widely used by millions of travellers worldwide daily. According to SPER Market Research study (2024) the global online travel booking platform will reach USD 1745.94 Billion by the year 2033 with a CAGR of 10.01%. With such huge market and growth rate there is a demand for a technological advancement and better customer experience in each element of travel. According to a research survey done by McKinsey (2022) Customers link personalization with a positive experience which makes them feel special. According to Harvard business review article (2022) states that over 50% of the survey respondents believe in customer personalisation as an important way for increasing revenue and profits. Technology integration in the industry of tourism is reshaping the way people travel. Travelers now days seek more than just mere customization but evolving in hyper personalization. They not just want to feel welcomed but also truly understood.

3.1 Hyper Personalisation and AI

Personalization proactively offers users options based on their historical behavior, often anticipating their needs before they become explicitly aware of them. By continuously presenting users with customized content and suggestions that reflect their individual preferences, personalization shapes their daily routines and decision-making processes. This anticipatory approach enables digital platforms to respond to market fluctuations more effectively, allowing them to influence user decisions and preferences to some extent (Needham et al., 2016; Ng, 2020).

Hyper-personalization advances this concept by leveraging real-time digital data to provide users with instant, tailored product recommendations. This technique enhances flexibility in planning by dynamically adjusting suggestions based on users' current interactions and preferences. As a result, hyper-personalization enables a more adaptive and responsive approach, accommodating shifts in user needs and market conditions over shorter time frames (Walther, 1996). This real-time adaptability not only improves user experience but also allows digital platforms to maintain a competitive edge by staying aligned with rapidly changing consumer behaviors and preferences.

Digital technology has opened up new communication and distribution channels for both consumers and suppliers of travel services (Sharma et al., 2020). The proliferation of mobile apps has compelled educators to explore their efficacy in providing learning opportunities (Mittal et al., 2017). Hyper-personalisation has emerged as a breakthrough innovation essential for capturing consumers' attention amidst multiple touchpoints (Elsawy, 2023). It serves as a potent marketing tool that industries are increasingly leveraging to drive sales and foster customer loyalty. In today's consumer landscape, individuals crave significance and seek tailored experiences based on their unique tastes, preferences, and styles, whether it's receiving a customized shampoo or personalized movie recommendations on OTT platforms. According to a McKinsey report (2023), a staggering 71% of customers expect personalized interactions from businesses they engage with. Hyper-personalisation harnesses customer data and online interactions using AI to deliver bespoke products, services, and content. While personalisation has long been employed as a marketing tactic, it poses challenges in creating customer-centric strategies due to the constantly evolving nature of client needs. Hyper-personalisation addresses this gap by leveraging automation, artificial intelligence, and real-time analytics to enhance marketing strategies.

The integration of artificial intelligence extends beyond the e-commerce industry, catering to the demands of consumers across various sectors, including banking, healthcare, and e-commerce services. Recent research has focused on strategic marketing issues related to personalisation, such as incorporating unstructured data into existing marketing frameworks. Agarwal et al. (2020) explored the use of analytics to enhance consumer value in healthcare settings, while Balducci and Marinova (2018) highlighted the utilization of unstructured data across multiple marketing sectors. Similarly, Kumar et al. (2019) investigated the role of AI in improving client engagement through personalisation, while Tong et al. (2020) utilized machine learning techniques for predictive purposes in personalised mobile marketing. The potential for AI-powered personalization through chatbots and AI assistance is immense, leading to heightened user satisfaction and engagement (Singla, 2020). There is a growing demand for human-like interaction and assistance through AI for travellers to aid in holiday planning (Koo et al., 2023). This underscores the pivotal role of AI in enhancing the user experience and meeting the evolving needs of travellers in the digital age.

Salesforce study (2021) has found that 52% of the customers are expecting personalised experience while in the year 2023 this number has risen to 65%. A PWC study has noted that 63% to 82% American consumers are willing to share their personal info for a much better and valuable service. AI can increase efficiency in travel planning. AI can further analyse traveller preferences and travel style which can suggest personalized itinerary it can also eliminate the time-consuming task for planning each detail or segment of the trip. Further, AI can take advantage of its predictive analytics which can take into account historic data of customers and travellers to forecast trends related to flight prices, hotel rates and peak times for alerting customers regarding these timelines and help them potentially save money by avoiding peak travel seasons.

3.2 Indian Travel Industry

The Indian travel industry witnesses significant reliance on Online Travel Agencies (OTAs) and booking platforms such as Booking.com, MakeMyTrip, and Airbnb among travellers. Post the COVID-19 pandemic, the sector is experiencing notable growth and transformation. Projections indicate a robust growth rate of 11.7% from 2022 to 2027, with the market size forecasted to reach USD 13,462 million (Yahoo Finance, 2023). This growth is propelled by a surge in demand for travel, particularly in domestic tourism, focusing on meaningful experiences like wellness retreats and outdoor adventures. Concurrently, there has been a rise in Staycations, coworking spaces, and unique stay options, reflecting a shift towards flexible, authentic, and secure travel experiences. A study conducted by PWC (2023) underscores the on-going transformation within the travel industry, characterized by traditional players grappling with the adoption of digital technologies while new businesses enter the market with innovative, consumer-centric services. Amidst stiff competition, key players such as Airbnb, Cleartrip, and Booking.com are implementing aggressive pricing strategies to capture market share. In this landscape, there is a pressing need for travel companies to differentiate themselves by offering user-friendly and personalized experiences tailored to individual preferences. This entails building a loyal customer base by delivering seamless digital interactions and sustainable travel options that meet the evolving expectations of modern travellers.

The Online booking segment is estimated to see a growth in upcoming period. Websites and mobile apps have played an important role in the growth of travel industry by making it easier for booking flights, bus, trains, hotels and stays. Due to high internet penetration and use of smartphones, India had 749 million internet users, where consumers rely on online search using various websites, blogs, social media and recommendations.

3.3 Competitive Landscape

According to a study conducted by *PWC (2023)*, Travel industry in currently going through a constant transformation where traditional players are going through adoption difficulty of digital technologies to their business and new business are entering into the market with innovative consumer centric services. The online travel services have few key players in the market which includes Airbnb, cleartrip, Bookings.com etc. due to high competition and market fragmentation there is aggressive pricing strategy implemented by market players. There is a need for travel companies to come up with differentiating factors for its users to make sure they build a loyal customer base and provide an experience which is user friendly and personalised to each one of their needs. The Indian travel booking platforms is currently dominated by established players which offers various ranges of services. MMT (MakeMyTrip) is the leader with 60% market share providing various services from flight bookings, hotels, car rental etc. Yatra is another major competitor of MMT focuses on customer loyalty through its discount offers. Cleartrip is another player which offers corporate travel solutions. Booking.com is another travel agency focusing on hotel bookings and stays option.

3.4 Traveler's Concerns

The travel industry is witnessing a digital transformation from the use of AR/VR to online bookings. The online booking platforms have changed the way people search, research, book and manage their trips. Even with such convenience created by the booking platforms they face various challenges which hinders personalized experience of travel.

Discontent With Standardized Experiences

Pre-packaged tours establish a familiar and controlled setting for travelers, effectively shielding them from the unfamiliar aspects of the host environment (Larsen & Urry, 2011). Tour packages typically consist of multiple service components sold together, often involving various providers to deliver each part, creating a value chain. Numerous studies have explored how individual components impact overall tourist satisfaction, revealing that some elements contribute more significantly than others. For instance, research by Chan et al., (2015) and Räikkönen & Honkanen (2013) highlights those specific aspects, such as accommodation quality and guided tours, can significantly influence the overall satisfaction of tourists. These findings suggest that while every component contributes to the travel experience, certain elements have a more pronounced effect on the perceived value and enjoyment of the trip.

Despite the varying contributions of individual components, there is a general agreement among researchers that tourists generally perceive tour packages as cohesive products. This holistic view means that tourists tend to evaluate their experiences in an integrated manner, considering the package as a single entity rather than assessing each component separately. Zach and Racherla (2011) support this perspective, noting that the overall impression of the tour package plays a crucial role in shaping tourist satisfaction. This holistic evaluation underscores the importance of ensuring consistency and quality across all components of a tour package to enhance the overall travel experience. This curated experience allows tourists to navigate new destinations with a sense of comfort and security, minimizing exposure to potential cultural or environmental surprises. By doing so, these tours provide a seamless and predictable travel experience, fostering a sense of ease and reducing the potential stress associated with encountering unknown elements in a foreign setting. Travellers often find themselves disenchanted with generic experiences in the travel sector, feeling that they are merely going through the motions rather than embarking on a distinctive journey. Instead of feeling captivated and invigorated by tailored recommendations and experiences, they encounter cookie-cutter products that fail to address their individual needs, desires, and aspirations. A significant source of frustration stems from the formulaic nature of many travel packages and itineraries. These pre-packaged solutions, designed to appeal to a broad audience, lack the personal touch and authenticity that travellers seek. For example, participating in generic sightseeing tours or staying in standardized hotel chains can leave visitors feeling disconnected from the local surroundings and culture. The repetition of these mundane experiences can lead travellers to feel as though they have missed out on opportunities for exploration and discovery. Rather than immersing themselves in the authenticity of a destination, they find themselves following the well-trodden tourist paths, devoid of genuine connection.

The desire for uniqueness and self-expression plays a pivotal role in travellers' dissatisfaction with generic situations. Travel is often regarded as a means of self-discovery and personal growth. Self-image encompasses a broad spectrum of elements, including personal attributes, preferences, and even fantasies. Individuals often seek destinations that allow them to express their identity and align with their self-concept (Hosey & Martin, 2012). This drive for self-expression through travel choices underscores the importance of destinations that resonate on a personal level, offering a sense of connection and authenticity to the traveler. Research indicates that the alignment between a consumer's self-image and the perceived image of a product significantly influences both initial purchase decisions and long-term loyalty (Sparks et al., 2011). When consumers perceive a strong congruence between their self-image and a product's image, they are more likely to form a lasting attachment to the brand. This self-congruence, combined with the functional consistency of the product, plays a crucial role in understanding consumer behavior. By recognizing these dynamics, marketers can develop more effective strategies that cater to the personal and functional needs of consumers, ultimately fostering deeper brand loyalty and more successful marketing outcomes (Sirgy & Su, 2000). When experiences fail to resonate with their individual interests, values, and identity, travellers may feel constrained and disillusioned. For instance, a passionate food enthusiast may find themselves disappointed by restaurants that do not cater to their unique palate, while an adventure seeker may yearn for experiences that offer greater excitement and challenge. In essence, the lack of personalized and authentic experiences can hinder travellers from fully realizing the transformative potential of their journeys.

Singla et.al, (2021) highlights the travellers of today who have various needs and are a diverse group with different preferences. Various booking platforms offer "One size fit all" approach, which presents a generic search results and limited customization options. There is a gap created due to impersonal experience and failure to address individual travel styles, interests, budgets which leads wasting time. As Morgan et al, (2018) states in their research that travellers focus on completing transactions which overshadows the goal of facilitating a memorable experience. Travelers are observed in their booking journey to rush in the process without any guidance or support to create ideal trip.

Navigating Information Overload

In the digital age, the sheer volume of information available presents a significant challenge for travellers. With countless websites, travel forums, social media platforms, and online booking systems vying for attention, individuals often find themselves overwhelmed by choice (Castañeda et al., 2020; Zhang et al., 2022). Sorting through this vast array of sources to find relevant and reliable information can be a daunting and time-consuming task. Compounding this challenge is the variability in quality and dependability across different sources, ranging from sponsored content to user-generated reviews. Discerning travellers must exercise critical thinking skills to distinguish between factual information and promotional content. This process requires sifting through sponsored posts, advertisements, and expert reviews to uncover authentic insights. However, the lack of personalization in online search experiences exacerbates the difficulty. Generic search results often fail to account for individuals' unique preferences, interests, and travel objectives, resulting in mismatches between the information provided and their actual needs. Furthermore, accessing pertinent information may be hindered by linguistic barriers, cultural differences, and accessibility issues, particularly when researching destinations outside one's familiar territory. Travelers may struggle to find content that resonates with their expectations and preferences without personalized recommendations tailored to their profiles. The limitations in internet connectivity and access to digital devices further impede travellers' ability to leverage online resources effectively, particularly in remote or underserved areas. These challenges underscore the importance of personalized and user-centric approaches to information dissemination in the travel industry, ensuring that travellers can access relevant and reliable information tailored to their specific needs and circumstances. The trustworthiness of travel and tourism information on social media is a topic of debate in the literature. Some scholars argue that social media sources are more reliable (Senecal & Nantel, 2004; Buhalis, 2003; Fotis et al., 2012; Akehurst, 2009; Chung & Buhalis, 2008; Weiss et al., 2008; Gretzel et al., 2008; Xiang & Gretzel, 2010; O'Connor, 2008; Park et al., 2007). However, other studies suggest these sources are less credible (Cox et al., 2009; Tham et al., 2013; Yoo et al., 2009). This lack of consensus on the credibility of travel 2.0 applications (Munar & Jacobsen, 2014) indicates that the trustworthiness of online travel and tourism information remains a contentious and widely debated issue among scholars and commentators.

As highlighted by Gretzel & Huang et al, (2018) Travelers do face decision fatigue due to the overwhelmed choices as they are not able to find a tailored recommendation for their specific travel needs. There are a lot of information and options to choose from including deals and reviews which makes it difficult for the users to make an informed decision faster. They have also mentioned the problem of inconsistency in data presentation across various platforms which makes it difficult for the travellers to compare options effectively and find the best deal for themselves. (Xiang et al, 2019) is furthermore creating generic recommendations which is just based popularity and is not really aligned with travellers preferences which stagger them to find a relevant suggestions of irrelevant choices.

Untapped Exploration

Travelers often miss out on the opportunity to explore the authentic and lesser-known aspects of a destination for various reasons, thereby limiting the depth and richness of their travel experiences. The dominance of mainstream tourist attractions and activities geared towards mass tourism plays a significant role in diverting attention away from hidden treasures that offer a more immersive and genuine glimpse into the destination's culture and heritage. Consequently, travellers may overlook opportunities to uncover undiscovered gems, explore off-the-beaten-path areas, and engage in meaningful interactions with local communities. A quite interesting study (Serhat & Uzuncan, 2021) found that the existential divergence through experiential differentiation is hindered by public narratives shaped by online content, which limit genuine unknown experiences to predefined representations. Consequently, the excitement of exploring the unknown is reduced to consuming previously designed and familiar representations.

Strict travel schedules and time constraints further contribute to missed exploration opportunities. Despite the mediating role of leisure on stress, evidence suggests that leisure per se may cause stress (Iwasaki & Mannell, 2000; Schuster et al., 2023). In the recreation setting, for example, recreation hassles have been identified as a form of stress (Schuster, Hammitt, & Moore, 2003). With limited time available, many tourists prioritize visiting must-see sites and iconic landmarks, often at the expense of more obscure or unconventional experiences. Additionally, pre-planned itineraries and organized trips may impose rigid schedules that leave little room for spontaneous discoveries or impromptu detours. The lack of flexibility in these itineraries inhibits travellers from fully immersing themselves in the destination's unique offerings and serendipitous encounters. The absence of intimate local knowledge and perspectives presents another barrier to discovering hidden gems. Without access to reliable recommendations and insider insights, travellers struggle to uncover authentic experiences that are not heavily promoted by the tourism industry. Language barriers, cultural differences, and limited access to local resources further compound this challenge, hindering travellers' ability to navigate and explore a destination's lesser-known attractions with confidence and ease. Addressing these barriers to exploration requires a multifaceted approach that emphasizes personalized recommendations, flexible travel itineraries, and access to local expertise. By empowering travellers with the tools and resources needed to venture off the beaten path, destinations can ensure that visitors have the opportunity to immerse themselves fully in the authentic and diverse experiences that each location has to offer. Current platforms are just focusing on basic data points like travel dates, destination & pricing with limited filters, platforms are missing to cater travel style – backpacking, luxury, adventure etc. travel purpose – Business trip, vacation, workcation, leisure trips etc. and desired experiences – cultural immersion, encountering wildlife, food fest etc.

Privacy Concerns

Privacy concerns significantly arise among travelers, especially regarding the collection and utilization of personal data by online booking platforms and travel agencies (Ioannou et al., 2021; Ioannou et al., 2020). Travelers worry about how their personal information is gathered, stored, and used, which can influence their trust and willingness to engage with these platforms. The potential for misuse of data and lack of transparency in data handling practices further exacerbate these concerns. As a result, addressing privacy issues is crucial for maintaining consumer trust and ensuring the success of personalized travel services. While travellers willingly provide information such as their name, contact details, payment information, and travel preferences for booking purposes and personalized services, they harbour apprehensions about the transparency and security of their data within these organizations. In the literature there have been some studies that explored the magnitude and reasons for privacy concerns. The literature has underscored the importance of examining travellers' privacy concerns (Anuar & Gretzel, 2011), yet there is a scarcity of studies specifically addressing privacy in the travel context (Lee &

Cranage, 2011; Tussyadiah et al., 2019; Wozniak et al., 2018). Existing research has typically focused on issues such as privacy breaches related to location-based social media and publicly available data (Vu et al., 2018), the significance of security and privacy in smart tourism destinations (Jeong & Shin, 2019), the influence of psychological factors on consumer behavior while traveling (Wozniak et al., 2018), online transaction intentions (Ponte et al., 2015; Liang & Shiau, 2018), and the creation of user-generated content (Hew et al., 2017). The spectre of data breaches and unauthorized access looms large, given the sensitive nature of the information held by travel agencies, including bank details and trip schedules. The travel sector's susceptibility to cyberattacks further exacerbates these fears, as high-profile data breaches have underscored the vulnerability of personal data and the potential ramifications of its misuse or illegal access. Beyond external threats, travellers also express unease about how travel agencies share and monetize their personal information. While tailored recommendations and targeted advertisements can enhance the travel experience, individuals may feel uneasy about the extent to which their data is leveraged for marketing purposes without explicit consent. Moreover, privacy concerns extend to the adoption of new technologies in travel services, such as location tracking, biometric scanning, and facial recognition. While these innovations offer efficiency and convenience, they raise red flags regarding individual autonomy and privacy. The prospect of constant surveillance and the perceived loss of control over personal data evoke anxieties among travellers, who fear being continuously monitored and tracked during their journeys. Navigating these privacy concerns requires a delicate balance between leveraging data to enhance the travel experience and safeguarding individuals' rights to privacy and autonomy. Travel agencies and online platforms must prioritize transparency, consent, and robust data protection measures to assuage travellers' fears and foster trust in the digital ecosystem of travel services. By championing responsible data practices and empowering travellers with greater control over their personal information, the industry can cultivate a more secure and privacy-respecting environment for all stakeholders involved. Singala et al., (2021) has pointed out concerns regarding security as a significant challenge in online booking regarding sharing financial and personal information. There is usually a hidden fee or platform fee charged which is associated with the bookings such kind of unclarity leads to mis communication and lack of trust built with users on the platform. In the era of AI-driven tourism start-ups, one of the paramount challenges revolves around data privacy and security (Ghouse & Chaudhary, 2024).

Embracing Authenticity in Travel

The concept of authenticity has been a long-standing yet contested topic within tourism theory and research, maintaining a dominant role in practice despite its elusive nature. Authenticity's polymorphism, intangibility, and ineffability have been widely discussed, with Cohen and Cohen (2012) noting the lack of consensus that prevents it from anchoring a general tourism paradigm. Despite subsequent conceptual and empirical advancements (e.g., Knudsen et al., 2016; Rickly & McCabe, 2017; Sarial-Abi et al., 2020; Tiberghien et al., 2017, 2020), authenticity remains theoretically debated. Practically, it is extensively used to market tourism products and evaluate a broad range of goods and experiences beyond tourism. Some scholars argue that consumers prioritize authenticity (MacCannell, 1976; Pine & Gilmore, 2011). There is a need for the continued relevance of authenticity in tourism studies by exploring its dynamic nature as a network of relationships between objects, places, and people. Authenticity is seen as a negotiation process that embeds individuals within these networks, emphasizing emotional and performative aspects of tourist experiences. This negotiation extends to the authentic self, where feelings of authenticity arise from social relationships rather than a fixed true self. Discarding the concept would overlook its role in connecting tourists to their environment and the broader human experience. Therefore, authenticity remains a crucial concept for researchers, practitioners, and tourists, highlighting key social and cultural processes in tourism. However, understanding its utility for tourism supply and demand remains complex due to varying interpretations and the lack of a firm theoretical consensus. Thus, while authenticity is indispensable and influential in practice, its theoretical clarity remains unresolved.

Travelers today are increasingly drawn to genuine, immersive experiences that offer a deep dive into the history, customs, and way of life of their destination. This growing appreciation for authenticity reflects a shift towards seeking meaningful encounters over superficial or commercialized travel options. At the heart of this quest lies a desire for genuine cultural immersion, where travellers actively seek opportunities to engage with local populations, traditions, and daily life. Previous research has underscored the significance of understanding national culture when engaging with international tourists (Dai et al., 2019; Fernández et al., 2020). However, these studies often concentrate primarily on aspects such as the performance of the tourism and hotel industries (Nazarian et al., 2017; Sunny, Patrick, & Rob, 2019) and staff training (e.g., Robinson, Martins, Solnet, & Baum, 2019; Tracey & Swart, 2020).

Cultural immersion takes many forms, from participating in cooking classes and artisan workshops to attending cultural festivals and patronizing locally run establishments. By embedding themselves in the fabric of the community, travellers gain a richer understanding of the destination and forge lasting connections with its inhabitants. The pursuit of authenticity extends to culinary experiences, with travellers eager to sample the region's authentic cuisine made from locally sourced ingredients. Whether indulging in farm-to-table dining experiences or savouring street food delicacies, food plays a pivotal role in capturing the essence of a place's identity and culture. In addition to cultural encounters, travellers seek authentic outdoor experiences that allow them to connect with nature responsibly. Whether trekking through untouched wilderness, exploring remote landscapes, or observing wildlife in their natural habitats, travellers value destinations that prioritize sustainability and ethical tourism practices. Avoiding heavily marketed tourist traps, they gravitate towards off-the-beaten-path locations and untamed landscapes that offer genuine encounters with nature. By embracing authenticity in their travel choices, tourists not only enrich their own experiences but also contribute to the preservation of cultural heritage and natural landscapes. Supporting local businesses and initiatives, they play a vital role in fostering sustainable tourism practices and ensuring that future generations can continue to enjoy the authentic charm of diverse destinations around the globe.

There is limited integration of customer data across various touch points like pre booking, post booking which creates fragmented travel journey. Platforms are not considering leveraging the past behaviour and preferences for tailoring recommendations, offers and support in a traveller's journey causing a hindrance in user experience.

This research chapter aims to provide valuable insights into the dynamics of hyper personalization and AI-driven solutions in the online travel services sector, with a focus on understanding consumer perceptions, preferences, and satisfaction levels (Fig 1). By addressing these objectives, the study seeks to inform industry stakeholders and decision-makers about the strategies and technologies that can drive greater customer engagement and loyalty in the competitive landscape of online travel. The three independent variables are Personalized Marketing (the practice of tailoring marketing efforts to individual consumer preferences and behaviours); Impact of AI (the use of artificial intelligence technologies to analyze consumer data, predict behaviours, and automate personalized interactions and Hyper Personalization (personalization that goes beyond traditional personalized marketing by using real-time data and AI to deliver highly customized experiences.

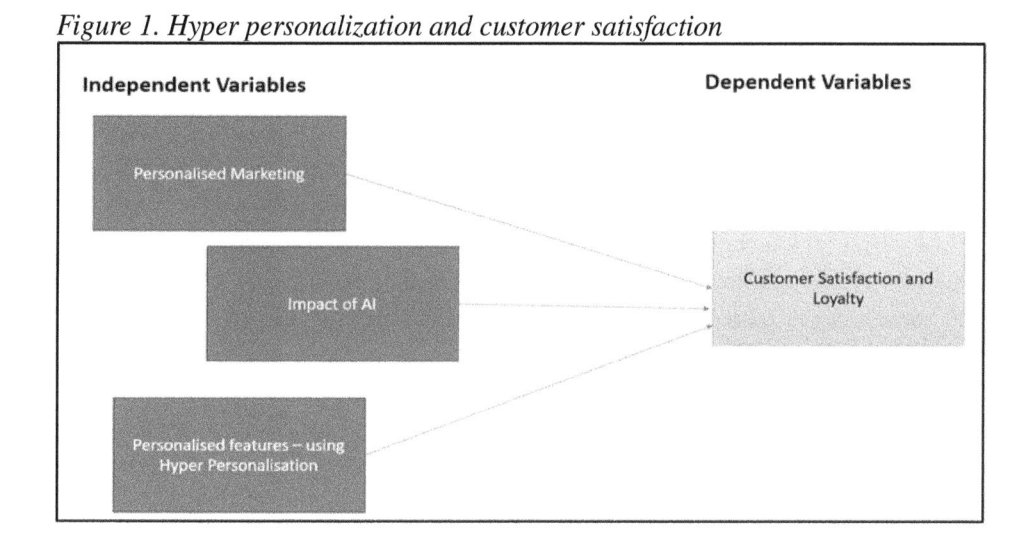

Figure 1. Hyper personalization and customer satisfaction

4. METHODS

In the chosen research methodology, a mixed-methods approach is employed to provide a holistic understanding of consumer behavior and preferences within the dynamic landscape of the travel industry. The decision to utilize a mixed-methods design stems from the recognition of the multifaceted nature of consumer decision-making processes in this domain. By combining qualitative and quantitative methodologies, the research aims to capture both the depth and breadth of consumer experiences, ensuring a comprehensive analysis that goes beyond surface-level insights.

4.1 Qualitative Data Collection

Focus group discussions are selected as the qualitative data collection method due to their effectiveness in facilitating in-depth exploration and contextual understanding of consumer perspectives. This approach allows researchers to engage participants in open-ended discussions, enabling the exploration of nuanced motivations, perceptions, and attitudes related to various aspects of travel planning and personalized service utilization. By delving into participants' lived experiences and subjective viewpoints, rich qualitative data is generated, providing valuable insights into the underlying factors shaping consumer behavior.

Thematic analysis is employed as the primary analytical framework for interpreting the qualitative data (Guest et al., 2012; Berbekova et al., 2021). Inspired by the six-step Thematic Analysis approach outlined by Braun and Clarke (2006), this work follows the systematic methodology used by Nikitas et al. (2019). Thematic Analysis is a technique for identifying, organizing, and interpreting patterns or themes within qualitative data. It involves systematically coding and analyzing data, connecting it to broader theoretical concepts to provide deeper insights. This systematic approach enables researchers to identify recurring themes, patterns, and relationships within the data, ensuring rigor and reliability in the analysis process. By organizing and categorizing qualitative data according to key themes and concepts, researchers can extract meaningful insights and draw robust conclusions that inform theory and practice in the travel industry.

4.2 Quantitative Data Collection

Surveys conducted using Google Forms are utilized for quantitative data collection, leveraging their capacity to gather structured data from a diverse sample of respondents in a scalable and efficient manner. Surveys offer the advantage of reaching a large audience and collecting data on a wide range of variables related to consumer preferences and behavior. This quantitative data complements the qualitative insights obtained from focus group discussions, providing a comprehensive understanding of consumer trends and patterns.

Statistical analysis techniques are employed to analyze the quantitative data, allowing researchers to identify correlations, trends, and associations within the dataset. By applying statistical methods such as descriptive analysis, inferential statistics, and regression analysis, researchers can uncover meaningful insights and quantify the relationships between variables. This methodological approach enhances the robustness and generalizability of the findings, enabling researchers to draw evidence-based conclusions and recommendations for stakeholders in the travel industry.

Sampling and Respondents: The research employs a stratified random sampling strategy to ensure representation across different demographic segments within the target population. The sample comprises online travel service users aged between 18 to 50 in India, reflecting the diverse user base of the industry. By selecting participants from various demographic backgrounds and geographic regions, the research aims to minimize biases and capture a broad spectrum of perspectives. This sampling approach enhances the validity and generalizability of the findings, enabling researchers to draw meaningful conclusions about consumer behavior in the context of online travel services.

5. FINDINGS

5.1 Quantitative Findings

The analysis of quantitative data reveals several key insights into the usage patterns, preferences, and satisfaction levels of respondents regarding online travel platforms and personalized services.

Usage Patterns: The majority of respondents use online travel platforms occasionally for making bookings and planning their travel. This suggests that while online platforms are commonly utilized, they may not be the primary method for all travellers.

Current Satisfaction Levels: The average satisfaction rating reported by users is 3, with the mode being 2, indicating that most participants rated their satisfaction as moderate. This suggests that there is room for improvement in the overall user experience provided by online travel platforms.

Perception of Personalization: Approximately 41.9% of respondents feel that the marketing messages or ads they receive are slightly personalized to their interests and preferences. However, a significant majority (60.5%) express a strong likelihood to engage with personalized offers and ads based on their past behavior and interests (Fig. 2).

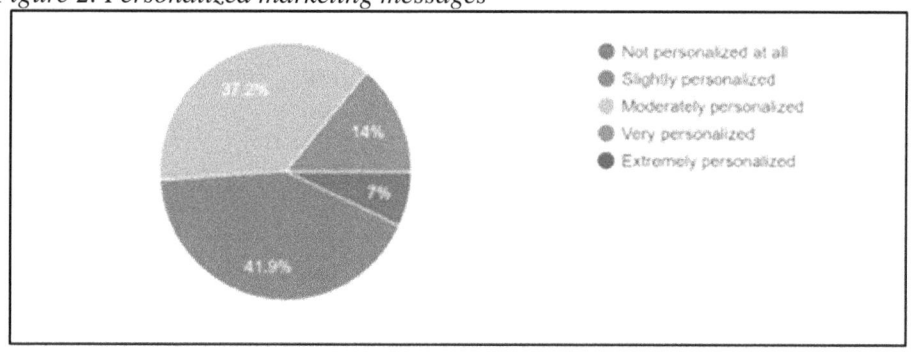

Figure 2. Personalized marketing messages

Utilization of AI: Around 51% of respondents report having used AI while planning a trip, with over 50% preferring to use AI tools on travel platforms for better assistance and time-saving benefits. This highlights a growing acceptance and reliance on AI-driven features among users.

Demand for Personalized Features: The most demanded feature on travel platforms, as indicated by respondents, is personalized itinerary, along with other features deemed valuable and essential. This underscores the importance of personalized experiences in enhancing user satisfaction and engagement (Fig. 3).

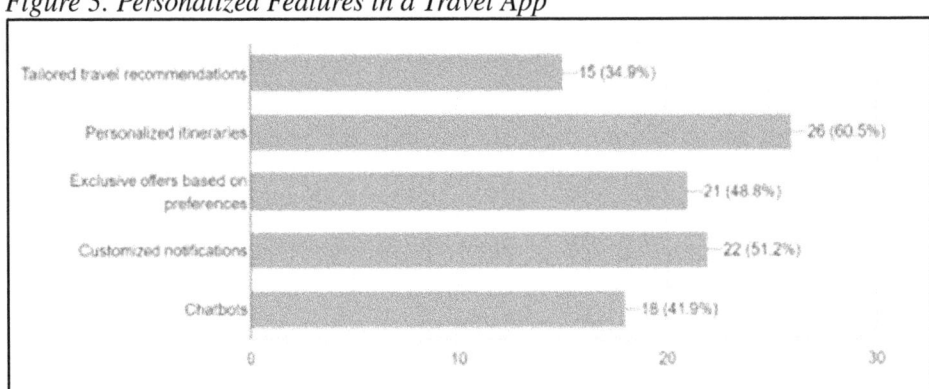

Figure 3. Personalized Features in a Travel App

Feature	Count (%)
Tailored travel recommendations	15 (34.9%)
Personalized itineraries	26 (60.5%)
Exclusive offers based on preferences	21 (48.8%)
Customized notifications	22 (51.2%)
Chatbots	18 (41.9%)

Impact of Personalization and AI on Satisfaction: Multi regression analysis reveals that personalized marketing, AI presence, and hyper-personalization significantly impact customer satisfaction and loyalty. The obtained R-square value of 0.55 indicates a moderately good fit of the model, while the p-values for all three variables (0.002, 0.008, 0.0001) are below the significance threshold of 0.05, indicating their significant influence on customer satisfaction and loyalty (Table 1).

Table 1. Regression Analysis and significant beta values

SUMMARY OUTPUT				
Regression Statistics				
Multiple R	0.741790032			
R Square	0.550252452			
Adjusted R Square	0.514746066			
Standard Error	0.563046444			

continued on following page

Table 1. Continued

SUMMARY OUTPUT				
Observations	42			
ANOVA				
	df	SS	MS	F
Regression	3	14.738905	4.912968318	15.49728156
Residual	38	12.046809	0.317021298	
Total	41	26.785714		
	Coefficients	Standard Error	t Stat	P-value
Intercept	0.115382966	0.6555766	0.176002277	0.86122676
personalised marketing	0.33255425	0.1014822	3.276971111	0.002246275
AI	0.202555965	0.1568042	0.192951382	0.008480246
personalised Features	0.669847328	0.161292	4.153010462	0.000178872

These findings underscore the importance of personalized services and AI integration in enhancing user satisfaction and loyalty within the online travel industry. By understanding and leveraging these insights, travel platforms can better cater to the evolving needs and preferences of their users, ultimately driving improved user experiences and brand loyalty.

5.2 Qualitative Findings

The focus group discussions provided valuable qualitative insights that complemented and enriched the quantitative findings obtained from the survey data. Participants engaged in open-ended discussions, allowing for a deeper exploration of their attitudes, perceptions, and experiences related to online travel platforms and personalized services. The qualitative findings offer nuanced perspectives and shed light on the underlying motivations and considerations driving consumer behaviour in the context of travel planning and booking.

Questions asked in Focus group discussion:

Q1. What kind of personal information are you comfortable sharing with travel websites to get personalized experience? (for example – travel preferences, budget, travel style)

Q2. Experiencing a travel website which can anticipate your needs and preferences even before putting in many details. Do you find this appealing why or why not?

Q3. Have you experienced AI powered chatbots or features on travel Websites whicle making your bookings? How was your experience?

Q4. Suggestions or Recommendations in how travel websites can use personalization and AI to improve their services?

Q5. How comfortable will be you be with AI personalizing your travel experience?

Q6. Any further experience to be shared with regards the use of existing travel websites and AI integration in these websites?

Perception of Personalization: Participants expressed mixed feelings regarding the level of personalization offered by online travel platforms. While some acknowledged receiving personalized marketing messages and ads, others felt that the level of personalization was inadequate and generic. There was a consensus among participants that personalized recommendations based on past behavior and preferences would enhance their overall experience and engagement with travel platforms.

Utilization of AI: The discussions revealed a growing acceptance and interest in utilizing AI-driven features for trip planning and assistance. Participants appreciated the convenience and efficiency offered by AI tools, such as personalized itinerary planning and real-time recommendations. However, concerns were raised regarding the reliability and accuracy of AI-generated suggestions, highlighting the importance of maintaining a balance between automation and human oversight.

Demand for Personalized Features: Participants emphasized the importance of personalized features, such as customized itineraries and tailored recommendations, in enhancing their travel planning experience. They expressed a desire for greater flexibility and customization options to cater to their unique preferences and interests. Additionally, participants valued features that provided real-time updates and notifications, allowing for seamless and convenient travel experiences.

Impact on Satisfaction and Loyalty: Overall, participants agreed that personalized services and AI integration significantly influenced their satisfaction and loyalty towards online travel platforms. They perceived personalized experiences as a reflection of the platform's commitment to understanding and meeting their individual needs. Participants expressed a willingness to engage with platforms that offered personalized services and demonstrated a genuine understanding of their preferences, indicating a strong correlation between personalized experiences and user satisfaction.

The qualitative findings from the focus group discussions support the quantitative findings obtained from the survey data, providing a deeper understanding of consumer attitudes and behaviours within the online travel industry. These insights can inform the development of targeted strategies and initiatives aimed at enhancing user experiences and fostering brand loyalty in online travel platforms.

6. CONCLUSION

This chapter provides valuable insights into the impact of hyper-personalization and AI integration on customer satisfaction and loyalty within the online travel services industry in India. Through a mixed-methods approach combining qualitative focus group discussions and quantitative surveys, a comprehensive understanding of consumer behavior, preferences, and perceptions has been achieved.

The quantitative findings revealed that a significant proportion of respondents use online travel platforms occasionally, with moderate levels of satisfaction reported. There is a growing acceptance and preference for personalized marketing messages and AI-driven features among users, indicating a shift towards more tailored and efficient travel experiences. The demand for personalized features, such as personalized itineraries, highlights the importance of customization in meeting user needs and enhancing satisfaction.

The multi-regression analysis further confirmed the significant impact of personalized marketing, AI presence, and hyper-personalization on customer satisfaction and loyalty. These findings underscore the critical role of technological advancements and personalized services in shaping user experiences and driving brand loyalty within the online travel industry.

The qualitative findings from focus group discussions provided additional depth and context to the quantitative findings. Participants expressed a desire for more personalized and authentic travel experiences, emphasizing the importance of tailored recommendations and local immersion. Their insights shed light on the motivations, preferences, and challenges faced by users when utilizing online travel platforms, offering valuable guidance for industry stakeholders.

In conclusion, the findings of this study underscore the imperative for online travel platforms to prioritize personalization and AI integration to enhance user satisfaction and loyalty. The ability to leverage advanced technology to deliver tailored experiences that meet the specific needs of users is becoming increasingly critical in the competitive market landscape. The results indicate that platforms which can effectively utilize AI to understand and predict user preferences are better positioned to offer personalized services that not only satisfy customers but also foster long-term loyalty. This personalized approach can lead to higher engagement rates, repeat business, and positive word-of-mouth, all of which are crucial for sustaining competitive advantage.

Moving forward, continuous investment in innovative technologies and a customer-centric approach will be vital for driving growth and differentiation in the online travel services sector. As user expectations evolve, travel platforms must remain agile and responsive to these changes, ensuring that their technological capabilities are aligned with the demands of their customer base. By focusing on the integration of AI and personalization, companies can create more meaningful and efficient user experiences. This strategic focus will not only enhance customer satisfaction and loyalty but also position these platforms as leaders in the digital travel market. Ultimately, the success of online travel services will hinge on their ability to adapt to technological advancements and maintain a relentless focus on meeting the evolving needs of their users.

7. RECOMMENDATION AND IMPLICATIONS

The travel industry is experiencing a significant paradigm shift, particularly in the wake of the COVID-19 pandemic. The surge in demand for tourism has been accompanied by an equally strong demand for highly personalized and engaging travel experiences. As travelers seek more tailored and immersive journeys, the emphasis on hyper-personalization becomes increasingly pronounced. This shift is driven by a desire for travel experiences that cater to individual preferences, interests, and needs, reflecting a broader trend towards customized services across various sectors. In this evolving landscape, the ability of travel booking platforms to deliver such bespoke experiences will be crucial in distinguishing themselves from competitors.

Central to this differentiation is the effective utilization of data and artificial intelligence (AI). By harnessing advanced data analytics and AI technologies, travel platforms can offer highly personalized recommendations and craft travel itineraries that resonate with each user's unique profile. Hyper-personalization allows for the creation of bespoke travel schedules and recommendations based on an individual's past behaviors, preferences, and real-time feedback. This approach not only enhances the overall travel experience but also fosters a deeper connection between the traveler and the platform. As the industry continues to evolve, the integration of these advanced technologies will be a key factor in driving competitive advantage, ensuring that travel platforms can meet the growing expectations of their users while capitalizing on emerging opportunities in the post-pandemic era.

Enhance Personalized Efforts: Based on the findings indicating a high demand for personalized features and marketing messages, online travel platforms should prioritize the development and implementation of robust personalization strategies. This involves leveraging user data effectively to deliver tailored recommendations, itineraries, and promotional offers that align with individual preferences and interests.

Invest in AI Integration: Given the positive perception of AI-driven features among users, online travel platforms should invest in the integration of AI technologies to enhance user experiences. This includes the development of AI-powered tools such as intelligent chatbots, personalized trip planners, and real-time assistance to streamline the booking process and provide valuable support to users throughout their journey.

Focus on Authenticity and Local Immersion: Recognizing the desire for authentic and immersive travel experiences expressed by participants in the focus group discussions, travel platforms should prioritize partnerships with local businesses and initiatives that promote cultural immersion and sustainable tourism practices. Offering curated experiences that showcase the unique culture, cuisine, and attractions of each destination can help differentiate platforms and attract discerning travellers seeking authentic experiences.

Regular Feedback and Iteration: To ensure ongoing relevance and effectiveness, online travel platforms should establish mechanisms for collecting feedback from users and monitoring trends in consumer preferences and behaviours. By staying attuned to evolving user needs and preferences, platforms can iteratively refine their offerings and remain competitive in a rapidly changing market landscape.

Invest in User Education: Given the relatively low usage of AI features reported by some respondents, online travel platforms should invest in user education initiatives to increase awareness and adoption of AI-driven tools and features. Providing tutorials, guides, and demonstrations can help users understand the benefits of AI integration and feel more comfortable utilizing these technologies to enhance their travel experiences.

Data Privacy and Security: With the increasing collection and utilization of user data for personalized services, online travel platforms must prioritize data privacy and security. Implementing robust data protection measures, obtaining explicit user consent for data usage, and adhering to regulatory frameworks such as GDPR are essential to build trust and confidence among users and mitigate the risk of data breaches or misuse.

Collaboration with Industry Stakeholders: Collaboration with industry stakeholders, including hotels, airlines, tour operators, and local tourism boards, can facilitate the development of comprehensive and seamless travel experiences for users. By forging strategic partnerships and integrating third-party services and content, online travel platforms can offer greater value and convenience to users while expanding their offerings and market reach.

Omnichannel Personalisation: Implementing Omnichannel Personalisation, personalised experience should be extended across all the channels including website, App, email marketing for the purpose of creating seamless and consistent user experience. Travellers should get the same consistent recommendations and notifications related to their travel preferences across any of the platforms used.

Customer Segmentation: Segmenting the travellers based on demographics, travel style, corporate or leisure, family or solo, luxury or budget which will further allow to target travellers based on specific marketing campaigns.

Partnerships: Partnering with various other travel service providers which can help in collaborations with regards to targeting specific travellers. Integrating with platform loyalty programmes can help in customer retention and provide edge over competitors.

By implementing these recommendations, online travel platforms can enhance user satisfaction, foster brand loyalty, and differentiate themselves in a competitive marketplace, ultimately driving growth and success in the online travel services sector.

REFERENCES

Agarwal, R., Dugas, M., Gao, G., & Kannan, P. K. (2020). Emerging technologies and analytics for a new era of value-centered marketing in healthcare. *Journal of the Academy of Marketing Science*, 48(2), 9–23. DOI: 10.1007/s11747-019-00692-4

Akehurst, G. (2009). User generated content: The use of blogs for tourism organisations and tourism consumers. *Service Business*, 3(1), 51–61. DOI: 10.1007/s11628-008-0054-2

Anuar, F., & Gretzel, U. (2011, January). Privacy concerns in the context of location-based services for tourism. *ENTER 2011 Conference*.

Balducci, B., & Marinova, D. (2018). Unstructured data in marketing. *Journal of the Academy of Marketing Science*, 46(4), 557–590. DOI: 10.1007/s11747-018-0581-x

Berbekova, A., Uysal, M., & Assaf, A. G. (2021). A thematic analysis of crisis management in tourism: A theoretical perspective. *Tourism Management*, 86, 104342. DOI: 10.1016/j.tourman.2021.104342

Braun, V., & Clarke, V. (2006). Using thematic analysis in psychology. *Qualitative Research in Psychology*, 3(2), 77–101. DOI: 10.1191/1478088706qp063oa

Buhalis, D. (2003). *eTourism: Information technology for strategic tourism management*. Pearson Education.

Buhalis, D., & Law, R. (2020). Hyper-personalization in tourism: Time for a paradigm shift? *Journal of Hospitality and Tourism Technology Management*, 30(2), 381–392.

Castañeda, J. A., Rodríguez-Molina, M. Á., Frías-Jamilena, D. M., & García-Retamero, R. (2020). The role of numeracy and information load in the tourist decision-making process. *Psychology and Marketing*, 37(1), 27–40. DOI: 10.1002/mar.21278

Chan, A., Hsu, C. H., & Baum, T. (2015). The impact of tour service performance on tourist satisfaction and behavioral intentions: A study of Chinese tourists in Hong Kong. *Journal of Travel & Tourism Marketing*, 32(1-2), 18–33. DOI: 10.1080/10548408.2014.986010

Chung, J. Y., & Buhalis, D. (2008). Web 2.0: A study of online travel community. In *Information and communication technologies in tourism 2008* (pp. 70–81). Springer. DOI: 10.1007/978-3-211-77280-5_7

Cohen, E., & Cohen, S. A. (2012). Authentication: Hot and cool. *Annals of Tourism Research*, 39(3), 1295–1314. DOI: 10.1016/j.annals.2012.03.004

Constantinides, E., & Synodinos, C. (2018). A review of personalization in tourism. *Journal of Hospitality and Tourism Technology*, 9(2), 221–238.

Cox, C., Burgess, S., Sellitto, C., & Buultjens, J. (2009). The role of user-generated content in tourists' travel planning behavior. *Journal of Hospitality Marketing & Management*, 18(8), 743–764. DOI: 10.1080/19368620903235753

Dai, T., Hein, C., & Zhang, T. (2019). Understanding how Amsterdam City tourism marketing addresses cruise tourists' motivations regarding culture. *Tourism Management Perspectives*, 29, 157–165. DOI: 10.1016/j.tmp.2018.12.001

Deloitte. (2022). The AI Advantage in the Indian Travel and Hospitality Industry. https://www2.deloitte.com/in/en/pages/deloitte-analytics/articles/Deloitte-India-AI-Warriors.html

Dubey, R., & Singh, A. K. (2018). Personalized Tourism Recommendation Based on Cultural Preferences and Social Context in India. *ACM Transactions on Asian Language Information Processing*, 17(4), 1–18.

Elsawy, T. M. (2023). Beyond Passive Observance: Understanding Egyptian Domestic Tourists' Behaviour through Hyper-Personalised Digital Clienteling. *Pharos International Journal of Tourism and Hospitality*, 2(2), 1–15. DOI: 10.21608/pijth.2023.256371.1007

Fernández, J. A. S., Azevedo, P. S., Martín, J. M. M., & Martín, J. A. R. (2020). Determinants of tourism destination competitiveness in the countries most visited by international tourists: Proposal of a synthetic index. *Tourism Management Perspectives*, 33, 100582. DOI: 10.1016/j.tmp.2019.100582

Fotis, J., Buhalis, D., & Rossides, N. (2012). Social media use and impact during the holiday travel planning process. In *Information and communication technologies in tourism 2012* (pp. 13–24). Springer. DOI: 10.1007/978-3-7091-1142-0_2

Ghouse, S. M., & Chaudhary, M. (2024). Artificial Intelligence (AI) for Tourism Start-Ups. In *Innovative Technologies for Increasing Service Productivity* (pp. 161-178). IGI Global.

Gretzel, U., Kang, M., & Lee, W. (2008). Differences in consumer-generated media adoption and use: A cross-national perspective. *Journal of Hospitality & Leisure Marketing*, 17(1-2), 99–120. DOI: 10.1080/10507050801978240

Gretzel, U., & Yoo, K. H. (2020). Hyper-personalization in tourism: Conceptualization, applications, and research agenda. *Journal of Hospitality and Tourism Management*, 37(1), 100156.

Guest, G., MacQueen, K. M., & Namey, E. E. (2012). *Applied thematic analysis*. Sage.

Gupta, T., & Singh, J. (2019). Leveraging Hyper-personalization for Customer Engagement in the Indian Travel Industry: A Case Study of Yatra.com. *International Journal of Business Analytics*, 8(2), 100–112.

Hew, J. J., Tan, G. W. H., Lin, B., & Ooi, K. B. (2017). Generating travel-related contents through mobile social tourism: Does privacy paradox persist? *Telematics and Informatics*, 34(7), 914–935. DOI: 10.1016/j.tele.2017.04.001

Hosany, S., & Martin, D. (2012). Self-image congruence in consumer behavior. *Journal of Business Research*, 65(5), 685–691. DOI: 10.1016/j.jbusres.2011.03.015

Ioannou, A., Tussyadiah, I., & Lu, Y. (2020). Privacy concerns and disclosure of biometric and behavioral data for travel. *International Journal of Information Management*, 54, 102122. DOI: 10.1016/j.ijinfomgt.2020.102122

Ioannou, A., Tussyadiah, I., & Miller, G. (2021). That's private! Understanding travelers' privacy concerns and online data disclosure. *Journal of Travel Research*, 60(7), 1510–1526. DOI: 10.1177/0047287520951642

Iwasaki, Y., & Mannell, R. C. (2000). Hierarchical dimensions of leisure stress coping. *Leisure Sciences*, 22(3), 163–181. DOI: 10.1080/01490409950121843

Jeong, M., & Shin, H. H. (2020). Tourists' experiences with smart tourism technology at smart destinations and their behavior intentions. *Journal of Travel Research*, 59(8), 1464–1477. DOI: 10.1177/0047287519883034

Knudsen, D. C., Rickly, J. M., & Vidon, E. S. (2016). The fantasy of authenticity: Touring with Lacan. *Annals of Tourism Research*, 58, 33–45. DOI: 10.1016/j.annals.2016.02.003

Koo, C., Xiang, Z., Gretzel, U., & Sigala, M. (2021). Artificial intelligence (AI) and robotics in travel, hospitality and leisure. *Electronic Markets*, 31(3), 473–476. DOI: 10.1007/s12525-021-00494-z PMID: 35603226

KPMG. (2022). India's Travel & Hospitality Renaissance: Fuelled by Technology and Disruption. https://kpmg.com/us/en/webcasts/2023/travel-leisure-hospitality-industry.html

Kumar, A., & Kaur, R. (2017). Hyper-personalization: A New Paradigm for Indian Travel and Tourism Industry. *IUP Journal of Management Research*, 16(3), 45–52.

Kumar, V., Rajan, B., Venkatesan, R., & Lecinski, J. (2019). Understanding the role of artificial intelligence in personalized engagement marketing. *California Management Review*, 61(4), 135–155. DOI: 10.1177/0008125619859317

Lee, C. H., & Cranage, D. A. (2011). Personalisation–privacy paradox: The effects of personalisation and privacy assurance on customer responses to travel Web sites. *Tourism Management*, 32(5), 987–994. DOI: 10.1016/j.tourman.2010.08.011

Liang, C. C., & Shiau, W. L. (2018). Moderating effect of privacy concerns and subjective norms between satisfaction and repurchase of airline e-ticket through airline-ticket vendors. *Asia Pacific Journal of Tourism Research*, 23(12), 1142–1159. DOI: 10.1080/10941665.2018.1528290

MacCannell, D. (2013). *The tourist: A new theory of the leisure class*. Univ of California Press. DOI: 10.1525/9780520354050

Malik, A., & Jain, P. (2022). Understanding Travel Consumer Behaviour in India: A Study of Hyper-personalization and its Impact on Decision-Making. *International Journal of Hospitality Management*, 109, 104033.

Markets and Markets. (n.d.). Online travel booking platform market - global forecast to 2030. [Online]., from https://www.marketsandmarkets.com/Market-Reports/online-travel-booking-platform-market-115208171.html

McKinsey & Company. (2020). Artificial Intelligence in Travel & Hospitality. https://www.mckinsey.com/industries/travel-logistics-and-infrastructure/our-insights/the-promise-of-travel-in-the-age-of-ai

Mittal, N., Chaudhary, M., & Alavi, S. (2017). Learning management through mobile apps-a new buzzword. *International Journal of Business Innovation and Research*, 13(3), 271–287. DOI: 10.1504/IJBIR.2017.084419

Mittal, R., & Khan, M. A. (2020). The Role of Hyper-personalization in Enhancing Customer Experience in the Indian Travel and Tourism Industry. *Journal of Internet Commerce*, 23(3), 351–374.

Moore, K., Buchmann, A., Månsson, M., & Fisher, D. (2021). Authenticity in tourism theory and experience. Practically indispensable and theoretically mischievous? *Annals of Tourism Research*, 89, 103208. DOI: 10.1016/j.annals.2021.103208

Mordor Intelligence. (2024, February). India online travel market size, share & industry analysis. [Online]. https://www.mordorintelligence.com/industry-reports/online-travel-market-in-india/market-trends

Munar, A. M., & Jacobsen, J. K. S. (2014). Motivations for sharing tourism experiences through social media. *Tourism Management*, 43, 46–54. DOI: 10.1016/j.tourman.2014.01.012

Nazarian, A., Atkinson, P., & Foroudi, P. (2017). Influence of national culture and balanced organizational culture on the hotel industry's performance. *International Journal of Hospitality Management*, 63, 22–32. DOI: 10.1016/j.ijhm.2017.01.003

Needham, C., Allen, K., & Hall, K. (2016). Enacting personalisation on a micro scale. In *Micro-Enterprise and Personalisation* (pp. 111–128). Policy Press. DOI: 10.2307/j.ctt1t890w5.12

Ng, P. (2020). Platform Urbanism: Planning towards Hyper-Personalisation. *International Journal of Urban and Civil Engineering*, 14(7), 189–192.

Nikitas, A., Njoya, E. T., & Dani, S. (2019). Examining the myths of connected and autonomous vehicles: Analysing the pathway to a driverless mobility paradigm. *International Journal of Automotive Technology and Management*, 19(1-2), 10–30. DOI: 10.1504/IJATM.2019.098513

O'connor, P. (2008). User-generated content and travel: A case study on Tripadvisor. com. In *Information and communication technologies in tourism 2008* (pp. 47–58). Springer. DOI: 10.1007/978-3-211-77280-5_5

Park, D. H., Lee, J., & Han, I. (2007). The effect of on-line consumer reviews on consumer purchasing intention: The moderating role of involvement. *International Journal of Electronic Commerce*, 11(4), 125–148. DOI: 10.2753/JEC1086-4415110405

Pine, J. B., & Gilmore, J. H. (1999). The Experience Economy.

Ponte, E. B., Carvajal-Trujillo, E., & Escobar-Rodríguez, T. (2015). Influence of trust and perceived value on the intention to purchase travel online: Integrating the effects of assurance on trust antecedents. *Tourism Management*, 47, 286–302. DOI: 10.1016/j.tourman.2014.10.009

Räikkönen, J., & Honkanen, A. (2013). Does satisfaction with package tours lead to successful vacation experiences? *Journal of Destination Marketing & Management*, 2(2), 108–117. DOI: 10.1016/j.jdmm.2013.03.002

Rickly, J. M., & McCabe, S. (2017). Authenticity for tourism design and experience. *Design Science in tourism: Foundations of destination management*, 55-68.

Robinson, R. N., Martins, A., Solnet, D., & Baum, T. (2019). Sustaining precarity: Critically examining tourism and employment. *Journal of Sustainable Tourism*, 27(7), 1008–1025. DOI: 10.1080/09669582.2018.1538230

Sarial-Abi, G., Merdin-Uygur, E., & Gürhan-Canli, Z. (2020). Responses to replica (vs. genuine) touristic experiences. *Annals of Tourism Research*, 83, 102927. DOI: 10.1016/j.annals.2020.102927

Schuster, R., Buxton, R., Hanson, J. O., Binley, A. D., Pittman, J., Tulloch, V., La Sorte, F. A., Roehrdanz, P. R., Verburg, P. H., Rodewald, A. D., Wilson, S., Possingham, H. P., & Bennett, J. R. (2023). Protected area planning to conserve biodiversity in an uncertain future. *Conservation Biology*, 37(3), e14048. DOI: 10.1111/cobi.14048 PMID: 36661081

Senecal, S., & Nantel, J. (2004). The influence of online product recommendations on consumers' online choices. *Journal of Retailing*, 80(2), 159–169. DOI: 10.1016/j.jretai.2004.04.001

Serhat, G., & Uzuncan, B. (2021). Impossibility of authentic experience? The existential estrangement which turns to performance. *Journal of Tourism and Cultural Change*, 19(5), 681–695. DOI: 10.1080/14766825.2020.1748637

Sharma, A., Sharma, S., & Chaudhary, M. (2020). Are small travel agencies ready for digital marketing? Views of travel agency managers. *Tourism Management*, 79, 104078. DOI: 10.1016/j.tourman.2020.104078

Singla, S. (2020). AI and IoT in healthcare. *Internet of things use cases for the healthcare industry*, 1-23.

Sirgy, M. J., & Su, C. (2000). Destination image, self-congruity, and travel behavior: Toward an integrative model. *Journal of Travel Research*, 38(4), 340–352. DOI: 10.1177/004728750003800402

Skift. (2023, September 27). How AI can personalize the travel experience for every guest. [Online], from https://skift.com/insight/new-report-personalizing-the-travel-experience-using-data-and-ai/

Sparks, B., Bradley, G., & Jennings, G. (2011). Consumer value and self-image congruency at different stages of timeshare ownership. *Tourism Management*, 32(5), 1176–1185. DOI: 10.1016/j.tourman.2010.10.009

SPER Market Research. (2023, February 15). Online travel booking platform market size to reach usd 1745.94 billion by 2033 at a cagr of 10.01%, from https://www.linkedin.com/pulse/online-travel-booking-platform-market-igraf

Sunny, S., Patrick, L., & Rob, L. (2019). Impact of cultural values on technology acceptance and technology readiness. *International Journal of Hospitality Management*, 77, 89–96. DOI: 10.1016/j.ijhm.2018.06.017

Technavio. (2023, November 16). Indian travel and tourism market 2024-2028: growth, trends, covid-19 impact, and forecasts.

Tham, A., Croy, G., & Mair, J. (2013). Social media in destination choice: Distinctive electronic word-of-mouth dimensions. *Journal of Travel & Tourism Marketing*, 30(1-2), 144–155. DOI: 10.1080/10548408.2013.751272

Tiberghien, G., Bremner, H., & Milne, S. (2017). Performance and visitors' perception of authenticity in eco-cultural tourism. *Tourism Geographies*, 19(2), 287–300. DOI: 10.1080/14616688.2017.1285958

Tiberghien, G., Bremner, H., & Milne, S. (2020). Authenticity and disorientation in the tourism experience. *Journal of Outdoor Recreation and Tourism*, 30, 100283. DOI: 10.1016/j.jort.2020.100283

Tong, S., Luo, X., & Xu, B. (2020). Personalized mobile marketing strategies. *Journal of the Academy of Marketing Science*, 48(2), 64–78. DOI: 10.1007/s11747-019-00693-3

Tracey, B., & Swart, M. P. (2020). Training and development research in tourism and hospitality: A perspective paper. *Tourism Review*, 75(1), 256–259. DOI: 10.1108/TR-06-2019-0206

Travel + Leisure. (2023, August 11). How AI is transforming travel personalization. [Online], from https://blog.operasolutions.com/ai-is-reimagining-travel-personalisation

Tussyadiah, I., Li, S., & Miller, G. (2019). Privacy protection in tourism: Where we are and where we should be heading for. In *Information and Communication Technologies in Tourism 2019: Proceedings of the International Conference in Nicosia, Cyprus, January 30–February 1, 2019* (pp. 278-290). Springer International Publishing.

Urry, J., & Larsen, J. (2011). The tourist gaze 3.0.

Vu, H. Q., Law, R., & Li, G. (2019). Breach of traveller privacy in location-based social media. *Current Issues in Tourism*, 22(15), 1825–1840. DOI: 10.1080/13683500.2018.1553151

Walther, J. B. (1996). Computer-mediated communication: Impersonal, interpersonal, and hyperpersonal interaction. *Communication Research*, 23(1), 3–43. DOI: 10.1177/009365096023001001

Weiss, A. M., Lurie, N. H., & MacInnis, D. J. (2008). Listening to strangers: Whose responses are valuable, how valuable are they, and why? *JMR, Journal of Marketing Research*, 45(4), 425–436. DOI: 10.1509/jmkr.45.4.425

Wozniak, T., Schaffner, D., Stanoevska-Slabeva, K., & Lenz-Kesekamp, V. (2018). Psychological antecedents of mobile consumer behaviour and implications for customer journeys in tourism. *Information Technology & Tourism*, 18(1-4), 85–112. DOI: 10.1007/s40558-017-0101-8

Xiang, Z., & Gretzel, U. (2010). Role of social media in online travel information search. *Tourism Management*, 31(2), 179–188. DOI: 10.1016/j.tourman.2009.02.016

Xiang, Z., Gretzel, U., Gong, S., & Li, J. (2019). Understanding the dark side of personalization in tourism e-commerce: A conceptual framework and research agenda. *Journal of Hospitality and Tourism Technology*, 10(2), 434–452.

Yoo, K. H., Lee, Y., Gretzel, U., & Fesenmaier, D. R. (2009). Trust in travel-related consumer generated media. In *Information and communication technologies in tourism 2009* (pp. 49–59). Springer. DOI: 10.1007/978-3-211-93971-0_5

Zhang, X., Ding, X., & Ma, L. (2022). The influences of information overload and social overload on intention to switch in social media. *Behaviour & Information Technology*, 41(2), 228–241. DOI: 10.1080/0144929X.2020.1800820

Chapter 7
Harnessing OpenStreetMap for Smart Destination Mapping and Navigation

Kashif Mehmood Khan
 https://orcid.org/0000-0003-4888-2295
Department of Computer Science, SZABIST, Karachi, Pakistan

Remi Thomas
 https://orcid.org/0000-0002-4003-9941
Vishwakarma University, Pune, India

Munir Ahmad
 https://orcid.org/0000-0003-4836-6151
Survey of Pakistan, Pakistan

ABSTRACT

OpenStreetMap (OSM) offers a powerful and versatile alternative to traditional map providers for smart destinations. This chapter explored the key advantages of OSM, including its collaborative data model, open licensing, and integration potential. The chapter then delved into various applications of OSM for smart destinations. By leveraging OSM's data and integration capabilities, destinations can create detailed and user-centric maps, enhance navigation with real-time data, and tailor experiences for different visitor segments. Integration with mobile applications, public transit systems, and location-based services further enriches the visitor experience by providing a comprehensive navigation ecosystem and personalized recommendations. However, the chapter also acknowledged the challenges associ-

DOI: 10.4018/979-8-3693-5678-4.ch007

ated with using OSM. Data quality and consistency can vary across regions, and maintaining and updating the data requires dedicated resources. Integration with other platforms presents technical complexities that necessitate specific expertise.

INTRODUCTION

The rise of location-based services (LBS) has revolutionized the way we navigate and explore our surroundings (Kurtz et al., 2021; Molitor et al., 2020; Ruan et al., 2021; Singh & Singh, 2020). Smart destinations, which leverage LBS to provide a seamless and personalized experience for visitors, are becoming increasingly common. A critical component of smart destinations is the ability to create and utilize detailed and up-to-date maps. While traditional map providers offer valuable information, OpenStreetMap (OSM) presents a unique alternative due to its open, collaborative, and constantly evolving nature. Traditional map providers often face limitations in terms of data coverage, detail, and currency. Additionally, their closed ecosystems can restrict customization and integration with other platforms. OSM, on the other hand, is a free and editable world map created by a global community of volunteers (Bartzokas-Tsiompras, 2022; Grinberger et al., 2022; Sarkar & Anderson, 2022). This collaborative approach ensures that OSM data is constantly updated and reflects the latest changes in the physical environment (Zacharopoulou et al., 2021). Furthermore, the open nature of OSM allows for seamless integration with other platforms and the creation of customized map visualizations.

The significance of leveraging OSM for smart destination mapping and navigation lies in its ability to provide a more dynamic and user-centric experience. With OSM, destinations can create and maintain highly detailed maps that cater to the specific needs of their visitors. These maps can include information on points of interest, transportation networks, and pedestrian walkways, all of which are crucial for effective navigation (Balducci, 2021; Felício et al., 2022; Ferster et al., 2020). Moreover, the open nature of OSM allows for the integration of real-time data feeds, such as traffic congestion or public transit schedules, further enhancing the navigational experience (Klinkhardt et al., 2021).

This chapter explores OSM's potential for smart destination mapping and navigation. The structure of this chapter is as follows. The second section provides a detailed overview of OSM, its functionalities, and its advantages over traditional map providers. The third section explores the various applications of OSM for smart destination mapping and navigation. The fourth section discusses the integration of OSM with other platforms and services. The fifth section addresses the challenges associated with using OSM for smart destinations, followed by a discussion of potential solutions and future directions in the concluding section.

LITERATURE REVIEW

This section delves into the specifics of destination mapping and OpenStreetMap to provide a comprehensive understanding of these concepts to the readers of the chapter.

Destination Mapping

Destination mapping is usually used to describe the process of defining significant places or places of interest as destinations, for example, to go for a trip, to shop, or whatever its purpose may be, and to recognize how people or goods get to those destinations. It can be applied in planning and development, transport and supply chain management, business and marketing, and tourism. For example, in urban planning, destination mapping is applied to identify the people's movements in a city or a specific region to develop the best routes for transport, walking space, and other facilities (Rosa-Jiménez et al., 2016). Similarly, it can assist in the determination of the most efficient ways through which goods can be transported to their final destination (Farheen et al., 2024). Moreover, destination mapping can be applied in the retailer's studies as it helps determine the origin of customers and places frequented by consumers (Alawadi et al., 2022). In the context of tourism, maps are used to identify the most attractive places for tourists, tourists' mobility, and where and how facilities can be developed for their convenience (Masteriarsa & Riyanto, 2023). Further, destination mapping can also be fundamental when an emergency response method is being developed to decide on key destinations like hospitals or assembly points or safer areas and the best route to get there (Ostwald & Waller, 2024). The data for the formation of destination maps may be obtained from different sources, including GPS data, mobile telephone tracking data survey data, and geospatial data among others.

Destination Mapping for Tourism

Tourism hugely influences destination mapping mainly by focusing on certain destinations that contain or can contain huge tourism foot traffic. Tourist attractions, including famous geographical and historical sites, and recreation avenues are defined in the model as significant areas. Tourism trends are also acknowledged in emerging destinations to direct planners to utilize these unexplored places for upcoming developments. In this way, destination mapping reveals these key locations and offers guidance as to which areas of a town, city, region, or country should be targeted to build up infrastructure to support visitors in the tourism industry.

Destination mapping can reinforce through tourism the need for infrastructure development mainly transport and accommodation sectors (Masteriarsa & Riyanto, 2023). This helps to define and improve infrastructure by extending transport highways of airports, roads, and public transportation to enable tourists to access the appropriate areas. Moreover, mapping is significant for the proper siting of hotels, restaurants, and other services for guests to enhance their comfort while traveling. This planned infrastructure helps to localize the influx of tourists and is also beneficial for the development of the area in general.

Improving the tourist experience is one of the critical objectives of and practices involved in, destination mapping within the tourism context (Deng et al., 2021). With detailed maps and a navigation system, tourists and travelers can navigate unknown landscapes, find various attractions, and use opportunities. However, destination mapping might also encompass the cultural and historical background, this way enriching the experience and offering the opportunity to learn more about the place. It is an ideal method of tapping a loyal customer base while at the same time enhancing the customers' experience in a way that they will recommend the tour to others and revisit the destination.

Destination mapping also includes sustainable tourism planning, knowing that it is extremely important for any tourist destination (Masteriarsa & Riyanto, 2023; Wahyuningtyas et al., 2022). Thus, when evaluating external and internal environmental factors of certain areas, the planners can introduce methods to reduce adverse influences of tourism on the environment and contributing to the development of the communities. Destination mapping contributes to the reduction of tourist' flow by certain places by shifting them to other less crowded spots: this enables to ease pressure on attraction points and also enhances the regionalization of offerings among places. The approach adopted from this case ensures the sustainable development of tourism to meet the market needs while at the same time protecting the environment.

Destination mapping is an effective technique in promoting and marketing tourism and related services (Datiko, 2024). Due to identification of tourists' origins and their interests, it is easier for the tourism boards and marketers to develop campaigns for such tourists. This specific marketing makes it possible to reach the targeted clients; therefore, many visitors come from the targeted areas. On the same note, mapping facilitates the development of new specialized itineraries to suit different needs, thus boosting the destination's attraction more.

In tourism, the mapping of destinations is important in issues to do with crisis management and/or the formulation of emergency preparedness strategies (Cahigas et al., 2022). It aids in determining safe areas, medical facilities, and escape paths so that, both the tourists and inhabitants can be shielded in the occasion of an event.

Any time there must be a response to disasters that include natural disasters, political instabilities, or sickness outbreaks, there must be a map that guides the quickest and most efficient ways of reaching important places and getting or providing the relevant resources. Such preparedness ensures that the lives of people are protected during disasters and at the same time assists in preserving the image of the destination as a safe place for tourism.

Destination mapping also plays a pivotal role in providing detailed and beneficial information regarding tourists and their choices, impact contributions insightful results. This suggests that through the interpretation of movements, expenditure, and any other activities, stakeholders in the tourism sector will be in a position to determine the areas that are most suitable for investment and the right direction towards the development of more facilities to meet tourists' needs. This information is useful for grasping the impact of tourism on the Gross Domestic Product of certain territories and managing spatial development. Thus, these insights help with better and more accurate preparation of sustainable tourism plans.

OpenStreetMap

OpenStreetMap thrives on the passion and expertise of a global community of volunteers committed to enhancing and maintaining map data (Bartzokas-Tsiompras, 2022; Zhou, Wang, et al., 2022; Zhou, Zhang, et al., 2022). This decentralized model fosters a continuous cycle of improvement, seamlessly integrating diverse local perspectives and insights. Imagine a vibrant tapestry of contributors: urban cyclists meticulously mapping bike lanes and shortcuts through bustling cityscapes, nature enthusiasts capturing every twist and turn of trails in remote wilderness areas, and residents highlighting hidden gems and community landmarks.

Collaborative Mapping

This collective effort enriches OSM with intricate detail and ensures that maps evolve in real-time, reflecting the ever-changing landscape and user needs. Unlike traditional mapping services that rely on static data, OSM's collaborative approach captures the nuances of terrain, local knowledge, and community usage patterns with remarkable accuracy. By harnessing the power of community-driven mapping, OSM delivers dynamic and up-to-date maps that empower users worldwide, making it a truly invaluable resource for navigation, exploration, and community engagement.

Data Model and Attributes

OpenStreetMap adopts a robust and adaptable data model crafted to capture a broad spectrum of geographic elements with precision (Biljecki et al., 2023; Formica et al., 2020). Beyond foundational features like roads and buildings, OSM meticulously catalogs points of interest (POIs) that span from quaint cafes and cultural museums to significant historical landmarks. What sets OSM apart is its capacity to imbue each element with a rich tapestry of attributes, significantly enriching the map's functionality and relevance. This comprehensive approach can empower users to tailor their map interactions to specific needs and preferences, whether seeking a cozy spot for brunch, exploring local history, or planning accessible routes. By integrating such detailed and dynamic data, OSM continually enhances the user experience, making navigation more informed, engaging, and personally relevant.

Open Licensing and Community Governance

OpenStreetMap operates under a robust open licensing framework, primarily the Open Database License (ODbL), which enables unrestricted access, modification, and redistribution of its data. This open approach cultivates a fertile ground for innovation and customization, empowering individuals and organizations alike to enhance and adapt OSM data to meet diverse needs (Le Guilcher et al., 2022). Imagine a scenario where a local tourism board enriches OSM with detailed information on historical walking tours, bike rental locations, and cultural landmarks, tailoring the map precisely to the interests and requirements of visitors. This flexibility not only enriches the map's content but also fosters a deeper engagement with local communities and their unique offerings.

In addition to its open licensing, OSM prides itself on a governance structure rooted in collaboration and transparency. Decisions concerning platform development and policy are democratically made through a voting system where active contributors have a direct voice. This participatory model ensures that the OSM community drives its evolution, maintaining a high standard of accuracy, relevance, and inclusivity in its mapping efforts.

Comparison With Traditional Map Providers

When comparing OpenStreetMap to traditional map providers, several distinct advantages emerge.

- OSM benefits from its community-driven model, ensuring that map data is frequently updated and reflects changes in real time. New roads, businesses,

- and infrastructure developments are often added to OSM more swiftly than to commercially sourced maps.
- Unlike traditional providers that charge licensing fees for map data access, OSM offers its data freely under open licenses like the ODbL. This cost-saving advantage is particularly beneficial for smaller destinations or organizations with limited budgets, enabling them to access and utilize detailed map data without financial barriers.
- OSM's open nature allows for extensive customization of maps. Destinations can tailor map styles to match their branding or local aesthetics, highlight specific points of interest that matter most to their visitors, and integrate additional data layers such as local events or ecological information. This level of flexibility and customization is often limited with traditional providers whose maps are more standardized and less adaptable to specific community needs.
- OSM data is compatible with a wide range of platforms and services due to its open formats and APIs (Application Programming Interfaces). This seamless integration capability allows destinations to build comprehensive navigation ecosystems. Whether it's embedding maps on websites, developing mobile apps, or integrating with tourism services, OSM supports diverse applications that enhance visitor experiences and accessibility.

By understanding these key aspects, we can establish a strong foundation for appreciating the potential of OSM in the context of smart destination mapping and navigation. OSM's collaborative approach, rich data model, open licensing, and integration potential make it a powerful tool for creating dynamic and user-centric maps for smart destinations.

APPLICATIONS OF OSM FOR SMART DESTINATIONS

Building upon the understanding of OSM established in Section 2, this section delves into the various applications of OSM data for smart destination mapping and navigation.

Creating Detailed and User-Centric Maps

OpenStreetMap excels in providing highly detailed maps that cater specifically to the diverse needs of visitors and outdoor enthusiasts. Consider a historic city utilizing OSM to offer more than just a standard map. With OSM, destinations can spotlight iconic landmarks such as the Colosseum and Trevi Fountain alongside lesser-known treasures like secluded piazzas, cozy cafes, and unique walking tours curated by local contributors. This approach encourages tourists to venture off the beaten path, uncovering authentic cultural experiences and hidden gems that enrich their visit beyond typical tourist routes (Ahmad, 2023; Bustamante et al., 2021; Calka & Moscicka, 2022).

National parks and hiking destinations leverage OSM to craft comprehensive trail maps tailored to outdoor enthusiasts. These maps not only outline trail networks but also provide vital details such as trail difficulty ratings, elevation profiles, and notable points of interest like scenic viewpoints or cascading waterfalls. Moreover, OSM supports the integration of user-generated content, enabling hikers to share firsthand experiences, update trail conditions, and contribute photos—all of which enhance the accuracy and usefulness of the maps over time (Balducci, 2021; Calka & Moscicka, 2022; Smirnov et al., 2020).

By harnessing the flexibility and collaborative spirit of OSM, destinations can create maps that are not only informative but also engaging and responsive to the diverse interests and preferences of their visitors. This approach not only enhances navigation but also fosters deeper connections between travelers and the places they explore, promoting a more enriching and memorable journey.

Enhancing Navigation With Real-Time Data Integration

OpenStreetMap can serve as a versatile foundation for integrating real-time data feeds, enhancing navigation with up-to-the-minute information, and improving user experiences in various scenarios (Dai et al., 2020; Li et al., 2022). For example, a bustling city wants to integrate live traffic updates into its OSM-based map. By overlaying real-time data on congestion, road closures, and construction, visitors can navigate efficiently, avoiding delays and selecting optimal routes. This feature proves invaluable during major events or peak tourist seasons when traffic conditions fluctuate, empowering users to make informed decisions and reach their destinations with minimal hassle.

Cities with robust public transportation networks leverage OSM to integrate live bus and train schedules. Travelers can access real-time arrival and departure information directly on the map, facilitating seamless trip planning and minimizing wait times. Whether navigating unfamiliar routes or commuting regularly, this integration ensures reliable and efficient use of public transit services, enhancing overall mobility experiences. By leveraging OSM's adaptable framework for real-time data integration, destinations can offer visitors enhanced navigation tools that adapt to changing conditions, improve journey predictability, and ultimately elevate the travel experience through enhanced convenience and efficiency.

Tailored Experiences for Different User Segments

OpenStreetMap offers unparalleled flexibility, enabling destinations to create personalized map experiences tailored to the unique needs of various visitor segments. For example, for business travelers, a customized OSM map can serve as a strategic tool by highlighting essential locations such as business centers, co-working spaces, and conference venues. Integrating real-time data on ride-hailing service availability enhances convenience, allowing travelers to efficiently arrange transportation for meetings and appointments. This integration not only saves time but also enhances productivity during business trips.

OSM can support the creation of accessibility-focused maps designed to meet the needs of visitors with diverse mobility requirements (Biagi et al., 2020; Hill et al., 2024). These maps can prominently feature amenities such as wheelchair-accessible ramps, elevators in public buildings, and designated disabled parking zones. By providing clear and detailed accessibility information, OSM enables individuals with disabilities to navigate the destination confidently, ensuring equal access to facilities and services.

INTEGRATION WITH OTHER PLATFORMS AND SERVICES

Unlocking the full potential of OSM for smart destinations lies in its seamless integration with other platforms and services. This collaborative approach fosters a comprehensive navigation ecosystem that empowers visitors with a rich and informative experience.

Integration With Mobile Applications

Imagine a visitor arriving in a new city and accessing a dedicated mobile app powered by OpenStreetMap, offering a suite of features that enhance their exploration and navigation experience. An interactive map app can present a user-friendly map utilizing OSM data, enabling visitors to effortlessly explore points of interest, navigate public transportation networks, and uncover local recommendations from the community. Whether discovering cultural landmarks or charming cafes off the beaten path, the interactive map provides comprehensive insights to enrich the visitor's journey.

Moreover, integrated navigation functionalities can guide visitors through unfamiliar streets with precision. Leveraging real-time traffic updates and OSM's detailed mapping, the app offers clear turn-by-turn directions that adapt to pedestrian pathways, one-way streets, and local traffic conditions. This ensures efficient and stress-free navigation, particularly in historic districts or bustling urban centers.

Furthermore, the app can also enhance the visitor experience by overlaying real-time updates directly on the OSM map. This includes live information on public transit schedules, current restaurant hours, availability of tickets for popular attractions, and more. By providing up-to-date insights, visitors can make informed decisions on the go, optimizing their itinerary and maximizing their time exploring the destination.

Connection With Public Transit Systems

Integrating OSM data seamlessly with public transit systems enhances navigation capabilities and improves the overall travel experience. In this regard, OSM can display real-time bus and train schedules directly on digital maps within mobile apps or at transit hubs. This integration eliminates the need for visitors to use separate transit apps or rely on printed schedules, providing convenient access to up-to-date departure times and route information. Whether planning a journey or checking schedules on the go, travelers benefit from streamlined journey planning and reduced wait times.

Moreover, by combining real-time traffic data with public transit schedules, OSM facilitates route optimization tailored to individual travel needs. For example, when a visitor wishes to reach a museum, the system can recommend the most efficient travel route based on current traffic conditions and transit schedules. This might include a combination of bus routes and walking paths optimized to minimize travel time and navigate around potential delays or congestion points.

By leveraging OSM's comprehensive dataset and its integration capabilities with public transit systems, destinations can offer visitors enhanced convenience, efficiency, and reliability in navigating urban environments. This integration not only simplifies travel logistics but also supports sustainable mobility practices by promoting the use of public transportation as a viable and accessible option for exploring and experiencing the destination.

Interoperability With Location-Based Services

OpenStreetMap can serve as a versatile foundation for integrating with a network of interconnected LBS, enhancing the visitor experience in various ways. For example, a visitor using a restaurant recommendation app powered by OSM data. The app can utilize OSM's extensive points of interest dataset, combined with real-time user reviews and ratings, to suggest top-rated restaurants near the visitor's current location. This personalized approach helps travelers discover authentic dining experiences, uncover hidden culinary gems, and avoid tourist traps, enhancing their overall satisfaction and enjoyment.

Moreover, an events app integrated with OSM data can dynamically display upcoming events based on the visitor's location. By leveraging OSM's detailed mapping of venues and event spaces, the app provides timely information on local festivals, concerts, art exhibitions, and other cultural events. This feature not only enriches the visitor's itinerary with unique experiences but also fosters a deeper connection with the destination's cultural and social fabric.

By leveraging OSM's robust and continually updated dataset, LBS can deliver tailored recommendations and real-time event information that enhance visitor engagement, support informed decision-making, and contribute to a more enriching travel experience. This interoperability underscores OSM's role as a foundational resource for creating dynamic and user-centric applications that connect travelers with the diverse offerings of a destination.

CHALLENGES AND CONSIDERATIONS FOR USING OSM

While OSM offers a wealth of benefits for smart destinations, it's important to acknowledge the challenges and considerations associated with its use.

Data Quality and Consistency

OpenStreetMap derives its strength from a global community of volunteers, but this decentralized model also poses challenges in maintaining consistent data quality across different regions. In highly populated areas with active communities, OSM often features detailed and regularly updated information. However, rural or less populated regions may exhibit inconsistencies or gaps in data coverage, impacting the map's completeness and accuracy. Several strategies can help address these challenges and enhance data quality (Antoniou, 2023; Basiri et al., 2019; Biljecki et al., 2023; Moradi et al., 2022; Yamashita et al., 2019).

- Destinations can deploy automated data validation tools to detect and rectify inconsistencies, such as missing or outdated information. These tools analyze OSM data against predefined criteria, highlighting potential errors for community review and correction.
- Engaging with local OSM contributors proves invaluable in improving data accuracy and completeness. Destinations can actively involve community members in mapping initiatives, encouraging them to contribute local knowledge, update map features, and fill data gaps specific to their area. This

collaborative approach ensures that the map reflects current conditions and meets the needs of both residents and visitors.
- Providing training sessions and support resources to local volunteers fosters a better understanding of mapping standards and techniques. This empowers contributors to maintain high data standards and adhere to best practices in data collection and verification.

By implementing these strategies, destinations can leverage OSM's community-driven model to enhance data quality, address regional disparities, and ensure the map remains a reliable and comprehensive resource for navigation, exploration, and community engagement.

Resource Requirements

Maintaining and updating OSM data requires dedicated resources, balancing volunteer contributions with strategic resource management approaches tailored to the scale and complexity of the destination's needs.

- Engaging with existing OSM volunteer communities and local chapters can significantly augment data maintenance efforts. These networks often include passionate individuals with local knowledge and mapping expertise, eager to contribute to their community's map accuracy and completeness.
- Collaborating with local OSM chapters or user groups establishes ongoing relationships and facilitates coordinated efforts in data collection and validation. Such partnerships leverage collective knowledge and resources, enhancing the efficiency and effectiveness of data management initiatives.
- Implementing tools like bulk editing software and automated validation processes optimizes data management workflows. These tools streamline tasks such as identifying errors, updating large datasets, and maintaining consistency across different map features. By automating routine tasks, destinations can allocate resources more strategically toward quality assurance and community engagement.
- Investing in training programs and capacity-building initiatives empowers local contributors with skills in mapping techniques, data validation, and best practices. This investment fosters a knowledgeable and motivated community capable of sustaining high data standards and adapting to evolving mapping needs.

By adopting these resource management approaches, destinations can effectively support the ongoing maintenance and enhancement of OSM data, ensuring the map remains accurate, comprehensive, and relevant to both residents and visitors alike. This collaborative effort strengthens community engagement and reinforces OSM's role as a dynamic and reliable platform for geographic information worldwide.

Integration Complexity

Integrating OpenStreetMap data with other platforms and services offers substantial benefits but can present technical challenges that require specialized expertise.

- Adhering to established best practices is crucial for seamless integration. This includes using standardized data formats, such as GeoJSON or XML, which facilitate compatibility and interoperability across different systems. Ensuring data consistency and accuracy through regular updates and validation processes is also essential to maintain the reliability of integrated services.
- Leveraging well-documented APIs (Application Programming Interfaces) provided by OSM simplifies the process of accessing and utilizing map data. These APIs allow developers to retrieve specific geographic information, perform spatial queries, and incorporate dynamic map features into applications without needing to handle raw data directly.
- Exploring open-source software libraries and integration tools tailored for OSM can streamline development efforts. These tools often include functionalities for data visualization, routing optimization, and real-time updates, reducing the complexity of coding from scratch and accelerating the deployment of integrated solutions.
- Engaging with the OSM community and participating in forums or developer groups can provide valuable insights, troubleshooting assistance, and collaborative opportunities. Community-driven initiatives often contribute to the evolution of integration standards and the development of new tools, benefiting both developers and end-users.

By following these best practices and leveraging available tools and resources, destinations and developers can effectively navigate the technical complexities of integrating OSM data. This approach not only enhances the functionality and usability of integrated services but also promotes innovation and collaboration within the broader geographic information community.

CONCLUSION

OpenStreetMap stands out as a compelling alternative to traditional map providers for smart destinations. This chapter explored the reasons behind this, highlighting the key advantages of OSM. These include its collaborative data model, where a global community continuously updates and improves map data, ensuring its accuracy and relevance for navigation. Additionally, open licensing allows destinations to freely customize maps to their specific needs and branding. Finally, OSM's integration potential empowers destinations to create a comprehensive navigation ecosystem by seamlessly connecting with mobile apps, public transit systems, and location-based services, offering visitors a rich and informative experience.

The chapter further delved into various applications of OSM for smart destinations. By leveraging OSM's data and integration capabilities, destinations can create detailed maps that cater to diverse visitor needs. Imagine a historic city showcasing iconic landmarks alongside hidden gems curated by local contributors, encouraging tourists to explore beyond the beaten path. National parks can benefit similarly, crafting comprehensive trail maps with real-time data on conditions and user reviews, enriching the outdoor experience.

Furthermore, OSM integrates with real-time data feeds, providing up-to-date information on traffic, public transit schedules, and even restaurant hours. This empowers visitors to navigate efficiently, make informed decisions, and optimize their itineraries, eliminating the guesswork often associated with travel. Additionally, destinations can create personalized map experiences for different visitor segments. Business travelers can benefit from maps highlighting business centers and co-working spaces, while accessibility-focused maps can empower visitors with specific mobility requirements.

However, the chapter also acknowledged that using OSM comes with challenges. Data quality can vary across regions. To address this, destinations can deploy automated validation tools and collaborate with local OSM communities to leverage their local knowledge. Additionally, training programs on mapping standards can help ensure data consistency. Maintaining and updating OSM data requires dedicated resources. Destinations can address this by collaborating with existing OSM communities and leveraging bulk editing software. Investing in training programs empowers local contributors, fostering a knowledgeable and motivated community. Finally, integration with other platforms can be technically complex. Here, standardized data formats, well-documented APIs, and open-source libraries can streamline the process. Engaging with the OSM community provides valuable insights and fosters collaboration, benefiting both developers and end-users.

REFERENCES

Ahmad, M. (2023). Exploring the Role of OpenStreetMap in Mapping Religious Tourism in Pakistan for Sustainable Development. In J. P. D. M. Vítor, A. G. da R. N. João, L. de J. P. Maria, & A. de M. C. Liliana (Eds.), *Experiences, Advantages, and Economic Dimensions of Pilgrimage Routes* (pp. 23–40). IGI Global. DOI: 10.4018/978-1-6684-9923-8.ch002

Alawadi, K., Hernandez Striedinger, V., Maghelal, P., & Khanal, A. (2022). Assessing walkability in hot arid regions: The case of downtown Abu Dhabi. *URBAN DESIGN International*, 27(3), 211–231. Advance online publication. DOI: 10.1057/s41289-021-00150-0

Antoniou, V. (2023). On volunteered geographic information quality: a framework for sharing data quality information. In *Geoinformatics for Geosciences: Advanced Geospatial Analysis using RS*. GIS and Soft Computing. DOI: 10.1016/B978-0-323-98983-1.00009-0

Balducci, F. (2021). Is OpenStreetMap a good source of information for cultural statistics? The case of Italian museums. *Environment and Planning. B, Urban Analytics and City Science*, 48(3), 503–520. Advance online publication. DOI: 10.1177/2399808319876949

Bartzokas-Tsiompras, A. (2022). Utilizing OpenStreetMap data to measure and compare pedestrian street lengths in 992 cities around the world. *European Journal of Geography*, 13(2), 127–141. Advance online publication. DOI: 10.48088/ejg.a.bar.13.2.127.138

Basiri, A., Haklay, M., Foody, G., & Mooney, P. (2019). Crowdsourced geospatial data quality: challenges and future directions. In *International Journal of Geographical Information Science* (Vol. 33, Issue 8). DOI: 10.1080/13658816.2019.1593422

Biagi, L., Brovelli, M. A., & Stucchi, L. (2020). Mapping the accessibility in openstreetmap: A comparison of different techniques. *International Archives of the Photogrammetry, Remote Sensing and Spatial Information Sciences - ISPRS Archives, 43*(B4). DOI: 10.5194/isprs-archives-XLIII-B4-2020-229-2020

Biljecki, F., Chow, Y. S., & Lee, K. (2023). Quality of crowdsourced geospatial building information: A global assessment of OpenStreetMap attributes. *Building and Environment*, 237, 110295. Advance online publication. DOI: 10.1016/j.buildenv.2023.110295

Bustamante, A., Sebastia, L., & Onaindia, E. (2021). On the representativeness of openstreetmap for the evaluation of country tourism competitiveness. *ISPRS International Journal of Geo-Information*, 10(5), 301. Advance online publication. DOI: 10.3390/ijgi10050301

Cahigas, M. M. L., Prasetyo, Y. T., Alexander, J., Sutapa, P. L., Wiratama, S., Arvin, V., Nadlifatin, R., & Persada, S. F. (2022). Factors Affecting Visiting Behavior to Bali during the COVID-19 Pandemic: An Extended Theory of Planned Behavior Approach. *Sustainability (Basel)*, 14(16), 10424. Advance online publication. DOI: 10.3390/su141610424

Calka, B., & Moscicka, A. (2022). Usefulness of OSM and BDOT10k Data for Developing Tactile Maps of Historic Parks. *Applied Sciences (Basel, Switzerland)*, 12(19), 9731. Advance online publication. DOI: 10.3390/app12199731

Dai, J., Li, C., Zuo, Y., & Ai, H. (2020). An osm data-driven method for road-positive sample creation. *Remote Sensing (Basel)*, 12(21), 3612. Advance online publication. DOI: 10.3390/rs12213612

Datiko, D. B. (2024). The customer-centric-marketing (CCM) perspectives in the tourism and hospitality sector: Insight from a developing country. *International Journal of Tourism Policy*, 14(1), 37–53. Advance online publication. DOI: 10.1504/IJTP.2024.135429

Deng, B., Xu, J., & Wei, X. (2021). Tourism Destination Preference Prediction Based on Edge Computing. *Mobile Information Systems*, 2021, 1–11. Advance online publication. DOI: 10.1155/2021/5512008

Farheen, N. S. S., Badiger, C. S., Kishore, L., Dheeraj, V., & Rajendran, S. R. (2024). A Future Look at Artificial Intelligence in the World of Tourism. In *Marketing and Big Data Analytics in Tourism and Events* (pp. 1–16). IGI Global. DOI: 10.4018/979-8-3693-3310-5.ch001

Felício, S., Hora, J., Ferreira, M. C., Abrantes, D., Costa, P. D., Dangelo, C., Silva, J., & Galvão, T. (2022). Handling OpenStreetMap georeferenced data for route planning. *Transportation Research Procedia*, 62, 189–196. Advance online publication. DOI: 10.1016/j.trpro.2022.02.024

Ferster, C., Fischer, J., Manaugh, K., Nelson, T., & Winters, M. (2020). Using OpenStreetMap to inventory bicycle infrastructure: A comparison with open data from cities. *International Journal of Sustainable Transportation*, 14(1), 64–73. Advance online publication. DOI: 10.1080/15568318.2018.1519746

Formica, A., Mazzei, M., Pourabbas, E., & Rafanelli, M. (2020). Approximate Query Answering Based on Topological Neighborhood and Semantic Similarity in OpenStreetMap. *IEEE Access : Practical Innovations, Open Solutions*, 8, 87011–87030. Advance online publication. DOI: 10.1109/ACCESS.2020.2992202

Grinberger, A. Y., Minghini, M., Yeboah, G., Juhász, L., & Mooney, P. (2022). Bridges and Barriers: An Exploration of Engagements of the Research Community with the OpenStreetMap Community. *ISPRS International Journal of Geo-Information*, 11(1), 54. Advance online publication. DOI: 10.3390/ijgi11010054

Hill, C., Young, M., Blainey, S., Cavazzi, S., Emberson, C., & Sadler, J. (2024). An integrated geospatial data model for active travel infrastructure. *Journal of Transport Geography*, 117, 103889. DOI: 10.1016/j.jtrangeo.2024.103889

Klinkhardt, C., Woerle, T., Briem, L., Heilig, M., Kagerbauer, M., & Vortisch, P. (2021). Using openstreetmap as a data source for attractiveness in travel demand models. In *Transportation Research Record* (Vol. 2675, Issue 8). DOI: 10.1177/0361198121997415

Kurtz, O. T., Wirtz, B. W., & Langer, P. F. (2021). An Empirical Analysis of Location-Based Mobile Advertising—Determinants, Success Factors, and Moderating Effects. *Journal of Interactive Marketing*, 54, 69–85. Advance online publication. DOI: 10.1016/j.intmar.2020.08.001

Le Guilcher, A., Olteanu-Raimond, A. M., & Balde, M. B. (2022). Analysis of massive imports of open data in openstreetmap database: A study case for france. *ISPRS Annals of the Photogrammetry, Remote Sensing and Spatial Information Sciences*, 5(4), 99–106. Advance online publication. DOI: 10.5194/isprs-annals-V-4-2022-99-2022

Li, J., Qin, H., Wang, J., & Li, J. (2022). OpenStreetMap-Based Autonomous Navigation for the Four Wheel-Legged Robot Via 3D-Lidar and CCD Camera. *IEEE Transactions on Industrial Electronics*, 69(3), 2708–2717. Advance online publication. DOI: 10.1109/TIE.2021.3070508

Masteriarsa, M. F., & Riyanto, R. (2023). Tourism Destination Mapping Based on Tourism Characteristics and Carrying Capacity of Province in Indonesia. *Jurnal Perencanaan Pembangunan: The Indonesian Journal of Development Planning*, 7(3), 344–361. Advance online publication. DOI: 10.36574/jpp.v7i3.460

Molitor, D., Spann, M., Ghose, A., & Reichhart, P. (2020). Effectiveness of Location-Based Advertising and the Impact of Interface Design. *Journal of Management Information Systems*, 37(2), 431–456. Advance online publication. DOI: 10.1080/07421222.2020.1759922

Moradi, M., Roche, S., & Mostafavi, M. A. (2022). Exploring five indicators for the quality of OpenStreetMap road networks: A case study of Québec, Canada. *Geomatica*, 75(4), 178–208. Advance online publication. DOI: 10.1139/geomat-2021-0012

Ostwald, M. J., & Waller, S. T. (2024). Rehearsing Emergency Scenarios: Using Space Syntax and Intelligent Mobility Modelling for Scenario Visualisation and Disaster Preparedness. *Climate Disaster Preparedness: Reimagining Extreme Events through Art and Technology*, 151–165.

Rosa-Jiménez, C., Reyes-Corredera, S., & Nogueira-Bernárdez, B. (2016). New possibilities of GIS for mapping a mature destination: A case in Benalmádena, Spain. *Anatolia*, 27(1), 82–90. Advance online publication. DOI: 10.1080/13032917.2015.1083211

Ruan, L., Long, Y., Zhang, L., & Lv, G. (2021). A platform and its applied modes for geography fieldwork in higher education based on location services. *ISPRS International Journal of Geo-Information*, 10(4), 225. Advance online publication. DOI: 10.3390/ijgi10040225

Sarkar, D., & Anderson, J. T. (2022). Corporate editors in OpenStreetMap: Investigating co-editing patterns. *Transactions in GIS*, 26(4), 1879–1897. Advance online publication. DOI: 10.1111/tgis.12910

Singh, S., & Singh, J. (2020). Location Driven Edge Assisted Device and Solutions for Intelligent Transportation. In *Fog*. Edge, and Pervasive Computing in Intelligent IoT Driven Applications., DOI: 10.1002/9781119670087.ch7

Smirnov, A., Kashevnik, A., Mikhailov, S., Shilov, N., Orlova, D., Gusikhin, O., & Martinez, H. (2020). Context-Driven Tourist Trip Planning Support System: An Approach and OpenStreetMap-Based Attraction Database Formation. *Advances in Geographic Information Science*, 1, 139–154. Advance online publication. DOI: 10.1007/978-3-030-31608-2_10

Wahyuningtyas, N., Yaniafari, R. P., Ratnawati, N., Megasari, R., Aini, D. N., Dewi, K., & Rosita, F. A. D. (2022). Development e-tourism as an effort to support tourism charm programme in Indonesia. *Geo Journal of Tourism and Geosites*, 42(2 supplement), 759–766. Advance online publication. DOI: 10.30892/gtg.422spl15-886

Yamashita, J., Seto, T., Nishimura, Y., & Iwasaki, N. (2019). VGI contributors' awareness of geographic information quality and its effect on data quality: a case study from Japan. *International Journal of Cartography*. DOI: 10.1080/23729333.2019.1613086

Zacharopoulou, D., Skopeliti, A., & Nakos, B. (2021). Assessment and visualization of osm consistency for european cities. *ISPRS International Journal of Geo-Information*, 10(6), 361. Advance online publication. DOI: 10.3390/ijgi10060361

Zhou, Q., Wang, S., & Liu, Y. (2022). Exploring the accuracy and completeness patterns of global land-cover/land-use data in OpenStreetMap. *Applied Geography (Sevenoaks, England)*, 145, 102742. Advance online publication. DOI: 10.1016/j.apgeog.2022.102742

Zhou, Q., Zhang, Y., Chang, K., & Brovelli, M. A. (2022). Assessing OSM building completeness for almost 13,000 cities globally. *International Journal of Digital Earth*, 15(1), 2400–2421. Advance online publication. DOI: 10.1080/17538947.2022.2159550

KEY TERMS AND DEFINITIONS

Collaborative Mapping: Refers to the process of map production and updating involving the contributions of different people usually via the Internet. This approach involves the utilization of a community of volunteers, locals, and specialists, to guarantee that maps are correct, up to date, and contain numerous details of the community. OpenStreetMap is one of the collaborative mappings where people can provide and edit maps in real-time.

Destination Mapping: Can therefore be defined as the identification of, and the analysis of the flow towards major objectives or targets, which could be tourist attractions, stores, other facilities, or any other landmarks that may be of importance. It is applied in sectors such as tourism, urban planning, logistics, and marketing where it facilitates efficient design of structures, improvement of the access to services or places as well as decision making.

Location-Based Services (LBS): Is a mobile service or other related service that utilizes the positioning of a specific technological device and the supply of relevant information or a particular set of functions. Some of the LBS are used in navigation applications, advertisements, social networks where individuals notify their friends about their location, emergency where help is provided at the user's location, etc. LBSs are applied in many spheres such as retail trade, tourism, transportation, and security and defense.

OpenStreetMap (OSM): Aims to gather and share free geographic data and map services any people or group of people requesting it. This is an openly accessible platform where users and members of the community can report and modify road designs or new forms of trails, buildings, and other geographical features. OSM is applied in different fields including navigation, and scientific research, and acts as the foundation map of applications and services that are based on geography.

Smart Tourism: Is the utilization of IoT, big data, and other mobile technologies in modern tourist environments to positively transform/revise the tourists' experience and in turn, boost the viability and effectiveness of tourism destinations. It entails employing information technology in offering tailored services, up-to-date information, and easy and efficient access to the tourists; and in improving the Efficient management of limited resources for the benefit of destinations, supervising the visitors, and enhancing the sustainable management of the environmental resources.

Spatial or Geospatial Data: Means information which has a locational or spatial reference, that is, the information being collected or dealt with can be located or plotted on the earth's surface. This data involves the coordinates either geographical which involve latitude and longitude or the geographical names which include addresses or any other data that may describe the location and configuration of physical objects or geographical regions. Spatial data is used in areas such as GIS (Geographic Information Systems), city planning, environment management, and transport and distribution.

Chapter 8
Redefining Success of the Tourism Sector Through Technological Advancements

Hafizullah Dar
https://orcid.org/0000-0003-2388-9474
Lovely Professional University, India

Mudasir Ahmad Dar
IGNOU, India

ABSTRACT

This study focuses on the transformational impact of technology on the tourism sector. The contribution of digital platforms, social media, and virtual reality on destination marketing strategies and the promotion of active traveler participation is explored in this study. The role of smart tourism technologies enhancing personalization and improved customer service in tourism sector is also studied. The importance of inclusive design, assistive technology, and digital accessibility in providing equal opportunities to individuals with disabilities or unique needs is further examined. Besides, the study considers the role of technology in optimizing operational and management functions within the tourism sector. This includes process transformation and workflow optimization, improved performance expectations, and the ability to make data-driven decisions. Furthermore, this study reiterates the importance of responsible innovation that is focused on sustainability, inclusiveness, and ethical equity in redefining the notion of tourism success in digital times.

DOI: 10.4018/979-8-3693-5678-4.ch008

INTRODUCTION

Traditionally, success in the tourism sector is often defined based on the number of visitors, revenue generated by the industry, and destination-based popularity. However, with the rise of technology and its dynamics, the achievement of success is more than quantitative measures (Shin, et al., 2023; García-Madurga & Grilló-Méndez, 2023). Technology allows the tourism industry to redefine success based on the qualitative aspects that include the concept of visitor experience, sustainability, and accessibility (Li, et al., 2023; Sustacha, et al., 2023). For example, technology has allowed the provision of virtual reality experiences that make tourists feel like they are in distant places and the data-driven analytics that help in making the right decisions (Arici, et al., 2023). Therefore, technological development has been incorporated as a tool to foster development in the industry. Re-defining success in the tourism industry with regard to technology includes embracing entrepreneurship that fosters economic development and sustainability (Rane, et al., 2023). Ultimately, by harnessing the power of technology, stakeholders can create more meaningful and impactful tourism experiences that transcend conventional notions of success.

Technology plays a crucial role in transforming various aspects of the tourism industry. To begin with, it revolutionizes destination marketing through the provision of interactive platforms, social media engagement, and virtual reality experiences (Qumsieh-Mussalam, & Tajeddini, 2019). These advancements enable destinations to effectively reach and attract a global audience. Furthermore, technological innovations such as mobile apps, IoT devices, and data analytics greatly enhance the overall customer experience (Ekka & Dhall, 2023; Montero, et al., 2023; Aguirre Montero, et al., 2023; Theofanous, et al., 2024). They accomplish this by offering personalized services, seamless bookings, and real-time assistance. Moreover, technology supports sustainable tourism practices by promoting renewable energy solutions, conservation efforts, and eco-friendly initiatives. By doing so, it ensures responsible development in the tourism sector. Likewise, advancements in accessibility technologies make travel more inclusive and accessible to individuals with disabilities or special needs (Chan & Agapito, 2022). Overall, technology empowers stakeholders to optimize operations, improve efficiency, and foster innovation, eventually shaping a more resilient and competitive tourism industry.

The purpose of the book chapter is to explore how technological advancements are reshaping the tourism sector's concept of success. It highlights the transformative impact of technology on destination marketing, customer experiences, accessibility, operational efficiency, and sustainability, emphasizing the need for responsible innovation to redefine success in the digital age.

To accomplish the objectives of this book chapter, secondary data has been collected from various sources including journals, books, articles, websites, reports and other published materials.

Secondary data was used in the book chapter to provide wide-ranging insights from current research, industry reports, and other publications. This approach facilitated a broad analysis of technologies, trends, and best practices within the tourism industry. It also enabled a time-efficient technique to evaluate technological impacts, confirming that the discussion was grounded in pre-existing data, reliable, and real-world applications. During data collection process, some principle words and terminologies were used such as, digital age, tourism services, enhancing customer experience, tourism development, digital accessibility of tourism, tourism technology, digital tourism operation management, challenges and ethical issues in tourism during digital era, and social media for tourism to accomplish the study objectives and draw a comprehensive outcome for the stakeholders in tourism sector.

TECHNOLOGICAL INNOVATIONS IN DESTINATION MARKETING

Digital platforms, social media, and virtual reality (VR) have revolutionized destination marketing strategies by providing innovative avenues to engage and captivate audiences (Qumsieh-Mussalam, & Tajeddini, 2019). Digital platforms such as websites, mobile apps, and online travel agencies enable destinations to showcase their attractions, accommodations, and activities to a global audience, facilitating seamless bookings and transactions (Ekka & Dhall, 2023). Social media platforms offer interactive channels for destination promotion, leveraging user-generated content, influencer partnerships, and targeted advertising to amplify brand visibility and engagement (Çeltek & İhan, 2018; Sinha, et al., 2020). Moreover, virtual reality technologies immerse prospective travelers in virtual experiences, allowing them to explore destinations, accommodations, and attractions from the comfort of their homes, finally inspiring travel decisions and driving visitor interest in a more immersive and experiential manner (Qumsieh-Mussalam, & Tajeddini, 2019; Sorokina, et al, 2022).

Tourism Australia's "Virtual Reef" project is a noteworthy instance of a technologically innovative destination marketing campaign that has proven to be successful (Marasco, et al, 2028). Through the use of virtual reality technology, the campaign provided consumers with an immersive experience that highlighted the biodiversity and beauty of the Great Barrier Reef. Tourism Australia distributed VR headsets and produced a 360-degree video experience on YouTube and social media by teaming with Google and Samsung. The advertisement attracted a lot of attention, capturing the interest of viewers everywhere and encouraging visit to the Great Barrier Reef. Tourism Australia efficiently presented the destination's natural marvels through this creative use of technology, increasing interest in and visits to the famous reef system.

Enhancing Customer Experience With Smart Tourism

In the tourism business, smart tourism technologies—such as wearables, smartphone apps, and Internet of Things devices—are essential for improving the overall visitor experience (Babu, & Subramoniam, 2016; Muniz, et al., 2021). Travelers can enhance their convenience and accessibility by using mobile apps, which offer personalized recommendations, real-time navigation assistance, and seamless booking possibilities. Travelers may maximize their comfort and safety while on the go with wearable devices like fitness trackers and smartwatches, which also provide interactive tour guides, contactless payment alternatives, and health and activity monitoring (Phutela, 2022). IoT devices also improve the quality of the guest experience by enabling automation and connectivity in lodgings ([1]Dar & Kashyap, 2023; [2]Dar & Kashyap, 2023; Sahar & Dar, 2024). This allows for smart room controls, personalized services, and energy efficiency. Tourism stakeholders may enhance tourist pleasure and loyalty by implementing these smart technologies to offer more seamless, personalized, and immersive experiences (Chung, et al., 2017; Zhang, et al, 2022; Torabi, et al., 2022).

Smart technologies are being used by businesses in the tourism sector to streamline operations and personalize offerings (Torabi, et al., 2022). For example, hotel chains are using mobile apps to provide guests with personalized concierge services, easy check-in and check-out procedures, and options for customizing their rooms. Similar to this, wearable technology is being used by airlines to offer customers personalized entertainment choices, in-flight meal selections based on dietary requirements, and real-time flight information (Muniz, et al., 2021). Additionally, to enhance tourist pleasure and engagement while maximizing operational efficiency, attractions and tour operators are implementing IoT devices to detect visitor movements, improve crowd flow, and provide tailored audio tours or augmented reality experiences (Torabi, et al., 2022). These illustrations show how individualized experiences and enhanced operating procedures provided by smart tourism technologies are revolutionizing the sector.

Improving Accessibility and Inclusivity Through Tech

Enhancing accessibility and inclusivity for travelers with special needs or impairments is made possible in large part by technology (Tlili, et al., 2021). Accessibility features in mobile apps and websites, like voice navigation, alternative text descriptions, and screen readers, allow people who are blind or visually impaired to independently book trips and obtain travel information (Montero, et al., 2023; Aguirre Montero, et al., 2023; Theofanous, et al., 2024). Additionally, real-time navigation direction, tactile feedback, and audio announcements are provided by wearable technology and Internet of Things sensors embedded in transportation hubs and tourist locations, making navigation easier for those with mobility impairments. Virtual reality technology also provides virtual tours and simulations that lower barriers and uncertainty by allowing people with sensory impairments to preview locations and lodging before making a reservation (Lam, et al., 2020; Theofanous, et al., 2024). Furthermore, in order to improve the infrastructure, services, and accommodations for travelers with disabilities, online platforms and community-driven initiatives are promoting greater inclusivity and equal access to travel experiences by educating the public about accessible travel options, exchanging resources, and encouraging collaboration among stakeholders (Dar, 2022; Chan & Agapito, 2022).

Tourism products are changing to meet the demands of a wider range of consumers thanks to initiatives like digital accessibility features, assistive technologies, and inclusive design (Scheyvens & Biddulph, 2018). The creation of infrastructure and accommodations that accommodate people with different abilities is guided by the concepts of inclusive design. Mobility aids, hearing aids, and braille signage are examples of assistive technologies that improve accessibility in transportation hubs, tourist destinations, and lodging facilities (Chan & Agapito, 2022). Furthermore, digital accessibility features guarantee equal access to travel opportunities and improve the inclusivity of tourism experiences by enabling people with disabilities to access and interact with online travel platforms, booking systems, and destination information through features like screen readers, captioning, and voice commands (Lam, et al., 2020; Chan & Agapito, 2022).

Managing Tourism Operations Efficiently

Technology enhances decision-making, efficiency, and workflows in the tourism industry. It also streamlines management and operations procedures (Giotis & Papadionysiou, 2022). For instance, data analytics technologies help organizations estimate demand, identify customer preferences, and optimize pricing strategies by analyzing massive amounts of data to extract relevant insights (Shmarkov, et al., 2019; Golja & Paulišić, 2021). Automation technologies reduce manual workloads and minimize errors by automating repetitive operations like inventory management, booking confirmations, and customer support questions. AI-driven systems also make use of machine learning algorithms to offer customized experiences, personalize marketing efforts, and allocate resources as efficiently as possible. In addition, cloud-based solutions enable real-time communication, centralize data management, and promote stakeholder engagement. These features ultimately optimize operational proficiency and improve the overall visitor experience in the tourist sector.

The tourism business may improve productivity, resource allocation, and decision-making by implementing automation, data analytics, and AI-driven solutions (Giotis & Papadionysiou, 2022). Automating repetitive operations reduces operating expenses and frees up personnel time. Examples of these duties include customer service and booking administration (Bayram, 2020). Large-scale data is analyzed by data analytics technologies in order to spot patterns, project demand, and improve pricing tactics (Shmarkov, et al., 2019). Artificial Intelligence (AI)-powered solutions leverage machine learning algorithms to customize marketing campaigns, suggest customized experiences, and maximize resource distribution, leading to enhanced operational efficiency and more informed decision-making across the tourism industry (Giotis & Papadionysiou, 2022; Sahar & Dar, 2024).

Overcoming Challenges and Ethical Considerations

Stakeholders in the industry must acknowledge and carefully analyze the problems and ethical issues raised by the extensive use of technology in the tourism sector (Dar, 2024). One issue is the "digital divide," which refers to how various groups' or areas' access to technology might worsen existing discrepancies in information availability and traveler engagement. Furthermore, when travel agencies gather and retain enormous volumes of personal information about visitors, issues about data security and privacy surface. These concerns center on the moral implications of data use, sharing, and protection.

The emergence of technology-driven platforms and sharing economy models in the travel industry, like Airbnb and Uber, have disrupted tourism ecosystems, resulting in difficulties with regulations, problems with tax evasion, and disputes with local communities over things like overtourism and the cost of housing. The possibility of job displacement in the tourism sector as a result of automation and AI-driven solutions is another ethical concern (Prahadeeswaran, 2023; Dar, 2024). Although technology can improve productivity and simplify processes, it can also result in job losses for employees whose jobs are automated. Furthermore, the use of technology in tourism operations makes businesses and tourists alike more vulnerable to cybersecurity concerns including ransomware attacks, data breaches, and online fraud.

There are moral conundrums with regard to the application of cutting-edge technologies in the travel industry, such as biometric scanning and facial recognition, which raise issues with privacy invasion, monitoring, and the exploitation of personal data (Gössling, 2021). In addition, the commercialization of local communities and cultural heritage through technology-mediated tourism experiences can lead to moral dilemmas with sustainability, authenticity, and civil interaction with host communities (Saleem, et al., 2024). The carbon footprint of technology infrastructure, including data centers and transportation networks, raises questions about environmental sustainability. Another problem is the impact of e-waste, which is produced by the quick turnover of electronic gadgets in the tourism industry.

When it comes to the adoption and application of technology in the tourism sector, transparency, accountability, inclusion, and sustainability must be given top priority in order to address these issues and ethical concerns (Dar, 2024). In order to create moral guidelines, rules, and best practices that protect the interests of all parties involved and maximize the transformative power of technology for the advancement of tourism and society as a whole, industry stakeholders, policy-makers, and civil society must work together (Buhalis, et al, 2019).

Issues such as data privacy, overtourism, digital divide, and the need for responsible innovation are critical considerations in the context of technology adoption in the tourism sector. Large volumes of personal data about tourists are collected and processed by tourism businesses, raising concerns about data privacy and requiring strong security measures to maintain compliance with privacy laws such as GDPR. In popular areas, overtourism exacerbates environmental degradation, overcrowding, and strain on local infrastructure and resources (Buhalis, et al, 2019). It is mostly caused by the ease with which travel may be booked using digital platforms. In order to combat overtourism, sustainable tourism management techniques are needed, such as stakeholder cooperation, tourist dispersion, and destination diversification (Souza, et al, 2020).

The digital gap disadvantages vulnerable populations with limited access to technology and online resources by exacerbating disparities in tourism engagement and information availability (Hassan & Quader, 2022). Enhancing digital literacy, boosting internet connectivity, and encouraging equitable access to technology for all populations are necessary steps toward closing the digital divide. Sustainable practices, ethical thinking (Dar, 2024), and community involvement are all necessary for responsible innovation in tourist technology to maximize positive effects on the environment, society, and culture while maximizing benefits to all parties involved (Dar, 2022).

Future Trends and Opportunities

Enhancing personalization, sustainability, and immersive experiences are likely to be the main focuses of future developments in technology-driven tourism advances (Yang & Wang, 2023). Through the use of AI algorithms and advanced data analytics, travel agencies will be able to provide highly personalized experiences and suggestions based on individual tastes (Alyasiri, et al., 2024). With the continued development of virtual reality and augmented reality technologies, passengers will be able to experience immersive previews of destinations, lodging, and activities. Furthermore, advancements in tourism technology will place an increasing focus on sustainability, with the goal of lowering environmental impact, encouraging responsible travel, and lowering carbon footprints (Wider, et al., 2023). This could involve the broad use of environmentally friendly technologies, like sustainable accommodation designs, green transportation options, and renewable energy sources. Furthermore, the use of blockchain technology has the potential to transform other facets of the tourist sector, such as safe and transparent transactions, identity validation, and safeguarding of travelers' confidential information (Díaz, et al., 2023). To suit the changing demands and tastes of passengers while maintaining ethical tourism practices, personalization, sustainability, and immersive experiences will be given priority in future technology-driven tourism advancements (Raji, et al., 2024).

As technology advances and changes the nature of travel, there are several new chances for cooperation, innovation, and expansion within the tourist sector (Raji, et al., 2024). The development of creative solutions that improve tourist experiences while advancing sustainability and inclusion can be achieved through cross-industry alliances, which bring together tourism companies with technology companies, sustainability organizations, and local communities (Ariza-Colpas, et al., 2023). More flexibility, diversity, and affordability in lodging options are made possible by the chances for cooperation that the sharing economy's emergence offers between established travel agencies and peer-to-peer platforms (Troisi, et al., 2023; Fahlevi, 2023). Additionally, the incorporation of cutting-edge technologies like blockchain, AI, and IoT creates new opportunities for innovation in fields like smart destination management, customized experiences, and environmentally friendly travel methods (^{2}Dar & Kashyap, 2023).

The limit of technology in the tourism sector goes wider as there are opportunities for growth through destination diversification, as emerging markets and lesser-known destinations gain prominence and attract travelers seeking unique and authentic experiences (Farid, et al., 2023). Likewise, collaboration with government agencies and policymakers can facilitate the development of supportive regulatory frameworks, infrastructure investments, and destination management strategies that foster sustainable growth and mitigate challenges such as overtourism. Overall, emerging opportunities for collaboration, innovation, and growth within the tourism industry are vast and diverse, offering stakeholders the chance to leverage technology, sustainability, and community engagement to create more resilient, inclusive, and enjoyable travel experiences for travelers worldwide (Dar, 2022).

CONCLUSION

The book chapter examines how technology is revolutionizing the travel and tourism sector in a number of ways. It demonstrates how destination marketing methods have changed as a result of digital platforms, social media, and virtual reality, increasing engagement and motivating travel decisions. The chapter also covers how wearables, mobile apps, and Internet of Things (IoT) devices can enhance the entire consumer experience by personalizing services. Additionally, it discusses how crucial inclusive design, assistive technology, and digital accessibility features are to guaranteeing that people with special needs or impairments have equitable access to travel possibilities. The chapter also looks at how technology streamlines workflows, increases productivity, and permits data-driven decision-making in the operations and administration of tourism. Throughout the discussion, the chapter emphasizes the need for responsible innovation that prioritizes sustainability, inclusivity, and ethical considerations to redefine success in the tourism sector in the digital age.

Technology is changing the tourism industry, and embracing this change will help stakeholders develop, adapt, and prosper in a digital environment that is changing quickly. Tourism companies may improve consumer experiences, expedite processes, and advance sustainability by utilizing technology. Technology also makes individualized services possible, promotes inclusion, and creates new avenues for growth and collaboration. It is not only advantageous, but also necessary to stay competitive and resilient in the face of changing traveler demands and expectations in order to shape a more sustainable and inclusive tourism business going forward. This is especially true in the highly competitive tourist industry of today.

To ensure the tourism industry's long-term success and resilience, stakeholders must be encouraged to prioritize sustainability, inclusion, and responsible innovation in their technology-driven efforts. Stakeholders may limit harmful effects on the environment, society, and culture while maximizing positive outcomes for all by embracing responsible innovation, fostering diversity, and implementing sustainable practices. Travelers, host communities, and future generations will all gain from our collaborative efforts to build a more inventive, egalitarian, and sustainable tourism environment. For a better future, let's give sustainability, inclusivity, and responsible innovation top priority in our technology-driven projects.

REFERENCES

Aguirre Montero, A., Hernández Sales, L., Youbi Idrissi, M., & López Sánchez, J. A. (2023). Web accessibility and inclusivity of tourist destinations at social media management. *An intercultural analysis of Andalusia and Northern Morocco.*

Alyasiri, O. M., Selvaraj, K., Younis, H. A., Sahib, T. M., Almasoodi, M. F., & Hayder, I. M. (2024). A Survey on the Potential of Artificial Intelligence Tools in Tourism Information Services. *Babylonian Journal of Artificial Intelligence*, 2024, 1–8. DOI: 10.58496/BJAI/2024/001

Arici, H. E., Saydam, M. B., & Koseoglu, M. A. (2023). How do customers react to technology in the hospitality and tourism industry? *Journal of Hospitality & Tourism Research (Washington, D.C.)*, 10963480231168609.

Ariza-Colpas, P. P., Piñeres-Melo, M. A., Morales-Ortega, R. C., Rodriguez-Bonilla, A. F., Butt-Aziz, S., Naz, S., del Carmen Contreras-Chinchilla, L., Romero-Mestre, M., & Ascanio, R. A. V. (2023). Augmented Reality and Tourism: A Bibliometric Analysis of New Technological Bets in the Post-COVID Era. *Sustainability (Basel)*, 15(21), 15358. DOI: 10.3390/su152115358

Babu, S., & Subramoniam, S. (2016). Tourism management in internet of things era. *Journal of Information Technology and Economic Development*, 7(1).

Bayram, G. E. (2020). Impact of information technology on tourism. In *The emerald handbook of ICT in tourism and hospitality* (pp. 243–257). Emerald Publishing Limited. DOI: 10.1108/978-1-83982-688-720201015

Buhalis, D., Harwood, T., Bogicevic, V., Viglia, G., Beldona, S., & Hofacker, C. (2019). Technological disruptions in services: Lessons from tourism and hospitality. *Journal of Service Management*, 30(4), 484–506. DOI: 10.1108/JOSM-12-2018-0398

Çeltek, E., & İhan, . (2018). Innovations in destination marketing. In *The Routledge handbook of destination marketing* (pp. 417–428). Routledge. DOI: 10.4324/9781315101163-32

Chan, C. S., & Agapito, D. (2022). Managing destination experience design for tourists with disabilities: ICT and accessibility. In *Handbook on the Tourist Experience* (pp. 226–245). Edward Elgar Publishing.

Chung, N., Tyan, I., & Han, H. (2017). Enhancing the smart tourism experience through geotag. *Information Systems Frontiers*, 19(4), 731–742. DOI: 10.1007/s10796-016-9710-6

Dar, H. (2022). Conceptualizing the smart community in the ages of smart tourism: A literature perspective. *Revista Turismo & Desenvolvimento (RT&D)/Journal of Tourism & Development*, (39).

Dar, H. (2024). Sustainable Measures Deterring Ethical and Decent Dilemmas in Tourism. In *Managing Tourism and Hospitality Sectors for Sustainable Global Transformation* (pp. 219–229). IGI Global. DOI: 10.4018/979-8-3693-6260-0.ch016

Dar, H., & Kashyap, K. (2023a). Indian Medical Tourism: COVID-19 Situation, Planning and Reviving Approaches. In *Tourism and Hospitality in Asia: Crisis, Resilience and Recovery* (pp. 97–111). Springer Nature Singapore.

Dar, H., & Kashyap, K. (2023b). Smart healthcare system (SHS): Medical tourism delivering, consumption, and elevating tool in the ages of smart technologies. *Tourism Planning & Development*, 20(3), 397–415. DOI: 10.1080/21568316.2022.2109206

Díaz, E., Esteban, Á., Koutra, C., Almeida, S., & Carranza, R. (2023). Co-creation of value in smart ecosystems: Past trends and future directions in tourism literature. *Journal of Hospitality and Tourism Technology*, 14(3), 365–383. DOI: 10.1108/JHTT-04-2021-0122

Ekka, P. M., & Dhall, R. (2023). Technology, destination marketing and tourism: What, why and way forward. *Smart Tourism*, 4(2), 2447. DOI: 10.54517/st.v4i2.2447

Fahlevi, M. (2023). A Systematic Literature Review on Marine Tourism in Business Management: State of the Art and Future Research Agenda. *Journal of Tourism and Services*, 14(27), 299–321. DOI: 10.29036/jots.v14i27.549

Farid, S., Boudia, M. A., & Mwangi, G. (2023). Revolutionizing Tourism: Harnessing the Power of IoT in Smart Destinations. *Journal of Digital Marketing and Communication*, 3(2), 91–99. DOI: 10.53623/jdmc.v3i2.360

García-Madurga, M. Á., & Grilló-Méndez, A. J. (2023). Artificial Intelligence in the tourism industry: An overview of reviews. *Administrative Sciences*, 13(8), 172. DOI: 10.3390/admsci13080172

Giotis, G., & Papadionysiou, E. (2022). The role of managerial and technological innovations in the Tourism industry: A review of the empirical literature. *Sustainability (Basel)*, 14(9), 5182. DOI: 10.3390/su14095182

Golja, T., & Paulišić, M. (2021). Managing-technology enhanced tourist experience: The case of scattered hotels in Istria. *Management*, 26(1), 63–95. DOI: 10.30924/mjcmi.26.1.5

Gössling, S. (2021). Tourism, technology and ICT: A critical review of affordances and concessions. *Journal of Sustainable Tourism*, 29(5), 733–750. DOI: 10.1080/09669582.2021.1873353

Hassan, H. K., & Quader, M. S. (2022). Tourism Events, Festivals and Digital Technology Applications in Asia: Socio-Cultural Drawbacks and Ways to Overcome. In *Technology Application in Tourism Fairs, Festivals and Events in Asia* (pp. 345–362). Springer Singapore. DOI: 10.1007/978-981-16-8070-0_21

Lam, K. L., Chan, C. S., & Peters, M. (2020). Understanding technological contributions to accessible tourism from the perspective of destination design for visually impaired visitors in Hong Kong. *Journal of Destination Marketing & Management*, 17, 100434. DOI: 10.1016/j.jdmm.2020.100434

Li, P., Zhou, Y., & Huang, S. (2023). Role of information technology in the development of e- tourism marketing: A contextual suggestion. *Economic Analysis and Policy*, 78, 307–318. DOI: 10.1016/j.eap.2023.03.010

Marasco, A., Buonincontri, P., Van Niekerk, M., Orlowski, M., & Okumus, F. (2018). Exploring the role of next-generation virtual technologies in destination marketing. *Journal of Destination Marketing & Management*, 9, 138–148. DOI: 10.1016/j.jdmm.2017.12.002

Montero, A. A., Sales, L. H., Idrissi, M. Y., & López-Sánchez, J. A. (2023). Web accessibility and inclusivity of tourist destinations at social media management. An intercultural analysis of Andalusia and Northern Morocco. *Universal Access in the Information Society*, •••, 1–17. DOI: 10.1007/s10209-023-01020-y

Muniz, E. C. L., Dandolini, G. A., Biz, A. A., & Ribeiro, A. C. (2021). Customer knowledge management and smart tourism destinations: A framework for the smart management of the tourist experience–SMARTUR. *Journal of Knowledge Management*, 25(5), 1336–1361. DOI: 10.1108/JKM-07-2020-0529

Phutela, N. (2022). Drivers of Customer Experience (CX) in Smart Tourism-A Qualitative Study. *Journal of Positive School Psychology*, 6(2), 871–881.

Prahadeeswaran, R. (2023). A Comprehensive Review: The Convergence of Artificial Intelligence and Tourism. *International Journal for Multidimensional Research Perspectives*, 1(2), 12–24.

Qumsieh-Mussalam, G., & Tajeddini, K. (2019). Innovation in tourism destination marketing. In *Tourism, hospitality and digital transformation* (pp. 165–174). Routledge. DOI: 10.4324/9780429054396-10

Raji, M. A., Olodo, H. B., Oke, T. T., Addy, W. A., Ofodile, O. C., & Oyewole, A. T. (2024). Digital marketing in tourism: A review of practices in the USA and Africa. *International Journal of Applied Research in Social Sciences*, 6(3), 393–408. DOI: 10.51594/ijarss.v6i3.896

Rane, N., Choudhary, S., & Rane, J. (2023). Sustainable tourism development using leading-edge Artificial Intelligence (AI), Blockchain, Internet of Things (IoT), Augmented Reality (AR) and Virtual Reality (VR) technologies. *Blockchain, Internet of Things (IoT), Augmented Reality (AR) and Virtual Reality (VR) technologies.*

Sahar, S. N., & Dar, H. (2024). Artificial Intelligence-Enhanced Global Healthcare: The Future of Medical Tourism. In *Impact of AI and Robotics on the Medical Tourism Industry* (pp. 194-216). IGI Global.

Saleem, M., Shah, M. J., Wajid, M., Akhter, M., & Malik, J. A. (2024). A Comprehensive Study of AI and IoT's Impact on Smart Tourism Destinations. *Journal of Computing & Biomedical Informatics*.

Scheyvens, R., & Biddulph, R. (2018). Inclusive tourism development. *Tourism Geographies*, 20(4), 589–609. DOI: 10.1080/14616688.2017.1381985

Shin, H. H., Shin, S., & Gim, J. (2023). Looking back three decades of hospitality and tourism technology research: A bibliometric approach. *International Journal of Contemporary Hospitality Management*, 35(2), 563–588. DOI: 10.1108/IJCHM-03-2022-0376

Shmarkov, M. S., Shmarkova, L. I., & Shmarkova, E. A. (2019, May). Digital technologies in the organization and management of tourist organizations. In *1st International Scientific Conference" Modern Management Trends and the Digital Economy: from Regional Development to Global Economic Growth"(MTDE 2019)* (pp. 98-101). Atlantis Press. DOI: 10.2991/mtde-19.2019.18

Sinha, R., Hassan, A., & Ghosh, R. K. (2020). Changes in tourism destination promotion with the technological innovation. In *The Emerald handbook of ICT in tourism and hospitality* (pp. 213–228). Emerald Publishing Limited. DOI: 10.1108/978-1-83982-688-720201014

Sorokina, E., Wang, Y., Fyall, A., Lugosi, P., Torres, E., & Jung, T. (2022). Constructing a smart destination framework: A destination marketing organization perspective. *Journal of Destination Marketing & Management*, 23, 100688. DOI: 10.1016/j.jdmm.2021.100688

Souza, V. S., Marques, S. R. B. D. V., & Veríssimo, M. (2020). How can gamification contribute to achieve SDGs? Exploring the opportunities and challenges of ecogamification for tourism. *Journal of Hospitality and Tourism Technology*, 11(2), 255–276. DOI: 10.1108/JHTT-05-2019-0081

Sustacha, I., Banos-Pino, J. F., & Del Valle, E. (2023). The role of technology in enhancing the tourism experience in smart destinations: A meta-analysis. *Journal of Destination Marketing & Management*, 30, 100817. DOI: 10.1016/j.jdmm.2023.100817

Theofanous, G., Thrassou, A., & Uzunboylu, N. (2024). Digital Inclusivity: Advancing Accessible Tourism via Sustainable E-Commerce and Marketing Strategies. *Sustainability (Basel)*, 16(4), 1680. DOI: 10.3390/su16041680

Tlili, A., Altinay, F., Altinay, Z., & Zhang, Y. (2021). Envisioning the future of technology integration for accessible hospitality and tourism. *International Journal of Contemporary Hospitality Management*, 33(12), 4460–4482. DOI: 10.1108/IJCHM-03-2021-0321

Torabi, Z. A., Shalbafian, A. A., Allam, Z., Ghaderi, Z., Murgante, B., & Khavarian-Garmsir, A. R. (2022). Enhancing memorable experiences, tourist satisfaction, and revisit intention through smart tourism technologies. *Sustainability (Basel)*, 14(5), 2721. DOI: 10.3390/su14052721

Troisi, O., Visvizi, A., & Grimaldi, M. (2023). Digitalizing business models in hospitality ecosystems: Toward data-driven innovation. *European Journal of Innovation Management*, 26(7), 242–277. DOI: 10.1108/EJIM-09-2022-0540

Wider, W., Gao, Y., Chan, C. K., Lin, J., Li, J., Tanucan, J. C. M., & Fauzi, M. A. (2023). Unveiling trends in digital tourism research: A bibliometric analysis of co-citation and co-word analysis. *Environmental and Sustainability Indicators*, 20, 100308. DOI: 10.1016/j.indic.2023.100308

Yang, F. X., & Wang, Y. (2023). Rethinking metaverse tourism: A taxonomy and an agenda for future research. *Journal of Hospitality & Tourism Research (Washington, D.C.)*. DOI: 10.1177/10963480231163509

Zhang, Y., Sotiriadis, M., & Shen, S. (2022). Investigating the impact of smart tourism technologies on tourists' experiences. *Sustainability (Basel)*, 14(5), 3048. DOI: 10.3390/su14053048

Chapter 9
Sentiment Analysis and Machine Learning for Tourism Feedback Data Analysis:
An Overview of Trends, Techniques, and Applications

Dhivya Bino
Middle East College, Oman

V. Dhanalakshmi
Sultan Qaboos University, Oman

Prakash Kumar Udupi
Middle East College, Oman

ABSTRACT

This chapter gives a bird's eye view of the different approaches and techniques for applying machine learning and sentiment analysis models on tourism review data. The literature review section examines different approaches and frameworks for sentiment analysis with respect to the tourism sector. The methodology followed includes the basic implementation of different techniques of sentiment analysis and machine learning. The sentiment analysis has been performed using a transformer-based model on a data set of user feedback publicly available from Kaggle. Its performance was evaluated using accuracy, precision, recall, and F1 score, and results were found to be comparable with similar studies done. The chapter also includes a demonstration of feature extraction using lexicon-based method as well

DOI: 10.4018/979-8-3693-5678-4.ch009

as performance comparison of different machine learning algorithms. The insights gained from these analyses can be useful for businesses, governments, and individuals connected with the tourism sector, aiding them in making decisions influenced by public sentiment.

INTRODUCTION

The tourism industry has a major impact on all the development goals of a nation. A thriving tourism sector acts as a powerful driver for a nation's economic growth contributing to revenue generation through foreign exchange, aiding job creation and infrastructure development (Rasool et al., 2021). It also generates cultural appreciation creating an overall positive global image for a nation. Hence developing the tourism sector through diverse mechanisms is a key strategic direction and a policy priority for countries worldwide. Expanding the tourist base requires well thought of actions including rolling out new tourism products and services that cater to different interest groups, running effective marketing and promotional activities, and ensuring memorable experiences for the tourists. Traveler experiences are influenced by multiple factors, a) the product itself which is no longer based on traditional sight-seeing model but on a repackaged format which falls in different categories like nature tourism, cultural tourism, adventure tourism, medical/wellness tourism, gastronomic tourism to name a few. b) services that are linked to these products like smooth visa processing, convenient modes of transportation networks (air, rail, road, sea), comfortable hotel and lodging facilities, good quality communication systems and utilities (internet, electricity, water supply), food and hospitality, safety and security, multilingual language support. c)Eco friendly facilities that emphasize sustainability also play a key role in the travelers' experience all together. Jabbar et al (2022) summarizes these under the umbrella categories of a) Attractions b) Amenities and c) Accessibility.

Significance of Sentiment Analysis and Its Practical Applications for Tourism Industry

It's imperative that all involved in the tourism ecosystem are provided with timely and accurate feedback on their products and services to add extra value and attain competitive advantage. Different stakeholders like tourism ministries, travel agencies and restaurants are keen to find out what tourists think about their products and services at the individual and public level. Such opinions act as measuring rods using which the service providers gauge the effectiveness of their services, improve themselves and emerge as key players in the market. It is in this context that Sentimental Analysis (SA) is presented, a case of Natural Language Processing, a subfield of Artificial Intelligence that is gaining traction. SA seeks to understand the "opinions" or "sentiments" of people through analyzing their feedback which is expressed in a natural language format typically considered as unstructured format in computer terms. SA has the potential to overhaul tourism businesses and their management by making it more efficient, personalized and accessible for everyone.

Traditionally, various participants of tourism industry resorted to 'pull' technology wherein the feedback of tourists was sought explicitly through surveys, observation, interviews and so on and analyzed manually. However, these days, due to the exponential use of social media and proliferation of websites like TripAdvisor and apps that facilitate computerized customer feedback collection, customer opinion is 'pushed' to the service providers without the need of initiating a manual feedback collection. Such opinions can be expressed through multiple modalities (text, image, audio, video) and can indicate their emotions, attitudes, beliefs (in short how they feel) about a specific individual, product, service, event, or organization related to their tourism experience. In fact, opinion related to travel and tourism is one of the most expressed types of feedback that can be found on social media these days. User generated content (UGC) available on social media and on other travel related apps are trustworthy opinion of customers representing their true sentiments regarding their experiences because most of the times they are given impromptu without any kind of nudging. However, since they are not subjected to any kind of approvals, the veracity of opinion is also often thought to be questionable and subjective even though Jabbar et al.(2022) indicates that such reviews can be reliable.

Sentimental analysis, data analysis and machine learning play an important role in enhancing customer experience, planning of strategies and optimizing operational efficiencies in tourism industries. Using these analysis, tourism businesses and governments can become profitable by understanding valuable insights into travelers' need, preference, concern, behavior and satisfaction. These user sentiments are not only useful for various service providers of tourism industry but also influence the tourists' decision making regarding a place they should travel or in choosing other related services. Thomaz et al. (2016) as cited in Renganathan & Upadhya (2021) show that the opinions of other tourists particularly the ones expressed through social media play an impactful role in influencing the tourism related purchases of people.

Collecting real time feedback for improving services would be the first step as part of a real-world application of sentiment analysis and machine learning in tourism. By monitoring social media and feedback from review sites, tourism service providers can identify common issues and areas for improvements. Tools such as Talkwalker and Brandwatch can be used to analyze travel related social media information and to understand customer sentiments.

Enhancing customer experience is one of the practical examples of using sentimental analysis and machine learning in tourism industries. Based on data collections and algorithmic learning implementations, recommendations are generated, which helps the tourists to focus better on their tourism requirements thereby enhancing customer engagement. Platforms such as Expedia and TripAdvisor use machine learning for analyzing customer preferences and history and suggest personalized options for each traveler.

Marketing strategy optimization is another important application for the tourism sector based on sentiment analysis and machine learning. Targeted advertising extensively uses machine learning and sentiment analysis for customer segmentation, targeted campaigns, programmatic advertising and email marketing there by helping to increase return on investments (ROI) for tourism business. Platforms such as Google Ads use various data and information to deliver targeted ads to the customer or user based on their behavior and interests to deliver the right offers and promotions to right customers.

Operational efficiency improvement is another key aspect, which can be achieved by sentiment analysis and machine learning in tourism industries. Analyzing occupancy rates, booking data, queries and email data can help to allocate and manage resources efficiently which helps to achieve better customer satisfaction.

The study conducted by Kusumawardani et al. (2024) using Indonesian tourism review data evidence the significance of SA in helping the governments in effective utilization of funds for the implementation of national level policies aimed at improving the tourist sector. This study found that there were differences in public attitudes pre and post covid towards priority destinations. They also discovered that the main aspects frequently discussed by tourists included food, scenery, staff, some specific attractions like temples. They further found out which tourist destination received the greatest number of positive reviews, helping them understand the most popular tourist destination. Based on understanding customer sentiments properly, this study concluded that government funds can be channelized effectively for the advancement of the places classified strategically as super priority destinations.

In short, advances in sentiment analysis can greatly benefit the tourism sector, where analyzing online reviews and social media posts provides deep insights into consumer behavior. This can lead to improved decision-making particularly with respect to modifying marketing and sales strategies including better recommendation systems, enhanced customer relationship and experience, overall social media reputation as well as brand management (Manosso & Domareski Ruiz, 2021). SA has become essential for businesses to understand public sentiment and make informed decisions. While machine learning has enhanced the precision of these analyses, the rise of big data and social media has driven the need for sophisticated analytical methods. The COVID-19 pandemic further underscored the importance of sentiment analysis in adapting to changing tourist behaviors and refining industry strategies.

Tourism Feedback Platforms

Tourism Review feedback platforms are vital in collecting, analyzing and utilizing tourist opinions. These range from sites dedicated to travel and tourism like TripAdvisor to general purpose products like Facebook and Instagram. They differ in the type and nature of data and the purpose for which it is collected, depth of analysis and mode of presentations. Some of the key characteristics are given below.

Booking Websites and Apps. TripAdvisor, Booking, AirBnB, Yelp and Agoda, Expedia, VirtualTourist, LonelyPlanet are some popular sites that enable tourists to book tourism related products and services. Their popularity and extent of use might vary depending on geographical location or specific category of users. There is no clear evidence indicating who is the most dominant player in the market even though some studies point out that TripAdvisor could be the most popular one. These sites also facilitate feedback collection on the services availed.

Tripadvisor collects qualitative (written reviews, photographs) and quantitative data(ratings). The reviews are collected on multiple aspects like accommodation, restaurants and tourist attractions. The platform also employs ranking machine learning algorithms which prioritize listings based on volume, recency and quality of user experience based on the review. Because of the anonymity of the reviews and the lack of necessary controls to verify the authenticity of the user, the veracity of the feedback data collected is often questionable, however due to their specific reputation management system, the number of reliable reviews overpowers fake reviews (Fuentes et al., 2018).

Booking.Com primarily collects reviews from users on accommodations who have actually completed a stay. Data includes ratings on different aspects like cleanliness, comfort and service. Since only verified users can leave reviews, the feedback is highly credible. Unlike TripAdvisor which collects feedback in a free format, Booking.com encourages users to provide both positive and negative comments (Fuentes et al., 2018). It also provides complex search facilities wherein tourists can filter facilities based on feedback on specific aspects like solo travel or cleanliness or budget.

Airbnb collects mutual reviews from both tourists and service providers which includes both quantitative ratings and qualitative detailed written feedback. The dual review system by both the guests and the hosts promotes accountability on both sides.

Yelp offers similar feedback collection mechanism as others mentioned above; however, they attempt to segregate authentic reviews from fake and biased reviews using their advanced machine learning algorithms. Detailed demographic data of the users is collected along with the review to provide better context and improve credibility.

Microblogging and Social Media Platforms. Facebook, X(previously Twitter), Instagram are some of the most popular platforms where feedback related to travel experiences is shared casually. The content related to travel is shared in an unstructured format in the form of status updates, tweets, posts and reels. Since platforms like TripAdvisor are specifically designed for travel related services and the feedback collected is more structured, the analysis and comparison of products and services is much easier. Also, the data quality and veracity is higher because of additional inbuilt verification systems. They also enable Aspect based SA since feedback collection also focuses on specific aspects like accommodation, food and so on. However, social media and microblogging platforms have a larger audience which utilized properly can help tourism businesses and governments to tap into a large pool of tourists and their preferences.

LITERATURE REVIEW

Sentiment Analysis as a Subfield of Natural Language Processing

AI, a branch of Computer Science encompasses various theoretical frameworks, technologies and techniques that enable computers to behave like human beings. In other words, it aims to build 'intelligent' and 'smart' devices that can mimic different sensory, physical, and intellectual capabilities of human beings. The combination of Robotics (Zlatanov & Popesku, 2019), Computer Vision (Zhang et al., 2024) and Natural Language Processing (NLP) (Alvarez-Carmona et al., 2022), three main subfields of AI is creating new horizons for businesses including the tourism industry. NLP makes devices human language proficient whereby they can interpret and respond to both oral and written communications in a useful manner for human beings. Like any other revolutionary technology, NLP based tools ease tasks based on human-human communication via human-machine communication. Techniques like tokenization, named entity recognition, syntactic parsing and part of speech tagging are commonly engaged for NLP based tasks. Information Extraction, Language Translation, Text Classification and Summarization and SA are some applications based on NLP (Khurana et al., 2022). In fact, SA, a particular category of Text Mining/Classification domain "is the computational process of understanding the emotions and attitudes of people expressed through their opinion regarding a particular experience or concept (Liu, 2012).

SA essentially identifies the polarity and intensity of emotions in the feedback and quantifies it for appropriate classification. Most of the research work aims at projecting SA as a binary classification task which determines whether an opinion is positive or negative. Some studies have attempted ternary classification of sentiments as positive, negative and neutral whereas certain others have focused on multi classification of sentiments as happy, sad, angry, bored and so on which comes under the umbrella of emotion detection. However, as indicated by Nandwani & Verma (2021) understanding the right emotion behind a written text is a challenging task even for human beings with chances of wrong interpretation being quite high. The right interpretation of the intent hidden in a text/ opinion depends on multiple factors like the type of words used, its contextual use, symbols and emojis showing expressions, tones based on sentence construction. Sentiment analysis as a computational problem therefore is a complex phenomenon with its roots in computing, psychology and linguistics and statistics.

Foundations and Evolution of Sentiment Analysis

The evolution of sentiment analysis has been fundamentally shaped by pioneering research, which established the theoretical and methodological frameworks that underpin current advancements in the field. Early work by Osgood et al. (1975), on the relationship between language and sentiment laid the groundwork by investigating how linguistic elements convey emotions, a precursor to what would later be formalized as sentiment analysis.

The early 2000s marked a significant turning point with the introduction of key methodologies by researchers like Turney et al. (2002) and Pang et al. (2002). Their pivotal contributions focused on opinion polarity, utilizing techniques such as unsupervised learning to classify text as positive, negative, or neutral. This period also saw the application of sentiment analysis primarily to product and service reviews, providing a practical context for these emerging methodologies.

Technological advancements, particularly in machine learning (ML) and natural language processing (NLP), have played a critical role in advancing the field. Early ML techniques, including Naive Bayes classifiers, provided a foundation for sentiment classification. The subsequent introduction of deep learning models significantly enhanced the precision and scalability of sentiment analysis, enabling more complex and context-aware sentiment detection.

One such pioneering advancement came with the introduction of deep learning techniques like Convolutional Neural Networks (CNN) and Recursive Neural Networks (RNN), which transformed the way sentiment is analyzed in text. Socher et al.

(2013) was among the first to apply recursive neural networks to sentiment analysis, enabling more sophisticated and context-sensitive interpretation of sentiments. This work marked a significant shift towards deep learning approaches, which have since become central to the field. Another pioneering technology is the introduction of BERT (Bidirectional Encoder Representations from Transformers) by Devlin et al. (2019). BERT set new standards in context-aware sentiment analysis by capturing the nuances of word usage in different contexts, thereby improving the accuracy and depth of sentiment analysis across various applications. In the specific context of tourism, recent research by Ni et al. (2024) has further advanced sentiment analysis by proposing a hybrid approach that combines lexicon-based methods with active learning support vector machines. This method addresses the challenges of big data in tourism, providing enhanced precision in sentiment classification and making it highly relevant for analyzing large volumes of user-generated content on platforms like social media.

Interdisciplinary approaches have further enriched sentiment analysis, incorporating insights from fields such as linguistics, psychology, and cognitive science. This integration has facilitated the development of more sophisticated models capable of handling multimodal and conversational data, expanding the applicability of sentiment analysis to complex real-world scenarios such as user profiling and mental health monitoring.

The explosion of social media has introduced new challenges and opportunities, necessitating the development of advanced tools capable of real-time sentiment analysis across massive datasets. The integration of Graph Neural Networks (GNNs) represents a significant evolution in sentiment analysis techniques, providing enhanced interpretability and the ability to model intricate data structures.

Recent advancements in Sentiment Analysis (SA) have significantly enhanced the ability to interpret and leverage large volumes of textual and multimodal data. Additionally, the exploration of temporal dynamics in sentiment has highlighted the importance of understanding how sentiment evolves in response to specific events, adding a temporal dimension to traditional sentiment analysis frameworks.

The development of sentiment analysis, particularly within the field of natural language processing (NLP), has been significantly shaped by several pioneering research papers that introduced innovative methodologies based on machine learning, deep learning as well as hybrid techniques advancing the field's capabilities. These trends are particularly relevant to the tourism sector, where understanding tourist sentiments is crucial for improving services and maintaining a positive reputation. The foundational studies and subsequent technological innovations have established a robust, multifaceted framework for sentiment analysis. This framework continues to drive current research trends, fostering the ongoing evolution of the field and expanding its application across various domains, including social media analytics, political discourse, and consumer behavior analysis.

Sentiment Analysis Approaches and Frameworks

Sentiment analysis has been explored on multiple levels: Document Level, Sentence Level, Phrase Level, and Aspect Level (Wankhade et al., 2022). At each of these levels, sentiment analysis examines opinions and emotions with varying degrees of granularity.

Document Level Sentiment Analysis. Document level SA views one document as an individual unit attaching a single polarity for classifying it as positive or negative. In the tourism sector, document-level sentiment analysis serves as a powerful tool for evaluating customer feedback from diverse sources such as travel blogs, review websites, and social media platforms. For instance, a tourism board aiming to understand the overall perception of a newly promoted tourist destination can utilize this method to analyze comprehensive reviews and articles. This approach allows them to assess general sentiment and identify recurring themes, such as satisfaction with accommodations, dining experiences, and local attractions. The insights garnered from this analysis enable the tourism board to make informed decisions regarding marketing strategies and necessary improvements to enhance visitor experiences. The tourism-based websites such as Tripadvisor.com collect extensive reviews from popular travel websites, social media posts, and detailed travel blog entries. These sources provide a wealth of information at the document level, capturing a range of visitor experiences. Using document-level sentiment analysis, the management of TripAdvisor.com processes the entire content of each review and blog post to determine the overall sentiment. This involves analyzing the text to categorize it as positive, negative, or neutral and identifying common themes. The findings of the analysis could be either on accommodation or any other relevant aspect. Many reviews highlight satisfaction with the range and quality of hotels and vacation rentals, indicating a positive sentiment toward accommodations. Dining Experiences: Several travel blogs and reviews mention the diverse and high-quality dining options available, showing a strong positive sentiment in this area. Local Attractions: Reviews are mixed regarding local attractions. While some visitors enjoyed the historical sites and beaches, others felt there was a lack of engaging activities for families and children, revealing both positive and negative sentiments. Transport and Accessibility: Numerous reviews express frustration with the town's transportation options, including limited public transport and congested roads, indicating a negative sentiment in this aspect.

After the analysis, the management will delve into decision-Making. Based on the document-level sentiment analysis, the TripAdvisor board can make informed decisions to enhance the visitor experience such as bringing in marketing strategies to emphasize the positive aspects, such as high-quality accommodations and diverse dining options, in future marketing campaigns. Improvement Initiatives: Address the negative feedback by developing more family-friendly attractions and improving transportation infrastructure to make the town more accessible and enjoyable for visitors.

By leveraging document-level sentiment analysis, the tourism board gains comprehensive insights into visitor perceptions, enabling them to refine their strategies and improve the overall appeal of the coastal town as a tourist destination.

Sentence level document Analysis. Understanding the sentiment of individual ideas within text reveals specific opinions and emotions, offering valuable insights into the overall sentiment of a document. Sentence-level sentiment analysis categorizes sentences as positive, negative, or neutral, with refined categories like very positive, very negative, or mixed sentiment sentences. This process involves analyzing syntactic and semantic features of sentences using machine learning and natural language processing (NLP) techniques (Jamin Rahman Jim et al., 2024).

In the tourism industry, traditional review analysis can be challenging, often providing a broad picture leaving the management with limited insights into specific areas of guest satisfaction. Sentence-level sentiment analysis addresses this by examining individual experiences within reviews. For example, a chain of hotels aiming to personalize guest experiences can use this granular approach to delve deeper into feedback. Analyzing sentences individually allows for precise identification of aspects that resonate with guests and areas needing improvement. For instance, a review might highlight positive sentiments towards a swimming pool and gym but negative sentiments about wait times for additional services. Another review might praise the taste of food but criticize portion sizes. This targeted approach empowers tourism stakeholders to prioritize enhancements, personalize experiences, and enhance guest satisfaction by addressing frequent pain points and leveraging positive feedback. By translating guest feedback into actionable insights, sentence-level sentiment analysis paves the way for more personalized and enjoyable experiences, ultimately leading to increased satisfaction and loyalty.

Phrase level and aspect level sentiment Analysis. In the context of tourism analysis, aspect-level sentiment analysis and phrase-level sentiment analysis offer different granularities of understanding tourist feedback. Aspect-level sentiment analysis, also known as feature-based sentiment analysis, involves identifying sentiments about specific aspects or features of an entity within a text (Bansal & Kumar, 2021). Instead of providing an overall sentiment score for the entire text, this method breaks down the text into different aspects and determines the sentiment for each one individually. For instance, consider tourist reviews about Oman on a travel website. A review might mention various aspects such as the hospitality, natural scenery, and cultural experiences. Aspect-level sentiment analysis would identify and analyze sentiments for each of these aspects separately. For example, a review might state, "The hospitality in Oman is exceptional, but the cultural tours could be better organized." In this case, the analysis would reveal a positive sentiment towards hospitality and a negative sentiment towards cultural tours.

On the other hand, phrase-level sentiment analysis focuses on identifying the sentiment of specific phrases within a text (Wilson et al., 2009). It is more granular than document-level sentiment analysis but less detailed than aspect-level analysis. Phrase-level sentiment analysis identifies sentiments associated with phrases without necessarily linking them to specific aspects. Using the same tourist reviews about Oman, phrase-level sentiment analysis would identify sentiment expressed in phrases without categorizing them under specific aspects. For instance, the review "The hospitality in Oman is exceptional, but the cultural tours could be better organized" would be broken down into phrases such as "The hospitality in Oman is exceptional" and "the cultural tours could be better organized," with sentiments identified as positive and negative, respectively categorizing it as mixed sentiment.

To illustrate the practical application of these methods, consider a research study on sentiment analysis for online tourist reviews of Oman. The study would start with data collection, gathering a dataset of tourist reviews from various travel platforms. After preprocessing the data to remove noise like Hyper Text Markup Language(HTML) tags and special characters, the study would proceed with aspect-level sentiment analysis. This involves using natural language processing (NLP) techniques to identify different aspects mentioned in the reviews, such as hospitality, natural scenery, and cultural experiences, followed by applying a sentiment analysis model to classify the sentiment for each identified aspect. Concurrently, phrase-level sentiment analysis would break down the reviews into meaningful phrases and classify the sentiment for each phrase. In the comparative analysis, aspect-level analysis might reveal that sentiments towards Oman's hospitality are overwhelmingly positive, while cultural tours receive mixed reviews. Conversely, phrase-level analysis would provide a broader sentiment distribution within the text, highlighting that many phrases express positive sentiments, while a smaller proportion reflecting negative or neutral sentiments.

SA Framework/Methodology

For performing sentiment analysis, the mentioned steps given in Figure 1 are required though some of them might be combined or done parallelly depending on the quality of the available data sets and the performance and accuracy requirements.

Figure 1. Sentiment Analysis Steps

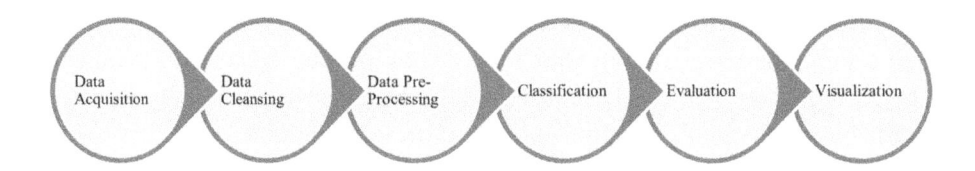

```
Data Acquisition → Data Cleansing → Data Pre-Processing → Classification → Evaluation → Visualization
```

Data Acquisition. This stage starts with the identification of the data sources from which data is extracted for further analyses. For instance, when a travel and tourism agency wants to assess public opinion of their services, they could target the data available from social media websites like FaceBook, X or Instagram or review websites like Trip Advisor or any other relevant text corpus. Data can be acquired by coding using appropriate programming software like Python or R. These utilize public Application Programming Interfaces (APIs) provided by the social media websites. By using the publicly available open source Tweepy library of the Python programming language, Leelawat et al.(2022) utilized Thailand tourism data available on X(Twitter) for conducting Sentiment analysis of tourism in Thailand during the COVID-19 pandemic. Another option is to do Web scraping as done by Nur et al.(2023), a mechanism by which patterned data usually in the form of tables or lists is extracted from webpages. It facilitates data extraction from multiple websites and search results. Such scraping tools also provide facilities like converting unstructured data to more structured format to be able to store in json databases or csv files. Screen Scraper, Web Harvey and Kimono are few examples of Webscraping software that provide both free and paid options, the free ones generally used by students/researchers while the paid ones utilized by business for commercial purposes (Haddaway, 2015). Both Adnan et al. (2019) & Khotimah & Sarno(2019) have scraped UGC using web Harvey from tourism sector review websites, Tripadvisor and Traveloka respectively as part of their research study that performed sentiment analysis on customer reviews on hotels/restaurants. Even though web scraping is by far, the most easiest, fastest and resource efficient means of data acquisition, the available data might be limited due to privacy policies governing the social media responsible use. So a third feasible mechanism would be to instead use the scraped and preprocessed data on the tourism sector provided by authorized data providers from data market places. Some of the popular data marketplaces include Amazon Webservices (AWS) Data Exchange, Microsoft Azure Marketplace, Google Cloud

Marketplace, Snowflake Data Market Place and IBM Cloud Pak for Data. By accessing vast amounts of data from reputable data provides all in one place, time and effort can be greatly saved.

Data Cleansing. This is a crucial step wherein the acquired data is cleansed by removing noise and transformed for further analysis. Noise is any discrepancy in the original data collected that can lead to decreased classification accuracy and biased results. The noise could be in the form of missing data values, erroneous data, wrongly labelled data and imbalanced data. The impact of wrongly classified data is much more than erroneous data values on the classification results (Hasan & Chu, 2022). In the context of text processing, unnecessary characters like punctuation or other special characters, URLs, non-alphanumeric characters, SPAM, ads related data are also considered as noise and must be removed. This process should also manage abbreviations and short forms. The work of Liu et al.(2022) points out that transformer based BERT model performs better in comparison to deep learning based CNN and FNN models with intrinsic noise and also highlights the significance of removing intrinsic noise for better accuracy of results.

Some common data cleaning techniques include the following stages.

1. Tokenization is the process of dividing text into subunits like individual characters or words or expressions or sentences suitable for deeper analysis(Choo & Kim, 2023). Different methods like white space tokenization, character tokenization, sentence tokenization, regular expression tokenization, unigram/bigram/n gram tokenization, PoS tokenization, Dictionary based tokenization treebank style, sentiment aware techniques can be used. The methods need to be chosen based on the required level of granularity and the type of analysis. White space tokenization is effective in case of languages with clear boundaries like English.
2. Stop Word removal

Any word that is insignificant in the context of NLP for a particular domain is considered as a stop Word and needs to be removed since they do not add value to analysis. They can also lead to inefficiency of the algorithm. Common stop words include words like "which", "is", "the", "and", "etc." .They occur very frequently in the text and are usually added for making text grammatically correct. There are different techniques for stop word removal. Comparison with precompiled stop wordlist and removing based on pattern matching, removing the most frequently occurring word, removing singleton and method based on word corpus are some common methods (Kaur & Buttar, 2018). NLTK library of the python programming language is commonly used which contains necessary classes and methods by which stop words can be removed easily. This is seen to be implemented by Leelawat et al.(2022) also as part of their research on sentiment classification of Thailand tourists. Special characters, URLs, any HTML tags or even proper words that do not make sense in the context (non-tourism data) also need to be removed.

3. Normalization is the process for reducing variation in the text by treating similar words identical, for instance, converting all text to lower case or uppercase. It can also include contraction or expansion whereby words like "don't" and "do not" are made consistent. The entire process improves consistency, thereby the accuracy of sentiment classification and analysis.
4. Stemming and Lemmatization is the process of reducing the words into their root form. Stemming cuts of prefixes and suffixes from a word based on some predefined rules whereas Lemmatization considers contextual information using morphological analysis and lexicon-based rules to reduce the word to its actual dictionary form. Lemmatization is more applicable in case of Sentiment analysis tasks and Word net Lemmatizer of python NLTK library is commonly used for carrying this out (Leelawat et al., 2022).
5. Part of Speech (PoS) Tagging is the process by which different words or phrases in a sentence are assigned the appropriate role it plays with respect to its context in the sentence. By grammatically classifying different words as nouns, verbs, adjectives and so on accurately, PoS tagging can reduce the error rates of the overall text classification task. Machine learning and deep learning based PoS techniques are found to improve accuracy and reduce false positive rates (Chiche & Yitagesu, 2022)
6. In the present generation, emojis and abbreviations are powerful indicators of sentiment compared to a normal text, however their meaning can vary depending on context. Managing abbreviations, slangs and negations and emojis and hashtags is challenge that needs to be addressed to improve the accuracy of sentiment classification. Emoji aware framework and techniques based on machine learning can significantly improve the performance of sentiment classification models(Alfreihat et al., 2024)

For a basic sentiment analysis, tokenization using white space followed by stop words removal (punction to start with) can be a foundational step. It can be combined with ngram (bigram or trigram) for capturing sentiments expressed through phrases topped with PoS tagging for further complex level of analysis.

Data Labelling. Following data cleaning, data needs to be labelled into the three basic categories for analysis as positive, negative and neutral. The quality of the labelled data can directly influence the accuracy of the results of sentiment analysis performed later. One option is to manually label the data set, use 80% of it to train the machine learning algorithm and use 20% of it to test/compare the performance of different algorithms. Leelawat et al.(2022) has followed this approach wherein 18,000 tweets out of the 150580 were assigned to different classification categories based on consensus of the 3 researchers involved. Such manual labelling which involves human annotators reading each line of text and assigning a label is very time consuming but the most accurate method. Clear guidelines should be provided to the various annotators in case of vast amounts of data to ensure that there is consistency followed in labelling and any human error is ruled out. It is also imperative to use metrics like Cohen's kappa to measure the level of agreement amongst the different annotators involved. In cases where manual labelling is impractical due to vast amounts of data and shortage of time and human resources, then automatic labelling can be carried out using pretrained sentiment analysis models. There are many annotation software tools. Doccano is such an open-source tool. Crowd sourcing is another option where companies like Amazon Mechanical Turk or Figure Eight with massive pool of employees can rapidly annotate huge data sets at cost effectively (Joshi et al., 2017)

Data Preprocessing. This stage is sometimes synonymous with Data Cleansing stage mentioned above or carried out separately depending on the type of classification algorithms used. Apart from the stages mentioned earlier as part of data cleansing, Feature selection and extraction is a main activity done as part of data preprocessing. Features are those words that are most indicative of sentiment in a text. For e.g. in the particular review sentence "The hotel ambience was out of the world, staff was friendly but room was a bit small", "out of the world, "Friendly" and "small" are potential features that can be extracted and represented numerically. There are different approaches like Bag of Words model, lexicon based models, unigrams, bigrams and N grams ("out of the world" since individually they would not make sense), POS tagging, TF-IDF and so on which are used traditionally. Term Frequency- Inverse Document Frequency (TF-IDF) method is used by Leelawat et al.(2022) in case of using SVM classifier which requires assigning numerical values to tokens corresponding to different feature sets. Document Term Matrix (DTM) to create a word of vectors which is followed by unigram and bigram feature extraction and term weighting using TF-IDF method is used by many researchers. DTM transforms a collection of documents or texts into a matrix where the different unique terms are highlighted with their frequency of occurrence at the intersection of a row and column. This is supposedly an efficient method for analyzing the term usage across the document set or review texts. However, Saraswathi et al.(2023) has pointed out that the traditional approaches do not perform well when performing challenging tasks like sentiment analysis and has proposed a linguistic rule based novel mechanism of feature extraction where filter-based feature selection method is combined with the wrapper-based forward feature selection method. The type of feature extraction method to be used depends on the type of text to be analyzed, the sentiment granularity expected and the availability of computational resources.

Apart from feature selection, in the case of using transformer models, it is a common practice to remove or truncate opinions with longer text for ensuring performance while training models. Again, data augmentation can also be performed to balance the dataset so that the performance of the model while training can be improved. Pérez Enríquez et al. (2022) used summarization approach for data augmentation on the Mexican tourist opinion data set obtained from Tripadvisor for doing a comparative analysis of the performance of classical machine learning approach, SVM with state of the art transformer based model.

Classification. The core of sentiment analysis lies in the selection and application of the appropriate classification algorithms to split the reviews into positive, neutral and negative and perform further analysis. Lexicon based, machine learning and deep learning and mixed approaches are commonly used by researchers for sentiment analysis tasks (Wankhade et al., 2022; Hashim et al., 2020). Of late, state of the art deep transformer-based approaches is providing promising results outperforming traditional approaches in accuracy.

1. Lexicon Based Approaches

Lexicons are prebuilt dictionaries which contain words and phrases along with their associated sentimental polarity and intensity. Polarity will be identified by labels of positive, negative and neutral whereas intensity will be denoted by attaching scores. Excellent and good are both positive words with excellent getting a higher score denoting its intensity. Lexicon based approaches generally use a rule-based framework which compares each word in the analyzed text with that of the lexicon. When a match is found, its sentiment score is added to the overall sentiment score. Based on the accumulated sentiment score, the sentence or the document is then classified as positive negative or neutral (Wankhade et al., 2022; Joshi et al., 2017). Among the two prominent lexicon based approaches, Dictionary based approach is considered more effective with many established dictionaries like Senticnet and SenticWordNet. Corpus based approach adds value by helping to discover contextual and domain focused sentiments (Akin Ozen, 2021).

2. Machine Learning and Deep Learning-Based Approaches

SA can be performed using machine learning (ML) based approaches offering better performance than pure lexicon-based approaches. Machine Learning uses labeled data to pretrain the algorithm to correctly classify a text (Lazrig & Humpherys, 2022). This comes under the category of Supervised machine learning.

Common algorithms include Naïve Bayes (NB), Support Vector Machine (SVM), Random Forest(RF) (Akin Ozen, 2021). Sentiment analysis of tourist reviews by Arun Wadhe & S. Suratkar (2020) compared the performance of different machine learning techniques NB, SVM and RF with the combination of feature extraction techniques of count vectorization and TF-IDF finding that TF-IDF with Random Forest classification achieved highest accuracy of 86%. Deep learning approaches like CNN and RNN provide better results when analyzing complex textual data. However, they are computationally expensive and require a much more amount of data for training in comparison to the traditional machine learning models. Transformer based models built on the neural network architecture are revolutionizing NLP tasks and SA. Pretrained models utilizing transfer learning made available by platforms like Hugging Face are also contributing significantly for advancing related research. Alonso-Mencía (2023) points out that Roberta, a particular implementation of the BERT model is effective for sentence level sentiment analysis, however different transformer-based models based on Roberta model can perform differently for classification of different variables and hence overall performance is heavily dependent on the right selection of the model.

Evaluation and Validation. A classification model must be evaluated using various metrics to ensure its effectiveness. A Confusion Matrix is widely employed for this purpose, which gives the total number of true positives, true negatives, false positives and false negatives. These values are further used for calculating other metrics like F1 score, accuracy, precision, recall among where accuracy is most often used. Receiver Operating Characteristic (ROC) metric provides the performance of the model at different classification thresholds and is helpful to find out the optimum threshold for a specific application (Bordoloi & Biswas, 2023)

Visualization. Depending on the level of SA performed, sentiment summarization will have to be undertaken to generate an overall sentiment. This can be done for document level or based on aspect levels. Sentiment visualization is a very useful subfield of Sentiment analysis that enables common users to make meaningful insights based on the analyzed opinions labels and scores., Some graphical models depict how sentiments towards a particular entity has evolved over time whereas some others highlight sentiments based on topics or aspects (Ameni Dhaoui Boumaiza, 2016)

Specific Challenges and Opportunities for Future Research

Despite great advancements, sentimental analysis and machine learning applications in the tourism industry also need to address various challenges. Some of these have already been touched upon in the previous section while discussing SA approaches and frameworks, however a more detailed discussion is provided in this section. This includes limitations directly arising from implementation of sentiment analysis processes. Understanding the context of data generally and with references to cultural differences, sarcasm, sentiments across different languages and dialects are quite challenging along with ethical issues such as data privacy and security. Wrong analyses stemming from low quality and less accurate data also could be a big limitation of sentiment analysis. Use of advanced NLP (Natural Language Processing) techniques are necessary to overcome these challenges which are often found to be very expensive. Some of the main challenges encountered and their potential solutions are covered below.

Multilingual Data. Tourism feedback data often comes from global sources involving multiple languages and dialects. Effective sentiment analysis hence becomes a complex process requiring machine understanding and learning of local expressions, slang and cultural nuances. Tourist feedback often contains mixed sentiments where they might praise one aspect of their experience (e.g., accommodation) while criticizing another (e.g. transportation). Sentiment analysis focused on assigning a single sentiment to an entire text or document may misrepresent true sentiments in this case.

Comprehensive labelled and annotated data sets supporting multiple languages are required for aiding multilingual SA. Also, this could add an extra layer of translation process if the final analysis is done in one base language or if the presentation layer of the system works in a different language than the one in which the feedback was originally collected. Mao et al. (2024) points out that this could have implications for the overall performance of the system. Ensemble of pretrained transformer-based BERT and GPT 3 models seems to achieve good accuracy in classifying translated texts while performing SA on multilingual data set of French, Chinese, Arabic and Italian (Ullah et al., 2024).

Metaphors, Sarcasm, Irony and colloquialism. Certain languages like English, Spanish, French are particularly rich in metaphors, sarcasm, irony and colloquialism owing to their cultural emphasis on humor, wit and social interaction whereas certain other languages like Arabic and Japanese use these more subtly reflecting cultural norms of politeness. Li et al.(2023) proposes a dual channel algorithm based on CNN and BiLSTM (bi directional Long Short Memory and attention mechanism to overcome the inaccuracy of semantic word vectors and the limitation of single neural networks in representing multiple associative features in this context. The model seems to be effective for creating more accurate and context aware word vectors for travel reviews in Chinese language.

Context and Ambiguity. The words and sentences expressing a sentiment can be highly context sensitive, leading to ambiguity. For example, a phrase like, "spine chilling experience" could be positive in the case of adventure tourism whereas negative in case of wellness tourism experience. Sentiment analysis algorithms often perform weakly in such contexts without additional information. Rezapour

(2024) claims that the traditional preprocessing methods like stop word and punctuation removal hinder the performance of transformer-based models in contextual understanding of words. So customized data preprocessing techniques depending on the SA methods employed can improve accuracy of the algorithm when faced with ambiguous data.

Sarcasm and Irony. Tourists may resort to using sarcasm and irony, especially if experiences are negative. This is more prominent when posting feedback using social media and microblogging sites because of the free format. The usage of positive words and phrases to denote a negative expression usually confuses traditional machine learning algorithms. Lack of an appropriate tone which facilitates sarcasm detection complicates the process. However, deep learning and transformer-based models (BERT) perform better in this context in comparison to traditional machine learning algorithms (Šandor & Bagić Babac, 2024).

Big Data (Rich and Unstructured Data). Tourism feedback data is characterized by the five Vs of Big Data i.e., Volume, Variety, Velocity, Veracity and Value which is highly complex for analysis. Data integration from various sources and platforms such as social media, email, feedback forms can create unstructured unreliable data. This can also lead to inconsistent data formats, imbalanced data, lack of meta data and platform specific data variations. Most of the sentiment analysis algorithms perform the analysis based only on the text feedback whereas the other type of data formats (text-structured and unstructured, audio, video, images) are often not taken into consideration by many. This leaves out the full picture of user experience limiting tourism service providers from tapping into valuable data. In such cases, application of Multimodal fusion techniques, the process of extracting, filtering and combining data features from different data sources is an additional step that needs to be implemented before SA (Gandhi et al., 2023). Any data that is missing, inconsistent, irrelevant, overlapping, temporal, or added only for the sake of grammatical correctness can be considered as noise. Chances of noisy data are also huge in the context of big data which needs to be adequately addressed using advanced data cleaning and noise removal techniques while analyzing sentiments.

Spam and Fake Reviews and Temporal Variability. Tourist platforms are susceptible to spam and fake reviews and manipulated content just like any other product reviews intended to either promote or damage brand reputation. Analyzing such sentiments extracted from platforms without proper verification and authentication mechanisms can lead to biased results (Gupta et al., 2024). Tourism is also an industry which is very prone to seasonal demands. Analyzing sentiments without considering the time aspect might lead to wrong conclusions, for instance, a destination may receive negative comments due to weather conditions in a particular season but positive ones otherwise.

Ethical implications. Privacy issues, biases, lack of transparency, misuse and manipulation of data are some of the areas that can have ethical implications (Karoo & Chitte, 2023). SA involves processing large amounts of user feedback data along with personal data for contextual analysis. Even if data is anonymized during the sentiment analysis process, there are many advanced data mining de identification techniques by which users can be reidentified compromising their privacy. Another issue that may arise is potential bias and discrimination due to imbalanced and biased data sets used during the training phase of the machine learning algorithms. This can lead to undue targeting or excluding certain groups over others in promotional campaigns. Manipulating tourist behavior by exploiting emotional responses for upselling solely for profit is another grey area of contention. Using bots or humans for creating manipulated reviews either for promoting or demoting certain brands is another unethical practice which can damage trust and risk overall reputation. Care must be taken to overcome challenges due to unauthorized access of customer data and breaches. Robust security measures and encryptions must be implemented to protect the data. Adhering to data protection laws and policies can further help in enhancement of data privacy and security. Compliance with data protection regulations like GDPR (General Data Protection Regulation) is essential to ensure that sensitive information shared by the users is safeguarded. Tourism businesses and websites must adopt ethical guidelines and prioritize user privacy and rights for ensuring trust and overall accountability.

Challenges in performing sentiment analysis stem from the multiplicity of languages used for feedback, other inherent language specific nuances like sarcasm, use of humor, metaphor and irony, nature of data as well as dynamic nature of tourist experiences depending on circumstances and seasons. Many of the above-mentioned challenges are now being addressed by using advanced and sophisticated deep learning algorithms and hybrid approaches. Use of advanced spam filtering mechanisms can improve data quality leading to better results. Along with basic data preprocessing techniques like stemming, lemmatization, stop word removal combining advanced data preprocessing techniques like data augmentation can reduce noise, ensure data standardization and balance and improve overall data quality. Additionally combining automated sentiment analysis with human oversight can improve the accuracy of such analysis, making them more reliable. Comparative studies of the quality of user feedback data collected by different tourism feedback data collection products would be much-required research that can help many governments, tourism service providers and tourists in using these data for strategic decisions. Some earlier studies have attempted to evaluate the trustworthiness of feedback data of two major platforms, TripAdvisor and booking.com. For instance, Zelenka et al. (2021) proposed a model for making the review data more credible, however with the addition of multiple new sites and apps, more studies in this area focusing on different aspects and parameters can be highly useful particularly for common users related to tourism for making accurate decisions. Another area that needs to be explored is noise learning and removal in the context of NLP applications. Gan et al. (2023) points out that transformer-based models perform better at noise removal than deep learning methods whereas Gochhait (2024) highlights deep learning methods over traditional machine learning for better preprocessing accuracy. In general, improving accuracy rates and reducing computational expenses in the context of specific challenges mentioned above like multilingual data, big data, context specific data, data with irony, sarcasm, metaphors, and so on are the key areas that requires further research

Methodology

Our experiment aims to showcase the use of different techniques mentioned above to classify the sentiments of tourists who visited different branches of Disneyland. It also intends to compare the performance of different classification techniques. We have particularly used a transformer-based model which is one of the latest techniques known to give better accuracy in classification considering the challenges mentioned above.

The performance of different machine learning models for predicting certain values associated with the data set was tabulated and compared. There are a variety of AI based software available using which tourism sector service providers can monitor tourist sentiments and analyze the polarity of the opinions expressed. Voyant and Orange are such free and easy to use tools available online which can be used by managers and other non-technical people for any quick data analyses. Apart from that, Python and R and programming languages with lot of built in libraries can be used by computer science students, technical professionals and researchers to determine the polarity and subjectivity of sentiments. Polarity indicates whether the sentiment is positive (1), neutral (0) or negative (-1). Subjectivity is indicated by a range of 0.0 to 1.0 where 0 is for a completely objective and 1 is for purely subjective statement. For instance, Text Blob is a basic library in Python which can be used to determine polarity and subjectivity of the text passed as input to its methods. Pipeline function in Transformer library of Python allows to carry out sentiment analysis using deep learning methods based on transformer models. For our study, we have used R, Python, Voyant and Orange tools.

Data Set

The data set originally contained 45000 records with review feedback data of tourists on different branches of Disneyland. This was downloaded from Kaggle (data science and machine learning community run by google with many free resources) as a csv file having five columns, a) Review_ID, b) Rating, c) Year_Month, d) Reviewer_Location, e) Review_Text, and f) Branch.

A sample view of the data set is given below in Figure 2. Except for the Review_Id column, all the other columns were used as input parameters for different methods mentioned below used as part of our experimentation. Sentiment Analysis using the transformer-based model was performed only using the column "Review_Text".

Figure 2. Sample Data

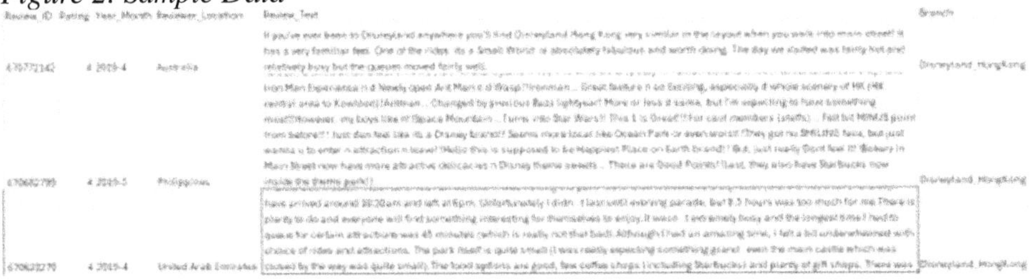

Methods

For the purposes of our experimentation, demonstration, analysis and discussion, the use of different methods for sentiment analysis that are commonly adopted by researchers was examined. This includes the classical lexicon based approach like TF- IDF method, as well as the state of the art deep learning transformer based methods.

i. At the onset, Document Term Matrix(DTM) was tabulated and also plotted as a bar graph with the extracted sub data set of 3000 rows using R programming software. DTM represents a document mathematically in the form of a matrix where the columns denote the different unique terms from the text along with their frequency of appearance.

ii. Word clouds are another powerful means for visually representing the most frequently used words using varying sizes wherein the most frequently used word is denoted by the highest size. Jamjuntr & Kaewyong (2021) have performed a word cloud analysis as part of their study of sentiments on Thailand tourism data. Such a visual representation of texts in the word cloud format helps to identify patterns, key themes and most frequently used words. Voyant was used in our study to generate the corresponding word cloud.

iii. Another method that is employed for analysis was finding out the correlation between frequently occurring words. In other words, it checks whether frequently appearing words occur more frequently at the same time or they tend to go up and down separately. The score of Pearsons correlation coefficient ranging from 1, 0 to -1 will indicate a positive, no correlation or negative correlation respectively. The value for significance indicates the confidence in the correlation coefficient value and it depends heavily on the extend to which the data is normally distributed. Values closer to 0 (.05 and less) denote a strong correlation. Voyant again provides easy to use interfaces for generating correlations easily. Topic modelling was also performed using the Voyant tool for discovering any hidden themes(topics). This works by grouping related words from a document or corpus into clusters. The process involves statistically assigning words to different topics using a technique called LDA (Latent Dirichlet Allocation) (Joshi et al., 2017). Each topic includes all the words in the document, however only the top 10 will be shown which are the most relevant ones. The order of the words also matters with the first one most indicative of the topic

iv. Sentiment classification and analysis was performed using R software as well as our algorithm which utilized the pipeline function in Python built on deep learning based transformed model. From the original data set, 3000 rows only were used as input to our algorithm. The pre trained transformer model defaulted to "distilbert/distilbert-base-uncased-finetuned-sst-2-english" was used to create the sentiment polarity labels "positive" and "negative". The performance of the model was evaluated using the metrics using Accuracy, Precision, Recall and F1 Score. The steps of our algorithm are as follows.

Step 1: Import required libraries
Step 2: Download the required NLTK resources
Step 3: Load Stop words List
Step 4: Load the Data from CSV file
Step 5: Extra the appropriate data column "Review_Text" for classification
Step 6: Perform Data Cleaning/Data Preprocessing on extracted column
Step 7: Perform sentiment classification using pre trained transformer model
Step 8: Extract the sentiment labels and score of each row
Step 9. Print the sentiment analysis results
Step 10: Evaluate the model performance using train(80%) and test(20%) data sets

v. Machine learning models KNN, SVM, Naive Bayes, Logistic Regression, Random Forest, Neural Network, Gradient Boosting and AdaBoost were implemented using the Orange Software to predict one of the columns "branch" using other columns Rating, Year_Month, and Reviewer_Location as input parameters as given in Figure 3. Their performance was evaluated using AUC, Accuracy, Precision, F1 Score and Recall metrics

Figure 3. Machine Learning models using Orange Software

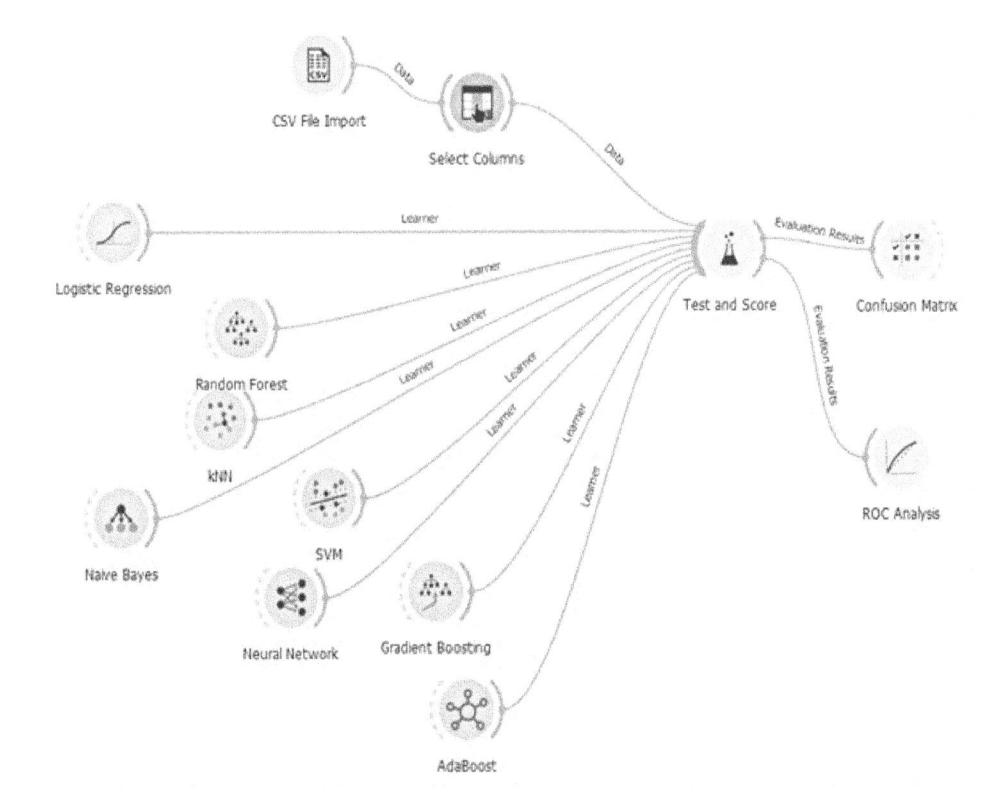

Results and Analysis

1. The DTM given in Table 1 highlights that the most frequently used term is "park" whereas "rides" is also frequently spoken about by the reviewers. It can also be seen that the review feedback mentions the words "day" and "time" quite frequently. While DTM itself does not determine the sentiment, it provides

a structured foundation for feature creation which can be used for subsequent sentiment classification and analysis.

Table 1. Document Term Matrix- First 10 most frequently used word (Using R)

	Word	Frequency
Park	Park	2947
Rides	Rides	2450
Disney	Disney	2427
Disneyland	Disneyland	2135
Day	Day	2011
Time	Time	1890
Get	Get	1533
One	One	1280
Can	Can	1216
Ride	Ride	1113

The same results were also graphically represented using a bar chart plotted using the R software as follows in Figure 4.

Figure 4. Plot for the most frequent words (Using R)

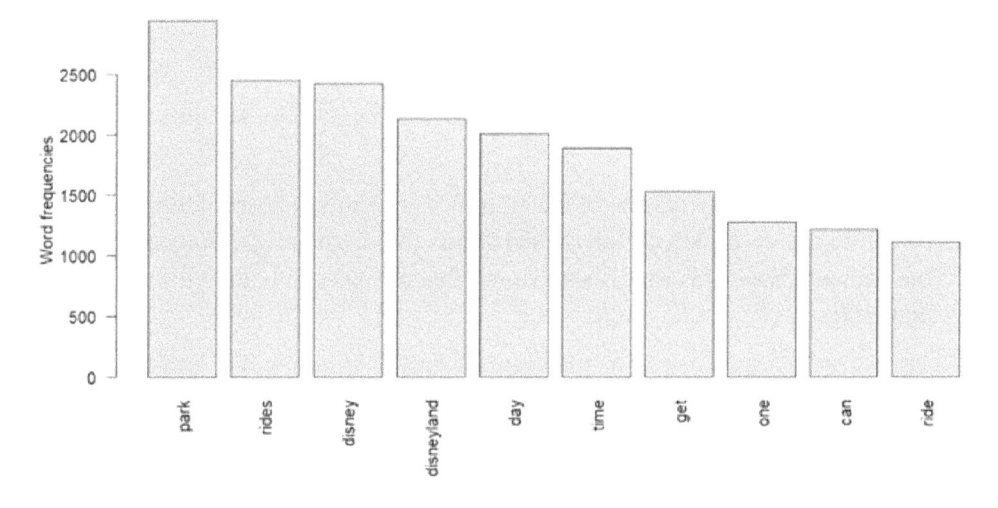

2. The word cloud generated by the open-source tool Voyant depicted in Figure 5 also shows park as one of the most frequently used word apart from the obvious word of Disney and Disneyland. The words "rides", and "time" also have been highlighted. Even though the results as mentioned in table 1 is not identical to the results displayed by the word cloud, they are still very much comparable because the words "park", "rides" and "times" have taken higher positions in both these result sets.

Figure 5. Word cloud with most frequently used words

3. The statistical representation of the 10 topics generated as part of topic modelling in Figure 6 showcases the related words that frequently occur together on the data set that it was run. It also shows that a word can belong to more than one topics

Figure 6. Topic Modelling

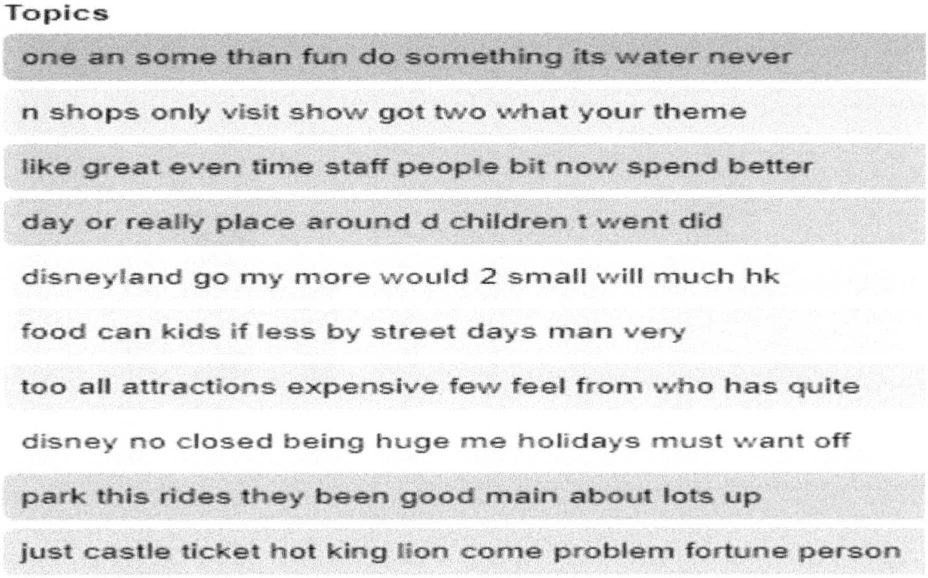

Topics

one an some than fun do something its water never
n shops only visit show got two what your theme
like great even time staff people bit now spend better
day or really place around d children t went did
disneyland go my more would 2 small will much hk
food can kids if less by street days man very
too all attractions expensive few feel from who has quite
disney no closed being huge me holidays must want off
park this rides they been good main about lots up
just castle ticket hot king lion come problem fortune person

4. Sentiment Classification and Analysis

The above representations have helped us to understand some key themes, patterns and topics of discussion as part of the reviews. However, they do not give us a clear picture of the actual sentiment (positive, negative, neutral) associated with these words. It is possible to attach sentiment scores to the reviews using natural language processing techniques.

i. The sentiment scores generated using R software highlights the occurrence of 8 different basic emotions as per Plutchik's wheel (Joshi et al., 2017) . Figure 7 below indicates "Anticipation", "Joy", "Trust" are the main positive emotions whereas "fear", anger", and "sadness" are some of negative emotions frequently expressed by the reviewers with regard to their Disneyland travel experiences. It clearly portrays that the positive comments are much higher than the negative ones

Figure 7. Sentiment Scores (Using R)

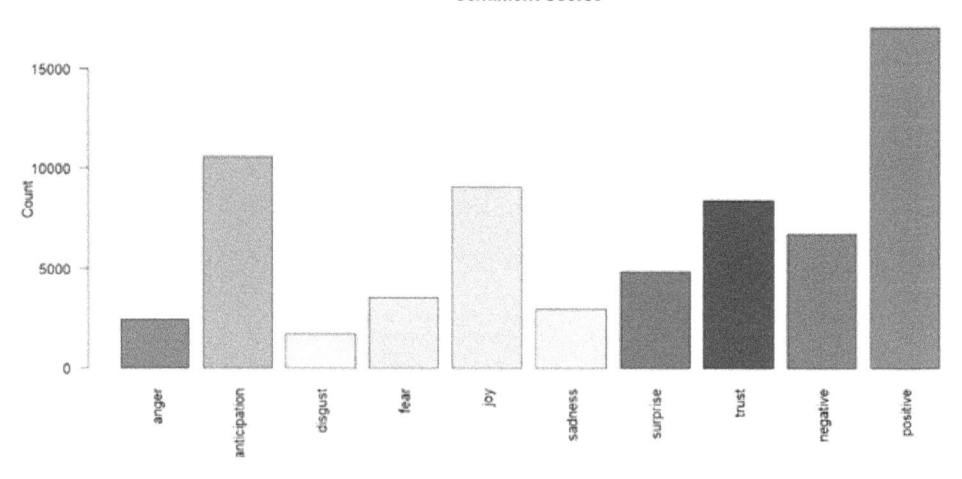

ii. Transformer Based Model

The sample results obtained for the sentiment label and scores using the transformer-based algorithm is as given in Figure 8.

Figure 8. Sample Result set with sentiment label and score

It can be seen that the review text by a traveler from Australia for the Disneyland Hongkong branch, "If you've ever been to Disneyland anywhere you'll find Disneyland Hong Kong very similar in the layout when you walk into main street! It has a very familiar feel. One of the rides its a Small World is absolutely fabulous and worth doing. The day we visited was fairly hot and relatively busy but the queues moved fairly well", has received a positive label with the sentiment score of 0.998917341. Another review text by a tourist from United Kingdom "the location is not in the city, took around 1 hour from Kowlon, my kids like disneyland so much, everything is fine. but its really crowded and hot in Hong Kong" has been classified as "negative" with sentiment score of 0.99285239.

Irrespective of the fallacies of grammar or the place of the traveler, the model has classified the sentiments quite accurately. From the overall 3000 rows input, 82.3% was classified as positive whereas only 17.7% was considered as negative. This is in alignment with the results displayed in Figure 8 which pointed out that positive sentiments were much higher than the negative sentiments.

The confusion matrix and the values of the evaluation metric, Accuracy, Recall, Precision and F1 Score generated is given in Figure 9.

Figure 9. Confusion Matrix and results of evaluation metrics

```
Accuracy: 0.8450
Recall: 0.8230
Precision: 0.7382
F1-score: 0.7657
```

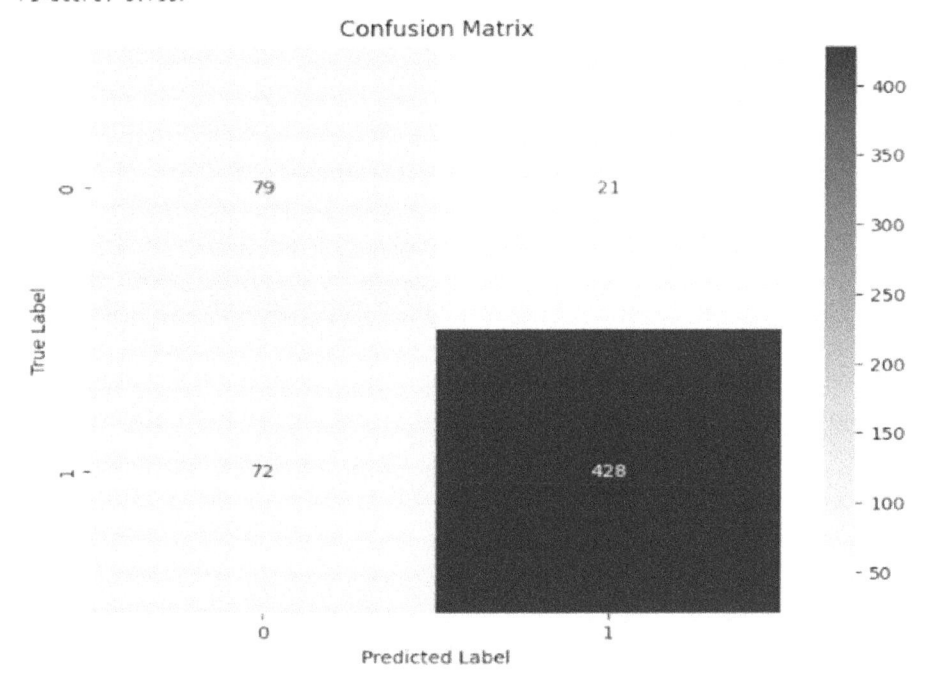

The top left quadrant and the bottom right quadrant of the confusion matrix indicate the true negative(TN) and true positive (TP) values whereas the bottom left and top right show the false negative(FN) and false positive(FP) values respectively. The total predictions (TP) based on the total 600 rows used as the test data(20% of the 3000 rows), the TN (79) and TP (428) are higher than the FN (21) and the FP(72). This means that the error rate is less and accuracy of the model in classifying the positive and negative sentiments is dependable.

The values of the confusion matrix can further be used for calculating other evaluation metrics.

Accuracy shows how often the model correctly classifies the positive and negative values. It is calculated as A= (TP+ TN)/TP. Recall, R, otherwise called Sensitivity is calculated as TP /(TP +FN) determines how good the model is in correctly identifying the positives. It is calculated as R = TP/(TP+FN. Precision is the percentage of truly positive values out of the total positively predicted values, P = TP/(TP+FP. F1 Score is the harmonic mean of precision and sensitivity. This evaluation metric is usually considered good for imbalanced data sets like the one used in this study, F1 Score = 2*((P *R)/(P+R)), The transformer-based model implemented has an accuracy of .85, Recall rate of .82, Precision of .74 and F1 Score of .77. The results obtained are comparable to the results in the study undertaken by Pérez Enríquez et al.(2022), however their accuracy and F1 score is higher than the present demonstrated results. The difference may be due to the different transformer model that they have used (Robertabase) as well as the additional data preprocessing performed. As part of preprocessing, they have balanced the data sets to bring positive, negative and neutral records to be of the same size as well as augmented the data to increase the size of the data sets for the performance of the model training phase to be better.

5. Machine Learning Models

The results of the evaluation metric for all the machine learning algorithms implemented are given in Table 2. Gradient Boosting and Naïve Bayes and Logistic Regression performed the best when considering all metrics together. Neural Network also closely followed suit, faring similar for AUC and Precision. SVM performed the worst amongst all. The study conducted by Puh & Bagić Babac (2022) achieved similar accuracy (.73) for the performance of Naïve Bayes.

Table 2. Performance evaluation of machine learning algorithms

Model	AUC	CA	F1	Prec	Recall
SVM	0.612	0.424	0.342	0.41	0.424
Random Forest	0.833	0.699	0.698	0.699	0.699
Neural Network	0.823	0.699	0.699	0.704	0.699
Naive Bayes	**0.856**	**0.719**	**0.72**	**0.723**	**0.719**
Logistic Regression	**0.855**	**0.722**	**0.722**	**0.724**	**0.722**
kNN	0.704	0.493	0.463	0.588	0.493
Gradient Boosting	**0.853**	**0.723**	**0.723**	**0.725**	**0.723**
AdaBoost	0.776	0.685	0.685	0.687	0.685

The results of experimentation mentioned above clearly indicate the overall tourist satisfaction about DisneyLand as positive. It also highlighted the aspects most frequently spoken about by the tourists and the main emotions expressed by the tourists based on their experience. These are valuable insights using which the related service providers can enhance tourist experience at the same time enable other tourists in their decision making for related tourism product purchases. The study also confirmed the efficacy of transformer-based models in accurately classifying the sentiments despite complexities like sarcasm and erroneous data. However, further research should evaluate the performance of the transformer-based models and its resource implications while handling big data, multilingual data and multimodal data.

CONCLUSION

Sentiment Analysis using different state of the art techniques offers manifold opportunities for governments and business to understand the customer pulse, improve the way tourism is envisioned and implement strategies and decisions for enhancing tourist experience. This chapter provided a general overview of the significance of sentiment analysis for developing the tourism sector along with various approaches including lexicon, machine learning based and transformer-based models. It also provided a basic implementation of the above approaches using different tools like Voyant, Orange, R and Python. Future work suggests exploring other transformer-based models with optimized settings combined with data preprocessing using data augmentation and data balancing. The insights gained from these analyses can be useful for businesses, governments, and individuals connected with the tourism sector, aiding them in making decisions influenced by public sentiment.

REFERENCES

Akin Ozen, I. (2021). Tourism Products and Sentiment Analysis. In C. Cobanoglu, S. Dogan, K. Berezina, & G. Collins (Eds.), *Advances in Hospitality and Tourism Information Technology*. University of South Florida M3 Publishing. https://digitalcommons.usf.edu/m3publishing/vol18/iss9781732127586/8/

Alfreihat, M., Saad Almousa, O., Tashtoush, Y., & AlSobeh, A. (2024). Emo-SL Framework: Emoji Sentiment Lexicon Using Text-Based Features and Machine Learning for Sentiment Analysis. *IEEE Access: Practical Innovations, Open Solutions*, 12, 81793–81812. Advance online publication. DOI: 10.1109/ACCESS.2024.3382836

Alonso-Mencía, J. (2023). *Unlocking Sentiments: Exploring the Power of NLP Transformers in Review Analysis*. https://ceur-ws.org/Vol-3496/restmex-paper12.pdf

Alvarez-Carmona, M. A., & Aranda, R. (2022). *Natural language processing applied to tourism research: A systematic review and future research directions*. DOI: 10.1016/j.jksuci.2022.10.010

Ameni Dhaoui Boumaiza. (2016). A Survey on Sentiment Analysis and Visualization. *Qatar Foundation Annual Research Conference Proceedings,* 2016(1). DOI: 10.5339/qfarc.2016.ICTPP1203

Arun Wadhe, A., & Suratkar, S., S. (2020, May 28). Tourist Place Reviews Sentiment Classification Using Machine Learning Techniques. *2020 International Conference on Industry 4.0 Technology (I4Tech)*. DOI: 10.1109/I4Tech48345.2020.9102673

Bansal, A., & Kumar, N. (2021). Aspect-Based Sentiment Analysis Using Attribute Extraction of Hospital Reviews. *New Generation Computing*. Advance online publication. DOI: 10.1007/s00354-021-00141-3 PMID: 34866746

Bordoloi, M., & Biswas, S. K. (2023). Sentiment analysis: A survey on design framework, applications and future scopes. *Artificial Intelligence Review*, 56(11), 12505–12560. Advance online publication. DOI: 10.1007/s10462-023-10442-2 PMID: 37362892

Chiche, A., & Yitagesu, B. (2022). Part of speech tagging: A systematic review of deep learning and machine learning approaches. *Journal of Big Data*, 9(1), 10. Advance online publication. DOI: 10.1186/s40537-022-00561-y

Choo, S., & Kim, W. (2023). A study on the evaluation of tokenizer performance in natural language processing. *Applied Artificial Intelligence*, 37(1), 2175112. Advance online publication. DOI: 10.1080/08839514.2023.2175112

Devlin, J., Chang, M.-W., Lee, K., & Toutanova, K. (2019). BERT: Pre-training of deep bidirectional transformers for language understanding. *Proceedings of the 2019 Conference of the North American Chapter of the Association for Computational Linguistics*, 4171-4186. DOI: 10.18653/v1/N19-1423

Fuentes, M., Carles, M. P., & Camon, F. (2018, March 14). Does verifying users influence rankings? Analyzing TripAdvisor and Booking.com. Udl.cat; Cognizant Communication Corporation. https://repositori.udl.cat/items/7d0e0fa2-c764-47d3-b462-9eafb462bdbc

Gan, L., Hu, L., Tan, X., & Du, X. (2023). TBNF:A Transformer-based Noise Filtering Method for Chinese Long-form Text Matching. *Applied Intelligence*, 53(19), 22313–22327. DOI: 10.1007/s10489-023-04607-3

Gandhi, A., Adhvaryu, K., Poria, S., Cambria, E., & Hussain, A. (2023). Multimodal sentiment analysis: A systematic review of history, datasets, multimodal fusion methods, applications, challenges and future directions. *Information Fusion*, 91, 424–444. DOI: 10.1016/j.inffus.2022.09.025

Gochhait, S. (2024). *Comparative Analysis of Machine and Deep Learning Techniques for Text Classification with Emphasis on Data Preprocessing*. Qeios., DOI: 10.32388/XHC9J1

Gupta, D., Bhargava, A., Agarwal, D., Alsharif, M. H., Uthansakul, P., Uthansakul, M., & Aly, A. A. (2024). Deep Learning-Based Truthful and Deceptive Hotel Reviews. *Sustainability (Basel)*, 16(11), 4514–4514. DOI: 10.3390/su16114514

Hasan, R., & Chu, C.-H. H. (2024). A Heterogeneous Ensemble Method for Handling Class Noise in Supervised Machine Learning. *SAC '24: Proceedings of the 39th ACM/SIGAPP Symposium on Applied Computing*, 902–909. DOI: 10.1145/3605098.3635936

Hashim, R., Omar, B., Saeed, N., Ba-Anqud, A., & Al-Samarraie, H. (2020). The application of sentiment analysis in tourism research: A brief review. *IJBTS International Journal of Business Tourism and Applied Sciences*, 8(1). http://www.ijbts-journal.com/images/column_1587487589/IJBTS%20V8%20no1%201_6%20Rohani%20Hashim%20Tokyo19.pdf

Jabbar, M., Dwi Okfantia, A., Widjanarti, A., & Zulen, A. (2022). *IFC-Bank of Italy Workshop on "Data Science in Central Banking: Applications and tools" Sentiment analysis of tourist reviews from online travel forum for improving Indonesia tourism sector 1*. https://www.bis.org/ifc/publ/ifcb59_18.pdf

Jamjuntr, P., & Kaewyong, P. (2021). Sentiment analysis with a textblob package implications for tourism. *Journal of Management Information and Decision Sciences*, 24(S6), 1–9. https://www.abacademies.org/articles/sentiment-analysis-with-a-text-blob-package-implications-for-tourism.pdf

Jim, J. R., Talukder, M. A. R., Malakar, P., Kabir, M. M., Nur, K., & Mridha, M. F.Jamin Rahman Jim. (2024). Recent advancements and challenges of NLP-based sentiment analysis: A state-of-the-art review. *Natural Language Processing Journal*, 6, 100059–100059. DOI: 10.1016/j.nlp.2024.100059

Joshi, A., Bhattacharyya, P., & Ahire, S. (2017). Sentiment Resources: Lexicons and Datasets. In E. Cambria, D. Das, S. Bandyopadhyay, & A. Feraco (Eds.), *A Practical Guide to Sentiment Analysis*. Springer Cham.

Karoo, K., & Chitte, V. (2023). Ethical Considerations in Sentiment Analysis: Navigating the Complex Landscape. *International Research Journal of Modernization in Engineering Technology and Science*, 5(2). Advance online publication. DOI: 10.56726/IRJMETS46811

Kaur, J., & Buttar, P. K. (2018, September 1). *Stopwords removal and its algorithms based on different methods. International Journal of Advanced Research in Computer Science | EBSCOhost*. https://openurl.ebsco.com/EPDB%3Agcd%3A14%3A27966862/detailv2?sid=ebsco%3Aplink%3Ascholar&id=ebsco%3Agcd%3A132911177&crl=c

Khurana, D., Koli, A., Khatter, K., & Singh, S. (2022). Natural Language processing: State of the art, Current Trends and Challenges. *Multimedia Tools and Applications*, 82(3), 3713–3744. DOI: 10.1007/s11042-022-13428-4 PMID: 35855771

Kusumawardani, R. P., Rahman, R. A., Wibowo, R. P., & Tjahjanto, A. (2024). Understanding Fine-Grained Sentiments of Super-Priority Destination Visitors using Multi-task Learning for Extraction of Aspect Terms and Polarity Classification on Reviews. *Procedia Computer Science*, 234, 602–613. DOI: 10.1016/j.procs.2024.03.045

Lazrig, I., & Humpherys, S. (2022). Using Machine Learning Sentiment Analysis to Evaluate Learning Impact. *Information Systems Education Journal*, 20(1). https://files.eric.ed.gov/fulltext/EJ1333895.pdf

Leelawat, N., Jariyapongpaiboon, S., Promjun, A., Boonyarak, S., Saengtabtim, K., Laosunthara, A., Yudha, A. K., & Tang, J. (2022). Twitter data sentiment analysis of tourism in Thailand during the COVID-19 pandemic using machine learning. *Heliyon*, 8(10), e10894. DOI: 10.1016/j.heliyon.2022.e10894 PMID: 36211996

Li, H., Li, W., Zhao, J., Yu, P., & Huang, Y. (2023). A sentiment analysis approach for travel-related Chinese online review content. *PeerJ. Computer Science*, 9, e1538–e1538. DOI: 10.7717/peerj-cs.1538 PMID: 37705661

Liu, B. (2012). Sentiment Analysis and Opinion Mining. In *Synthesis Lectures on Human Language Technologies*. Springer International Publishing. DOI: 10.1007/978-3-031-02145-9

Liu, B., Xu, W., Tencent, Y., Wu, X., Zhang, B., & Zhu, L. (2022). *Noise Learning for Text Classification: A Benchmark*. https://aclanthology.org/2022.coling-1.402.pdf

Manosso, F. C., & Domareski Ruiz, T. C. (2021, October 18). *Using Sentiment Analysis in Tourism Research: A Systematic, Bibliometric, and Integrative Review*. Social Science Research Network. https://papers.ssrn.com/sol3/papers.cfm?abstract_id=3938896

Mao, Y., Liu, Q., & Zhang, Y. (2024). Sentiment analysis methods, applications, and challenges: A systematic literature review. Journal of King Saud University. Computer and Information Sciences/Maǧalla ǧamʼa Al-Malīk Saud: Ùlm Al-ḥasib Wa Al-Maʼlumat, 36(4), 102048–102048. DOI: 10.1016/j.jksuci.2024.102048

Naik, G., Wani, S., Pawar, R., & Randhir, R. (2022). Tourist Place Reviews Sentiment Classification Using Machine Learning Techniques. *International Journal for Research in Engineering Application & Management*, 08, 2454–9150. DOI: 10.35291/2454-9150.2022.0161

Nandwani, P., & Verma, R. (2021). A review on sentiment analysis and emotion detection from text. *Social Network Analysis and Mining*, 11(1), 81. Advance online publication. DOI: 10.1007/s13278-021-00776-6 PMID: 34484462

Ni, W., Sumartini, S., Ketut, I., Putra, G. D., Sudarma, M., & Sukarsa, I. M. (2024). Enhance sentiment analysis in big data tourism using hybrid lexicon and active learning support vector machine. *Bulletin of Electrical Engineering and Informatics*. DOI: 10.11591/eei.v13i5.7807

Nur, Malik, & Nur. (2023). Sentiment classification from reviews for tourism analytics. *IJAIN (International Journal of Advances in Intelligent Informatics)*, 9(1), 108–108. https://doi.org/DOI: 10.26555/ijain.v9i1.1077

Osgood, C. E. (1975). *Cross-Cultural Universals of Affective Meaning*. University of Illinois Press.

Pang, B., Lee, L., & Vaithyanathan, S. (2002). Thumbs up?: Sentiment classification using machine learning techniques. *Proceedings of the ACL-02 Conference on Empirical Methods in Natural Language Processing*, 10, 79-86. DOI: 10.3115/1118693.1118704

Pérez Enríquez, M., Mencía, J., & Segura-Bedmar, I. (2022). *Transformers Approach for Sentiment Analysis: Classification of Mexican Tourists Reviews from TripAdvisor*. https://ceur-ws.org/Vol-3202/restmex-paper11.pdf

Puh, K., & Bagić Babac, M. (2022). Predicting sentiment and rating of tourist reviews using machine learning. *Journal of Hospitality and Tourism Insights*, 6(3), 1188–1204. DOI: 10.1108/JHTI-02-2022-0078

Rasool, H., Maqbool, S., & Tarique, M. (2021). The relationship between tourism and economic growth among BRICS countries: A panel cointegration analysis. *Future Business Journal*, 7(1), 1. Advance online publication. DOI: 10.1186/s43093-020-00048-3

Renganathan, V., & Upadhya, A. (2021). Dubai Restaurants: A Sentiment Analysis of Tourist Reviews. *ProQuest*. https://www.proquest.com/docview/2627538050?sourcetype=Scholarly%20Journals

Rezapour, M. (2024). Emotion Detection with Transformers: A Comparative Study. ArXiv.org. https://arxiv.org/abs/2403.15454

Rokade, P. P., & D, A. K. (2019). Business intelligence analytics using sentiment analysis-a survey. *International Journal of Electrical and Computer Engineering (IJECE)*, 9(1), 613–620. https://ijece.iaescore.com/index.php/IJECE/article/view/10540/11092

Šandor, D., & Bagić Babac, M. (2024). Sarcasm detection in online comments using machine learning. *Information Discovery and Delivery*, 52(2), 213–226. DOI: 10.1108/IDD-01-2023-0002

Saraswathi, N., Sasi Rooba, T., & Chakaravarthi, S. (2023). Improving the accuracy of sentiment analysis using a linguistic rule-based feature selection method in tourism reviews. *Measurement. Sensors*, 29, 100888. DOI: 10.1016/j.measen.2023.100888

Socher, R., Perelygin, A., Wu, J., Chuang, J., Manning, C. D., Ng, A. Y., & Potts, C. (2013). Recursive deep models for semantic compositionality over a sentiment treebank. *Proceedings of the 2013 Conference on Empirical Methods in Natural Language Processing*, 1631-1642.

Turney, P. D. (2002). Thumbs up or thumbs down?: Semantic orientation applied to unsupervised classification of reviews. *Proceedings of the 40th Annual Meeting of the Association for Computational Linguistics*, 417-424. DOI: 10.3115/1073083.1073153

Ullah, S. (2024). A multimodal approach to cross-lingual sentiment analysis with ensemble of transformer and LLM. *Scientific Reports*, 14(1), 9603. Advance online publication. DOI: 10.1038/s41598-024-60210-7 PMID: 38671064

Wankhade, M., Rao, A. C. S., & Kulkarni, C. (2022). A survey on sentiment analysis methods, applications, and challenges. *Artificial Intelligence Review*, 55(55), 5731–5780. Advance online publication. DOI: 10.1007/s10462-022-10144-1

Wilson, T., Wiebe, J., & Hoffmann, P. (2009). Recognizing Contextual Polarity: An Exploration of Features for Phrase-Level Sentiment Analysis. *Computational Linguistics*, 35(3), 399–433. DOI: 10.1162/coli.08-012-R1-06-90

Zelenka, J., Azubuike, T., & Pásková, M. (2021). Trust Model for Online Reviews of Tourism Services and Evaluation of Destinations. *Administrative Sciences*, 11(2), 34. DOI: 10.3390/admsci11020034

Zhang, Y., Diao, W., Nie, Y., & Wang, Q. (2024). Design of signage guidance system for tourist attractions based on computer vision technology. *Journal of Computational Methods in Sciences and Engineering*, 24(1), 413–426. DOI: 10.3233/JCM-237032

Zlatanov, S., & Popesku, J. (2019). Current Applications of Artificial Intelligence in Tourism and Hospitality. Proceedings of the International Scientific Conference - Sinteza 2019. DOI: 10.15308/Sinteza-2019-84-90

KEY TERMS AND DEFINITIONS

Artificial Intelligence (AI): A branch of Computer Science that is providing various theoretical frameworks, tools and technologies for enabling computers to behave like human beings.

Deep Learning: The advanced level of machine learning implemented using neural networks which uses context level and domain level information as part of learning complex information.

Machine Learning: A subfield of artificial intelligence that enables computers to memorize and learn from previous experiences and mistakes primarily taking the form of a training phase.

Natural Language Processing (NLP): A branch of artificial intelligence that enables computers to understand, interpret and respond to human language like English in formats including written, audio, and video.

Part of Speech (PoS) Tagging: The process by which different words or phrases in a sentence are assigned appropriate grammatical roles like noun, verb and so on with respect to its context in the sentence.

Sentiment: The attitude, beliefs or feelings of a person regarding anything with which they may have had a physical or intellectual experience. It can be about a person, product, service, location, concept and so on.

Sentiment Analysis: A subfield of the text classification domain by which the sentiment expressed via any medium of natural language can be classified as positive, negative or neutral.

Chapter 10
Smart Tourism and Co-Creation of the Tourism Experience:
Netnographic Possibilities and Technological Perspectives

Badr Bentalha
https://orcid.org/0000-0003-1339-542X
National School of Business and Management, Sidi Mohammed Ben Abdellah University, Morocco

ABSTRACT

With the union of information and communication technologies, tourism is continuing a genuine transition to e-tourism. This mutation of ICT and the advent of the virtual community are constantly transforming the behavior of both producers and consumers of tourism products. While tourism companies continue to make massive use of the media, particularly social networks, to win over new customers, tourists, on the other hand, are looking to use them as a lever to actively participate in the creation of experiential value. So, to what extent does the use of social networks encourage the co-creation of the tourist experience, and how can future technologies modify tourist experiences? Through a qualitative netnographic study, the authors found that social networks actively contribute to the co-creation of tourism value, especially via the informational, interactive, and curatorial dimensions.

INTRODUCTION

Consumers, and tourists in particular, are increasingly connected, and demand instant and rapid information. In this sense, digital technology predominates in travel planning. By 2022, 43% of the world's travelers will be planning their trips online (Fevad, 2023). In response to this trend, tourism companies need to implement a digital strategy to steer the deployment of their business on the web. The intelligent version of their marketing must imperatively take into account the characteristics of new media, in particular social networks. Social networks are new communication tools, with their specific audiences, uses, and new communication spaces. They foster a culture of sharing and exchanging information. Since then, these new tools have attracted a great deal of interest from the media, practitioners, and researchers alike.

Social networks have emerged as powerful platforms for tourism promotion and marketing. Tourism organizations, destinations, hotels, and travel companies leverage these platforms to showcase visually appealing content, including photographs, videos, and captivating stories, to inspire potential travelers. Social media influencers and travel bloggers with large followings play a crucial role in promoting destinations and travel experiences, often through sponsored partnerships or collaborations with tourism businesses. During and after their travels, tourists actively share their experiences on social networks through posts, photos, and videos. This user-generated content not only allows travelers to document and relive their memories but also serves as a form of word-of-mouth marketing for tourism businesses and destinations. Positive experiences shared on social media can inspire others to visit the same locations, creating a ripple effect of interest and potential bookings. For tourism businesses, social networks offer a direct communication channel with customers. These platforms allow businesses to address customer concerns, gather feedback, and provide real-time customer service. By monitoring social media conversations and analyzing user preferences and behavior, tourism organizations can gain valuable insights to improve their offerings, tailor marketing strategies, and stay ahead of emerging trends in the industry.

With the digital transition, tourism is undergoing a profound transformation with e-tourism, where the virtual community is constantly converting the behavior of both producers and consumers of tourism products. Tourists can share their experiences in real-time on social media while benefiting from the experiences and opinions of other customers or users. These technologies are used throughout the stay and are likely to enhance the visitor's experience. As a result, companies in the tourism sector need to embrace these new concerns and integrate them into their commercial and production strategies, to adapt and reinvent their business model. Today's digitalization is becoming an ideal framework for realizing opportunities to co-create memorable tourism experiences, through creative collaboration between the company and the online community. From this perspective, the concept of value co-creation is a striking reality that provides opportunities for tourists and businesses alike, thanks to creative collaboration through interactions in an online community.

Co-creation of value in tourism refers to the active involvement and collaboration between tourism service providers and customers in creating and shaping the overall tourism experience. It recognizes that the value of a tourism product or service is not solely determined by the provider but also by the customers' participation, input, and interactions. In this context, customers are viewed as co-creators rather than passive consumers, contributing to the design, delivery, and evaluation of tourism offerings. Netnographic analysis enables tourism organizations to identify emerging trends, unmet needs, and areas for innovation based on the conversations and interactions within online communities. By actively engaging with these communities and analyzing user-generated content, tourism businesses can co-create value by tailoring their products and services to better align with customer preferences and expectations, ultimately enhancing the overall tourism experience.

So, to what extent does the use of social networks foster the co-creation of customers' tourism experience, and how can current technologies modify tourism experiences?

To address this issue, this research paper deals respectively with the theoretical and conceptual framework (1), the methodological approach adopted (2), the results of the empirical study, and fundamental recommendations (3).

1. THEORETICAL AND CONCEPTUAL FRAMEWORK

1.1. Social Networks: A Lever for Analyzing the Consumer Experience

The digitization of an organization is a global transformation of the company, which must take place across its entire value chain. In the age of social networks, *"individuals have new ways of expressing themselves, protesting, testifying, supporting, debating, ..., in a friendly, interactive space of exchange, calling into question the hierarchy of subjects that create the news: there is a shift from a time when the media told people what they should debate to a time when people inspire the media, the subjects to be covered"* (Zammar, 2012, p 19).

Social networks are a real springboard for developing a company's visibility and therefore its reputation. It's a way of getting the company known. Using social networks is a solution for diversifying and increasing customer acquisition sources. It's a tool for sales prospecting, but also a lever in the customer loyalty process. With social networks, you can create a certain closeness with your contacts, creating special relationships and getting to know them better. Another advantage of social networks is that you can broadcast your messages in real-time. So, by communicating on social media, the company will reach an audience over a wide geographical area.

Marketing is a field that explicitly refers to the idea of experience production by the company. According to Cova & Cova (2009), the word "*experience*" is a buzzword used in all languages and sciences to designate any situation experienced daily by an individual. The concept of consumer experience has long since emerged in the field of marketing, following the pioneering work of Hirschman & Holbrook (1982a, 1982b). They emphasize the affective and symbolic aspects of consumer behavior. Their work marked the emergence of a new approach known as experiential marketing. Customer experience refers to all the emotions and feelings experienced by a customer before, during, and after the purchase of a product or service. For our part, we adopt Holbrook & Hirschman's (1982a) definition of consumer experience as "*a subjective state of consciousness accompanied by a variety of symbolic meanings, hedonic responses, and aesthetic criteria*". It is therefore the complex result of heterogeneous elements and factors involved in the customer journey. Experiential tourism includes the people we meet, the places we visit, and the activities we engage in. It presents reality and provides a genuine experience, enabling tourists to discover new cultures, ways of doing things, and activities.

Pine & Gilmore (1999), for example, define experience creation as "*a company intentionally using goods and services to engage individual customers to create a memorable event*". They propose an experiential wheel with five components: surprise, using the brand to serve the experiential, creating a bond, offering the extraordinary, and stimulating the five senses. The consumer experience is both individual and collective, subjective and objective (Lequin, 2002). It refers to the impressions and perceptions that customers have of all their interactions with a company. In reality, this concept reflects the entire customer journey, from the website to the shopping experience, interaction, sales support, technical assistance, etc. (Hmioui et al., 2022). Customer experience management is a program for delivering an optimized customer experience designed to improve loyalty.

Customer experience is seen as a source of influence on satisfaction and loyalty. It can be broken down into several experience phases of varying degrees of importance, depending on the field of activity. Arnould et al. (2002) unpack it into 4 main stages: the experience of anticipating consumption, the experience of buying, the experience of consuming, and the experience of remembering. Thus, the consumer is the unit of experience production, through the processing and interpretation of products and services. The experience involves both the cognitive and affective spheres and results from the interaction between person/object/situation. It goes beyond the purchase decision to take into account post-purchase psychological states, and in particular perceived value. We can therefore distinguish three components of experiential tourism: a first experience expected before the act of purchase, a second experience lived during the act of purchase, and a third experience memorized after the act of purchase. With a plethora of digital devices, consumers have new opportunities to express themselves, share, interact with each other and with the company, and thus co-create value (Neuhofer et al., 2013; Abbes & Hallem, 2016). Leclercq et al., (2016) advocate classifying the values perceived by the consumer of a co-creation experience along the three axes intrinsic/extrinsic, self-oriented/other-oriented, and active/reactive. For this purpose, Abbes & Hallem (2016) have synthesized the conceptualization of the perceived value of a co-creation experience, based on 14 types of values grouped into three categories (Table 1):

Table 1. Dimensions of the perceived value of the co-creation experience

Dimensions	Items	Content
Self-oriented intrinsic values	**Recreational value**	Entertaining aspects of the tourist's consumption of hotel activities and services: games, distractions, playfulness, fun, ...
	Value aesthetic-sensory	Sensory aspects of hotel activities and services (interaction with the tourist's "5 senses"): beauty, smell, aesthetics, looks, décor, taste, flavor, perception, etc.
	Emotional value	Affective aspects of consuming hotel activities and services: feelings, emotions, intuitions, happiness, contentment, pleasure, enchantment, enjoyment, etc.
	Psychological value	Psychological aspects of hospitality consumption: difficulty, mental, constraint, influence, creativity, initiative, innovation, etc.
	Spiritual value	Aspects relating to the tourist's beliefs and values when consuming hotel activities and services: lifestyle, way of life, values, traditions, etc.
	Escape value	Immersion aspects generated by the consumption of hotel activities and services: escape, overflow, immersion, navigation, ablution, etc.
	Appropriation value	Aspects linked to the appropriation of the setting and conditions for consuming hotel activities and services: orientation, handling of equipment, etc.

continued on following page

Table 1. Continued

Dimensions	Items	Content
Self-oriented extrinsic values	Freedom Value	Aspects of flexibility in the consumption of hotel services: freedom, choice, maneuverability, ease, speed, etc.
	Informational value	Aspects related to acquired informational skills about hotel activities and services: ingredients, production processes, hygiene and safety measures, etc.
	Optimization value	Aspects relating to the tourist's ability to optimize his or her choices in terms of hotel services: usefulness, costs, quality/price, budget, etc.
	Learning value	Aspects relating to the tourist's ability to accumulate knowledge to better enjoy hotel services: learning, accumulation, skills, expertise, etc.
	Reassurance value	Aspects of tourist reassurance when consuming hotel services: safety, hygiene, cleanliness, trust, sincerity, loyalty, honesty, etc.
	Convenience value	Aspects of practicality in the consumption of hotel services: ease of use, practicality of service, manipulability, etc.
Extrinsic, other-oriented values	Value of social ties within and outside the company	Relational aspects with contact personnel and other employees during hotel services: vis-à-vis, contact, suggestions, discussion, exchange, etc.

Source: Adapted from Abbes & Hallem (2016)

The table 1 categorizes the various sources of value that hotel guests derive from their overall experience. It covers both intrinsic values (inherent satisfaction) and extrinsic values (practical benefits). The self-oriented intrinsic values tap into the hedonic, sensory, and psychological needs of guests. Recreational, aesthetic, and emotional values are about providing entertaining, beautiful, and emotionally-resonant experiences that evoke feelings of pleasure, fun, and excitement. Psychological, spiritual, and escape values allow guests to engage in mentally-stimulating activities, connect with their beliefs/values, and achieve a sense of transportation away from daily life. These intrinsic values create a holistic experience that is highly memorable and impactful for guests on a personal level. They transform a hotel stay from just a night's lodging into something extraordinary and meaningful. The self-oriented extrinsic values focus on more practical and functional benefits for guests. This includes optimizing value for money, developing new skills, ensuring safety/trust, maximizing convenience, and having autonomy over their experience. These extrinsic aspects enhance the overall quality and satisfaction by removing friction points and equipping guests to make the most of their hotel journey. Finally, the other-oriented extrinsic value highlights the importance of social connections - both with hotel staff through personalized interactions as well as with other guests by facilitating networking opportunities. This social dimension elevates the experience beyond just transactions to more human-centric exchanges.

By holistically addressing these diverse sources of value across the self-oriented intrinsic/extrinsic and other-oriented categories, hotels can craft superior and multifaceted experiences tailored to the complete range of guest needs and desires. It provides a framework for exceeding expectations and delivering truly transformative hospitality. It would thus seem that the perceived values of the co-creation experience are rich and diverse, and can be further consolidated by the contribution of technology, especially digital technology.

1.2. The Co-Creation of Tourism Experiences and Intelligent Technologies

Co-creation involves collaboration between several actors, over a more or less variable period, to create economic, social, emotional, cultural, educational, organizational, or societal value (Guimont & Lapointe, 2015). The starting point for value co-creation is an invitation presented by an initiating actor, who submits to other actors a value proposition that, on the one hand, is sufficiently seductive to entice them to contribute to its enrichment (Desmarteau et al., 2017). Value co-creation implies the reciprocal and joint creation of value for both the customer and the company, and therefore the commitment of the consumer (Leclercq et al., 2016). This type of behavior requires the voluntary involvement of customers in one or more stages of the company's value chain, from product/service design to promotion and evaluation. Consumption is no longer seen as an act of passive reception of an autonomous offer, but as an act of production (Firat & Venkatesh, 1995), mainly through the creation of content, enabled by the interactive web technologies found on social platforms and blogs.

In the context of tourism, a specific stream of research has emerged to describe this phenomenon, dubbed original tourism, and conventionally referred to as "*creative tourism*" (Smith, 2009). It can be described as fundamentally experiential tourism. As a result, the value attached to products is approached holistically through the content of the experience lived during their consumption, thought of as a primary subjective state provoked by the symbolism, hedonism, and aestheticism of the product.

In tourism, the principle of pleasure is paramount in the satisfaction derived from the consumer experience (Bourgeon & Bouchet, 2007), where imagination and range play a major role. Digitization is applied to the domain to enhance the co-creation of tourism experiences both in terms of the intensity of customer collaboration and the scope of co-created experiential values. According to Tang (2016), with digital marketing, the purpose of the company's communication strategy is to "*create added value for the company*" and "*increase the value perceived by consumers*", enabling the radical transformation of the customer experience, while allowing them to inform, and buy online. Indeed, digital transformation has revolutionized consumer behaviors and habits by introducing new, dematerialized, interactive, and collaborative business models (Fayon & Tartar, 2014). Tourism consumers are now freer, more involved in their consumption, and co-creators of their value (Cova & Cova, 2009; Prahalad & Ramaswamy, 2004; Lusch & Vargo, 2006). Consolidated by the use of new technologies, several types of value can be distinguished to enrich the consumption experience: functional, monetary, informational, emotional, and social (Gummerus & Philström, 2011; Gonzalez et al., 2012).

The interactivity, ubiquity, and connectivity induced by mobile digital technologies enhance customer experiences (Zhou and Lu, 2011), giving them greater control to make them their own (Saarijarvi et al., 2014). Mobile technologies appear to open up as yet untapped avenues for enhancing co-creation experiences and generating value for the customer. According to Armano's model (2007), the success of a communication strategy, particularly via social networks, is measured by its ability to capture prospects and turn them into loyal customers. Thus, *"consumer behavior is like a spiral that begins with an interaction as opposed to a communication. The spiral amplifies as the consumer increases engagement"*. This process can be simplified to information, interaction, engagement, conversation, and participation.

When it comes to tourism services, which are characterized by high levels of customer interactivity (Gronroos, 1990; Langeard & Eiglier, 1987) and simultaneous production and consumption (Grove et al., 2000), the tourist is more at the heart of the service experience process, as a more or less active, more or less innovative actor. Customers generally feel more committed to the brand when the latter allows them to create and share content with it (Mangold & Faulds, 2009). In short, mobilizing the virtual community, notably via social networks, is a means of personalizing the offer and ensuring social connectivity (Lu & Hsiao, 2010), encourages innovations and improvements to the offer (Hirt & Willmott, 2014), ensures better listening to customer needs and enables targeted communication via social networks.

Thus, the more the prospected tourist is engaged by accessing the higher stages of Armano's spiral (engagement, retention, or participation), the greater his or her contribution to the creation of the tourism experience (Figure 1).

Figure 1. Levels of commitment and collaboration in the co-creation of tourism experiences

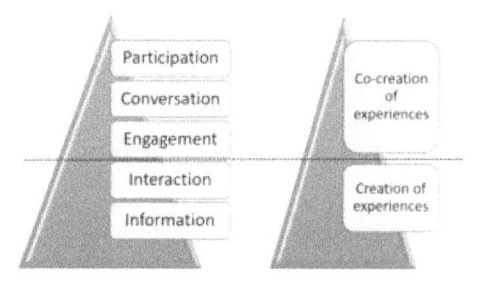

Source: own elaboration

Digital transformation has revolutionized consumer behaviors and habits, introducing new business models that are dematerialized, interactive, and collaborative (Fayon & Tartar, 2014). Consumers are now freer, more involved in their consumption (Firat & Dholakia, 2006), and co-creators of their value (Lusch & Vargo, 2006). Mobile technologies appear to be opening up as yet untapped avenues for enhancing co-creation experiences and generating value for the customer.

2. RESEARCH MODEL AND METHODOLOGY

The digitization of tourism communication is more than just a fad, it has gradually become a lever for improving the level of customer involvement in the experiential value creation process, particularly in the tourism sector.

In this sense, the use of digitalization, and especially digital social networks, is likely to increase the degree of tourist involvement in the purchasing process, and consequently the intensity of their co-creation of tourism experiences with the company. By becoming more involved in the tourist experience, the customer simultaneously improves the quality of his or her contributions to the creation of experiential value, by integrating as many of the dimensions in Table 1 as possible. Ultimately, approaching the interactions between the virtual community and the co-creation of the tourism experience comes down to analyzing the impact of the use of new digital media on the intensity and scope of the tourist's collaboration in the co-creation of experiential value (Figure 2).

Figure 2. Model for analyzing the impact of social networks on the co-creation of the tourism experience

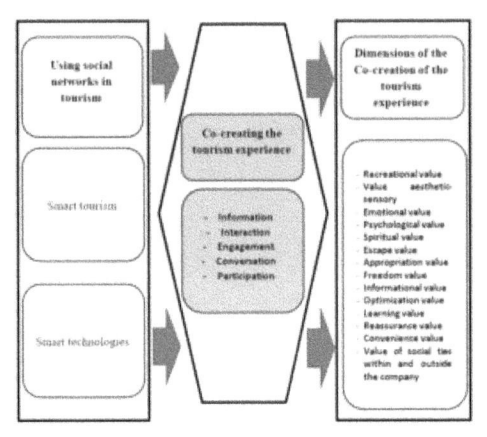

Source: own elaboration

Figure 2 presents a conceptual model that encapsulates the key elements involved in co-creating meaningful and valuable tourism experiences in the modern era. At its core, the model emphasizes the concept of "Co-creating the tourism experience" through active participation, engagement, and collaboration between tourists, service providers, and other stakeholders. This shift from a passive consumption model to one of co-creation recognizes the evolving role of tourists as active participants in shaping their own experiences. The model identifies five key aspects that facilitate this co-creation process: information sharing, interaction, engagement, conversation, and participation. These aspects underscore the importance of two-way communication, collaboration, and active involvement of tourists in the experience design and delivery process. The left side of the model highlights the role of "Using social networks in tourism" as a catalyst for co-creation. Social networks have emerged as powerful platforms for tourists to connect, share experiences, and actively participate in the tourism ecosystem. They enable real-time interactions, crowdsourcing of information, and the formation of virtual communities around travel and tourism. The right side presents the "Dimensions of the Co-creation of the tourism experience," which encompass a comprehensive range of intrinsic and extrinsic values that tourists seek. These dimensions span various aspects, including recreation, aesthetics, emotions, personal growth, freedom, information, optimization, learning, reassurance, convenience, and social connections. By actively involving tourists in the co-creation process, these diverse dimensions of value can be better addressed and tailored to individual preferences and needs.

The foundation of the model lies in "Smart tourism" enabled by "Smart technologies." These technologies, such as mobile apps, virtual reality, artificial intelligence, and the Internet of Things, serve as enablers for seamless information exchange, real-time interactions, and personalized experiences. They facilitate the flow of data, automation, and integration of various touchpoints in the tourism ecosystem, empowering both tourists and service providers to co-create unique and tailored experiences. This conceptual model captures the shift towards a more participatory and collaborative approach to tourism experiences. It recognizes the importance of leveraging social networks and smart technologies to facilitate co-creation, addressing the multidimensional nature of tourist values and expectations. The model for analyzing the impact of social networks on the co-creation of tourism experiences presupposes a satisfactory level of coherence and integration of the company's digital marketing communications approach.

The use of social networks leads to greater commitment on the part of the virtual community, by developing their participation in the creation of tourism experiences, their more active involvement in the purchasing process, and the enhancement of their consumption experiences and the development of their content. We now propose to focus on assessing the effectiveness of the approach by studying the virtual community's appreciation, via social networks, of its contribution to the process of co-creating tourism experiences. To explore the scope and effectiveness of the tourism marketing communication approach in the age of digitalization, notably through the use of social networks, we propose to analyze the opinions and comments of hotel guests, to report on their level of involvement in the purchase process of the establishments concerned in the city of Fez, Morocco.

Netnography is a combination of the two words Internet and Ethnography (Alla et al., 2019). Netnography emerged in the United States in the 1990s (Kozinets, 2015).

The advantage of using this method is that it puts the researcher in the position of an observer, without influencing the participant (Skandrani et al., 2009). All that's required is to monitor online communities using netnographic observation techniques, making the research method faster and more cost-effective. One of the main advantages of netnography is the ability to extend the geographical scope of the research field, connecting globally dispersed networks and increasing the researcher's accessibility to the population under study. This is particularly useful for hard-to-reach groups and sensitive research topics such as illegal acts, diseases, health concerns and interests, stigmatized phenomena, and groups (migrants, disabled, etc.). A major drawback of netnography is the researcher's inability to control the sampling structure, coupled with the lack of a predetermined questionnaire, interview schedule, observation plan, or any overarching research design for data collection (Lamsiah & Bentalha, 2023). Furthermore, a critical limitation of netnography stems from its incapacity to capture the full spectrum of offline interactions

(Morais et al., 2020). The selection of netnography as the methodological approach is warranted by the distinctive nature of the research question under investigation. Upon identifying and locating the relevant online community, the analysis will entail scrutinizing the opinions and comments posted on these platforms, aligning with the research inquiry. The initial step involves downloading all comments from multiple accounts pertinent to the research. Subsequently, in the second stage, the researchers will engage in double-coding the corpus to categorize the messages into thematic groupings. The overarching objective is to conduct a contextualized analysis of the various exchanges transpiring between members of the virtual community. The choice of Fez as the field of analysis is justified both by the city's reputation as a benchmark tourist destination and by the heritage, environmental, and social challenges inherent in this activity in the city. The empirical study takes the form of a survey of 412 customer reviews and comments, as posted on the Facebook accounts of Fez hotel establishment statements, during the study period (December 2022 and March 2023). For greater credibility, the reviews and comments analyzed were taken at random from Internet queries. Opinions and comments from the virtual community were statistically processed using TROPES and IRAMUTEQ software.

3. RESULTS AND DISCUSSION

Several academic works have already attempted to link the two parts of the empirical study. Tourism organizations greatly benefit from social media as a means to cultivate active engagement and connection with consumers. A well-executed social media strategy positively impacts the capacity for co-creation, specifically enhancing the ability to effectively leverage consumer knowledge and turn it into valuable resources for the organization (Tussyadiah & Zach, 2013).

Buhalis & Inversini (2014) demonstrated how the internet has enabled companies to profitably expand their customer base globally. Tourism businesses can access international customers and manage properties worldwide with ease, recognizing technology's importance for success and the need to manage their online presence holistically. Social media platforms facilitate the creation and exchange of user-generated content. Oliveira & Panyik (2015) analyzed tourist-generated content, which can produce value if integrated into destination branding strategies. Neuhofer (2016) studied how technological resources are integrated by examining the dichotomous relationship between value co-creation and co-destruction in connected tourism experiences. Through qualitative analysis, six dimensions were identified highlighting how connectivity can create or destroy value. Buonincontri & Micera (2016) examined how smart tourism destinations utilize technology to enhance co-creation of tourism experiences. Their interpretive framework explains how the technological components of smart destinations foster co-creation by encouraging interaction, active participation, and experience sharing among tourists.

Reichenberger (2017) explored value co-creation in tourism through the lens of social interactions among visitors. The study analyzed manifestations of these interactions, influencing factors, and types of value co-created, offering insights into relevant tourism interactions. Lee et al. (2017) investigated how interactive multimedia features on mobile travel services can enhance the tourist experience. Their findings suggest that multimedia interactivity on mobile travel apps has the potential to enrich co-creative experiences for tourists.

Gupta et al. (2020) suggested that utilizing augmented and virtual reality technologies at heritage sites can contribute to co-creating enhanced overall visitor tourism experiences. This can benefit stakeholders through increased spending and positive word-of-mouth. Buhalis et al. (2022) examined how the Metaverse can facilitate co-creation of tourism experiences by enabling consumers to engage with hotel organizations and other customers before, during, and after their visit. While the Metaverse presents both opportunities and challenges, hotel organizations must strategically leverage it to offer personalized experiences. Panhale et al. (2023) discussed using augmented reality in heritage tourism to facilitate visitors co-creating experiences. They identified five techniques for augmented reality-enabled co-creation and highlighted opportunities for this technology across other sectors. Garanti (2023) explored the concept of value co-creation within an intelligent tourism ecosystem, where all stakeholders participate in creating and sharing benefits from tourism products, services, and experiences. Intelligent tourism leverages ICTs to enhance experiences, with value co-creation involving all ecosystem stakeholders.

This literature review has enabled us to draw up an initial assessment of the importance of digital tools in the co-creation of the tourism experience. Following this literature review and the comments collected, we carried out a qualitative content analysis to identify the items involved in co-creating the tourism experience.

3.1. Use of Social Networks and Intensity of Co-Creation of Tourism Experiences

Statistical analysis via IRAMUTEQ of the opinions and comments of hotel guests using the Internet has enabled us to identify a panoply of fundamental items for assessing the level of their involvement in the process of creating tourist experiences during their stay in hotel establishments. The manual grouping of the above items enabled us to assess and extract 15 main dimensions for measuring the degree of customer involvement in the process of creating tourism experiences during their stay in Fez hotel establishments (Table 2).

Table 2. Degree of involvement of the virtual community in the process of consuming hotel services

Dimensions	Items	Description	Score		Percent (%)	
Information	General information	General destination and destination information	130	1727	2,0%	27,0%
	Hotel information	General information about the hotel and hotel services	472		7,4%	
	Hotel Reputation	Operating mode, labels, and certification, ...	74		1,2%	
	Conditions of stay	Type and length of stay, customer expectations, and specific needs, ...	424		6,6%	
	Hotel service attributes	Attributes of check-in, rooms, catering, entertainment, SPA, check-out, etc.	627		9,8%	
Interaction	Relationship quality	Presentation, skills, attitudes, and behavior of contact personnel	542	1266	8,5%	19,8%
	Service quality	Quality of reception, rooms, meals, SPA services, entertainment, etc.	606		9,5%	
	Brand image	Hotel reputation, media coverage, and brand awareness, ...	118		1,8%	
Engagement	Service effectiveness	Quality of reception, accommodation, catering, SPA, entertainment, ...	638	1114	10,0%	17,4%
	Relationship effectiveness	Availability, professionalism, communication efficiency of contact personnel, ...	338		5,3%	
	Risk management	Anticipation and handling of risks, ...	138		2,2%	
Conservation	Satisfaction development	Customer intelligence and satisfaction, ...	750	1223	11,7%	19,1%
	Building loyalty	Customer delight and loyalty, ...	473		7,4%	
Participation	Developing participation	Promoting involvement, valuing participation, ...	356	829	5,6%	13,0%
	Developing value co-creation	Co-design, co-production, co-distribution, and stay, ...	707		11,1%	
			6 393		100%	

Source: survey data

While the above five functions are all crucial to the efficiency of the hotel experience, they also reflect varying degrees of customer involvement in the process of creating tourism experiences. Our study shows an average involvement of customers in the most advanced functions of the purchasing process, namely participation and conservation in the creation of tourism experiences, for 19.1% and 13% respectively, reflecting a trend - albeit insufficient but remarkable - towards the co-creation of experiences. It's worth noting that the other functions, which we describe as basic, namely information (27%), interaction (19.8%), and engagement (17.4%), remain essential prerequisites for developing tourism experiences, thereby encouraging the customer to collaborate in the process.

Overall, we can conclude that hotel guests in Fez remain appropriately involved in the process of creating tourism experiences, perhaps due to the potential of the destination and/or the specific profiles of the tourists attracted. This connectivity is a good indicator of the effectiveness of these entities' overall marketing communications approach, and not necessarily of their digitalization or use of social networks. Such conclusions can only be drawn by comparing them with the quality and nature of the messages delivered by these establishments on these same media.

3.2. The Use of Social Networks and the Scale of Co-Created Experiential Tourism Value

The result of the manual grouping of the above items by experiential value dimension co-created by the virtual community during their hotel stay in Fez is given in the following Table 3:

Table 3. Weight of co-created experiential tourism value dimensions

Dimensions	Items	Score		Percent (%)	
Self-oriented intrinsic values	Recreational value	111	1 944	3,0%	53,1%
	Value aesthetic-sensory	335		9,2%	
	Emotional value	446		12,2%	
	Psychological value	521		14,2%	
	Spiritual value	230		6,3%	
	Escape value	187		5,1%	
	Appropriation value	114		3,1%	
Self-oriented extrinsic values	Freedom Value	225	1 572	6,1%	43,0%
	Informational value	556		15,2%	
	Optimization value	109		3,0%	
	Learning value	227		6,2%	
	Reassurance value	273		7,5%	
	Convenience value	182		5,0%	
Extrinsic, other-oriented values	Value of social ties within and outside the company	143	143	3,9%	3,9%
		3 659		100,0%	

Source: survey data

All experiential dimensions - intrinsic and extrinsic, introverted and extroverted - remain very important in the process of co-creating tourism value. However, it is naturally more the intrinsic, self-oriented values first, then the extrinsic, self-oriented values that foster engagement in the creation of the experience (Marion, 2016). This is what the study reveals, with a predominance of the intrinsic, self-oriented dimension (53.1%), followed by the extrinsic, self-oriented dimension (43%), and finally the extrinsic, other-oriented dimension (3.9%). It's first and foremost the internal pleasure motives of sensation, embellishment, immersion, sensoriality, enhancement, etc. that drive us and guide our attitudes and behavior, mainly in a performance naturally marked by pleasure-seeking, delight, and enchantment.

To elucidate the attitudes that co-create tourist experiences for customers during their stay in Fez hotels, we present in Table 4 extracts of verbatim taken from hotel guests' reviews and comments.

Table 4. Customer verbatim excerpts to illustrate co-creation of experiences

Items	Illustrative verbatim
Recreational value	✓ "At the hotel lobby, we enjoy a good variety of magazines and journals, it's very entertaining while waiting for our turn at the counter!". ✓ "I really enjoy personally composing my salad, it's a lot of fun! ✓ "Forming a sports team for a tournament at the hotel club, ..."
Value aesthetic-sensory	✓ "It feels very nice to set my main course at the restaurant". ✓ "Oh, the result of my touches on the room decoration is really beautiful!" ✓ "I even freely chose the color, shape, and design of my plates at breakfast".
Emotional value	✓ "A small gesture of indulgence from the head chef, who put his cap on me as a reward for my 'excellent' dressing of my salad". ✓ "I was even invited to help prepare the pie for his birthday". ✓ "It's okay, I just did my very first belly dance thanks to the hotel".
Psychological value	✓ "From now on, I always greet the waiter in Arabic". ✓ "In this evening, I served champagne to my friends at the hotel discotheque". ✓ "I was invited to join in the group dance at a lively hotel party".
Spiritual value	✓ "With the panaché of juices, which I delicately composed myself, it takes me back to his last stay in Hawaii". ✓ "With the few ingredients I added myself, the result is a real Shabbat dish". ✓ "The table layout reminds me of a Fassi ftour. "
Escape value	✓ "The colors and flavors of the dish I have prepared invade all my senses. ✓ "The bouquet of flowers I've just composed takes me far away to paradise". ✓ "The soft music I've just listened to in my room makes me surf between the stars".
Appropriation value	✓ "Choosing between garden, terrace and dining room". ✓ "Choosing the type of flowers and vase design to place on your restaurant table".
Freedom Value	✓ "In the kitchen, I am free to season my meals as I wish". ✓ "In the hotel laundry, I can do the type of cleaning I want, when I want, and how I want. ✓ "Self-service in the restaurant saves me more time".
Informational value	✓ "My participation in the preparation of my birthday pie has enabled me to better differentiate between very similar ingredients". ✓ "By practicing cooking, you understand the importance of wearing your hat and gloves". ✓ "It's not at all easy to be a good host!"

continued on following page

Table 4. Continued

Items	Illustrative verbatim
Optimization value	✓ "With experience, you can avoid wasting ingredients in the restaurant business". ✓ "By serving myself with self-service, I only take what I want, without waste or abuse". ✓ "Sharing a self-made birthday pie with hotel guests".
Learning value	✓ It's an excellent opportunity to learn how to decorate your room properly. ✓ "It's a bit tricky at first, but gradually I'm getting better at composing my perfume during SPA treatments". ✓ "With time, I'm able to arrange my room's furnishings better".
Reassurance value	✓ "As a witness to the preparation of my room, the sterilization measures in the bathroom make me feel more reassured. ✓ "A little experience at the security gate made me feel more confident in the hotel! ✓ "A visit to the hotel control room really reassured me".
Convenience value	✓ "It's not really complicated to compose the Henan on your own legs". ✓ "The sofa in my bedroom is now multi-purpose". ✓ "With practice, the preparation of Moroccan tea is within reach".
Value of social ties within and outside the company	✓ "Self-service hasn't stopped me from developing a good relationship with the hotel's cooks". ✓ "Once, we invited some waiters to share a collective dinner". ✓ "Great sympathy with the waiter, to whom I even suggested changing the color of his tie".

Source: survey data

Tourism businesses must recognize the impact of the Web and social media on the co-creation of the tourism experience. Researchers and practitioners must acknowledge that listening to customer feedback is crucial in social media communication. With the evolution of social media, communication between consumers and organizations has become more integral, and tourism businesses must adapt to this change. To effectively create and maintain a positive co-creation of the tourism experience, tourism businesses must learn three key lessons. Firstly, they must listen to their customers. Social media platforms broadcast emotional information, and customers are exposed to both official and unofficial information. Tourism managers must engage with relevant audiences, establish a communication channel, and spread positive messages in the marketplace. This is essential to understand the mechanisms of co-creation and to foster a virtual circle of tourism value creation by and for the customer. Secondly, tourism businesses must tell emotional stories and recount events. Social media have transformed the Internet into a warm and engaging space, and emotional storytelling is an effective communication strategy for fostering an online reputation. Emotional stories lead to memorable experiences and encounters, making tourism a valuable engagement. Lastly, personalized experiences are essential in co-creating the tourism experience. These experiences are oriented towards others via a social link with and outside the tourism business. By recognizing the importance of these three lessons, tourism businesses can effectively create and maintain a positive co-creation of the tourism experience.

Co-creating the tourism experience means exploiting all the information available online to enhance the tourist experience. Far from being a foregone conclusion, consumers' recourse to digitalization, in this case via social networks, can only automatically promote them towards the co-creation of consumer experiences, via the virtual logic of the spiral of engagement and therefore of the transformation of the purchasing process. Psycho-cultural and practical obstacles stand in the way of this ascent, which can be sought by customers and companies alike. In fact, for a given hotel, the effectiveness of such an approach depends on the adoption of a more innovative and competitive communications policy by the establishment's marketing managers, by monitoring the appreciation and reactions of Internet users in this field, and by the continuous adaptation of such a strategy in line with the evolution of technologies, consumer purchasing behavior and competitive practices. Alongside these purely quantitative aspects, the attractiveness of a hotel establishment also and above all implies compliance with quality standards for the supply of tourist services, essentially through the relevance and effectiveness of the classification of tourist establishments, quality control, the improvement of staff qualifications, the renewal of management styles, the innovation of services and the quality of customer relations.

CONCLUSION

Travel experiences are always memorable events that transcend their particular setting. They succeed in finding their place in our lives. For tourism professionals, integrating experiential logic into day-to-day operations requires above all a change in thinking, for which they need a little time, imagination, and, above all, the right sensitivities. It's about understanding human emotion, having a real sense of hospitality, a little creativity, and a sense of showmanship while preserving a realistic, economic rationale. Digitalization is either a fad or a major trend. Social networks, in particular, are becoming more and more essential, and are constantly transforming their communication and marketing strategies. Prevéraud (2016) confirms that social networks are entering a new era. In this case, in the tourism and hotel sectors, the massive use of these media can be an excellent lever, mainly for building loyalty and winning over new customers, thus helping to improve the effectiveness of the company's marketing strategy.

By its very nature, the tourism service, by assuming simultaneity and intangibility, puts the tourist at the heart of the entire process, from conception to memorization; integration of the latter is both the guarantee of better satisfying his expectations, improving his satisfaction and delight and a tool for creative innovation and performance for the company, being based on customer intelligence. Our empirical study highlights this vocation, showing that hotels are keen to digitalize their marketing communications, in particular via social networks, to transform their sales process more effectively, by adapting it to the needs and expectations of Internet users.

Thanks to their autonomy and decision-making intelligence, customer-internauts can steal their attitudes and purchasing behaviors, helping to make or break the marketing efforts undertaken by a given tourism establishment's marketing managers. Tourism marketing is definitely in the web age. Despite the advantages of co-creating an experience with the customer, considerably accelerated by digitalization, studies are constantly highlighting the perverse effects of such an approach. Our work provides a theoretical and empirical basis for linking the co-creation of the tourism experience with digital technologies. It provides a conceptual and empirical link between the different facets of digital co-creation of the tourism experience, via a literature review and a qualitative study. In addition, the work focuses on a specific analysis of the Moroccan tourism market, which is a developing, African, and traditional part of the tourism sector. Finally, the study consolidates the importance of digital tools in the implementation and development of sustainable, shared tourism value creation.

Like any study, this research had certain constraints that subsequent investigations could address to broaden the relevance and practical applications of the results. The timeframe of the study and the number of comments analyzed seem to be obstacles to a generalization of the results. This study can therefore be taken further in several ways. A comparative analysis between different countries to identify contingency factors or divergence in the intensity of the facets identified by the study. Another option is a confirmatory quantitative analysis to numerically link the variables in the analysis model. Finally, a longitudinal study can be carried out to identify changes in trends over time and the factors influencing changes in tourism customers' perceptions of the use of social networks and the effects of these networks on the co-creation of the tourism experience.

REFERENCES

Abbes, I., & Hallem, Y. (2016). Co-création et technologie mobile au sein d'un espace marchand: Quelles valeurs pour le consommateur? Une application dans le secteur de la restauration. *Revue Française du Marketing*, (256), 81–98.

Alla, L., Hmioui, A., & Bentalha, B. (2020). La netnographie dans les recherches marketing: La communauté virtuelle comme consom'acteur vecteur d'efficacité marketing. Alternatives Managériales Economiques, 2(4), 631-652. DOI: DOI: 10.48374/IMIST.PRSM/ame-v2i4.23559

Armano, D. (2007). The marketing spiral. Logic+ Emotio [En ligne], https://darmano.typepad.com/logic_emotion/2007/08/the-marketing-s.html

Arnould E-J., Price L., & Zinkhan G. (2002), Consumers. McGraw-Hill.

Bourgeon D. et Bouchet P. (2007), Marketing expérientiel et analyse des logiques de consommation du spectacle sportif, Revue française du marketing, n°212.

Buhalis, D., & Inversini, A. (2014). Tourism branding, identity, reputation co-creation, and word-of-mouth in the age of social media. In Tourism Management, Marketing, and Development: Volume I: The Importance of Networks and ICTs (pp. 15-40). New York: Palgrave Macmillan US.

Buhalis, D., Lin, M. S., & Leung, D. (2022). Metaverse as a driver for customer experience and value co-creation: Implications for hospitality and tourism management and marketing. *International Journal of Contemporary Hospitality Management*, 35(2), 701–716. DOI: 10.1108/IJCHM-05-2022-0631

Buonincontri, P., & Micera, R. (2016). The experience co-creation in smart tourism destinations: A multiple case analysis of European destinations. *Information Technology & Tourism*, 16(3), 285–315. DOI: 10.1007/s40558-016-0060-5

Cova, B., & Cova, V. (2009). Les figures du nouveau consommateur: Une genèse de la gouvernementalité du consommateur. *Recherche et Applications en Marketing*, 24(3), 82–100. DOI: 10.1177/076737010902400305

Desmarteau, R., Saives, A.-L., Schieb-Bienfait, N., Emin, S., Boldrini, J.-C., & Urbain, C. (2017), La création de valeur: glas ou Graal? Revue et modélisation du concept, XXVIe Conférence Internationale de Management Stratégique, Lyon, 7-9 juin 2017.

Fayon, D., & Tartar, M. (2014). *Transformation digitale: 5 leviers pour l'entreprise*. Pearson.

FEVAD (Fédération E-commerce et Vente À Distance). (2023), Chiffres Clés 2023, 8 pages.[En ligne]: https://www.fevad.com

Firat, A. F., & Dholakia, N. (2006). Theoretical and philosophical implications of postmodern debates: Some challenges to modern marketing. *Marketing Theory*, 6(2), 123–162. DOI: 10.1177/1470593106063981

Firat, F., & Venkatesh, A. (1995). Liberatory postmodernism and the reenchantement of consumption. *The Journal of Consumer Research*, 22(3), 239. DOI: 10.1086/209448

Garanti, Z. (2023). Value co-creation in smart tourism destinations. *Worldwide Hospitality and Tourism Themes*, 15(5), 468–475. DOI: 10.1108/WHATT-06-2023-0070

Gonzalez, C., Hure, E., & Picot-Coupey, K. (2012), Usages et valeurs des applications mobiles pour les consommateurs: quelles implications pour les distributeurs? *Colloque Etienne Thill*, 2012, Lille.

Guimont D. et Lapointe D. (2015), Co-creation of a tourist experience enhanced by technology, in the context of a Living Lab.

Gummerus, J., & Pihlström, M. (2011). Context and mobile services' value-in-use. *Journal of Retailing and Consumer Services*, 18(6), 521–533. DOI: 10.1016/j.jretconser.2011.07.002

Gupta, V., Sajnani, M., & Dixit, S. K. (2020). Impact of augmented and virtual reality on the value co-creation of visitor's tourism experience: A case of heritage sites in Delhi. In *Tourism in Asian Cities* (pp. 263–277). Routledge. DOI: 10.4324/9780429264801-19

Hirschman, E.-C., & Holbrook, M.-B. (1982a). Hedonic consumption: Emerging concepts, methods and propositions. *Journal of Marketing*, 46(3), 92–101. DOI: 10.1177/002224298204600314

Hirschman, E.-C., & Holbrook, M.-B. (1982b). The experiential aspects of consumption: Consumer fantasies, feelings and fun. *The Journal of Consumer Research*, 9(2).

Hirt, M., & Willmott, P. (2014). Strategic principles for competing in the digital age. *The McKinsey Quarterly*, 5(1), 1–13.

Hmioui, A., Alla, L., & Bentalha, B. (2022). Perception du tourisme durable par les clients étrangers: Cas du séjour dans un établissement hôtelier. Reconfigurations du tourisme en contexte de la crise du Covid-19: Quelles démarches pour quelles résiliences au Maroc et ailleurs?, 1(1), 5-38.

Kozinets, R. V. (2015). Netnography: Redefined. *Sage (Atlanta, Ga.)*.

Lamsiah, A., & Bentalha, B. (2023). 2022 Qatar World Cup: A Netnographic Analysis of the Relationship Between Sport, Media and Politic. Réflexions sportives, 1(3), 69-95.

Leclercq, T., Poncin, I., & Hammedi, W. (2016). Dix ans de co-création de valeur: Une revue intégrative. *Recherche et Applications en Marketing*, 31(3), 1–38. DOI: 10.1177/0767370116638270

Lee, L. S., Shaharuddin, S. S., Ng, G. W., & Wan-Busrah, S. F. (2017). Co-creation tourism experience in perceived usability of interactive multimedia features on mobile travel application. Journal of Telecommunication, Electronic and Computer Engineering (JTEC), 9(2-9), 155-161.

Lequin, M. (2002). L'écotourisme. Expérience d'une interaction nature-culture. *Téoros*, 21(3), 38–42. DOI: 10.7202/1072501ar

Lu, H. P., & Hsiao, K. L. (2010). The influence of extro/introversion on the intention to pay for social networking sites. *Information & Management*, 47(3), 150–157. DOI: 10.1016/j.im.2010.01.003

Lusch, R.-F., & Vargo, S.-L. (2006). Service-Dominant Logic: Reactions, Reflections and Refinements. *Marketing Theory*, 6(3), 281–288. DOI: 10.1177/1470593106066781

Mangold, W. G., & Faulds, D. J. (2009). Social media: The new hybrid element of the promotion mix. *Business Horizons*, 52(4), 357–365. DOI: 10.1016/j.bushor.2009.03.002

Marion, G. (2016). *Le consommateur coproducteur de valeur. L'axiologie de la consommation.* Cormelles-le-Royal, Editions EMS. DOI: 10.3917/ems.mario.2016.01

Morais, G. M., Santos, V. F., & Gonçalves, C. A. (2020). Netnography: Origins, Foundations, Evolution and Axiological and Methodological Developments and Trends. *The Qualitative Report*, 25(1), 441–455. DOI: 10.46743/2160-3715/2020.4227

Neuhofer, B. (2016). Value co-creation and co-destruction in connected tourist experiences. In Information and Communication Technologies in Tourism 2016: Proceedings of the International Conference in Bilbao, Spain, February 2-5, 2016 (pp. 779-792). Springer International Publishing. DOI: 10.1007/978-3-319-28231-2_56

Neuhofer, B., Buhalis, D., & Ladkin, A. (2013), Experiences, co-creation and technology: a conceptual approach to enhance tourism experiences, Tourism and Global Change: On the Edge of Something Big, *Conference Proceeding*.

Oliveira, E., & Panyik, E. (2015). Content, context and co-creation: Digital challenges in destination branding with references to Portugal as a tourist destination. *Journal of Vacation Marketing*, 21(1), 53–74. DOI: 10.1177/1356766714544235

Panhale, T., Bryce, D., & Tsougkou, E. (2023). Augmented reality and experience co-creation in heritage settings. *Journal of Marketing Management*, 39(5-6), 470–497. DOI: 10.1080/0267257X.2022.2120061

Pine, B. J., II. & Gilmore, J. H. 1999. The Experience Economy. Work is Theatre and Every Business a Stage. Harvard Business School Press. Boston

Prevéraud, J.-F. (2016), Réseaux sociaux: quels sont les risques pour les entreprises? https://www.industrie-techno.com/reseaux-sociaux-quels-sont-les-risques-pour-les-entreprises.9703

Reichenberger, I. (2017). C2C value co-creation through social interactions in tourism. *International Journal of Tourism Research*, 19(6), 629–638. DOI: 10.1002/jtr.2135

Skandrani, H., Touzani, L., & Touzani, M. (2009). *Identification des perceptions et des déterminants de l'image d'une destination touristique: une application de l'approche netnographique*. Revue Marocaine de Recherche en Management et Marketing.

Smith M. K. (2009). Issues in Cultural Tourism Studies. Routledge.

Tang, J. (2016), *Comment définir sa stratégie digitale?* http://www.jacques-tang.fr/comment-mettre-en-place-sa-strategie-digitale

Tussyadiah, I., & Zach, F. (2013). Social media strategy and capacity for consumer co-creation among destination marketing organizations. In Information and Communication Technologies in Tourism 2013: Proceedings of the International Conference in Innsbruck, Austria, January 22-25, 2013 (pp. 242-253). Springer Berlin Heidelberg. DOI: 10.1007/978-3-642-36309-2_21

Zammar, N. (2012), Réseaux Sociaux numériques: essai de catégorisation et cartographie des controverses. Thèse de doctorat en Sociologie. Université Européenne de Bretagne, Rennes 2, France.

Zhou, T., & Lu, Y. (2011). The effect of interactivity on the flow experience of mobile commerce user. *International Journal of Mobile Communications*, 9(3), 225–242. DOI: 10.1504/IJMC.2011.040604

Chapter 11
The Transformative Impact of Artificial Intelligence on Tourism Experience:
Analysis of Trends and Perspectives

Mourad Aarabe
https://orcid.org/0009-0003-9772-6683
National School of Business and Management of Fez, Morocco

Meryem Bouizgar
https://orcid.org/0009-0009-0943-2057
National School of Business and Management of Fez, Morocco

Nouhaila Ben Khizzou
National School of Business and Management of Fez, Morocco

Lhoussaine Alla
https://orcid.org/0000-0002-7238-1792
National School of Applied Sciences of Fez, Morocco

Ahmed Benjelloun
https://orcid.org/0009-0004-9673-2747
National School of Business and Management of Fez, Morocco

ABSTRACT

In today's turbulent and hyper-connected global environment, the integration of

DOI: 10.4018/979-8-3693-5678-4.ch011

emerging technologies has become a necessity rather than a choice. The aim of this research is to identify the trends, benefits, challenges, practical, and theoretical implications of artificial intelligence on the tourism experience, focusing the attention on the transformative potential of AI. With this perspective, the authors propose a rigorous systematic literature review following the PRISMA protocol. The results of this rigorous analysis, carried out using Nvivo software, reveal the growing role and transformative impact of artificial intelligence in enhancing the tourism experience.

INTRODUCTION

In a world that is in a constant state of evolution and highly interconnected, modern marketing has been significantly affected by the fast development of new technologies (Grewal et al., 2020; Kumar et al., 2021a; Shah & Murthi, 2021). Today, both theorists and practitioners are confronted with novel opportunities and challenges related to using technologies such as artificial intelligence in marketing. Among many sectors, the tourism industry is one of the most profoundly impacted by these advancements (Tussyadiah, 2020). This has led to the appearance of a novel concept termed "smart tourism"(Buhalis & Amaranggana, 2015a; Buhalis & Leung, 2018).

The tourism industry has become smarter as a result of the advent of new technologies (Knani et al., 2022) by using AI solutions to improve customer service (Lacárcel, 2022). This trend has attracted both scientists and professionals, who want to understand how AI changes consumer behavior, redefines interactions with tourist sites, and affects the experiences of travelers worldwide (Buhalis & Moldavska, 2022).

Despite the value of the topic, research on the use of artificial intelligence in the tourism industry remains underexplored. This is evident in the lack of attention given to key areas such as the identification of issues, opportunities, risks, and marketing performance outcomes. There is also a dearth of research examining the actual achievements of adopting and integrating solutions provided by this technology (Koo et al., 2023).

Our contribution aims to fill this gap by conducting a systematic review of the literature on the most relevant research regarding how the adoption of artificial intelligence can improve the quality of the customer experience in the tourism sector. The main objective is to identify trends, benefits, challenges, managerial and theoretical implications of the marketing adoption of this technology and its transformative impact. To achieve this, our research focuses on the following central question: What are the main marketing applications of artificial intelligence, and what is its impact on the tourism experience?

In order to achieve this objective, a systematic approach has been adopted for the literature review, based on an overall view. This approach will facilitate the coverage of a wide range of artificial intelligence applications. Secondly, the systematic literature search will adhere to the PRISMA protocol in order to select relevant studies from reliable academic databases. Finally, the collected data will be analyzed using the software Nvivo.

To find answers to our question, we will start by presenting a literature review that focuses on the structure of concepts regarding artificial intelligence, the tourism experience, and its transformative impact, followed by an examination of the current state of the interrelationship between these concepts. Next, we will present the methodology employed in our literature review. We will then present the main results and discussion, before summarizing the key implications, challenges, the structure of concepts, and future research prospects.

1. BACKGROUND AND LITERATURE REVIEW

Recent studies have illuminated the transformative impact of artificial intelligence on the tourism industry, particularly in the development of smart tourism destinations through the integration of the Internet of Things and artificial intelligence (Aliyah et al., 2023). Artificial intelligence applications cover various areas, including robotics, conversational systems, and predictive tools with a focus on sustainability (Dalipi et al., 2023). The adoption and implementation of AI in the tourism and hospitality industry has significantly changed marketing strategies and practices (Kim et al., 2024). According to Saydam et al., (2022), emerging themes in AI and tourism research include anthropomorphism, robotic services, and customer and employee perspectives on AI technologies. While AI offers several opportunities to improve the visitor experience and destination management, several challenges persist, including those related to privacy and personal data protection, as well as ethical and deontological considerations (Aliyah et al., 2023; Dalipi et al., 2023). In this section, we will attempt to conceptualize the key terms of our research beginning with artificial intelligence (1.1.1), the tourism experience (1.1.2), the smart tourism experience (1.1.3), and the transformative impact (1.1.4). We will then proceed to present a review of the current state of the art on artificial intelligence and tourist experience (1.2).

1.1. A Conceptual Approach to the Research

1.1.1. Artificial Intelligence

The term "artificial intelligence", or AI, was first introduced in 1956 at the Dartmouth Conference by a group of scientists and mathematicians (Hildebrand, 2019). It's a part of computer systems that aims to develop human-like intelligence abilities, including those pertaining to perception, reasoning, learning, and interaction with the environment (Huang & Rust, 2018). Through the use of algorithms and machine learning models, AI can analyze data and solve problems autonomously (Davenport et al., 2019, 2020). According to Bag et al., (2021), artificial intelligence refers to a set of devices that have been designed to emulate human intelligence in performing tasks or solving problems based on data generated by other technological advancements.

According to Kumar et al., (2021), the application of artificial intelligence helps to automate and improve marketing practices. Algorithms, machine learning, and other AI-powered technologies can analyze data to make relevant marketing decisions and give information about customer buying behavior (Stone et al., 2020). AI offers several possibilities for use in marketing, such as customization, predictive analysis, and chatbots, to improve efficiency, productivity, customer experience, revenue, and profitability (Asi et al., 2023).

Artificial intelligence is increasingly used to improve the traveler experience and optimize the operations of tourism businesses (Ghesh et al., 2023). Its applications in tourism include personalized travel recommendations, reservation management, price optimization, and traveler assistance throughout their journey (Prahadeeswaran, 2023). Through AI, tourism businesses can provide services that are more closely aligned with the specific needs of individual travelers, which can boost customer satisfaction and optimize revenue generation. AI can also contribute to customer engagement, simplify booking processes, and generate new revenue (Bilgihan & Ricci, 2023; Ku & Chen, 2024).

1.1.2. Tourism Experience

The tourism experience is a complex concept that has so many dimensions, such as individual motivations and interactions with the tourist environment. Many researchers have studied this concept, providing us with a deep understanding of its dimensions and specific mechanisms (Table 1).

Table 1. Summary of definitions of customer experience according to authors

Authors	Definitions
(Holbrook & Hirschman, 1982)	The customer experience is the combination of enjoyable and immersive elements such as the atmosphere, the presentation of the offer, and the layout of the store.
(Arnould & Price, 1993)	The customer experience is a cognitive process of making sense through social interactions between consumers and their environments during all stages of consumption (before, during, and after).
(Pine & Gilmore, 1998)	It's a unique, enjoyable, and sensory event that includes various memorable activities and impressions.
(Schmitt, 1999)	It results from interactions between an individual and an environment, including senses, emotions, actions, and thoughts.
(Chen & Tsai, 2007)	The tourism experience is a cognitive development that relies on sensory, emotional, and behavioral understandings.
(Rashid, 2013)	The tourism experience is diverse and includes various behavioral, social, cognitive, and emotional dimensions.
(Tung & Law, 2017)	The tourism experience is about the social, cognitive, and behavioral interactions during a journey.

Source: Authors

The tourism experience is a dynamic and personal process based on how people interact with their tourist surroundings (Witell et al., 2020). Besides using products or services, Holbrook & Hirschman, (1982) describe it as an experimental phenomenon involving both cognitive and emotional immersion. Zhou et al., (2023) viewed the quality of tourist services and visitor satisfactions are pivotal determinants of the tourism experience. Similarly, according to Knani et al., (2022), suggest that social media and other forms of technology may also influence travelers' expectations and experiences.

1.1.3. Smart Tourism Experience

Several authors (Aarabe et al., 2024; Buhalis & Amaranggana, 2015b; Kumar et al., 2023; Lee & Jan, 2023; Pai et al., 2020; Sustacha et al., 2023) have sought to conceptualize the notion of a smart tourism experience from a multidisciplinary perspective. This encompasses domains such as tourism, marketing, technology, and sustainability. As posited by Sustacha et al., (2023), the smart tourism experience involves the deployment of technological advancements to enhance the quality and personalization of trips. Buhalis & Amaranggana, (2015) postulate that the tourism experience encompasses both pre- and post-stay aspects and extends beyond the stay itself. Moreover, (Lee & Jan, 2023) examined the attributes of the smart tourism experience, including the utility and hedonic experience offered by emerging technologies such as virtual and augmented reality.

The literature indicates a growing interest in the smart tourism experience, with particular attention to emerging technologies such as augmented reality (Kounavis et al., 2012), artificial intelligence (Bhaskar & Sharma, 2022), the Internet of Things, and big data (Alla et al., 2022) to provide innovative and personalized solutions that enhance the tourism experience. The following table summarizes the main dimensions of smart tourism experiences by type of adopted emerging technology.

Table 2. Summary of the main mechanisms of the smart tourism experience

Authors	Mechanisms of the smart tourism experience
(Kounavis et al., 2012)	Using AR/VR technology and mobile devices makes natural resources look better.
(Gretzel et al., 2015)	Using advanced technology and involving tourists make the tourism experience better.
(Buhalis & Amaranggana, 2015b)	Planning resources better and giving people special services makes costs lower and makes businesses better.
(Chung et al., 2017)	Geolocation is a new technology in smart tourism that helps travelers have better experiences.
(Femenia-Serra & Neuhofer, 2018)	Smart tourism experiences happen when smart decisions are made with technology, like using data, real-time info, working together, and knowing the situation.
(Tussyadiah, 2020)	People in tourism are using new technology more to help them make decisions.
(H. Kim et al., 2021)	Making travel less stressful and better for tourists with the use of efficient and smart transportation systems.
(van Esch et al., 2022)	Making travel better with technology like electronic payments, and virtual reality, and knowing what traffic is like right now.
(Shin et al., 2022)	Reliable technology promotes memorable experiences and positive behavioral intentions.
(Li et al., 2023)	Optimizing travel through modeling the tourist transport system using a holistic approach to reduce waiting time and transportation expenses while considering the dynamics of tourist travel demands.
(X. Wang et al., 2016; Y. Wang et al., 2016)	Making online reservations and payments, using virtual reality, smart cards, and other services to promote interactions between tourists and improve the tourism experience. Thus, technology readiness is an indicator of satisfaction with travel technologies.

Source: inspired by (Aarabe et al., 2024)

1.1.4. Transformative Impact

- **Impact**

According to the Oxford dictionary, the term "impact" has two distinct meanings. First, this term is used to describe when one thing striking another with considerable force, resulting in a sudden and intense disturbance. Second, it means a big effect or influence, which can be either beneficial or detrimental, and can affect many different things. Different kinds of impact can be put into groups based on different criteria and can affect many different parts of life, from the sciences to society at large.

The examination of disparate types of impact, including those pertaining to cultural influence, societal transformation, and organizational dynamics, is of paramount importance in a multitude of fields. The cultural impacts of tourism can make local culture better or worse, especially for rural and minority groups (Reed & Fazey, 2021). The social impacts of sports include making people healthier, reducing crime, and helping students do better in school, with a focus on how people feel and many different social effects (Taylor et al., 2015). Organizational impact, which is about how companies work, affects how well a company does and if it can keep its values, showing how different kinds of companies are important for being successful (Sivasankaran, 2016).

In this way of thinking, it's important to understand and deal with these different impacts to solve big problems in society, make good changes, and make sure that people and groups can keep working together well.

- **Transformation**

According to the Large-Scale Change (LSC) theory (Wigboldus et al., 2020), change processes can be categorized into three different types: gradual change, change through reform, and transformation. Gradual change focuses on slowly adjustment of existing systems, aiming to make them stronger or weaker in some areas while keeping them largely the same overall (Waddell et al., 2015). It's about making small changes within the system without questioning its basic principles or overall structure. Reform involves shifting power or control among different parts of a connected system. This happens when one group or part of the system gains more influence, sometimes at the expense of others, changing how power works within the system (Schein, 2010). This also happens within the existing system without changing its basic principles. Transformation is a deep and widespread change resulting from a new understanding of what's possible and different ways of doing things. It's not just about making small adjustments or changing who's in charge, but about completely changing the way things work. So, it's the most significant change, affecting the very foundations of a system or society. It's not just about adjusting surface-level things, but about changing the basic rules and assumptions by which the system operates.

The Large system change (LSC) theory, as explained by (Dentoni et al., 2017), helps manage transformations by adding two important parts: understanding why people do what they do and handling disagreements. The first part is about understanding why people act the way they do. The LSC theory helps us understand the key things that make lasting changes successful (Dentoni et al., 2017). It shows how people start doing things differently and how to ensure that these changes are sustainable. The second part is about managing disagreement. The LSC theory says that big changes can cause arguments and disagreements between different groups of people. It says it's important to manage with these arguments in a way that makes everyone feel heard. It also suggests finding solutions that work for everyone.

- **Transformative impact**

Transformative Impact refers to significant changes that have a transformative effect, altering perspectives, values, structures of personal experience, and even the phenomenal nature of individual lifestyles (Guitart, 2022). Transformative change is defined by (Haxeltine et al., 2016) as *"change that questions, modifies, and/or replaces established (and/or dominant) institutions in a specific socio-material context."* It is characterized by a profound alteration of values, perceptions, and behaviors within a society.

This transformation is more than a mere superficial change (Waddell et al., 2015) and is distinct from simple modification of a single dimension of the socio-material context (like XYZ). In order to discuss a transformative impact, it is necessary to consider a simultaneous and extensive restructuring across multiple dimensions of the socio-material context. This restructuring must break with previous patterns in order to shape a new social reality. Strasser et al., (2019) employed the theory of transformative social innovation (STI) to delineate the dimensions of organizational transformative impact, which are depth, width, and length as detailed in the table below.

Table 3. Dimensions of Transformative Impact/Change according to STI Theory by (Strasser et al., 2020)

Dimension	Mechanisms
Depth	It can happen at different levels of depth, from gradual changes to complete reform or transformation.
Width	The width of the change means how big and far-reaching it is. Transformation can happen on different levels, from local to global, and affect lots of areas of activity, sectors, or groups of people.

continued on following page

Table 3. Continued

Dimension	Mechanisms
Length	It's about how well the change lasts over time and deals with future challenges and changes, while being able to adapt and keep its positive impact for a long time.

Source: Authors

1.2. State of the Art: Artificial Intelligence and Tourism Experience

Different fields, such as architecture, citizen science, and urban planning, explore transformative impacts. For example, the COVID-19 pandemic highlighted the transformative impact on user behavior, space arrangement, and socio-political aspects in urban areas (Rosni & Zainol, 2022).

The concept of transformative impact has many aspects and is always evolving, as shown by various researches. These include exploring the challenges of moving beyond traditional architectural practices (Von Gönner et al., 2023) to create socially and environmentally fair built environments (Guitart, 2022), applying the theory of transformative learning in high-impact educational experiences for effective measurement and documentation (Acheson et al., 2022), or developing a transformative leadership program with global reach and cultural adaptability (Barstow Hernandez, 2018).

Dafoe, (2018) defined transformative AI as "advanced AI that could lead to radical changes in well-being, wealth, or power." The discussion on transformative AI highlights the potential societal implications of advanced AI technologies beyond traditional notions of general artificial intelligence, emphasizing the need to anticipate and reduce extreme impacts on society (Gruetzemacher & Whittlestone, 2019).

Several authors have shown growing interest in research on integrating artificial intelligence into the tourism industry (Knani et al., 2022). An agreement on the opportunities offered by AI to improve various aspects of the tourism experience has been shown by several authors (Li et al., 2021; Prahadeeswaran, 2023; Zheng & Wu, 2023).

The work of (Gretzel et al., 2015) highlighted the rise of "smart tourism," a concept that tries to use technological advances to improve the tourism experience and generate economic benefits (Bilgihan & Ricci, 2023). AI plays a key role in developing smart systems capable of analyzing tourist data, recommending personalized destinations and activities (Grundner & Neuhofer, 2021), and optimizing the management of tourist resources (Kashem et al., 2023).

Artificial intelligence can be used in various marketing strategies related to tourism (Lacárcel, 2022). This includes machine learning for data analysis and customer segmentation, decision support systems to optimize advertising campaigns and personalized offers (Bhaskar & Sharma, 2022), social media analysis to understand traveler trends and preferences, AI algorithms to recommend destinations and activities, and using virtual reality and chatbots to improve user experience and provide more efficient customer service (Ku & Chen, 2024).

The integration of artificial intelligence into the tourism industry offers significant opportunities to improve visitor satisfaction (Ku & Chen, 2024; Manthiou & Klaus, 2022), optimize the management of tourist resources (Kashem et al., 2023), and enhance the competitiveness of destinations (Grundner & Neuhofer, 2021). However, to fully benefit from these advantages, it is essential to prioritize traveler data security and privacy (Bhaskar & Sharma, 2022; Buhalis & Moldavska, 2022; Sustacha et al., 2023).

In this section, a conceptual and theoretical framework was discussed by delving into the key concepts related to our study, namely artificial intelligence, tourism experience, and smart tourism experience, while emphasizing the concept of transformative impact. The latter made it possible to establish a link between artificial intelligence and tourist experience in the state-of-the-art subsection. In order to provide a response to this relationship, a rigorous methodological approach was adopted, as will be explained in the following section.

2. METHODOLOGICAL APPROACH

This systematic literature review (de Almeida Biolchini et al., 2007) examines the relationship between artificial intelligence and tourism experience. To gather our reference sample, we carefully followed the PRISMA protocol (Moher et al., 2009; PRISMA-P Group et al., 2015; Shamseer et al., 2015). This method follows strict standards and guidelines to ensure the relevance of the selected references (Mateo, 2020). A thorough search in well-known scientific databases such as SCOPUS, Web of Science (WOS), Springer, and Science Direct was conducted using relevant keywords ("tourist experience"; "tourism experience"; "AI"; "Artificial intelligence"; "transformative impact"…), resulting in a group of 568 articles. After improving the search, through the research domain filter and relevance filter (excluding references not matched with our issue, based on examination of titles, abstracts, and keywords), our collection was reduced to 35 articles (Figure 1).

To maximize our collection and capture references not identified in the search engines, we will use a reverse snowballing approach. This involves examining and selecting references from the initial sample based on their relevance, using the same inclusion and exclusion criteria as before (Wohlin, 2014).

Figure 1. PRISMA Flow Diagram

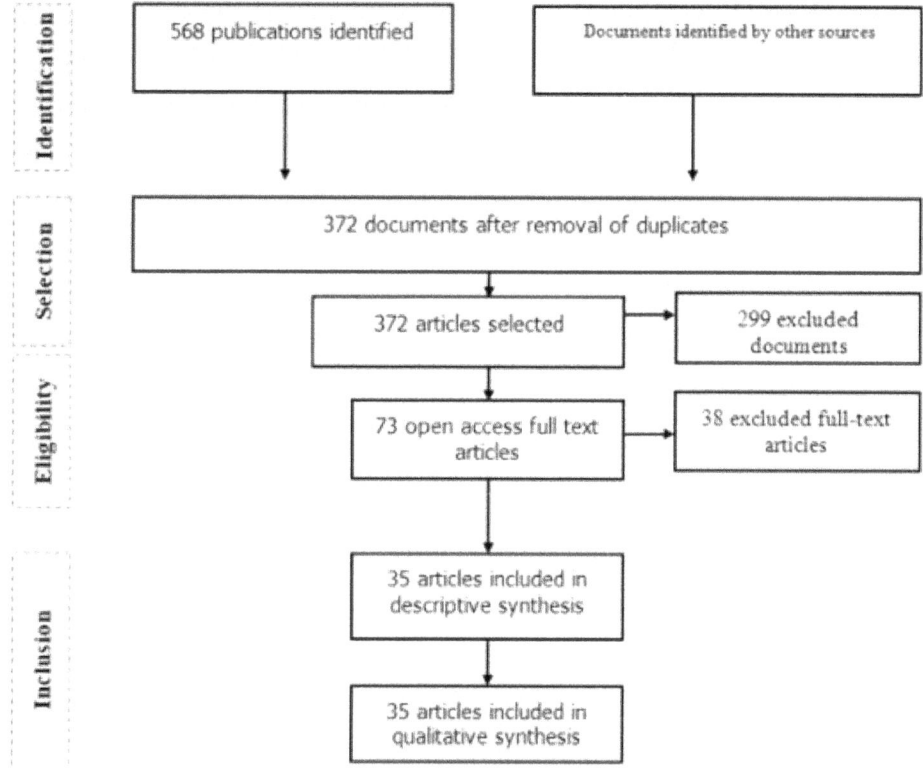

```
Identification:
  [568 publications identified]    [Documents identified by other sources]
                    ↓                           ↓
Selection:
         [372 documents after removal of duplicates]
                            ↓
              [372 articles selected] → [299 excluded documents]
                            ↓
Eligibility:
         [73 open access full text articles] → [38 excluded full-text articles]
                            ↓
Inclusion:
         [35 articles included in descriptive synthesis]
                            ↓
         [35 articles included in qualitative synthesis]
```

Source: Adapted from Moher et al., (2009)

We carefully analyzed this final sample, identifying theoretical patterns, research methods, results, and specific contributions to understanding the relationship between artificial intelligence and tourism experience.

3. RESULTS AND DISCUSSION

This section will provide an opportunity to discuss the main findings of our literature review. It will commence with a descriptive analysis (3.1), followed by a qualitative analysis (3.2) of the theories mobilized by the literature (3.2.1) and the main applications of artificial intelligence and their transformative impact on the tourist experience (3.2.2), as well as the challenges associated with the adoption of these technologies (3.2.3). This section will present an analytical model to summarize the main implications and suggest directions for future research to advance the understanding of this subject (3.3).

3.1. Descriptive Analysis

The 35 articles were published in 26 different journals since 2016. Figure 2 shows the distribution of our references by year, while Table 4 displays the distribution by journal title.

Figure 2. Distribution of References by Year

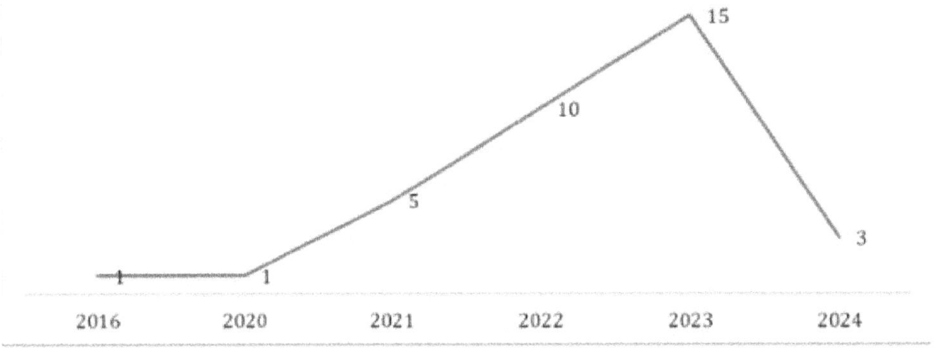

Source: Authors

The results show an increasing trend in publications from 2016, reaching a peak of 15 publications in 2023, representing 43% of our corpus.

Table 4. Distribution of References by Journal Title

Secondary title	Number of Corresponding Sources	Frequencies
Annals of Tourism Research	4	11%
International Journal of Hospitality Management	3	9%
Tourism Management	3	9%
Journal of Hospitality and Tourism Technology	2	6%
Journal of Destination Marketing & Management	2	6%
Technological Forecasting and Social Change	2	6%
Computers in Human Behavior	1	3%
Journal of Hospitality and Tourism Management	1	3%
Heliyon	1	3%
Tourism Review	1	3%
The Service Industries Journal	1	3%
PloS one	1	3%

continued on following page

Table 4. Continued

Secondary title	Number of Corresponding Sources	Frequencies
A Refereed Monthly International Journal of Management	1	3%
JOURNAL OF TOURISM SUSTAINABILITY AND WELL-BEING	1	3%
Journal of Environmental Management and Tourism	1	3%
International Journal of Information Management	1	3%
Journal of Retailing and Consumer Services	1	3%
International Journal of Information Management Data Insights	1	3%
Cities	1	3%
Journal of Business Research	1	3%
Journal of Sustainable Tourism	1	3%
International Journal for Multidimensional Research Perspectives	1	3%
Administrative Development 'A Journal of HIPA, Shimla'	1	3%
Innovative: Journal Of Social Science Research	1	3%
Worldwide Hospitality and Tourism Themes	1	3%
Total	35	100%

Source: Authors

Nearly half of the dataset comes from six main journals out of a total of 25 journals: "Annals of Tourism Research", "International Journal of Hospitality Management", "Tourism Management", "Journal of Hospitality and Tourism Technology", "Journal of Destination Marketing & Management", "Technological Forecasting and Social Change". The following table lists the top 20 most used keywords.

Table 5. Top 20 Most Frequent Keywords

Rang	Word	Number	Rang	Word	Number
1	tourism	4365	11	technology	2198
2	ai	2759	12	research	2530
3	tourist	1545	13	effect	2245
4	service	3132	14	customer	1821
5	hotel	1163	15	positive	2326
6	hospitality	1133	16	management	1994
7	data	1690	17	analysis	561
8	behavior	994	18	factors	658

continued on following page

Table 5. Continued

Rang	Word	Number	Rang	Word	Number
9	experience	2586	19	human	1222
10	industry	784	20	social	934

Source: Authors

The results show that authors focus on artificial intelligence, tourism, tourist behavior, technology, and tourism experience. This is evident from the use of terms such as "tourism", "artificial intelligence", "tourist", "service", "hotel", "data", "behavior", "experience", and "technology". The frequency of these key terms, as shown in the word cloud (Figure 3), indicates the relevance of the corpus used.

Figure 3. Word Cloud

Source: NVivo V12

3.2. Qualitative Analysis

3.2.1. Theoretical Models and Theories Applied to the Research

Our research carefully examines the impact of artificial intelligence on the tourism experience. It relies on a strong theoretical structure that considers various perspectives and contexts. During our work, different models have been proposed to explain the mechanisms of the tourism experience and how it can be improved by artificial intelligence. The following table provides a summary of the different theoretical structures used in this review.

Table 6. Summary of the main theories used in the literature

Authors	Used theories	Results
(Goel et al., 2022)	The Technology Acceptance Model (TAM), the Theory of Planned Behavior (TPB), Motivated Consumer Innovativeness (MCI),	Several factors influence the adoption of AI and robot technologies in the tourism and hotel services sector, including individual factors, service-related factors, technical factors, and social factors. There are obstacles to adoption, such as psychological, social, financial, technical, and functional factors.
(Yin et al., 2023)	Affordance Theory, Self-alignment Theory	AI environments can influence customer engagement behaviors, regulated by the level of technological readiness. The relationship is guided by alignment with the ideal self and trust.
(Koo et al., 2023)	Stimulus-Organism-Response (SOR) Theory	The study revealed four factors that contribute to the brand experiences of smart hotels: anthropomorphism, affectivity, entertainment, and escapism. These experiences are significant predictors of brand love and loyalty.
(Kim et al., 2024)	Theory of Value-Attitude-Behavior	Awareness of artificial intelligence affects the attitudes, social norms, and personal norms of potential consumers, leading to differences in behavior based on their sustainability goals.
(El Archi & BENBBA, 2023)	Technology Acceptance Model (TAM) Unified Theory of Acceptance and Use of Technology (UTAUT)	The TAM and UTAUT models are frequently used in research on tourism and hotels, especially in the fields of mobile applications and social media marketing.
(Manthiou & Klaus, 2022)	De Keyser et al. (2020) conceptualization	Robots significantly influence customer touchpoints in the customer journey. The context of the tourism experience with robots shapes the customer journey. The characteristics of tourism's experience with robots involve interaction, dimensionality, temporal flow, valence, and the ordinary aspect of the experience.

Source: Authors

3.2.2. Transformative Impact of AI on Tourism Experience

The tourism industry has undergone significant transformations due to the integration of AI with emerging technologies such as IoT, blockchain, and AR/VR. AI and IoT have enhanced smart tourism destinations by facilitating personalization and recommendation, as well as instant data collection (Aliyah et al., 2023). The potential of blockchain technology has been explored in energy distribution systems, enabling an impact on tourism infrastructure (Diantoro et al., 2023). AI tools have led to innovations in the tourism and hospitality industry with marketing applications (Table 7) such as demand forecasting, increased satisfaction and loyalty, and the co-creation of immersive experiences (Aarabe et al., 2024; Nannelli et al., 2023). The use of AI and robotics has improved service quality and customer experience with technologies such as chatbots, virtual reality, and language translation tools (Samala et al., 2020).

Table 7. Practical applications of AI

Authors	Dimensions	Practices
(Christou et al., 2023; Lacárcel, 2022)	Digital Marketing and Data Analysis	● Optimizing advertising campaigns ● Demand forecasting ● Analyzing social data ● Customer segmentation ● Understanding traveler trends and preferences ● Proactively managing online reputation
(Bilgihan & Ricci, 2023; Buhalis & Moldavska, 2022; Kumar et al., 2021)	Operational Optimization	● Operational Efficiency ● Improving hotel operations ● Simplifying booking processes ● Unlocking new sources of revenue

Source: Authors

Following the presentation of practical applications of artificial intelligence in the tourism domain to optimize operations and enhance the services offered (Table 7), the scope is extended by analyzing the transformative impact of AI on the tourism experience. This is done while examining the mechanisms for redefining consumer expectations and interactions (Table 8).

Table 8. Transformative impact of AI on tourism experience

Authors	Dimensions	Mechanisms
(Bhaskar & Sharma, 2022; Grundner & Neuhofer, 2021; Prahadeeswaran, 2023; Tussyadiah, 2020)	Service Personalization and automation	● Recommendation of tourism activities and destinations ● Offering experiences tailored to individual traveler needs ● Sustainable tourism ● Management of tourist attractions
(Bilgihan & Ricci, 2023; Manthiou & Klaus, 2022)	Interaction and Engagement	● Using chatbots for personalized traveler assistance from planning to the travel experience ● Guiding and assisting tourists through robots ● Promoting engagement by simplifying interactions (voice search, AR, VR...)
(Lacárcel, 2022; Verma et al., 2022)	Immersive Experiences	● Utilizing technologies such as VR and AR to create immersive experiences for tourists ● Adopting virtual tourism as an alternative to physical travel

continued on following page

Table 8. Continued

Authors	Dimensions	Mechanisms
(Ku & Chen, 2024; Manthiou & Klaus, 2022)	Customer Well-being and Satisfaction	● Positive Impact on Customer Engagement and Satisfaction ● Impact on the Quality of the Tourism Experience

Source: Authors

3.2.3. Challenges of AI Adoption

Several researches have demonstrated the growing impact of artificial intelligence in the tourism and hospitality industry, which has shown how it can enhance personalization and recommendation, and encourage initiatives related to sustainability and crisis management (García-Madurga & Grilló-Méndez, 2023; Gretzel et al., 2015). The advent of AI technologies such as search engines and chatbots has transformed processes and influenced consumer trust and brand engagement (Gajić et al., 2024; Goel et al., 2022). However, the authors have identified a significant need for research to elucidate consumer behavior in the tourism sector from a sustainability and intelligence perspective with a particular focus on confidentiality, data protection and privacy (Benjelloun & Kabak, 2024; Cain & Webster, 2023; Ghandour & Woodford, 2023; Lauterbach, 2019; Lo, 2023; Spalević et al., 2024). The following table summarizes the key challenges of adopting AI in the tourism sector, including ethical, cultural, sustainability, and regulatory considerations.

Table 9. Challenges of AI adoption

Authors	Dimensions	Mechanisms and dimensions
(Akter et al., 2023; Bhaskar & Sharma, 2022; Buhalis & Moldavska, 2022; Sustacha et al., 2023)	Ethical Considerations	● Data Confidentiality and Security ● Human Dependency ● Security and Privacy ● Algorithmic bias
(Gajić et al., 2024; Goel et al., 2022)	Barriers to Adoption	● Individual or psychological, functional, technical, and social factors influence consumers adoption of AI ● Customer trust, ● Brand engagement, ● Electronic Word-Of-Mouth (eWOM), ● Tourists' willingness to use AI technologies

continued on following page

Table 9. Continued

Authors	Dimensions	Mechanisms and dimensions
(S. Chen et al., 2023)	Cross-cultural Perspectives	● Individualism versus collectivism, ● Power distance, ● Masculinity versus femininity, ● Uncertainty avoidance, ● Long-term versus short-term orientation, ● Indulgence versus restraint
(García-Madurga & Grilló-Méndez, 2023; Gretzel, 2021)	Sustainability and Crisis Management	● Sustainable and inclusive manner post-pandemic ● Integration of sustainable practices ● Environmental conservation ● Reducing the industry's ecological footprint ● Optimizing resource allocation ● Enhancing waste management ● Reducing carbon emissions, ● Promoting responsible tourism behavior, ● Enhancing conservation efforts ● Over tourism
(Cain & Webster, 2023; Ghandour & Woodford, 2023; Lauterbach, 2019; Lo, 2023; Spalević et al., 2024)	Policy and Regulatory Frameworks	● Liability, ● Transparency ● Product Safety, ● Privacy ● Intellectual Property. ● Conditions of competition ● Macroeconomic policies, ● Regulatory powers

Source: Authors

3.3. Discussion

The application of artificial intelligence has profoundly transformed the tourism and hospitality industry, resulting in notable improvements in service quality, customer satisfaction, and operational efficiency. This advancement has been achieved through the adoption of AI-powered applications such including engines, virtual agents, and chatbots (Huang et al., 2022). These technologies provide personalized and automated travel services, consequently improving the overall tourist experience (Samala et al., 2020). The service-profit-role chain is an analytical tool used by Ruel & Njoku, (2021) to assess the impact of new technology adoption in the tourism industry on employee engagement, retention, and productivity, which in turn affects service quality and customer satisfaction. AI applications have been implemented across various domains within the tourism sector, including demand forecasting, destination management, and behavioral analysis (Doborjeh et al., 2021).

The results of our literature review highlight the growing potential of artificial intelligence (AI) in the tourism industry and how it can significantly transform the customer experience. This technology can use a large amount of data on travelers' preferences (Yin et al., 2023) and behaviors to provide relevant insights for tourism professionals to offer personalized services tailored to the specific needs of each customer (Manthiou & Klaus, 2022).

In this context, Goel et al., (2022) drew several conclusions regarding the adoption of artificial intelligence in the hospitality, aviation, tourism, and service sectors. They found that consumers face various obstacles to adopting these technologies, including psychological, social, financial, technical, and functional barriers that may hamper adoption. Yin et al., (2023) suggest that AI environments influence customer engagement behaviors (Bilgihan & Ricci, 2023), which is moderated by the technological readiness of customers. Trust and alignment with the ideal self-play a mediating role in this relationship. Koo et al., (2023) identified several predictive factors of brand love and loyalty in smart hotels, including anthropomorphism, affective experiences, entertaining experiences, and escapism. (Manthiou & Klaus, 2022) developed three theoretical propositions for the tourism experience with robots, emphasizing the importance of touchpoints, context, and qualities.

Although AI applications have resulted in notable enhancements in service quality and experiences, the human touch in this field remains ever important and cannot be supplanted by these technologies (Samala et al., 2020). In addition, the ongoing development of AI presents a duality of opportunities and challenges for the tourism and hospitality industry, including ethical, cultural, managerial, sustainability, and regulatory considerations.

For this reason, the intersection of travel experiences and the application of new technologies, including AI, represents a rapidly growing field with significant implications for tourism. These intelligent technologies are indispensable for the promotion of sustainable tourism practices. In conclusion, while there is ample evidence of a mutually reinforcing relationship between travel experiences and technology adoption, there are still gaps in our understanding. It would be beneficial for future studies to aim to provide more comprehensive insights into how these interactions occur in different contexts and among different populations.

The study presents a model that highlights the interdependence between tourist data, AI technologies, and digital platforms. The data is then subjected to analysis, personalization, automation, and recommendation process with the objective of improving the tourism experience, leading to customer satisfaction and loyalty. We put forth an (Figure 4) with the objective of integrating AI technologies and their implications for enhancing the tourism experience through automation and personalization.

Figure 4. Sketch of the Research Conceptual Model

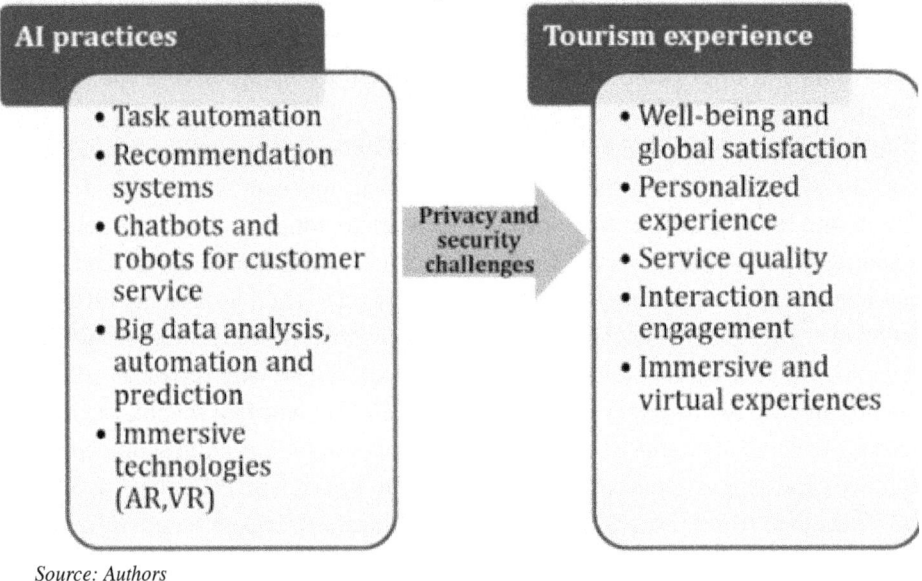

AI practices
- Task automation
- Recommendation systems
- Chatbots and robots for customer service
- Big data analysis, automation and prediction
- Immersive technologies (AR,VR)

Privacy and security challenges →

Tourism experience
- Well-being and global satisfaction
- Personalized experience
- Service quality
- Interaction and engagement
- Immersive and virtual experiences

Source: Authors

We assume that using artificial intelligence allows for collecting and analyzing a large amount of data on travelers' preferences and behaviors. As a result, there are personalized recommendations and services, which improve the travel experience and foster customer loyalty. Additionally, the use of AI simplifies processes in the tourism industry, such as booking, payment processing, and itinerary management, improving operational efficiency and creating a smooth experience. Performance analysis, feedback, and interactions with customers provide a basis for adjusting services in real time for continuous improvement. The ability to adapt in real time allows businesses to respond quickly to customer needs and offer immediate solutions, therefore improving customer satisfaction and the perception of the travel experience.

Contributions, Limitations, and Future Directions

In conclusion, this literature review attempts to understand how adopting artificial intelligence affects and deeply changes the travel experience. It influences not only current practices and models but also the basic principles that support this field. The results show that using artificial intelligence and related technologies, like robots, is important in the tourism industry. However, it is important to note that the transformative impact of AI comes with challenges such as psychological, social, financial, and technical barriers. AI environments affect customer engagement behaviors, so it is crucial to understand how these technologies shape travel interactions. The study also highlights the importance of making robots seem human and creating emotional experiences to build brand love and loyalty in smart hotels.

However, this study has limitations. Further research is needed to address them. The results may not be applicable everywhere due to the specific cultural, geographic, and economic contexts of the sample. Additionally, subjective measures of variables can introduce potential biases, and other unexplored factors might impact the travel experience in the long run.

The study provides valuable insights for future research. More analysis is required to elucidate the psychological mechanisms that may influence the relationship between the adoption of this technology and the quality of the experience. Longitudinal studies could track the evolution of the smart travel experience over time. This would entail examining how traveler perceptions and expectations change as they become accustomed to intelligent technologies. Comparative research between different tourist destinations could help better in understanding the contextual factors that influence the transformative impact of artificial intelligence on the travel experience. These studies could analyze the impact of local culture on the acceptance of AI technologies by tourists and local tourism stakeholders, by examining the success and failure cases of adoption in diverse cultural contexts. A comprehensive study of the smart travel experience is essential, integrating various emerging technologies to benefit from their synergy and complementarity. Ultimately, it is necessary to empirically test the proposed model in order to verify and refine its components.

Future research should focus on the integration of new technologies and innovative strategies to promote sustainability in the tourism industry. This will help raise awareness and the engagement of stakeholders, in addition to enabling the monitoring and prediction of their behavior. Furthermore, discussions about the impact of these technologies on employment are also necessary in the tourism sector. This must encompass a balanced examination of both the beneficial implications associated with the generation of new employment opportunities and the adverse effects pertaining to the displacement of certain manual and human responsibilities by these technological advancements. In light of the findings of this study, we intend to refine our conceptual model through qualitative and exploratory research. Subsequently, empirical survey will be conducted to validate the model and gain deeper insight into the relationship between the travel experience and the adoption of emerging technologies, including artificial intelligence. In conclusion, this study makes a significant contribution to the tourism field, establishing a foundation for future research and practical applications.

REFERENCES

Aarabe, M., Khizzou, N. B., Alla, L., & Benjelloun, A. (2024). Smart Tourism Experience and Responsible Travelers' Behavior : A Systematic Literature Review. In *Promoting Responsible Tourism With Digital Platforms* (p. 128-147). IGI Global. DOI: 10.4018/979-8-3693-3286-3.ch008

Acheson, K., Dirkx, J. M., & Shealy, C. N. (2022). High impact learning in higher education : Operationalizing the self-constructive outcomes of transformative learning theory. In *Transformative Learning Theory and Praxis*. Routledge. DOI: 10.4324/9780429450600-15

Akter, S., Sultana, S., Mariani, M., Wamba, S. F., Spanaki, K., & Dwivedi, Y. K. (2023). Advancing algorithmic bias management capabilities in AI-driven marketing analytics research. *Industrial Marketing Management*, 114, 243–261. DOI: 10.1016/j.indmarman.2023.08.013

Aliyah, L., Lukita, C., Pangilinan, G., Chakim, M., & Saputra, D. (2023). Examining the impact of artificial intelligence and internet of things on smart tourism destinations : A comprehensive study. *Aptisi Transactions on Technopreneurship*, 5(2sp), 135–145. DOI: 10.34306/att.v5i2sp.332

Alla, L., Kamal, M., & Bouhtati, N. (2022). Big data et efficacité marketing des entreprises touristiques : Une revue de littérature. *Alternatives Managériales Economiques,* 4(0), Article 0. DOI: 10.48374/IMIST.PRSM/ame-v1i0.36928

Arnould, E. J., & Price, L. L. (1993). River Magic : Extraordinary Experience and the Extended Service Encounter. *The Journal of Consumer Research*, 20(1), 24–45. DOI: 10.1086/209331

Asi, L., Mojjada, H., Prasanna, M., & Deepika, Y. (2023). *A Study on Artificial Intelligence in Marketing.* 5, 1-15. DOI: 10.36948/ijfmr.2023.v05i03.3789

Bag, S., Gupta, S., Kumar, A., & Sivarajah, U. (2021). An integrated artificial intelligence framework for knowledge creation and B2B marketing rational decision making for improving firm performance. *Industrial Marketing Management*, 92, 178–189. DOI: 10.1016/j.indmarman.2020.12.001

Barstow Hernandez, J. (2018). Transformative Leadership : Its Evolution and Impact. *The Journal of Bahá'í Studies*, 28(3), 55–85. DOI: 10.31581/jbs-28.3.3(2018)

Benjelloun, A., & Kabak, S. (2024). Ethical Challenges and Managerial Implications of Artificial Intelligence in Digital Marketing. In S. Kumar, K. Balachandran, J. H. Kim, & J. C. Bansal (Éds.), *Fourth Congress on Intelligent Systems* (Vol. 869, p. 439-445). Springer Nature Singapore. DOI: 10.1007/978-981-99-9040-5_32

Bhaskar, P., & Sharma, K. (2022). A Critical Insight into the Role of Artificial Intelligence (AI) in Tourism and Hospitality Industries. *A Refereed Monthly. International Journal of Management*, 15, 76–85.

Bilgihan, A., & Ricci, P. (2023). The new era of hotel marketing : Integrating cutting-edge technologies with core marketing principles New era of hotel marketing. *Journal of Hospitality and Tourism Technology*. Advance online publication. DOI: 10.1108/JHTT-04-2023-0095

Buhalis, D., & Amaranggana, A. (2015a). *Information and Communication Technologies in Tourism 2015* (Tussyadiah, I., & Inversini, A., Eds.). Springer International Publishing. DOI: 10.1007/978-3-319-14343-9_28

Buhalis, D., & Amaranggana, A. (2015b). Smart Tourism Destinations Enhancing Tourism Experience Through Personalisation of Services. In Tussyadiah, I., & Inversini, A. (Eds.), *Information and Communication Technologies in Tourism 2015* (pp. 377–389). Springer International Publishing. DOI: 10.1007/978-3-319-14343-9_28

Buhalis, D., & Leung, R. (2018). Smart hospitality—Interconnectivity and interoperability towards an ecosystem. *International Journal of Hospitality Management*, 71, 41–50. DOI: 10.1016/j.ijhm.2017.11.011

Buhalis, D., & Moldavska, I. (2022). Voice assistants in hospitality : Using artificial intelligence for customer service. *Journal of Hospitality and Tourism Technology*, 13(3), 386–403. DOI: 10.1108/JHTT-03-2021-0104

Cain, L., & Webster, C. (2023). The origin, rationale, and impacts of regulations on robots and AI in tourism and hospitality. *Proceedings INNODOCT/22. International Conference on Innovation, Documentation and Education*, 111-118. https://riunet.upv.es/handle/10251/193157

Chen, C.-F., & Tsai, D. (2007). How destination image and evaluative factors affect behavioral intentions? *Tourism Management*, 28(4), 1115–1122. DOI: 10.1016/j.tourman.2006.07.007

Chen, S., Zhang, K., Li, X., Ye, H., Lin, K. J., & Law, R. (2023). ChatGPT : Cross cultural tourism research imperative. *Journal of Economics and Management*, 45, 137–146. DOI: 10.22367/jem.2023.45.07

Christou, P., Hadjielias, E., Simillidou, A., & Kvasova, O. (2023). The use of intelligent automation as a form of digital transformation in tourism : Towards a hybrid experiential offering. *Journal of Business Research*, 155, 113415. DOI: 10.1016/j.jbusres.2022.113415

Chung, N., Tyan, I., & Han, H. (2017). Enhancing the smart tourism experience through geotag. *Information Systems Frontiers*, 19(4), 731–742. DOI: 10.1007/s10796-016-9710-6

Dafoe, A. (2018). AI governance : A research agenda. *Governance of AI Program, Future of Humanity Institute, University of Oxford: Oxford, UK, 1442*, 1443.

Dalipi, F., Kastrati, Z., & Öberg, T. (2023). The Impact of Artificial Intelligence on Tourism Sustainability : A Systematic Mapping Review. *2023 International Conference on Computational Intelligence and Knowledge Economy (ICCIKE)*, 119-125. https://ieeexplore.ieee.org/abstract/document/10131818/

Davenport, T., Guha, A., Grewal, D., & Bressgott, T. (2019). How artificial intelligence will change the future of marketing. *Journal of the Academy of Marketing Science*, 48(1), 1–19. DOI: 10.1007/s11747-019-00696-0

Davenport, T., Guha, A., Grewal, D., & Bressgott, T. (2020). How artificial intelligence will change the future of marketing. *Journal of the Academy of Marketing Science*, 48(1), 24–42. DOI: 10.1007/s11747-019-00696-0

de Almeida Biolchini, J. C., Mian, P. G., Natali, A. C. C., Conte, T. U., & Travassos, G. H. (2007). Scientific research ontology to support systematic review in software engineering. *Advanced Engineering Informatics*, 21(2), 133–151. DOI: 10.1016/j.aei.2006.11.006

Dentoni, D., Waddell, S., & Waddock, S. (2017). Pathways of transformation in global food and agricultural systems : Implications from a large systems change theory perspective. *Current Opinion in Environmental Sustainability*, 29, 8–13. DOI: 10.1016/j.cosust.2017.10.003

Diantoro, K., Supriyanti, D., Sanjaya, Y. P. A., & Watini, S. (2023). Implications of distributed energy development in blockchain-based institutional environment. *Aptisi Transactions on Technopreneurship*, 5(2sp), 209–220. DOI: 10.34306/att.v5i2sp.343

Doborjeh, Z., Hemmington, N., Doborjeh, M., & Kasabov, N. (2021). Artificial intelligence : A systematic review of methods and applications in hospitality and tourism. *International Journal of Contemporary Hospitality Management*, 34(3), 1154–1176. DOI: 10.1108/IJCHM-06-2021-0767

El Archi, Y., & Benbba, B. (2023). The Applications of Technology Acceptance Models in Tourism and Hospitality Research : A Systematic Literature Review. *Journal of Environmental Management and Tourism*, 14(2), 379. DOI: 10.14505/jemt.v14.2(66).08

Femenia-Serra, F., & Neuhofer, B. (2018). *Smart tourism experiences : Conceptualisation, key dimensions and research agenda.*

Gajić, T., Ranjbaran, A., Vukolić, D., Bugarčić, J., Spasojević, A., Đorđević Boljanović, J., Vujačić, D., Mandarić, M., Kostić, M., Sekulić, D., Bugarčić, M., Drašković, B. D., & Rakić, S. R. (2024). Tourists' Willingness to Adopt AI in Hospitality—Assumption of Sustainability in Developing Countries. *Sustainability (Basel)*, 16(9), 3663. DOI: 10.3390/su16093663

García-Madurga, M.-Á., & Grilló-Méndez, A.-J. (2023). Battlefield Tourism : Exploring the Successful Marriage of History and Unforgettable Experiences : A Systematic Review. *Tourism and Hospitality*, 4(2), 307–320. DOI: 10.3390/tourhosp4020019

Ghandour, A., & Woodford, B. J. (2023). Guidelines to Develop AI Ethics Policy in Organizations : Perspectives Informed from Two Different Countries' Laws. *2023 24th International Arab Conference on Information Technology (ACIT)*, 1-9. https://ieeexplore.ieee.org/abstract/document/10453750/

Ghesh, N., Alexander, M., & Davis, A. (2023). The artificial intelligence-enabled customer experience in tourism : A systematic literature review. *Tourism Review*. Advance online publication. DOI: 10.1108/TR-04-2023-0255

Goel, P., Kaushik, N., Sivathanu, B., Pillai, R., & George, J. (2022). Consumer's Adoption of Artificial Intelligence and Robotics in Hospitality and Tourism Sector : Literature Review and Future Research Agenda. *Tourism Review*. DOI: 10.1108/TR-03-2021-0138

Gretzel, U. (2021). Technological Solutions to Overtourism : Potential and Limits. In Mandić, A., & Petrić, L. (Eds.), *Mediterranean Protected Areas in the Era of Overtourism* (pp. 337–349). Springer International Publishing. DOI: 10.1007/978-3-030-69193-6_17

Gretzel, U., Sigala, M., Xiang, Z., & Koo, C. (2015). Smart tourism : Foundations and developments. *Electronic Markets*, 25(3), 179–188. DOI: 10.1007/s12525-015-0196-8

Grewal, D., Hulland, J., Kopalle, P. K., & Karahanna, E. (2020). The future of technology and marketing : A multidisciplinary perspective. *Journal of the Academy of Marketing Science*, 48(1), 1–8. DOI: 10.1007/s11747-019-00711-4

Gruetzemacher, R., & Whittlestone, J. (2019). *Defining and Unpacking Transformative AI*.

Grundner, L., & Neuhofer, B. (2021). The bright and dark sides of artificial intelligence : A futures perspective on tourist destination experiences. *Journal of Destination Marketing & Management*, 19, 100511. DOI: 10.1016/j.jdmm.2020.100511

Guitart, M. (2022). *Approaching Architecture : Three Fields, One Discipline* (1ʳᵉ éd.). Routledge. DOI: 10.4324/9781003195535

Haxeltine, A., Avelino, F., Pel, B., & Adina, D. (2016). *A framework for Transformative Social Innovation*. http://www.transitsocialinnovation.eu/content/original/Book%20covers/Local%20PDFs/240%20TRANSIT_WorkingPaper_no5_TSI%20framework_Haxeltine%20et%20al_November2016_AH041116.pdf

Hildebrand, C. (2019). The Machine Age of Marketing : How Artificial Intelligence Changes the Way People Think, Act, and Decide. *NIM Marketing Intelligence Review*, 11(2), 10–17. DOI: 10.2478/nimmir-2019-0010

Holbrook, M. B., & Hirschman, E. C. (1982). The Experiential Aspects of Consumption : Consumer Fantasies, Feelings, and Fun. *The Journal of Consumer Research*, 9(2), 132–140. DOI: 10.1086/208906

Huang, A., Chao, Y., de la Mora Velasco, E., Bilgihan, A., & Wei, W. (2022). When artificial intelligence meets the hospitality and tourism industry : An assessment framework to inform theory and management. *Journal of Hospitality and Tourism Insights*, 5(5), 1080–1100. DOI: 10.1108/JHTI-01-2021-0021

Huang, M.-H., & Rust, R. T. (2018). Artificial Intelligence in Service. *Journal of Service Research*, 21(2), 155–172. DOI: 10.1177/1094670517752459

Kashem, M. A., Shamsuddoha, M., Nasir, T., & Chowdhury, A. A. (2023). The role of artificial intelligence and blockchain technologies in sustainable tourism in the Middle East. *Worldwide Hospitality and Tourism Themes*, 15(2), 178–191. DOI: 10.1108/WHATT-10-2022-0116

Kim, H., Koo, C., & Chung, N. (2021). The role of mobility apps in memorable tourism experiences of Korean tourists : Stress-coping theory perspective. *Journal of Hospitality and Tourism Management*, 49, 548–557. DOI: 10.1016/j.jhtm.2021.11.003

Kim, H., So, K. K. F., Shin, S., & Li, J. (2024). Artificial Intelligence in Hospitality and Tourism : Insights From Industry Practices, Research Literature, and Expert Opinions. *Journal of Hospitality & Tourism Research (Washington, D.C.)*. Advance online publication. DOI: 10.1177/10963480241229235

Kim, M. J., Hall, C. M., Kwon, O., & Sohn, K. (2024). Space tourism : Value-attitude-behavior theory, artificial intelligence, and sustainability. *Journal of Retailing and Consumer Services*, 77, 103654. DOI: 10.1016/j.jretconser.2023.103654

Knani, M., Echchakoui, S., & Ladhari, R. (2022). Artificial intelligence in tourism and hospitality : Bibliometric analysis and research agenda. *International Journal of Hospitality Management*, 107, 103317. DOI: 10.1016/j.ijhm.2022.103317

Koo, B., Curtis, C., Ryan, B., Chung, Y., & Khojasteh, J. (2023). Psychometric approaches to exploring the characteristics of smart hotel brand experiences : Scale development and validation. *Journal of Hospitality and Tourism Management*, 56, 385–395. DOI: 10.1016/j.jhtm.2023.07.012

Kounavis, C. D., Kasimati, A. E., & Zamani, E. D. (2012). Enhancing the Tourism Experience through Mobile Augmented Reality : Challenges and Prospects. *International Journal of Engineering Business Management*, 4, 10. DOI: 10.5772/51644

Ku, E. C. S., & Chen, C.-D. (2024). Artificial intelligence innovation of tourism businesses : From satisfied tourists to continued service usage intention. *International Journal of Information Management*, 102757, 102757. Advance online publication. DOI: 10.1016/j.ijinfomgt.2024.102757

Kumar, N. R., Pavithra, R., Yuvaraj, V., & Kumar, T. M. (2023). The role of smart tourism in India for optimizing visitor experiences through technology. *JIMS8I International Journal of Information Communication and Computing Technology*, *11*(2), 692-701.

Kumar, S., Kumar, V., & Attri, K. (2021). Impact of artificial intelligence and service robots in tourism and hospitality sector : Current use & future trends. *Administrative Development « A Journal of HIPA, Shimla »*, *8*(SI-1), 59-83. DOI: 10.53338/ADHIPA2021.V08.Si01.04

Kumar, V., Ramachandran, D., & Kumar, B. (2021a). Influence of new-age technologies on marketing : A research agenda. *Journal of Business Research*, 125, 864–877. DOI: 10.1016/j.jbusres.2020.01.007

Kumar, V., Ramachandran, D., & Kumar, B. (2021b). Influence of new-age technologies on marketing : A research agenda. *Journal of Business Research*, 125, 864–877. DOI: 10.1016/j.jbusres.2020.01.007

Lacárcel, F. (2022). Main Uses of Artificial Intelligence in Digital Marketing Strategies Linked to Tourism. *Journal Of Tourism Sustainability And Well-Being, 10*(3), 215-226. DOI: 10.34623/mppf-r253

Lauterbach, A. (2019). Artificial intelligence and policy : Quo vadis? *Digital Policy. Regulation & Governance*, 21(3), 238–263. DOI: 10.1108/DPRG-09-2018-0054

Lee, T. H., & Jan, F.-H. (2023). How do smart tourism experiences affect visitors' environmentally responsible behavior? Influence analysis of nature-based tourists in Taiwan. *Journal of Hospitality and Tourism Management*, 55, 1–10. DOI: 10.1016/j.jhtm.2023.02.016

Li, C., Zheng, W., Zhuang, X., & Chen, F. (2023). Intelligent transport design with a dual focus : Tourist experience and operating cost. *Annals of Tourism Research*, 101, 103597. DOI: 10.1016/j.annals.2023.103597

Li, M., Yin, D., Qiu, H., & Bai, B. (2021). A systematic review of AI technology-based service encounters : Implications for hospitality and tourism operations. *International Journal of Hospitality Management*, 95, 102930. DOI: 10.1016/j.ijhm.2021.102930

Lo, L. S. (2023). AI policies across the globe : Implications and recommendations for libraries. *IFLA Journal*, 49(4), 645–649. DOI: 10.1177/03400352231196172

Manthiou, A., & Klaus, P. (2022). The interplaying factors of the robotic tourism experience : The customer journey's touchpoints, context, and qualities. *Technological Forecasting and Social Change*, 177, 121552. DOI: 10.1016/j.techfore.2022.121552

Mateo, S. (2020). Procédure pour conduire avec succès une revue de littérature selon la méthode PRISMA. *Kinésithérapie, la Revue*, 20(226), 29–37. DOI: 10.1016/j.kine.2020.05.019

Moher, D., Liberati, A., Tetzlaff, J., & Altman, D. G.The PRISMA Group. (2009). Preferred Reporting Items for Systematic Reviews and Meta-Analyses : The PRISMA Statement. *PLoS Medicine*, 6(7), e1000097. DOI: 10.1371/journal.pmed.1000097 PMID: 19621072

Moher, D., Shamseer, L., Clarke, M., Ghersi, D., Liberati, A., Petticrew, M., Shekelle, P., & Stewart, L. A.PRISMA-P Group. (2015). Preferred reporting items for systematic review and meta-analysis protocols (PRISMA-P) 2015 statement. *Systematic Reviews*, 4(1), 1. DOI: 10.1186/2046-4053-4-1 PMID: 25554246

Nannelli, M., Capone, F., & Lazzeretti, L. (2023). Artificial intelligence in hospitality and tourism. State of the art and future research avenues. *European Planning Studies*, 31(7), 1325–1344. DOI: 10.1080/09654313.2023.2180321

Pai, C.-K., Liu, Y., Kang, S., & Dai, A. (2020). The Role of Perceived Smart Tourism Technology Experience for Tourist Satisfaction, Happiness and Revisit Intention. *Sustainability (Basel)*, 12(16), 16. Advance online publication. DOI: 10.3390/su12166592

Pine, B. J., & Gilmore, J. H. (1998). *Welcome to the experience economy* (Vol. 76). Harvard Business Review Press Cambridge. https://enlillebid.dk/mmd/wp-content/uploads/2012/03/Welcome-to-the-Experience-Economy-Pine-and-Gilmore.pdf

Prahadeeswaran, R. (2023). A Comprehensive Review : The Convergence of Artificial Intelligence and Tourism. *International Journal for Multidimensional Research Perspectives*, 1(2), 2.

Rashid, B. (2013). *The Role of Affective Dimensions on Tourist Visit Experience.* https://www.academia.edu/download/86273203/78487609.pdf

Reed, M. S., & Fazey, I. (2021). Impact Culture : Transforming How Universities Tackle Twenty First Century Challenges. *Frontiers in Sustainability*, 2, 662296. DOI: 10.3389/frsus.2021.662296

Rosni, N. A., & Zainol, R. (2022). Transformative impact of covid 19 pandemic on the urban public spaces. *Planning Malaysia*, 20. Advance online publication. DOI: 10.21837/pm.v20i24.1205

Ruel, H., & Njoku, E. (2021). AI redefining the hospitality industry. *Journal of Tourism Futures*, 7(1), 53–66. DOI: 10.1108/JTF-03-2020-0032

Samala, N., Katkam, B. S., Bellamkonda, R. S., & Rodriguez, R. V. (2020). Impact of AI and robotics in the tourism sector : A critical insight. *Journal of Tourism Futures*, 8(1), 73–87. DOI: 10.1108/JTF-07-2019-0065

Saydam, M. B., Arici, H. E., & Koseoglu, M. A. (2022). How does the tourism and hospitality industry use artificial intelligence? A review of empirical studies and future research agenda. *Journal of Hospitality Marketing & Management*, 31(8), 908–936. DOI: 10.1080/19368623.2022.2118923

Schein, E. H. (2010). *Organizational Culture and Leadership*. John Wiley & Sons.

Schmitt, B. (1999). Experiential Marketing. *Journal of Marketing Management*, 15(1-3), 53–67. DOI: 10.1362/026725799784870496

Shah, D., & Murthi, B. P. S. (2021). Marketing in a data-driven digital world : Implications for the role and scope of marketing. *Journal of Business Research*, 125, 772–779. DOI: 10.1016/j.jbusres.2020.06.062

Shamseer, L., Moher, D., Clarke, M., Ghersi, D., Liberati, A., Petticrew, M., Shekelle, P., Stewart, L. A., & the PRISMA-P Group. (2015). Preferred reporting items for systematic review and meta-analysis protocols (PRISMA-P) 2015 : Elaboration and explanation. *BMJ, 349*(1), g7647-g7647. DOI: 10.1136/bmj.g7647

Shin, H. H., Jeong, M., So, K. K. F., & DiPietro, R. (2022). Consumers' experience with hospitality and tourism technologies : Measurement development and validation. *International Journal of Hospitality Management*, 106, 103297. DOI: 10.1016/j.ijhm.2022.103297

Sivasankaran, E. S. (2016). *Impact of culture in human resource management—ProQuest*. https://www.proquest.com/openview/32a26afa2a906de973f07d725586ab43/1?pq-origsite=gscholar&cbl=2030322

Spalević, Ž., Milosavljević, B., & Marković, S. (2024). Legal Basis of Educational Processes of Artificial Intelligence Algorithms in E-tourism. *International Journal of Cognitive Research in Science. Engineering and Education*, 12(1), 209–217.

Stone, M., Aravopoulou, E., Ekinci, Y., Evans, G., Hobbs, M., Labib, A., Laughlin, P., Machtynger, J., & Machtynger, L. (2020). Artificial intelligence (AI) in strategic marketing decision-making : A research agenda. *The Bottom Line (New York, N.Y.)*, 33(2), 183–200. DOI: 10.1108/BL-03-2020-0022

Strasser, T., de Kraker, J., & Kemp, R. (2019). Developing the Transformative Capacity of Social Innovation through Learning : A Conceptual Framework and Research Agenda for the Roles of Network Leadership. *Sustainability (Basel)*, 11(5), 5. Advance online publication. DOI: 10.3390/su11051304

Strasser, T., de Kraker, J., & Kemp, R. (2020). Three Dimensions of Transformative Impact and Capacity : A Conceptual Framework Applied in Social Innovation Practice. *Sustainability (Basel)*, 12(11), 11. Advance online publication. DOI: 10.3390/su12114742

Sustacha, I., Baños-Pino, J. F., & Del Valle, E. (2023). The role of technology in enhancing the tourism experience in smart destinations : A meta-analysis. *Journal of Destination Marketing & Management*, 30, 100817. DOI: 10.1016/j.jdmm.2023.100817

Taylor, P., Davies, L. E., Wells, P., Gilbertson, J., & Tayleur, W. (2015). *A review of the Social Impacts of Culture and Sport*.

Tung, V. W. S., & Law, R. (2017). The potential for tourism and hospitality experience research in human-robot interactions. *International Journal of Contemporary Hospitality Management*, 29(10), 2498–2513. DOI: 10.1108/IJCHM-09-2016-0520

Tussyadiah, I. (2020). A review of research into automation in tourism : Launching the Annals of Tourism Research Curated Collection on Artificial Intelligence and Robotics in Tourism. *Annals of Tourism Research*, 81, 102883. DOI: 10.1016/j.annals.2020.102883

van Esch, P., Cui, Y., Das, G., Jain, S. P., & Wirtz, J. (2022). Tourists and AI : A political ideology perspective. *Annals of Tourism Research*, 97, 103471. DOI: 10.1016/j.annals.2022.103471

Verma, S., Warrier, L., Bolia, B., & Mehta, S. (2022). Past, present, and future of virtual tourism-a literature review. *International Journal of Information Management Data Insights*, 2(2), 100085. DOI: 10.1016/j.jjimei.2022.100085

Von Gönner, J., Herrmann, T. M., Bruckermann, T., Eichinger, M., Hecker, S., Klan, F., Lorke, J., Richter, A., Sturm, U., Voigt-Heucke, S., Brink, W., Liedtke, C., Premke-Kraus, M., Altmann, C., Bauhus, W., Bengtsson, L., Büermann, A., Dietrich, P., Dörler, D., & Bonn, A. (2023). Citizen science's transformative impact on science, citizen empowerment and socio-political processes. *Socio-Ecological Practice Research*, 5(1), 11–33. DOI: 10.1007/s42532-022-00136-4

Waddell, S., Waddock, S., Cornell, S., Dentoni, D., McLachlan, M., & Meszoely, G. (2015). Large Systems Change : An Emerging Field of Transformation and Transitions. *Journal of Corporate Citizenship*, 2015(58), 5–30. DOI: 10.9774/GLEAF.4700.2015.ju.00003

Wang, X., Li, X., Zhen, F., & Zhang, J. H. (2016). How smart is your tourist attraction?: Measuring tourist preferences of smart tourism attractions via a FCEM-AHP and IPA approach. *Tourism Management*, 54, 309–320. DOI: 10.1016/j.tourman.2015.12.003

Wang, Y., So, K. K. F., & Sparks, B. A. (2016). Technology Readiness and Customer Satisfaction with Travel Technologies : A Cross-Country Investigation. *Journal of Travel Research*, 56(5), 563–577. DOI: 10.1177/0047287516657891

Wigboldus, S., Brouwers, J., & Snel, H. (2020). How a Strategic Scoping Canvas Can Facilitate Collaboration between Partners in Sustainability Transitions. *Sustainability (Basel)*, 12(1), 1. Advance online publication. DOI: 10.3390/su12010168

Witell, L., Kowalkowski, C., Perks, H., Raddats, C., Schwabe, M., Benedettini, O., & Burton, J. (2020). Characterizing customer experience management in business markets. *Journal of Business Research*, 116, 420–430. DOI: 10.1016/j.jbusres.2019.08.050

Wohlin, C. (2014). Guidelines for snowballing in systematic literature studies and a replication in software engineering. *Proceedings of the 18th International Conference on Evaluation and Assessment in Software Engineering*, 1-10. DOI: 10.1145/2601248.2601268

Yin, D., Li, M., & Qiu, H. (2023). Do customers exhibit engagement behaviors in AI environments? The role of psychological benefits and technology readiness. *Tourism Management*, 97, 104745. DOI: 10.1016/j.tourman.2023.104745

Zheng, Y., & Wu, Y. (2023). An investigation of how perceived smart tourism technologies affect tourists' well-being in marine tourism. *PLoS One*, 18(8), e0290539. DOI: 10.1371/journal.pone.0290539 PMID: 37624780

Zhou, G., Liu, Y., Hu, J., & Cao, X. (2023). The effect of tourist-to-tourist interaction on tourists' behavior : The mediating effects of positive emotions and memorable tourism experiences. *Journal of Hospitality and Tourism Management*, 55, 161–168. DOI: 10.1016/j.jhtm.2023.03.005

ADDITIONAL READING

Bouhtati, N., Alla, L., & Bentalha, B. (2023). Marketing Big Data Analytics and Customer Relationship Management: A Fuzzy Approach. In Integrating Intelligence and Sustainability in Supply Chains (pp. 75-86). IGI Global. DOI: 10.4018/979-8-3693-0225-5.ch004

Bouhtati, N., Alla, L., & Ed-Daakouri, I. (2024). Smart Data Analysis and Prediction of Responsible Customer Behaviour in Tourism: An Exploratory Review of the Literature. Promoting Responsible Tourism With Digital Platforms, 189-212.

Bouhtati, N., Kamal, M., & Alla, L. (2022, November). Big Data and the Effectiveness of Tourism Marketing: A Prospective Review of the Literature. In *The International Conference on Artificial Intelligence and Smart Environment* (pp. 287-292). Cham: Springer International Publishing.

Bulchand-Gidumal, J. (2022). Impact of artificial intelligence in travel, tourism, and hospitality. In *Handbook of e-Tourism* (pp. 1943–1962). Springer International Publishing. DOI: 10.1007/978-3-030-48652-5_110

Doğan, S., & Niyet, İ. Z. (2024). Artificial Intelligence (AI) in Tourism. In Future Tourism Trends Volume 2: Technology Advancement, Trends and Innovations for the Future in Tourism (pp. 3-21). Emerald Publishing Limited.

Dwivedi, Y. K., Pandey, N., Currie, W., & Micu, A. (2024). Leveraging ChatGPT and other generative artificial intelligence (AI)-based applications in the hospitality and tourism industry: Practices, challenges and research agenda. *International Journal of Contemporary Hospitality Management*, 36(1), 1–12. DOI: 10.1108/IJCHM-05-2023-0686

Filieri, R., D'Amico, E., Destefanis, A., Paolucci, E., & Raguseo, E. (2021). Artificial intelligence (AI) for tourism: An European-based study on successful AI tourism start-ups. *International Journal of Contemporary Hospitality Management*, 33(11), 4099–4125. DOI: 10.1108/IJCHM-02-2021-0220

Ghouse, S. M., & Chaudhary, M. (2024). Artificial Intelligence (AI) for Tourism Start-Ups. In Innovative Technologies for Increasing Service Productivity (pp. 161-178). IGI Global.

Guha, S., Mandal, A., Kujur, F., Poddar, S., & Chakrabarti, S. (2024). Innovation in Tourism and Startups in Eastern India. In *Sustainable Partnership and Investment Strategies for Startups and SMEs* (pp. 92–105). IGI Global. DOI: 10.4018/979-8-3693-2197-3.ch006

Jabeen, F., Al Zaidi, S., & Al Dhaheri, M. H. (2022). Automation and artificial intelligence in hospitality and tourism. *Tourism Review*, 77(4), 1043–1061. DOI: 10.1108/TR-09-2019-0360

Kazak, A. N., Chetyrbok, P. V., & Oleinikov, N. N. (2020). Artificial intelligence in the tourism sphere. []. IOP Publishing.]. *IOP Conference Series. Earth and Environmental Science*, 421(4), 042020. DOI: 10.1088/1755-1315/421/4/042020

Skavronskaya, L., Hadinejad, A., & Cotterell, D. (2023). Reversing the threat of artificial intelligence to opportunity: A discussion of ChatGPT in tourism education. *Journal of Teaching in Travel & Tourism*, 23(2), 253–258. DOI: 10.1080/15313220.2023.2196658

Solakis, K., Katsoni, V., Mahmoud, A. B., & Grigoriou, N. (2024). Factors affecting value co-creation through artificial intelligence in tourism: A general literature review. *Journal of Tourism Futures*, 10(1), 116–130. DOI: 10.1108/JTF-06-2021-0157

Zsarnoczky, M. (2017). How does artificial intelligence affect the tourism industry? *Vadyba*, 31(2), 85–90.

Compilation of References

Aarabe, M., Khizzou, N. B., Alla, L., & Benjelloun, A. (2024). Smart Tourism Experience and Responsible Travelers' Behavior : A Systematic Literature Review. In *Promoting Responsible Tourism With Digital Platforms* (p. 128-147). IGI Global. DOI: 10.4018/979-8-3693-3286-3.ch008

Abbes, I., & Hallem, Y. (2016). Co-création et technologie mobile au sein d'un espace marchand: Quelles valeurs pour le consommateur? Une application dans le secteur de la restauration. *Revue Française du Marketing*, (256), 81–98.

Abubakar, A. I., Omeke, K. G., Ozturk, M., Hussain, S., & Imran, M. A. (2020). The Role of Artificial Intelligence Driven 5G Networks in COVID-19 Outbreak: Opportunities, Challenges, and Future Outlook. *Frontiers in Communications and Networks*, 1, 575065. DOI: 10.3389/frcmn.2020.575065

Acheson, K., Dirkx, J. M., & Shealy, C. N. (2022). High impact learning in higher education : Operationalizing the self-constructive outcomes of transformative learning theory. In *Transformative Learning Theory and Praxis*. Routledge. DOI: 10.4324/9780429450600-15

Ade, M., Harahap, K., Muna, A., Ausat, A., Rachman, A., Riady, Y., & Azzaakiyyah, H. K. (2023). Overview of ChatGPT Technology and its Potential in Improving Tourism Information Services. *JurnalMinfoPolgan*, 12(2). Advance online publication. DOI: 10.33395/jmp.v12i2.12416

Agarwal, R., Dugas, M., Gao, G., & Kannan, P. K. (2020). Emerging technologies and analytics for a new era of value-centered marketing in healthcare. *Journal of the Academy of Marketing Science*, 48(2), 9–23. DOI: 10.1007/s11747-019-00692-4

Aguirre Montero, A., Hernández Sales, L., Youbi Idrissi, M., & López Sánchez, J. A. (2023). Web accessibility and inclusivity of tourist destinations at social media management. *An intercultural analysis of Andalusia and Northern Morocco.*

Ahmad, M. (2023). Exploring the Role of OpenStreetMap in Mapping Religious Tourism in Pakistan for Sustainable Development. In J. P. D. M. Vítor, A. G. da R. N. João, L. de J. P. Maria, & A. de M. C. Liliana (Eds.), *Experiences, Advantages, and Economic Dimensions of Pilgrimage Routes* (pp. 23–40). IGI Global. DOI: 10.4018/978-1-6684-9923-8.ch002

Akehurst, G. (2009). User generated content: The use of blogs for tourism organisations and tourism consumers. *Service Business*, 3(1), 51–61. DOI: 10.1007/s11628-008-0054-2

Akin Ozen, I. (2021). Tourism Products and Sentiment Analysis. In C. Cobanoglu, S. Dogan, K. Berezina, & G. Collins (Eds.), *Advances in Hospitality and Tourism Information Technology*. University of South Florida M3 Publishing. https://digitalcommons.usf.edu/m3publishing/vol18/iss9781732127586/8/

Akter, S., Sultana, S., Mariani, M., Wamba, S. F., Spanaki, K., & Dwivedi, Y. K. (2023). Advancing algorithmic bias management capabilities in AI-driven marketing analytics research. *Industrial Marketing Management*, 114, 243–261. DOI: 10.1016/j.indmarman.2023.08.013

Al Fararni, K., Nafis, F., Aghoutane, B., Yahyaouy, A., Riffi, J., & Sabri, A. (2021). Hybrid recommender system for tourism based on big data and AI: A conceptual framework. *Big Data Mining and Analytics*, 4(1), 47–55. DOI: 10.26599/BDMA.2020.9020015

Al Husban, S. A. M., Al Husban, A. A. S., & Al Betawi, Y. (2021). The Impact of the Cultural Beliefs on Forming and Designing Spatial Organizations, Spaces Hierarchy, and Privacy of Detached Houses and Apartments in Jordan. *Space and Culture*, 24(1), 66–82. DOI: 10.1177/1206331218791934

Alawadi, K., Hernandez Striedinger, V., Maghelal, P., & Khanal, A. (2022). Assessing walkability in hot arid regions: The case of downtown Abu Dhabi. *URBAN DESIGN International*, 27(3), 211–231. Advance online publication. DOI: 10.1057/s41289-021-00150-0

Alblooshi, H., & Shafii, H. (2024). Impact of Artificial Intelligence (AI) on Environmental Security (ES) of Post-Pandemic Covid-19: A Literature Review Study. *Research in Management of Technology and Business*, 5(1), 1–14.

Alfreihat, M., Saad Almousa, O., Tashtoush, Y., & AlSobeh, A. (2024). Emo-SL Framework: Emoji Sentiment Lexicon Using Text-Based Features and Machine Learning for Sentiment Analysis. *IEEE Access: Practical Innovations, Open Solutions*, 12, 81793–81812. Advance online publication. DOI: 10.1109/ACCESS.2024.3382836

Aliyah, L., Lukita, C., Pangilinan, G., Chakim, M., & Saputra, D. (2023). Examining the impact of artificial intelligence and internet of things on smart tourism destinations : A comprehensive study. *Aptisi Transactions on Technopreneurship*, 5(2sp), 135–145. DOI: 10.34306/att.v5i2sp.332

Alla, L., Hmioui, A., & Bentalha, B. (2020). La netnographie dans les recherches marketing: La communauté virtuelle comme consom'acteur vecteur d'efficacité marketing. Alternatives Managériales Economiques, 2(4), 631-652. DOI: DOI: 10.48374/IMIST.PRSM/ame-v2i4.23559

Alla, L., Kamal, M., & Bouhtati, N. (2022). Big data et efficacité marketing des entreprises touristiques : Une revue de littérature. *Alternatives Managériales Economiques, 4*(0), Article 0. DOI: 10.48374/IMIST.PRSM/ame-v1i0.36928

Al-Mansoori, F., & Hamdan, A. (2023). Integrating indigenous knowledge systems into environmental education for biodiversity conservation: A study of sociocultural perspectives and ecological outcomes. *AI. IoT and the Fourth Industrial Revolution Review*, 13(7), 61–74.

Almenar Fernández, L., & Belenguer González, A. (2022). The Transformation of Private Space in the Later Middle Ages: Rooms and Living Standards in the Kingdom of Valencia (1280-1450). *Journal of Urban History*, 48(4), 782–806. DOI: 10.1177/0096144220967990

Alonso-Mencía, J. (2023). *Unlocking Sentiments: Exploring the Power of NLP Transformers in Review Analysis*. https://ceur-ws.org/Vol-3496/restmex-paper12.pdf

Alotaibi, R., Ali, A., Alharthi, H., & Almehamadi, R. (2020). AI Chatbot for Tourism Recommendations A Case Study in the City of Jeddah, Saudi Arabia. *International Journal of Interactive Mobile Technologies*, 14(19), 18–30. DOI: 10.3991/ijim.v14i19.17201

Alrawadieh, Z., Alrawadieh, Z., & Cetin, G. (2021). Digital transformation and revenue management: Evidence from the hotel industry. *Tourism Economics*, 27(2), 328–345. DOI: 10.1177/1354816620901928

Alvarez-Carmona, M. A., & Aranda, R. (2022). *Natural language processing applied to tourism research: A systematic review and future research directions*. DOI: 10.1016/j.jksuci.2022.10.010

Alyasiri, O. M., Selvaraj, K., Younis, H. A., Sahib, T. M., Almasoodi, M. F., & Hayder, I. M. (2024). A Survey on the Potential of Artificial Intelligence Tools in Tourism Information Services. *Babylonian Journal of Artificial Intelligence*, 2024, 1–8. DOI: 10.58496/BJAI/2024/001

Ameni Dhaoui Boumaiza. (2016). A Survey on Sentiment Analysis and Visualization. *Qatar Foundation Annual Research Conference Proceedings,* 2016(1). DOI: 10.5339/qfarc.2016.ICTPP1203

Antoniou, V. (2023). On volunteered geographic information quality: a framework for sharing data quality information. In *Geoinformatics for Geosciences: Advanced Geospatial Analysis using RS.* GIS and Soft Computing. DOI: 10.1016/B978-0-323-98983-1.00009-0

Anuar, F., & Gretzel, U. (2011, January). Privacy concerns in the context of location-based services for tourism. *ENTER 2011 Conference.*

Arici, H. E., Saydam, M. B., & Koseoglu, M. A. (2023). How do customers react to technology in the hospitality and tourism industry? *Journal of Hospitality & Tourism Research (Washington, D.C.)*, 10963480231168609.

Ariza-Colpas, P. P., Piñeres-Melo, M. A., Morales-Ortega, R. C., Rodriguez-Bonilla, A. F., Butt-Aziz, S., Naz, S., del Carmen Contreras-Chinchilla, L., Romero-Mestre, M., & Ascanio, R. A. V. (2023). Augmented Reality and Tourism: A Bibliometric Analysis of New Technological Bets in the Post-COVID Era. *Sustainability (Basel)*, 15(21), 15358. DOI: 10.3390/su152115358

Arkinstall, C. A., FitzGibbon, S. I., Bradley, K. J., Moseby, K. E., & Murray, P. J. (2022). Using microchip-reading antennas to passively monitor a mammal reintroduction in south-west Queensland. *Australian Mammalogy*, 45(1), 98–107. DOI: 10.1071/AM22005

Armano, D. (2007). The marketing spiral. Logic+Emotio [En ligne], https://darmano.typepad.com/logic_emotion/2007/08/the-marketing-s.html

Arnould E-J., Price L., & Zinkhan G. (2002), Consumers. McGraw-Hill.

Arnould, E. J., & Price, L. L. (1993). River Magic : Extraordinary Experience and the Extended Service Encounter. *The Journal of Consumer Research*, 20(1), 24–45. DOI: 10.1086/209331

Arora, M., & Chandel, M. (2024). Role of artificial intelligence in promoting green destinations for sustainable tourism development. In A. Alnoor, G. E. Bayram, C. XinYing, & S. H. A. Shah (Eds.), *The role of artificial intelligence in regenerative tourism and green destinations (new perspectives in tourism and hospitality management)* (pp. 247–260). Emerald Publishing Limited. DOI: 10.1108/978-1-83753-746-420241016

Arora, M., & Chandel, M. (2024). *The Role of Artificial Intelligence in Regenerative Tourism and Green Destinations.* Emerald Publishing Limited.

Arun Wadhe, A., & Suratkar, S., S. (2020, May 28). Tourist Place Reviews Sentiment Classification Using Machine Learning Techniques. *2020 International Conference on Industry 4.0 Technology (I4Tech)*. DOI: 10.1109/I4Tech48345.2020.9102673

Asi, L., Mojjada, H., Prasanna, M., & Deepika, Y. (2023). *A Study on Artificial Intelligence in Marketing. 5*, 1-15. DOI: 10.36948/ijfmr.2023.v05i03.3789

Babu, S., & Subramoniam, S. (2016). Tourism management in internet of things era. *Journal of Information Technology and Economic Development*, 7(1).

Badruddoza Talukder, M., Kumar, S., Misra, L. I., & Firoj Kabir, . (2024). Determining the role of eco-tourism service quality, tourist satisfaction, and destination loyalty: A case study of Kuakata beach. *Acta Scientiarum Polonorum. Administratio Locorum*, 23(1), 133–151. DOI: 10.31648/aspal.9275

Bag, S., Gupta, S., Kumar, A., & Sivarajah, U. (2021). An integrated artificial intelligence framework for knowledge creation and B2B marketing rational decision making for improving firm performance. *Industrial Marketing Management*, 92, 178–189. DOI: 10.1016/j.indmarman.2020.12.001

Balducci, B., & Marinova, D. (2018). Unstructured data in marketing. *Journal of the Academy of Marketing Science*, 46(4), 557–590. DOI: 10.1007/s11747-018-0581-x

Balducci, F. (2021). Is OpenStreetMap a good source of information for cultural statistics? The case of Italian museums. *Environment and Planning. B, Urban Analytics and City Science*, 48(3), 503–520. Advance online publication. DOI: 10.1177/2399808319876949

Bansal, A., & Kumar, N. (2021). Aspect-Based Sentiment Analysis Using Attribute Extraction of Hospital Reviews. *New Generation Computing*. Advance online publication. DOI: 10.1007/s00354-021-00141-3 PMID: 34866746

Barrachina, P. (2024). AI-infused tourism: Enhancing travel experiences with smart sights. *International Journal of Computer Science & Information System*.

Barstow Hernandez, J. (2018). Transformative Leadership : Its Evolution and Impact. *The Journal of Bahá'í Studies*, 28(3), 55–85. DOI: 10.31581/jbs-28.3.3(2018)

Bartzokas-Tsiompras, A. (2022). Utilizing OpenStreetMap data to measure and compare pedestrian street lengths in 992 cities around the world. *European Journal of Geography*, 13(2), 127–141. Advance online publication. DOI: 10.48088/ejg.a.bar.13.2.127.138

Basiri, A., Haklay, M., Foody, G., & Mooney, P. (2019). Crowdsourced geospatial data quality: challenges and future directions. In *International Journal of Geographical Information Science* (Vol. 33, Issue 8). DOI: 10.1080/13658816.2019.1593422

Bayram, G. E. (2020). Impact of information technology on tourism. In *The emerald handbook of ICT in tourism and hospitality* (pp. 243–257). Emerald Publishing Limited. DOI: 10.1108/978-1-83982-688-720201015

Becken, S., & Patterson, M. (2018). Reducing plastic waste in tourism: A multi-stakeholder approach. *Journal of Sustainable Tourism*, 26(1), 141–159.

Belousova, V., Bondarenko, O., Chichkanov, N., Lebedev, D., & Miles, I. (2022). Coping with Greenhouse Gas Emissions: Insights from Digital Business Services. *Energies*, 15(8), 2745. DOI: 10.3390/en15082745

Benjelloun, A., & Kabak, S. (2024). Ethical Challenges and Managerial Implications of Artificial Intelligence in Digital Marketing. In S. Kumar, K. Balachandran, J. H. Kim, & J. C. Bansal (Éds.), *Fourth Congress on Intelligent Systems* (Vol. 869, p. 439-445). Springer Nature Singapore. DOI: 10.1007/978-981-99-9040-5_32

Berbekova, A., Uysal, M., & Assaf, A. G. (2021). A thematic analysis of crisis management in tourism: A theoretical perspective. *Tourism Management*, 86, 104342. DOI: 10.1016/j.tourman.2021.104342

Bertella, G., Fumagalli, M., & Williams-Grey, V. (2019). Wildlife tourism through the co-creation lens. *Tourism Recreation Research*, 44(3), 300–310. DOI: 10.1080/02508281.2019.1606977

Bharwani, S., & Mathews, D. (2021). Techno-business strategies for enhancing guest experience in luxury hotels: A managerial perspective. *Worldwide Hospitality and Tourism Themes*, 13(2), 168–185. DOI: 10.1108/WHATT-09-2020-0121

Bhaskar, P., & Sharma, K. (2022). A Critical Insight into the Role of Artificial Intelligence (AI) in Tourism and Hospitality Industries. *A Refereed Monthly. International Journal of Management*, 15, 76–85.

Biagi, L., Brovelli, M. A., & Stucchi, L. (2020). Mapping the accessibility in openstreetmap: A comparison of different techniques. *International Archives of the Photogrammetry, Remote Sensing and Spatial Information Sciences - ISPRS Archives, 43*(B4). DOI: 10.5194/isprs-archives-XLIII-B4-2020-229-2020

Bilgihan, A., & Ricci, P. (2023). The new era of hotel marketing : Integrating cutting-edge technologies with core marketing principles New era of hotel marketing. *Journal of Hospitality and Tourism Technology*. Advance online publication. DOI: 10.1108/JHTT-04-2023-0095

Biljecki, F., Chow, Y. S., & Lee, K. (2023). Quality of crowdsourced geospatial building information: A global assessment of OpenStreetMap attributes. *Building and Environment*, 237, 110295. Advance online publication. DOI: 10.1016/j.buildenv.2023.110295

Bordoloi, M., & Biswas, S. K. (2023). Sentiment analysis: A survey on design framework, applications and future scopes. *Artificial Intelligence Review*, 56(11), 12505–12560. Advance online publication. DOI: 10.1007/s10462-023-10442-2 PMID: 37362892

Bourgeon D. et Bouchet P. (2007), Marketing expérientiel et analyse des logiques de consommation du spectacle sportif, Revue française du marketing, n°212.

Braun, V., & Clarke, V. (2006). Using thematic analysis in psychology. *Qualitative Research in Psychology*, 3(2), 77–101. DOI: 10.1191/1478088706qp063oa

Brickson, L., Zhang, L., Vollrath, F., Douglas-Hamilton, I., & Titus, A. J. (2023). Elephants and algorithms: A review of the current and future role of AI in elephant monitoring. *Journal of the Royal Society, Interface*, 20(208), 20230367. Advance online publication. DOI: 10.1098/rsif.2023.0367 PMID: 37963556

Buckley, R. (2016). *Conservation tourism*. Routledge.

Buhalis, D. (2003). *eTourism: Information technology for strategic tourism management*. Pearson Education.

Buhalis, D., & Inversini, A. (2014). Tourism branding, identity, reputation co-creation, and word-of-mouth in the age of social media. In Tourism Management, Marketing, and Development: Volume I: The Importance of Networks and ICTs (pp. 15-40). New York: Palgrave Macmillan US.

Buhalis, D., & Amaranggana, A. (2015a). *Information and Communication Technologies in Tourism 2015* (Tussyadiah, I., & Inversini, A., Eds.). Springer International Publishing. DOI: 10.1007/978-3-319-14343-9_28

Buhalis, D., Harwood, T., Bogicevic, V., Viglia, G., Beldona, S., & Hofacker, C. (2019). Technological disruptions in services: Lessons from tourism and hospitality. *Journal of Service Management*, 30(4), 484–506. DOI: 10.1108/JOSM-12-2018-0398

Buhalis, D., & Law, R. (2020). Hyper-personalization in tourism: Time for a paradigm shift? *Journal of Hospitality and Tourism Technology Management*, 30(2), 381–392.

Buhalis, D., & Leung, R. (2018). Smart hospitality—Interconnectivity and interoperability towards an ecosystem. *International Journal of Hospitality Management*, 71, 41–50. DOI: 10.1016/j.ijhm.2017.11.011

Buhalis, D., Lin, M. S., & Leung, D. (2022). Metaverse as a driver for customer experience and value co-creation: Implications for hospitality and tourism management and marketing. *International Journal of Contemporary Hospitality Management*, 35(2), 701–716. DOI: 10.1108/IJCHM-05-2022-0631

Buhalis, D., & Moldavska, I. (2022). Voice assistants in hospitality: Using artificial intelligence for customer service. *Journal of Hospitality and Tourism Technology*, 13(3), 386–403. DOI: 10.1108/JHTT-03-2021-0104

Buhalis, D., & Sinclair, M. T. (2020). Artificial intelligence in tourism: A critical review. *International Journal of Hospitality Management*, 87, 102688.

Bulchand-Gidumal, J. (2022). Impact of artificial intelligence in travel, tourism, and hospitality. In *Handbook of e-Tourism* (pp. 1943–1962). Springer International Publishing. DOI: 10.1007/978-3-030-48652-5_110

Buonincontri, P., & Micera, R. (2016). The experience co-creation in smart tourism destinations: A multiple case analysis of European destinations. *Information Technology & Tourism*, 16(3), 285–315. DOI: 10.1007/s40558-016-0060-5

Burke, S., Pottier, P., Macartney, E. L., Drobniak, S. M., Lagisz, M., Ainsworth, T., & Nakagawa, S. (2022). Mapping literature reviews on coral health: Protocol for a review map, critical appraisal and bibliometric analysis. *Ecological Solutions and Evidence*, 3(4), e12190. Advance online publication. DOI: 10.1002/2688-8319.12190

Bustamante, A., Sebastia, L., & Onaindia, E. (2021). On the representativeness of openstreetmap for the evaluation of country tourism competitiveness. *ISPRS International Journal of Geo-Information*, 10(5), 301. Advance online publication. DOI: 10.3390/ijgi10050301

Cahigas, M. M. L., Prasetyo, Y. T., Alexander, J., Sutapa, P. L., Wiratama, S., Arvin, V., Nadlifatin, R., & Persada, S. F. (2022). Factors Affecting Visiting Behavior to Bali during the COVID-19 Pandemic: An Extended Theory of Planned Behavior Approach. *Sustainability (Basel)*, 14(16), 10424. Advance online publication. DOI: 10.3390/su141610424

Cain, L., & Webster, C. (2023). The origin, rationale, and impacts of regulations on robots and AI in tourism and hospitality. *Proceedings INNODOCT/22. International Conference on Innovation, Documentation and Education*, 111-118. https://riunet.upv.es/handle/10251/193157

Calka, B., & Moscicka, A. (2022). Usefulness of OSM and BDOT10k Data for Developing Tactile Maps of Historic Parks. *Applied Sciences (Basel, Switzerland)*, 12(19), 9731. Advance online publication. DOI: 10.3390/app12199731

Calleja, C., & Borg, B. (2012, February 14). Maltese hunters 'shooting protected birds' in Egypt. https://timesofmalta.com/article/Maltese-hunters-shooting-protected-birds-in-Egypt.406905

Cao, F., & Jian, Y. (2024). The role of integrating AI and VR in fostering environmental awareness and enhancing activism among college students. *The Science of the Total Environment*, 908, 168200. Advance online publication. DOI: 10.1016/j.scitotenv.2023.168200 PMID: 37918744

Carr, N., & Broom, D. M. (2018). *Tourism and animal welfare*. CABI Digital Library. DOI: 10.1079/9781786391858.0000

Casheekar, A., Lahiri, A., Rath, K., Prabhakar, K. S., & Srinivasan, K. (2024). A contemporary review on chatbots, AI-powered virtual conversational agents, ChatGPT: Applications, open challenges and future research directions. *Computer Science Review*, 52, 100632. DOI: 10.1016/j.cosrev.2024.100632

Castañeda, J. A., Rodríguez-Molina, M. Á., Frías-Jamilena, D. M., & García-Retamero, R. (2020). The role of numeracy and information load in the tourist decision-making process. *Psychology and Marketing*, 37(1), 27–40. DOI: 10.1002/mar.21278

Ceballos, G., Ehrlich, P. R., & Raven, P. H. (2020). Vertebrates on the brink as indicators of biological annihilation and the sixth mass extinction. *Proceedings of the National Academy of Sciences of the United States of America*, 117(24), 13596–13602. DOI: 10.1073/pnas.1922686117 PMID: 32482862

Çeltek, E., & İhan, . (2018). Innovations in destination marketing. In *The Routledge handbook of destination marketing* (pp. 417–428). Routledge. DOI: 10.4324/9781315101163-32

Center for Responsible Travel. (2017). *The case for responsible travel: Trends and statistics 2017*. https://www.responsibletravel.org/wp-content/uploads/sites/213/2021/03/trends-and-statistics-2017.pdf

Chan, A., Hsu, C. H., & Baum, T. (2015). The impact of tour service performance on tourist satisfaction and behavioral intentions: A study of Chinese tourists in Hong Kong. *Journal of Travel & Tourism Marketing*, 32(1-2), 18–33. DOI: 10.1080/10548408.2014.986010

Chan, C. S., & Agapito, D. (2022). Managing destination experience design for tourists with disabilities: ICT and accessibility. In *Handbook on the Tourist Experience* (pp. 226–245). Edward Elgar Publishing.

Chavan, P., Havale, D. S., & Khang, A. (2024). Artificial intelligence and tourism: A bibliometric analysis of trends and gaps. *Revolutionizing the AI-Digital Landscape*, 332–344. DOI: 10.4324/9781032688305-24

Chen, C.-F., & Tsai, D. (2007). How destination image and evaluative factors affect behavioral intentions? *Tourism Management*, 28(4), 1115–1122. DOI: 10.1016/j.tourman.2006.07.007

Chen, J., Luo, Y., Liu, H., Qin, J., & Chen, E. (2023). Algorithmic bias in AI-driven tourism: A review and future research directions. *Annals of Tourism Research*, 90, 103357.

Chen, R., Little, R., Mihaylova, L., Delahay, R., & Cox, R. (2019). Wildlife surveillance using deep learning methods. *Ecology and Evolution*, 9(17), 9453–9466. DOI: 10.1002/ece3.5410 PMID: 31534668

Chen, S., Zhang, K., Li, X., Ye, H., Lin, K. J., & Law, R. (2023). ChatGPT : Cross cultural tourism research imperative. *Journal of Economics and Management*, 45, 137–146. DOI: 10.22367/jem.2023.45.07

Chiche, A., & Yitagesu, B. (2022). Part of speech tagging: A systematic review of deep learning and machine learning approaches. *Journal of Big Data*, 9(1), 10. Advance online publication. DOI: 10.1186/s40537-022-00561-y

Chisom, O. N., Biu, P. W., Umoh, A. A., Obaedo, B. O., Adegbite, A. O., & Abatan, A. (2024). Reviewing the role of AI in environmental monitoring and conservation: A data-driven revolution for our planet. *World Journal of Advanced Research and Reviews*, 21(1), 161–171. DOI: 10.30574/wjarr.2024.21.1.2720

Choo, S., & Kim, W. (2023). A study on the evaluation of tokenizer performance in natural language processing. *Applied Artificial Intelligence*, 37(1), 2175112. Advance online publication. DOI: 10.1080/08839514.2023.2175112

Christou, P., Hadjielias, E., Simillidou, A., & Kvasova, O. (2023). The use of intelligent automation as a form of digital transformation in tourism : Towards a hybrid experiential offering. *Journal of Business Research*, 155, 113415. DOI: 10.1016/j.jbusres.2022.113415

Chung, J. Y., & Buhalis, D. (2008). Web 2.0: A study of online travel community. In *Information and communication technologies in tourism 2008* (pp. 70–81). Springer. DOI: 10.1007/978-3-211-77280-5_7

Chung, N., Tyan, I., & Han, H. (2017). Enhancing the smart tourism experience through geotag. *Information Systems Frontiers*, 19(4), 731–742. DOI: 10.1007/s10796-016-9710-6

Clapham, M., Miller, E., Nguyen, M., & Darimont, C. T. (2020). Automated facial recognition for wildlife that lack unique markings: A deep learning approach for brown bears. *Ecology and Evolution*, 10(23), 12883–12892. DOI: 10.1002/ece3.6840 PMID: 33304501

Clapham, M., Miller, E., Nguyen, M., & Van Horn, R. C. (2022). Multispecies facial detection for individual identification of wildlife: A case study across ursids. *Mammalian Biology*, 102(3), 943–955. DOI: 10.1007/s42991-021-00168-5 PMID: 36164481

Coetzee, B. W. T., & Chown, S. L. (2016). A meta-analysis of human disturbance impacts on Antarctic wildlife. *Biological Reviews of the Cambridge Philosophical Society*, 91(3), 578–596. DOI: 10.1111/brv.12184 PMID: 25923885

Coghlan, S., & Parker, C. (2023). Harm to nonhuman animals from AI: A systematic account and framework. *Philosophy & Technology*, 36(25), 25. Advance online publication. DOI: 10.1007/s13347-023-00627-6

Cohen, E. (2018). The philosophical, ethical and theological groundings of tourism – an exploratory inquiry. *Journal of Ecotourism*, 17(4), 359–382. DOI: 10.1080/14724049.2018.1522477

Cohen, E., & Cohen, S. A. (2012). Authentication: Hot and cool. *Annals of Tourism Research*, 39(3), 1295–1314. DOI: 10.1016/j.annals.2012.03.004

Cohen, M., Gaston, G., & Goeldner, J. (2019). *Tourism and development revisited: Critical issues for a new century*. Routledge.

Constantinides, E., & Synodinos, C. (2018). A review of personalization in tourism. *Journal of Hospitality and Tourism Technology*, 9(2), 221–238.

Coughlin, C. E., & van Heezik, Y. (2015). Weighed down by science: Do collar-mounted devices affect domestic cat behaviour and movement? *Wildlife Research*, 41(7), 606–614. DOI: 10.1071/WR14160

Cova, B., & Cova, V. (2009). Les figures du nouveau consommateur: Une genèse de la gouvernementalité du consommateur. *Recherche et Applications en Marketing*, 24(3), 82–100. DOI: 10.1177/076737010902400305

Cox, C., Burgess, S., Sellitto, C., & Buultjens, J. (2009). The role of user-generated content in tourists' travel planning behavior. *Journal of Hospitality Marketing & Management*, 18(8), 743–764. DOI: 10.1080/19368620903235753

Dafoe, A. (2018). AI governance : A research agenda. *Governance of AI Program, Future of Humanity Institute, University of Oxford: Oxford, UK, 1442*, 1443.

Dai, J., Li, C., Zuo, Y., & Ai, H. (2020). An osm data-driven method for road-positive sample creation. *Remote Sensing (Basel)*, 12(21), 3612. Advance online publication. DOI: 10.3390/rs12213612

Dai, T., Hein, C., & Zhang, T. (2019). Understanding how Amsterdam City tourism marketing addresses cruise tourists' motivations regarding culture. *Tourism Management Perspectives*, 29, 157–165. DOI: 10.1016/j.tmp.2018.12.001

Dalipi, F., Kastrati, Z., & Öberg, T. (2023). The Impact of Artificial Intelligence on Tourism Sustainability : A Systematic Mapping Review. *2023 International Conference on Computational Intelligence and Knowledge Economy (ICCIKE)*, 119-125. https://ieeexplore.ieee.org/abstract/document/10131818/

Dar, H. (2022). Conceptualizing the smart community in the ages of smart tourism: A literature perspective. *Revista Turismo & Desenvolvimento (RT&D)/Journal of Tourism & Development*, (39).

Dar, H. (2024). Sustainable Measures Deterring Ethical and Decent Dilemmas in Tourism. In *Managing Tourism and Hospitality Sectors for Sustainable Global Transformation* (pp. 219–229). IGI Global. DOI: 10.4018/979-8-3693-6260-0.ch016

Dar, H., & Kashyap, K. (2023a). Indian Medical Tourism: COVID-19 Situation, Planning and Reviving Approaches. In *Tourism and Hospitality in Asia: Crisis, Resilience and Recovery* (pp. 97–111). Springer Nature Singapore.

Dar, H., & Kashyap, K. (2023b). Smart healthcare system (SHS): Medical tourism delivering, consumption, and elevating tool in the ages of smart technologies. *Tourism Planning & Development*, 20(3), 397–415. DOI: 10.1080/21568316.2022.2109206

Das, I. R., Talukder, M. B., & Kumar, S. (2024). Implication of Artificial Intelligence in Hospitality Marketing. *Utilizing Smart Technology and AI in Hybrid Tourism and Hospitality*. IGI Global. DOI: 10.4018/979-8-3693-1978-9.ch014

Dash, S., & Kalamdhad, A. S. (2021). Science mapping approach to critical reviewing of published literature on water quality indexing. *Ecological Indicators*, 128, 107862. Advance online publication. DOI: 10.1016/j.ecolind.2021.107862

Datiko, D. B. (2024). The customer-centric-marketing (CCM) perspectives in the tourism and hospitality sector: Insight from a developing country. *International Journal of Tourism Policy*, 14(1), 37–53. Advance online publication. DOI: 10.1504/IJTP.2024.135429

Davenport, T., Guha, A., Grewal, D., & Bressgott, T. (2019). How artificial intelligence will change the future of marketing. *Journal of the Academy of Marketing Science*, 48(1), 1–19. DOI: 10.1007/s11747-019-00696-0

Davis, F. D. (1989). Technology acceptance model: TAM. *Information Seeking Behavior and Technology Adoption*, 205, 219.

de Almeida Biolchini, J. C., Mian, P. G., Natali, A. C. C., Conte, T. U., & Travassos, G. H. (2007). Scientific research ontology to support systematic review in software engineering. *Advanced Engineering Informatics*, 21(2), 133–151. DOI: 10.1016/j.aei.2006.11.006

De Kloet, M., & Yang, S. (2022). The effects of anthropomorphism and multimodal biometric authentication on the user experience of voice intelligence. *Frontiers in Artificial Intelligence*, 5, 831046. DOI: 10.3389/frai.2022.831046 PMID: 36062266

Deb, D., Wiper, S., Gong, S., Shi, Y., Tymoszek, C., Fletcher, A., & Jain, A. K. (2018). Face recognition: Primates in the wild. In *2018 IEEE 9th International Conference on Biometrics Theory, Applications and Systems, BTAS 2018* (pp. 1–10). IEEE. DOI: 10.1109/BTAS.2018.8698538

Deloitte. (2022). The AI Advantage in the Indian Travel and Hospitality Industry. https://www2.deloitte.com/in/en/pages/deloitte-analytics/articles/Deloitte-India-AI-Warriors.html

Deng, B., Xu, J., & Wei, X. (2021). Tourism Destination Preference Prediction Based on Edge Computing. *Mobile Information Systems*, 2021, 1–11. Advance online publication. DOI: 10.1155/2021/5512008

Dentoni, D., Waddell, S., & Waddock, S. (2017). Pathways of transformation in global food and agricultural systems : Implications from a large systems change theory perspective. *Current Opinion in Environmental Sustainability*, 29, 8–13. DOI: 10.1016/j.cosust.2017.10.003

Desmarteau, R., Saives, A.-L., Schieb-Bienfait, N., Emin, S., Boldrini, J.-C., & Urbain, C. (2017), La création de valeur: glas ou Graal? Revue et modélisation du concept, XXVIe Conférence Internationale de Management Stratégique, Lyon, 7-9 juin 2017.

Devlin, J., Chang, M.-W., Lee, K., & Toutanova, K. (2019). BERT: Pre-training of deep bidirectional transformers for language understanding. *Proceedings of the 2019 Conference of the North American Chapter of the Association for Computational Linguistics*, 4171-4186. DOI: 10.18653/v1/N19-1423

Diantoro, K., Supriyanti, D., Sanjaya, Y. P. A., & Watini, S. (2023). Implications of distributed energy development in blockchain-based institutional environment. *Aptisi Transactions on Technopreneurship*, 5(2sp), 209–220. DOI: 10.34306/att.v5i2sp.343

Díaz, E., Esteban, Á., Koutra, C., Almeida, S., & Carranza, R. (2023). Co-creation of value in smart ecosystems: Past trends and future directions in tourism literature. *Journal of Hospitality and Tourism Technology*, 14(3), 365–383. DOI: 10.1108/JHTT-04-2021-0122

Dickinson, J., & Bonney, R. (2012). *Citizen science: Public participation in environmental research.* Cornell University Press., DOI: 10.7591/cornell/9780801449116.001.0001

Ding, M. (2021). Research on Tourism Route Planning Based on Artificial Intelligence Technology. *Wireless Communications and Mobile Computing*, 2021(1), 2227798. Advance online publication. DOI: 10.1155/2021/2227798

Dionisio, M., Mendes, M., Fernandez, M., Nisi, V., & Nunes, N. (2022). Aqua: Leveraging citizen science to enhance whale-watching activities and promote marine-biodiversity awareness. *Sustainability (Basel)*, 14(21), 14203. Advance online publication. DOI: 10.3390/su142114203

Doborjeh, Z., Hemmington, N., Doborjeh, M., & Kasabov, N. (2022). Artificial intelligence: A systematic review of methods and applications in hospitality and tourism. *International Journal of Contemporary Hospitality Management*, 34(3), 1154–1176. DOI: 10.1108/IJCHM-06-2021-0767

Doğan, S., & Niyet, İ. Z. (2024). *Artificial Intelligence (AI) in Tourism. Future Tourism Trends Volume 2: Technology Advancement, Trends and Innovations for the Future in Tourism.* Emerald Publishing Limited.

Dogan, S., & Niyet, I. Z. (2024). Artificial Intelligence (AI) in Tourism. In Future Tourism Trends Volume 2: Technology Advancement, Trends and Innovations for the Future in Tourism (pp. 3-21). Emerald Publishing Limited.

Dogru, T., Line, N., Mody, M., Hanks, L., Abbott, J. A., Acikgoz, F., Assaf, A., Bakir, S., Berbekova, A., Bilgihan, A., Dalton, A., Erkmen, E., Geronasso, M., Gomez, D., Graves, S., Iskender, A., Ivanov, S., Kizildag, M., Lee, M., & Zhang, T. (2023). Generative artificial intelligence in the hospitality and tourism industry: Developing a framework for future research. *Journal of Hospitality & Tourism Research (Washington, D.C.)*. DOI: 10.1177/10963480231188663

Dorfling, J., Siewert, S. B., Bruder, S., Aranzazu-Suescun, C., Rocha, K., Landon, P. D., Bondar, G., Pederson, T., Le, C., Mangar, R., Rawther, C., & Trahms, B. (2022, January 3–7). *Satellite, aerial, and ground sensor fusion experiment for management of elephants and rhinos and poaching prevention.* AIAA SCITECH 2022 Forum (p. 1270). DOI: 10.2514/6.2022-1270

Doull, K. E., Chalmers, C., Fergus, P., Longmore, S., Piel, A. K., & Wich, S. A. (2021). An evaluation of the factors affecting 'poacher' detection with drones and the efficacy of machine-learning for detection. *Sensors (Basel)*, 21(12), 4074. Advance online publication. DOI: 10.3390/s21124074 PMID: 34199208

Dou, X., & Day, J. (2020). Human-wildlife interactions for tourism: A systematic review. *Journal of Hospitality and Tourism Insights*, 3(5), 529–547. DOI: 10.1108/JHTI-01-2020-0007

Dubey, R., & Singh, A. K. (2018). Personalized Tourism Recommendation Based on Cultural Preferences and Social Context in India. *ACM Transactions on Asian Language Information Processing*, 17(4), 1–18.

Duffy, R., & Moore, L. (2011). Global regulations and local practices: The politics and governance of animal welfare in elephant tourism. *Journal of Sustainable Tourism*, 19(4-5), 589–604. DOI: 10.1080/09669582.2011.566927

Dykins, R. (2020, December 9). *AndBeyond sells live online safaris to fund conservation*. Globetrender. https://globetrender.com/2020/12/09/andbeyond-private-virtual-safaris-conservation/

Ekka, P. M., & Dhall, R. (2023). Technology, destination marketing and tourism: What, why and way forward. *Smart Tourism*, 4(2), 2447. DOI: 10.54517/st.v4i2.2447

El Archi, Y., & Benbba, B. (2023). The Applications of Technology Acceptance Models in Tourism and Hospitality Research : A Systematic Literature Review. *Journal of Environmental Management and Tourism*, 14(2), 379. DOI: 10.14505/jemt.v14.2(66).08

Elsawy, T. M. (2023). Beyond Passive Observance: Understanding Egyptian Domestic Tourists' Behaviour through Hyper-Personalised Digital Clienteling. *Pharos International Journal of Tourism and Hospitality*, 2(2), 1–15. DOI: 10.21608/pijth.2023.256371.1007

Fahlevi, M. (2023). A Systematic Literature Review on Marine Tourism in Business Management: State of the Art and Future Research Agenda. *Journal of Tourism and Services*, 14(27), 299–321. DOI: 10.29036/jots.v14i27.549

Fakiha, B. (2023). Enhancing cyber forensics with AI and machine learning: A study on automated threat analysis and classification. *International Journal of Safety and Security Engineering*, 13(4), 701–707. DOI: 10.18280/ijsse.130412

Far Eastern Federal University, & Shumakova, E. V. (2019). Apart-hotel as an innovative form of organization of a hotel business. *azimuth of scientific study: economics and administration,* 8(28). https://doi.org/DOI: 10.26140/anie-2019-0803-0093

Farheen, N. S. (2024). *A Future Look at Artificial Intelligence in the World of Tourism. Marketing and Big Data Analytics in Tourism and Events*. IGI Global.

Farheen, N. S. S., Badiger, C. S., Kishore, L., Dheeraj, V., & Rajendran, S. R. (2024). A Future Look at Artificial Intelligence in the World of Tourism. In *Marketing and Big Data Analytics in Tourism and Events* (pp. 1–16). IGI Global. DOI: 10.4018/979-8-3693-3310-5.ch001

Farid, S., Boudia, M. A., & Mwangi, G. (2023). Revolutionizing Tourism: Harnessing the Power of IoT in Smart Destinations. *Journal of Digital Marketing and Communication*, 3(2), 91–99. DOI: 10.53623/jdmc.v3i2.360

Farr, J. J., Haave-Audet, E., Thompson, P. R., & Mathot, K. (2021). No effect of passive integrated transponder tagging on survival or body condition of a northern population of black-capped Chikadees (*Poecile atricapillus*). *Ecology and Evolution*, 11(14), 9610–9620. DOI: 10.1002/ece3.7783 PMID: 34306647

Fayon, D., & Tartar, M. (2014). *Transformation digitale: 5 leviers pour l'entreprise*. Pearson.

Felício, S., Hora, J., Ferreira, M. C., Abrantes, D., Costa, P. D., Dangelo, C., Silva, J., & Galvão, T. (2022). Handling OpenStreetMap georeferenced data for route planning. *Transportation Research Procedia*, 62, 189–196. Advance online publication. DOI: 10.1016/j.trpro.2022.02.024

Femenia-Serra, F., & Neuhofer, B. (2018). *Smart tourism experiences : Conceptualisation, key dimensions and research agenda*.

Fernández, J. A. S., Azevedo, P. S., Martín, J. M. M., & Martín, J. A. R. (2020). Determinants of tourism destination competitiveness in the countries most visited by international tourists: Proposal of a synthetic index. *Tourism Management Perspectives*, 33, 100582. DOI: 10.1016/j.tmp.2019.100582

Ferràs, X., Hitchen, E. L., Tarrats-Pons, E., & Arimany-Serrat, N. (2020). Smart tourism empowered by artificial intelligence: The case of Lanzarote. *Journal of Cases on Information Technology*, 22(1), 1–13. DOI: 10.4018/JCIT.2020010101

Ferster, C., Fischer, J., Manaugh, K., Nelson, T., & Winters, M. (2020). Using OpenStreetMap to inventory bicycle infrastructure: A comparison with open data from cities. *International Journal of Sustainable Transportation*, 14(1), 64–73. Advance online publication. DOI: 10.1080/15568318.2018.1519746

FEVAD (Fédération E-commerce et Vente À Distance). (2023), Chiffres Clés 2023, 8 pages.[En ligne]: https://www.fevad.com

Firat, A. F., & Dholakia, N. (2006). Theoretical and philosophical implications of postmodern debates: Some challenges to modern marketing. *Marketing Theory*, 6(2), 123–162. DOI: 10.1177/1470593106063981

Firat, F., & Venkatesh, A. (1995). Liberatory postmodernism and the reenchantement of consumption. *The Journal of Consumer Research*, 22(3), 239. DOI: 10.1086/209448

Flandrin, P., Hellemans, C., Van Der Linden, J., & Van De Leemput, C. (2021, October 6). Smart technologies in hospitality: effects on activity, work design and employment. A case study about chatbot usage. *ACM International Conference Proceeding Series*. DOI: 10.1145/3486812.3486838

Flück, B., Mathon, L., Manel, S., Valentini, A., Dejean, T., Albouy, C., Mouillot, D., Thuiller, W., Murienne, J., Brosse, S., & Pellissier, L. (2022). Applying convolutional neural networks to speed up environmental DNA annotation in a highly diverse ecosystem. *Scientific Reports*, 12(1), 10247. Advance online publication. DOI: 10.1038/s41598-022-13412-w PMID: 35715444

Formica, A., Mazzei, M., Pourabbas, E., & Rafanelli, M. (2020). Approximate Query Answering Based on Topological Neighborhood and Semantic Similarity in OpenStreetMap. *IEEE Access : Practical Innovations, Open Solutions*, 8, 87011–87030. Advance online publication. DOI: 10.1109/ACCESS.2020.2992202

Fotis, J., Buhalis, D., & Rossides, N. (2012). Social media use and impact during the holiday travel planning process. In *Information and communication technologies in tourism 2012* (pp. 13–24). Springer. DOI: 10.1007/978-3-7091-1142-0_2

Foyet, M. A. (2024, March 5). *AI in conservation: Where we came from — and where we are heading*. World Economic Forum. https://www.weforum.org/agenda/2024/03/ai-in-conservation-where-we-came-from-and-where-we-are-heading/

Fuentes, M., Carles, M. P., & Camon, F. (2018, March 14). Does verifying users influence rankings? Analyzing TripAdvisor and Booking.com. Udl.cat; Cognizant Communication Corporation. https://repositori.udl.cat/items/7d0e0fa2-c764-47d3-b462-9eafb462bdbc

Gade, S. S., Dhole, R. M., & Sisodiya, D. S. (2023). Guardians of wild: Artificial intelligence for wildlife conservation. *International Journal of Advanced Research in Science. Tongxin Jishu*, 3(1), 107–110. https://ijarsct.co.in/Paper13616.pdf

Gajić, T., Ranjbaran, A., Vukolić, D., Bugarčić, J., Spasojević, A., Đorđević Boljanović, J., Vujačić, D., Mandarić, M., Kostić, M., Sekulić, D., Bugarčić, M., Drašković, B. D., & Rakić, S. R. (2024). Tourists' Willingness to Adopt AI in Hospitality—Assumption of Sustainability in Developing Countries. *Sustainability (Basel)*, 16(9), 3663. DOI: 10.3390/su16093663

Gandhi, A., Adhvaryu, K., Poria, S., Cambria, E., & Hussain, A. (2023). Multimodal sentiment analysis: A systematic review of history, datasets, multimodal fusion methods, applications, challenges and future directions. *Information Fusion*, 91, 424–444. DOI: 10.1016/j.inffus.2022.09.025

Gangwar, V. P., & Reddy, D. (2023). Hospitality Industry 5.0: Emerging Trends in Guest Perception and Experiences. In Dadwal, S., Kumar, P., Verma, R., & Singh, G. (Eds.), (pp. 185–211). Advances in Business Strategy and Competitive Advantage. IGI Global. DOI: 10.4018/978-1-6684-6403-8.ch010

Gan, L., Hu, L., Tan, X., & Du, X. (2023). TBNF: A Transformer-based Noise Filtering Method for Chinese Long-form Text Matching. *Applied Intelligence*, 53(19), 22313–22327. DOI: 10.1007/s10489-023-04607-3

Gantchoff, M. G., Hill, J. E., Kellner, K. F., Fowler, N. L., Petroelje, T. R., Conlee, L., & Belant, J. L. (2020). Mortality of a large wide-ranging mammal caused by anthropogenic activities. *Scientific Reports*, 10(1), 8498. Advance online publication. DOI: 10.1038/s41598-020-65290-9 PMID: 32444633

Garanti, Z. (2023). Value co-creation in smart tourism destinations. *Worldwide Hospitality and Tourism Themes*, 15(5), 468–475. DOI: 10.1108/WHATT-06-2023-0070

García-Madurga, M.-A., & Grilló-Méndez, A.-J. (2023). Artificial intelligence in the tourism industry: An overview of reviews. *Administrative Sciences*, 13(8), 172. Advance online publication. DOI: 10.3390/admsci13080172

García-Madurga, M.-Á., & Grilló-Méndez, A.-J. (2023). Battlefield Tourism: Exploring the Successful Marriage of History and Unforgettable Experiences: A Systematic Review. *Tourism and Hospitality*, 4(2), 307–320. DOI: 10.3390/tourhosp4020019

Gazta, K. (2018). Environmental impact of tourism. *AGU International Journal of Professional Studies and Research*, 6, 7–17. https://web.archive.org/web/20180409201650id_/http://aguijpsr.com/images/short_pdf/1512624000_Kajal_Gazta_2.pdf

Gbobaniyi, O., Tincani, D., & Emelone, P. (2024). *The Strategic Efficacy of Artificial Intelligence (AI) in Medical Tourism. Impact of AI and Robotics on the Medical Tourism Industry*. IGI Global.

Geels, F. W. (2011). The multi-level perspective on sustainability transitions: Responses to seven criticisms. *Environmental Innovation and Societal Transitions*, 1(1), 24–40. DOI: 10.1016/j.eist.2011.02.002

Ghandour, A., & Woodford, B. J. (2023). Guidelines to Develop AI Ethics Policy in Organizations : Perspectives Informed from Two Different Countries' Laws. *2023 24th International Arab Conference on Information Technology (ACIT)*, 1-9. https://ieeexplore.ieee.org/abstract/document/10453750/

Ghesh, N., Alexander, M., & Davis, A. (2023). The artificial intelligence-enabled customer experience in tourism : A systematic literature review. *Tourism Review*. Advance online publication. DOI: 10.1108/TR-04-2023-0255

Ghouse, S. M., & Chaudhary, M. (2024). Artificial Intelligence (AI) for Tourism Start-Ups. In Innovative Technologies for Increasing Service Productivity (pp. 161-178). IGI Global.

Giotis, G., & Papadionysiou, E. (2022). The role of managerial and technological innovations in the Tourism industry: A review of the empirical literature. *Sustainability (Basel)*, 14(9), 5182. DOI: 10.3390/su14095182

Global Partnership on Artificial Intelligence. (2022, November). *Biodiversity and artificial intelligence: Opportunities and recommendations for action* [Report]. Global Partnership on Artificial Intelligence.

Gochhait, S. (2024). *Comparative Analysis of Machine and Deep Learning Techniques for Text Classification with Emphasis on Data Preprocessing*. Qeios., DOI: 10.32388/XHC9J1

Goel, P., Kaushik, N., Sivathanu, B., Pillai, R., & George, J. (2022). Consumer's Adoption of Artificial Intelligence and Robotics in Hospitality and Tourism Sector : Literature Review and Future Research Agenda. *Tourism Review*. DOI: 10.1108/TR-03-2021-0138

Golja, T., & Paulišić, M. (2021). Managing-technology enhanced tourist experience: The case of scattered hotels in Istria. *Management*, 26(1), 63–95. DOI: 10.30924/mjcmi.26.1.5

Gonzalez, C., Hure, E., & Picot-Coupey, K. (2012), Usages et valeurs des applications mobiles pour les consommateurs: quelles implications pour les distributeurs? *Colloque Etienne Thill*, 2012, Lille.

Gössling, S. (2021). Tourism, technology and ICT: A critical review of affordances and concessions. *Journal of Sustainable Tourism*, 29(5), 733–750. DOI: 10.1080/09669582.2021.1873353

Granli, P., & Poole, J. (2022). Who's who and whereabouts: An integrated system for reidentifying and monitoring African elephants. *Pachyderm*, 63, 72–90. https://pachydermjournal.org/index.php/pachyderm/article/view/482

Grant, M. J., & Booth, A. (2009). A typology of reviews: An analysis of 14 review types and associated methodologies. *Health Information and Libraries Journal*, 26(2), 91–108. DOI: 10.1111/j.1471-1842.2009.00848.x PMID: 19490148

Gretzel, U. (2011). Intelligent systems in tourism. A Social Science Perspective. In Annals of Tourism Research (Vol. 38, Issue 3, pp. 757–779). DOI: 10.1016/j.annals.2011.04.014

Gretzel, U. (2021). Technological Solutions to Overtourism : Potential and Limits. In Mandić, A., & Petrić, L. (Eds.), *Mediterranean Protected Areas in the Era of Overtourism* (pp. 337–349). Springer International Publishing. DOI: 10.1007/978-3-030-69193-6_17

Gretzel, U., Kang, M., & Lee, W. (2008). Differences in consumer-generated media adoption and use: A cross-national perspective. *Journal of Hospitality & Leisure Marketing*, 17(1-2), 99–120. DOI: 10.1080/10507050801978240

Gretzel, U., Kim, W., Koo, C., & Park, J. (2022). Smart tourism: A conceptual model and a literature review. *Journal of Hospitality and Tourism Management*, 47, 102853.

Gretzel, U., Koo, C., Kim, W., & Yannopoulos, G. (2020). Smart tourism: A systematic literature review. *Journal of Hospitality and Tourism Management*, 40, 553–564.

Gretzel, U., Koo, C., & Shin, J. H. (2020). *Smart tourism: Foundations and applications*. Emerald Publishing Limited.

Gretzel, U., Sigala, M., Xiang, Z., & Koo, C. (2015). Smart tourism : Foundations and developments. *Electronic Markets*, 25(3), 179–188. DOI: 10.1007/s12525-015-0196-8

Gretzel, U., & Yoo, K. H. (2020). Hyper-personalization in tourism: Conceptualization, applications, and research agenda. *Journal of Hospitality and Tourism Management*, 37(1), 100156.

Grewal, D., Hulland, J., Kopalle, P. K., & Karahanna, E. (2020). The future of technology and marketing : A multidisciplinary perspective. *Journal of the Academy of Marketing Science*, 48(1), 1–8. DOI: 10.1007/s11747-019-00711-4

Grinberger, A. Y., Minghini, M., Yeboah, G., Juhász, L., & Mooney, P. (2022). Bridges and Barriers: An Exploration of Engagements of the Research Community with the OpenStreetMap Community. *ISPRS International Journal of Geo-Information*, 11(1), 54. Advance online publication. DOI: 10.3390/ijgi11010054

Gruetzemacher, R., & Whittlestone, J. (2019). *Defining and Unpacking Transformative AI*.

Grundner, L., & Neuhofer, B. (2021). The bright and dark sides of artificial intelligence : A futures perspective on tourist destination experiences. *Journal of Destination Marketing & Management*, 19, 100511. DOI: 10.1016/j.jdmm.2020.100511

Guest, G., MacQueen, K. M., & Namey, E. E. (2012). *Applied thematic analysis*. Sage.

Guimont D. et Lapointe D. (2015), Co-creation of a tourist experience enhanced by technology, in the context of a Living Lab.

Guitart, M. (2022). *Approaching Architecture : Three Fields, One Discipline* (1ʳᵉ éd.). Routledge. DOI: 10.4324/9781003195535

Gummerus, J., & Pihlström, M. (2011). Context and mobile services' value-in-use. *Journal of Retailing and Consumer Services*, 18(6), 521–533. DOI: 10.1016/j.jretconser.2011.07.002

Gupta, D., Bhargava, A., Agarwal, D., Alsharif, M. H., Uthansakul, P., Uthansakul, M., & Aly, A. A. (2024). Deep Learning-Based Truthful and Deceptive Hotel Reviews. *Sustainability (Basel)*, 16(11), 4514–4514. DOI: 10.3390/su16114514

Gupta, S., Modgil, S., Lee, C. K., & Sivarajah, U. (2023). The future is yesterday: Use of AI-driven facial recognition to enhance value in the travel and tourism industry. *Information Systems Frontiers*, 25(3), 1179–1195. DOI: 10.1007/s10796-022-10271-8 PMID: 35529102

Gupta, T., & Singh, J. (2019). Leveraging Hyper-personalization for Customer Engagement in the Indian Travel Industry: A Case Study of Yatra.com. *International Journal of Business Analytics*, 8(2), 100–112.

Gupta, V., Sajnani, M., & Dixit, S. K. (2020). Impact of augmented and virtual reality on the value co-creation of visitor's tourism experience: A case of heritage sites in Delhi. In *Tourism in Asian Cities* (pp. 263–277). Routledge. DOI: 10.4324/9780429264801-19

Haleem, A., Javaid, M., Asim Qadri, M., Pratap Singh, R., & Suman, R. (2022). Artificial intelligence (AI) applications for marketing: A literature-based study. *International Journal of Intelligent Networks*, 3, 119–132. DOI: 10.1016/j.ijin.2022.08.005

Hasan, R., & Chu, C.-H. H. (2024). A Heterogeneous Ensemble Method for Handling Class Noise in Supervised Machine Learning. *SAC '24: Proceedings of the 39th ACM/SIGAPP Symposium on Applied Computing*, 902–909. DOI: 10.1145/3605098.3635936

Hashim, R., Omar, B., Saeed, N., Ba-Anqud, A., & Al-Samarraie, H. (2020). The application of sentiment analysis in tourism research: A brief review. *IJBTS International Journal of Business Tourism and Applied Sciences, 8*(1). http://www.ijbts-journal.com/images/column_1587487589/IJBTS%20V8%20no1%201_6%20Rohani%20Hashim%20Tokyo19.pdf

Hasija, K. G., Desai, K., & Acharya, S. (2023). Artificial Intelligence and Robotic Automation Hit by the Pandemic: Reality or Myth. In Tyagi, P., Chilamkurti, N., Grima, S., Sood, K., & Balusamy, B. (Eds.), *The Adoption and Effect of Artificial Intelligence on Human Resources Management, Part B* (pp. 127–147). Emerald Publishing Limited. DOI: 10.1108/978-1-80455-662-720230009

Hassan, H. K., & Quader, M. S. (2022). Tourism Events, Festivals and Digital Technology Applications in Asia: Socio-Cultural Drawbacks and Ways to Overcome. In *Technology Application in Tourism Fairs, Festivals and Events in Asia* (pp. 345–362). Springer Singapore. DOI: 10.1007/978-981-16-8070-0_21

Hauenstein, S., Jassoy, N., Mupepele, A. C., Carroll, T., Kshatriya, M., Beale, C. M., & Dormann, C. F. (2022). A systematic map of demographic data from elephant populations throughout Africa: Implications for poaching and population analyses. *Mammal Review*, 52(3), 438–453. DOI: 10.1111/mam.12291

Haxeltine, A., Avelino, F., Pel, B., & Adina, D. (2016). *A framework for Transformative Social Innovation*. http://www.transitsocialinnovation.eu/content/original/Book%20covers/Local%20PDFs/240%20TRANSIT_WorkingPaper_no5_TSI%20framework_Haxeltine%20et%20al_November2016_AH041116.pdf

Hevner, A., & Storey, V. (2023). Study Challenges for the Design of Human-Artificial Intelligence Systems (HAIS). *ACM Transactions on Management Information Systems*, 14(1), 1–18. DOI: 10.1145/3549547

Hew, J. J., Tan, G. W. H., Lin, B., & Ooi, K. B. (2017). Generating travel-related contents through mobile social tourism: Does privacy paradox persist? *Telematics and Informatics*, 34(7), 914–935. DOI: 10.1016/j.tele.2017.04.001

Hildebrand, C. (2019). The Machine Age of Marketing : How Artificial Intelligence Changes the Way People Think, Act, and Decide. *NIM Marketing Intelligence Review*, 11(2), 10–17. DOI: 10.2478/nimmir-2019-0010

Hill, C., Young, M., Blainey, S., Cavazzi, S., Emberson, C., & Sadler, J. (2024). An integrated geospatial data model for active travel infrastructure. *Journal of Transport Geography*, 117, 103889. DOI: 10.1016/j.jtrangeo.2024.103889

Hirschman, E.-C., & Holbrook, M.-B. (1982a). Hedonic consumption: Emerging concepts, methods and propositions. *Journal of Marketing*, 46(3), 92–101. DOI: 10.1177/002224298204600314

Hirschman, E.-C., & Holbrook, M.-B. (1982b). The experiential aspects of consumption: Consumer fantasies, feelings and fun. *The Journal of Consumer Research*, 9(2).

Hirt, M., & Willmott, P. (2014). Strategic principles for competing in the digital age. *The McKinsey Quarterly*, 5(1), 1–13.

Hmioui, A., Alla, L., & Bentalha, B. (2022). Perception du tourisme durable par les clients étrangers: Cas du séjour dans un établissement hôtelier. Reconfigurations du tourisme en contexte de la crise du Covid-19: Quelles démarches pour quelles résiliences au Maroc et ailleurs?, 1(1), 5-38.

Holbrook, M. B., & Hirschman, E. C. (1982). The Experiential Aspects of Consumption : Consumer Fantasies, Feelings, and Fun. *The Journal of Consumer Research*, 9(2), 132–140. DOI: 10.1086/208906

Hosany, S., & Martin, D. (2012). Self-image congruence in consumer behavior. *Journal of Business Research*, 65(5), 685–691. DOI: 10.1016/j.jbusres.2011.03.015

Huang, A., Chao, Y., De La Mora Velasco, E., Bilgihan, A., & Wei, W. (2022). When artificial intelligence meets the hospitality and tourism industry: An assessment framework to inform theory and management. *Journal of Hospitality and Tourism Insights*, 5(5), 1080–1100. DOI: 10.1108/JHTI-01-2021-0021

Huang, M.-H., & Rust, R. T. (2018). Artificial Intelligence in Service. *Journal of Service Research*, 21(2), 155–172. DOI: 10.1177/1094670517752459

Huang, Z., Wu, J., Li, J., Zhao, Y., & Li, Z. (2023). Applications of artificial intelligence in tourism management: A literature review. *Sustainability (Switzerland)*, 15(6), 3442.

Huveneers, C., Meekan, M. G., Apps, K., Ferreira, L. C., Pannell, D., & Vianna, G. M. S. (2017). The economic value of shark-diving tourism in Australia. *Reviews in Fish Biology and Fisheries*, 27(3), 665–680. DOI: 10.1007/s11160-017-9486-x

Iglesias, M. I., Jenkins, M., & Morison, G. (2021). An enhanced photorealistic immersive system using augmented situated visualization within virtual reality. *Proceedings -2021 IEEE Conference on Virtual Reality and 3D User Interfaces Abstracts and Workshops, VRW 2021*, 514–515. DOI: 10.1109/VRW52623.2021.00139

IndutsryWired. (2022, February 18). *AI in wildlife conservation: Learn about the latest trends*. https://industrywired.com/ai-in-wildlife-conservation-learn-about-the-latest-trends/

Ioannou, A., Tussyadiah, I., & Lu, Y. (2020). Privacy concerns and disclosure of biometric and behavioral data for travel. *International Journal of Information Management*, 54, 102122. DOI: 10.1016/j.ijinfomgt.2020.102122

Ioannou, A., Tussyadiah, I., & Miller, G. (2021). That's private! Understanding travelers' privacy concerns and online data disclosure. *Journal of Travel Research*, 60(7), 1510–1526. DOI: 10.1177/0047287520951642

Isabelle, D. A., & Westerlund, M. (2022). A review and categorization of artificial intelligence-based opportunities in wildlife, ocean and land conservation. *Sustainability (Basel)*, 14(4), 1979. Advance online publication. DOI: 10.3390/su14041979

Ivars-Baidal, J., Casado-Díaz, A. B., Navarro-Ruiz, S., & Fuster-Uguet, M. (2024). Smart tourism city governance: Exploring the impact on stakeholder networks. *International Journal of Contemporary Hospitality Management*, 36(2), 582–601. DOI: 10.1108/IJCHM-03-2022-0322

Iwasaki, Y., & Mannell, R. C. (2000). Hierarchical dimensions of leisure stress coping. *Leisure Sciences*, 22(3), 163–181. DOI: 10.1080/01490409950121843

Jabbar, M., Dwi Okfantia, A., Widjanarti, A., & Zulen, A. (2022). *IFC-Bank of Italy Workshop on "Data Science in Central Banking: Applications and tools" Sentiment analysis of tourist reviews from online travel forum for improving Indonesia tourism sector 1*. https://www.bis.org/ifc/publ/ifcb59_18.pdf

Jamjuntr, P., & Kaewyong, P. (2021). Sentiment analysis with a textblob package implications for tourism. *Journal of Management Information and Decision Sciences*, 24(S6), 1–9. https://www.abacademies.org/articles/sentiment-analysis-with-a-text-blob-package-implications-for-tourism.pdf

Jatav, S. (2022). Current Trends in Sustainable Tourism in the Indian Context. In Sezerel, H., & Christiansen, B. (Eds.), *Advances in Hospitality, Tourism, and the Services Industry* (pp. 391–412). IGI Global. DOI: 10.4018/978-1-6684-4645-4.ch018

Javaid, M., Haleem, A., Singh, R. P., & Suman, R. (2022). Artificial Intelligence Applications for Industry 4.0: A Literature-Based Study. *Journal of Industrial Integration and Management*, 07(01), 83–111. DOI: 10.1142/S2424862221300040

Jeong, M., & Shin, H. H. (2020). Tourists' experiences with smart tourism technology at smart destinations and their behavior intentions. *Journal of Travel Research*, 59(8), 1464–1477. DOI: 10.1177/0047287519883034

Jiang, G., Gao, W., Xu, M., Tong, M., & Liu, Z. (2023). Geographic Information Visualization and Sustainable Development of Low-Carbon Rural Slow Tourism under Artificial Intelligence. *Sustainability (Basel)*, 15(4), 3846. Advance online publication. DOI: 10.3390/su15043846

Jim, J. R., Talukder, M. A. R., Malakar, P., Kabir, M. M., Nur, K., & Mridha, M. F.Jamin Rahman Jim. (2024). Recent advancements and challenges of NLP-based sentiment analysis: A state-of-the-art review. *Natural Language Processing Journal*, 6, 100059–100059. DOI: 10.1016/j.nlp.2024.100059

Joseph, S. (2023, December 3). *AI in wildlife conservation: Poaching prevention and ethics*. https://medium.com/@staneyjoseph.in/ai-in-wildlife-conservation-poaching-prevention-and-ethics-03e2076f1a3a

Joshi, A., Bhattacharyya, P., & Ahire, S. (2017). Sentiment Resources: Lexicons and Datasets. In E. Cambria, D. Das, S. Bandyopadhyay, & A. Feraco (Eds.), *A Practical Guide to Sentiment Analysis*. Springer Cham.

Kamminga, J., Ayele, E., Meratnia, N., & Havinga, P. (2018). Poaching detection technologies - A survey. *Sensors (Basel)*, 18(5), 1474. Advance online publication. DOI: 10.3390/s18051474 PMID: 29738501

Karanth, K. K., & Defries, R. (2010). Conservation and management in human dominated landscapes: Case studies from India. *Biological Conservation*, 143(12), 2865–2964. DOI: 10.1016/j.biocon.2010.05.002

Karoo, K., & Chitte, V. (2023). Ethical Considerations in Sentiment Analysis: Navigating the Complex Landscape. *International Research Journal of Modernization in Engineering Technology and Science*, 5(2). Advance online publication. DOI: 10.56726/IRJMETS46811

Kashem, M. A., Shamsuddoha, M., Nasir, T., & Chowdhury, A. A. (2023). The role of artificial intelligence and blockchain technologies in sustainable tourism in the Middle East. *Worldwide Hospitality and Tourism Themes*, 15(2), 178–191. DOI: 10.1108/WHATT-10-2022-0116

Kaur, J., & Buttar, P. K. (2018, September 1). *Stopwords removal and its algorithms based on different methods. International Journal of Advanced Research in Computer Science | EBSCOhost*. https://openurl.ebsco.com/EPDB%3Agcd%3A14%3A27966862/detailv2?sid=ebsco%3Aplink%3Ascholar&id=ebsco%3Agcd%3A132911177&crl=c

Kays, R., Crofoot, M. C., Jetz, W., & Wikelski, M. (2015). Terrestrial animal tracking as an eye on life and planet. *Science*, 348(6240), aaa2478. Advance online publication. DOI: 10.1126/science.aaa2478 PMID: 26068858

Kellenberger, B., Marcos, D., Lobry, S., & Tuai, D. (2019). Half a percent of labels is enough: Efficient animal detection in UAV imagery using deep CNNs and active learning. *IEEE Transactions on Geoscience and Remote Sensing*, 57(12), 9524–9533. DOI: 10.1109/TGRS.2019.2927393

Kelly, C. (2020). Beyond 'a trip to the seaside': Exploring emotions and family tourism experiences. *Tourism Geographies*, 1–22.

Kerns, A. J., Shepard, D. P., Bhatti, J. A., & Humphreys, T. E. (2014). Unmanned aircraft capture and control via GPS spoofing. *Journal of Field Robotics*, 31(4), 617–636. DOI: 10.1002/rob.21513

Kerry, R. G., Montalbo, F. J. P., Das, R., Patra, S., Mahapatra, G. P., Maurya, G. K., Nayak, V., Jena, A. B., Ukhurebor, K. E., Jena, R. C., Gouda, S., Majhi, S., & Rout, J. R. (2022). An overview of remote monitoring methods in biodiversity conservation. *Environmental Science and Pollution Research International*, 29(53), 80179–80221. DOI: 10.1007/s11356-022-23242-y PMID: 36197618

Khan, N., Khan, W., Humayun, M., & Naz, A. (2024). *Unlocking the potential: Artificial intelligence applications in sustainable tourism*, In A. Alnoor, G. E. Bayram, C. XinYing, & S. H. A. Shah (Eds.), *The role of artificial intelligence in regenerative tourism and green destinations* (pp. 303–316). Emerald Publishing Limited. DOI: 10.1108/978-1-83753-746-420241020

Khurana, D., Koli, A., Khatter, K., & Singh, S. (2022). Natural Language processing: State of the art, Current Trends and Challenges. *Multimedia Tools and Applications*, 82(3), 3713–3744. DOI: 10.1007/s11042-022-13428-4 PMID: 35855771

Kim, H., & Chen, J. S. (2019). The memorable travel experience and its reminiscence functions. *Journal of Travel Research*, 58(4), 637–649. DOI: 10.1177/0047287518772366

Kim, H., Kim, Y., & Fesenmaier, D. R. (2019). Artificial intelligence for personalized and sustainable tourism experiences: A review and research agenda. *Journal of Sustainable Tourism*, 28(8), 1427–1450.

Kim, H., Koo, C., & Chung, N. (2021). The role of mobility apps in memorable tourism experiences of Korean tourists : Stress-coping theory perspective. *Journal of Hospitality and Tourism Management*, 49, 548–557. DOI: 10.1016/j.jhtm.2021.11.003

Kim, H., Park, S., Jeong, S., & Lee, S. (2023). Ethical issues in artificial intelligence for customer experience: A case study in the tourism industry. *Journal of Travel Research*, 62(2), 370–384.

Kim, H., Park, Y., Jeong, S., & Lee, S. (2018). How does artificial intelligence contribute to customer experience? An exploratory study on the service industry. *Industrial Management & Data Systems*, 118(9), 1824–1838.

Kim, H., So, K. K. F., Shin, S., & Li, J. (2024). Artificial Intelligence in Hospitality and Tourism : Insights From Industry Practices, Research Literature, and Expert Opinions. *Journal of Hospitality & Tourism Research (Washington, D.C.)*. Advance online publication. DOI: 10.1177/10963480241229235

Kim, M. J., Hall, C. M., Kwon, O., & Sohn, K. (2024). Space tourism : Value-attitude-behavior theory, artificial intelligence, and sustainability. *Journal of Retailing and Consumer Services*, 77, 103654. DOI: 10.1016/j.jretconser.2023.103654

Kirtil, I. G., & Askun, V. (2021). Artificial intelligence in tourism: A review and bibliometrics research. *Advances in Hospitality and Tourism Research-AHTR*, 9(1), 205–233. DOI: 10.30519/ahtr.801690

Klegarth, A. R., Fuentes, A., Jones-Engel, L., Marshall, G., & Abernathy, K. (2019). The ethical implications, and practical consequences, of attaching remote telemetry apparatus to macaques. In Dolins, F. L., Shaffer, C., Porter, L., Hickey, J., & Nibbelink, N. (Eds.), *Spatial analysis in field primatology: Applying GIS at varying scales* (pp. 64–86). Cambridge University Press. DOI: 10.1017/9781107449824.005

Kline, C. (2018). *Animals, food, and tourism*. Routledge. DOI: 10.4324/9781315265209

Klinkhardt, C., Woerle, T., Briem, L., Heilig, M., Kagerbauer, M., & Vortisch, P. (2021). Using openstreetmap as a data source for attractiveness in travel demand models. In *Transportation Research Record* (Vol. 2675, Issue 8). DOI: 10.1177/0361198121997415

Knani, M., Echchakoui, S., & Ladhari, R. (2022). Artificial intelligence in tourism and hospitality : Bibliometric analysis and research agenda. *International Journal of Hospitality Management*, 107, 103317. DOI: 10.1016/j.ijhm.2022.103317

Knudsen, D. C., Rickly, J. M., & Vidon, E. S. (2016). The fantasy of authenticity: Touring with Lacan. *Annals of Tourism Research*, 58, 33–45. DOI: 10.1016/j.annals.2016.02.003

Kontogiannis, V., Skourtis, C., & Tsiotas, G. (2021). Technological advancements in tourism: A review of the literature. *International Journal of Tourism Cities*, 7(3), 326–343.

Kontogiannis, V., Skuras, D., & Petridis, P. (2021). A conceptual framework for over-tourism management: Insights from a tourism destination perspective. *Journal of Sustainable Tourism*, 29(4), 756–779.

Koo, C., Xiang, Z., Gretzel, U., & Sigala, M. (2021). Artificial intelligence (AI) and robotics in travel, hospitality, and leisure. In Electronic Markets (Vol. 31, Issue 3, pp. 473–476). Springer Science and Business Media Deutschland GmbH. DOI: 10.1007/s12525-021-00494-z

Koo, B., Curtis, C., Ryan, B., Chung, Y., & Khojasteh, J. (2023). Psychometric approaches to exploring the characteristics of smart hotel brand experiences : Scale development and validation. *Journal of Hospitality and Tourism Management*, 56, 385–395. DOI: 10.1016/j.jhtm.2023.07.012

Koprowski, J. L., & Krausman, P. R. (Eds.). (2019). *International Wildlife Management: Conservation challenges in a changing world*. JHU Press. DOI: 10.1353/book.67482

Korteling, J. E., van de Boer-Visschedijk, G. C., Blankendaal, R. A. M., Boonekamp, R. C., & Eikelboom, A. R. (2021). Human- versus Artificial Intelligence. *Frontiers in Artificial Intelligence*, 4, 622364. DOI: 10.3389/frai.2021.622364 PMID: 33981990

Kounavis, C. D., Kasimati, A. E., & Zamani, E. D. (2012). Enhancing the Tourism Experience through Mobile Augmented Reality : Challenges and Prospects. *International Journal of Engineering Business Management*, 4, 10. DOI: 10.5772/51644

Kozinets, R. V. (2015). Netnography: Redefined. *Sage (Atlanta, Ga.)*.

KPMG. (2022). India's Travel & Hospitality Renaissance: Fuelled by Technology and Disruption. https://kpmg.com/us/en/webcasts/2023/travel-leisure-hospitality-industry.html

Ku, E. C. S., & Chen, C.-D. (2024). Artificial intelligence innovation of tourism businesses : From satisfied tourists to continued service usage intention. *International Journal of Information Management*, 102757, 102757. Advance online publication. DOI: 10.1016/j.ijinfomgt.2024.102757

Kumar, N. R., Pavithra, R., Yuvaraj, V., & Kumar, T. M. (2023). The role of smart tourism in India for optimizing visitor experiences through technology. *JIMS8I International Journal of Information Communication and Computing Technology, 11*(2), 692-701.

Kumar, S., Kumar, V., & Attri, K. (2021). Impact of artificial intelligence and service robots in tourism and hospitality sector : Current use & future trends. *Administrative Development « A Journal of HIPA, Shimla », 8*(SI-1), 59-83. DOI: 10.53338/ADHIPA2021.V08.Si01.04

Kumar, S., Talukder, M. B., & Kaiser, F. (2024). Artificial Intelligence in Business: Negative Social Impacts. In *Demystifying the Dark Side of AI in Business* (pp. 81-97). IGI Global. DOI: 10.4018/979-8-3693-0724-3.ch005

Kumar, A., & Kaur, R. (2017). Hyper-personalization: A New Paradigm for Indian Travel and Tourism Industry. *IUP Journal of Management Research*, 16(3), 45–52.

Kumar, D., & Jakhar, S. D. (2022). Artificial intelligence in animal surveillance and conservation. In Balamurugan, S., Pathak, S., Jain, A., Gupta, S., Sharma, S., & Duggal, S. (Eds.), *Impact of artificial intelligence on organizational transformation*. Wiley. DOI: 10.1002/9781119710301.ch5

Kumar, S., Talukder, M. B., Kabir, F., & Kaiser, F. (2024). Challenges and Sustainability of Green Finance in the Tourism Industry: Evidence from Bangladesh. In Taneja, S., Kumar, P., Grima, S., Ozen, E., & Sood, K. (Eds.), (pp. 97–111). Advances in Finance, Accounting, and Economics. IGI Global. DOI: 10.4018/979-8-3693-1388-6.ch006

Kumar, S., Talukder, M. B., & Pego, A. (Eds.). (2024). *Utilizing Smart Technology and AI in Hybrid Tourism and Hospitality*. IGI Global. DOI: 10.4018/979-8-3693-1978-9

Kumar, V., Ashraf, A. R., & Nadeem, W. (2024). AI-powered marketing: What, where, and how? *International Journal of Information Management*, 77, 102783. DOI: 10.1016/j.ijinfomgt.2024.102783

Kumar, V., Rajan, B., Venkatesan, R., & Lecinski, J. (2019). Understanding the role of artificial intelligence in personalized engagement marketing. *California Management Review*, 61(4), 135–155. DOI: 10.1177/0008125619859317

Kumar, V., Ramachandran, D., & Kumar, B. (2021a). Influence of new-age technologies on marketing : A research agenda. *Journal of Business Research*, 125, 864–877. DOI: 10.1016/j.jbusres.2020.01.007

Kundu, A., Reddy, C. V., Singh, R. K., & Kalamdhad, A. S. (2023). Critical review with science mapping on the latest pre-treatment technologies of landfill leachate. *Journal of Environmental Management*, 336, 117727. Advance online publication. DOI: 10.1016/j.jenvman.2023.117727 PMID: 36924707

Kurtz, O. T., Wirtz, B. W., & Langer, P. F. (2021). An Empirical Analysis of Location-Based Mobile Advertising—Determinants, Success Factors, and Moderating Effects. *Journal of Interactive Marketing*, 54, 69–85. Advance online publication. DOI: 10.1016/j.intmar.2020.08.001

Kusumawardani, R. P., Rahman, R. A., Wibowo, R. P., & Tjahjanto, A. (2024). Understanding Fine-Grained Sentiments of Super-Priority Destination Visitors using Multi-task Learning for Extraction of Aspect Terms and Polarity Classification on Reviews. *Procedia Computer Science*, 234, 602–613. DOI: 10.1016/j.procs.2024.03.045

Kutschera, V. E., Bidon, T., Hailer, F., Rodi, J. L., Fain, S. R., & Janke, A. (2014). Bears in a forest of gene trees: Phylogenetic inference is complicated by incomplete lineage sorting and gene flow. *Molecular Biology and Evolution*, 3(8), 2004–2017. DOI: 10.1093/molbev/msu186 PMID: 24903145

Lacárcel, F. (2022). Main Uses of Artificial Intelligence in Digital Marketing Strategies Linked to Tourism. *Journal Of Tourism Sustainability And Well-Being, 10*(3), 215-226. DOI: 10.34623/mppf-r253

Lam, K. L., Chan, C. S., & Peters, M. (2020). Understanding technological contributions to accessible tourism from the perspective of destination design for visually impaired visitors in Hong Kong. *Journal of Destination Marketing & Management*, 17, 100434. DOI: 10.1016/j.jdmm.2020.100434

Lamsiah, A., & Bentalha, B. (2023). 2022 Qatar World Cup: A Netnographic Analysis of the Relationship Between Sport, Media and Politic. Réflexions sportives, 1(3), 69-95.

Lauterbach, A. (2019). Artificial intelligence and policy : Quo vadis? *Digital Policy. Regulation & Governance*, 21(3), 238–263. DOI: 10.1108/DPRG-09-2018-0054

Law, R., & Chen, S. (2024). Developments and implications of tourism information technology: A horizon 2050 paper. *Tourism Review*. Advance online publication. DOI: 10.1108/TR-12-2023-0846

Law, R., Fong, S., & Wu, F. (2021). Artificial intelligence for dynamic pricing in tourism: A review of the literature. *Journal of Travel Research*, 60(2), 394–412.

Lazrig, I., & Humpherys, S. (2022). Using Machine Learning Sentiment Analysis to Evaluate Learning Impact. *Information Systems Education Journal*, 20(1). https://files.eric.ed.gov/fulltext/EJ1333895.pdf

Le Guilcher, A., Olteanu-Raimond, A. M., & Balde, M. B. (2022). Analysis of massive imports of open data in openstreetmap database: A study case for france. *ISPRS Annals of the Photogrammetry, Remote Sensing and Spatial Information Sciences*, 5(4), 99–106. Advance online publication. DOI: 10.5194/isprs-annals-V-4-2022-99-2022

Leclercq, T., Poncin, I., & Hammedi, W. (2016). Dix ans de co-création de valeur: Une revue intégrative. *Recherche et Applications en Marketing*, 31(3), 1–38. DOI: 10.1177/0767370116638270

Le, D., Nguyen, T., Scholten, H., & Havinga, P. (2017). Symbiotic sensing for energy-intensive tasks in large-scale mobile sensing applications. *Sensors (Basel)*, 17(12), 2763. Advance online publication. DOI: 10.3390/s17122763 PMID: 29186037

Lee, L. S., Shaharuddin, S. S., Ng, G. W., & Wan-Busrah, S. F. (2017). Co-creation tourism experience in perceived usability of interactive multimedia features on mobile travel application. Journal of Telecommunication, Electronic and Computer Engineering (JTEC), 9(2-9), 155-161.

Lee, C. H., & Cranage, D. A. (2011). Personalisation–privacy paradox: The effects of personalisation and privacy assurance on customer responses to travel Web sites. *Tourism Management*, 32(5), 987–994. DOI: 10.1016/j.tourman.2010.08.011

Lee, J., & Kozinets, R. V. (2020). Algorithmic tourism: Personalization, power, and experiential consumption. *The Journal of Consumer Research*, 47(2), 313–340.

Leelawat, N., Jariyapongpaiboon, S., Promjun, A., Boonyarak, S., Saengtabtim, K., Laosunthara, A., Yudha, A. K., & Tang, J. (2022). Twitter data sentiment analysis of tourism in Thailand during the COVID-19 pandemic using machine learning. *Heliyon*, 8(10), e10894. DOI: 10.1016/j.heliyon.2022.e10894 PMID: 36211996

Lee, T. H., & Jan, F.-H. (2023). How do smart tourism experiences affect visitors' environmentally responsible behavior? Influence analysis of nature-based tourists in Taiwan. *Journal of Hospitality and Tourism Management*, 55, 1–10. DOI: 10.1016/j.jhtm.2023.02.016

Lekić Glavan, O., Nikolić, N., Folić, B., Vitošević, B., Mitrović, A., & Kosanović, S. (2022). COVID-19 and City Space: Impact and Perspectives. *Sustainability (Basel)*, 14(3), 1885. DOI: 10.3390/su14031885

Lequin, M. (2002). L'écotourisme. Expérience d'une interaction nature-culture. *Téoros*, 21(3), 38–42. DOI: 10.7202/1072501ar

Leyva, E. S., & Parra, D. P. (2021). Environmental approach in the hotel industry: Riding the wave of change. *Sustainable Futures : An Applied Journal of Technology, Environment and Society*, 3, 100050. DOI: 10.1016/j.sftr.2021.100050

Liang, C. C., & Shiau, W. L. (2018). Moderating effect of privacy concerns and subjective norms between satisfaction and repurchase of airline e-ticket through airline-ticket vendors. *Asia Pacific Journal of Tourism Research*, 23(12), 1142–1159. DOI: 10.1080/10941665.2018.1528290

Li, C., Zheng, W., Zhuang, X., & Chen, F. (2023). Intelligent transport design with a dual focus : Tourist experience and operating cost. *Annals of Tourism Research*, 101, 103597. DOI: 10.1016/j.annals.2023.103597

Li, H., Li, W., Zhao, J., Yu, P., & Huang, Y. (2023). A sentiment analysis approach for travel-related Chinese online review content. *PeerJ. Computer Science*, 9, e1538–e1538. DOI: 10.7717/peerj-cs.1538 PMID: 37705661

Li, J., Qin, H., Wang, J., & Li, J. (2022). OpenStreetMap-Based Autonomous Navigation for the Four Wheel-Legged Robot Via 3D-Lidar and CCD Camera. *IEEE Transactions on Industrial Electronics*, 69(3), 2708–2717. Advance online publication. DOI: 10.1109/TIE.2021.3070508

Li, J., Xu, Y., Zhao, Y., Li, Z., & Fu, Y. (2018). How can artificial intelligence benefit the tourism industry? *Sustainability (Switzerland)*, 10(12), 4528.

Li, M., Yin, D., Qiu, H., & Bai, B. (2021). A systematic review of AI technology-based service encounters : Implications for hospitality and tourism operations. *International Journal of Hospitality Management*, 95, 102930. DOI: 10.1016/j.ijhm.2021.102930

Limna, P. (2023). Artificial Intelligence (AI) in the Hospitality Industry: A Review Article. *International Journal of Computing Sciences Research*, 7, 1306–1317. DOI: 10.25147/ijcsr.2017.001.1.103

Li, P., Zhou, Y., & Huang, S. (2023). Role of information technology in the development of e- tourism marketing: A contextual suggestion. *Economic Analysis and Policy*, 78, 307–318. DOI: 10.1016/j.eap.2023.03.010

Liu, B. (2012). Sentiment Analysis and Opinion Mining. In *Synthesis Lectures on Human Language Technologies*. Springer International Publishing. DOI: 10.1007/978-3-031-02145-9

Liu, B., Xu, W., Tencent, Y., Wu, X., Zhang, B., & Zhu, L. (2022). *Noise Learning for Text Classification: A Benchmark*. https://aclanthology.org/2022.coling-1.402.pdf

Liu, Z., Li, J., Ye, B., Li, Y., & Yan, J. (2022). Artificial intelligence and tourism: A review and future directions. *Annals of Tourism Research*, 88, 103242.

Li, X., Wang, Y., & Li, J. (2023). A review of intelligent tourism research: Literature analysis using CiteSpace. *Sustainability*, 15(4), 2324.

Lo, L. S. (2023). AI policies across the globe : Implications and recommendations for libraries. *IFLA Journal*, 49(4), 645–649. DOI: 10.1177/03400352231196172

Lu, H. P., & Hsiao, K. L. (2010). The influence of extro/introversion on the intention to pay for social networking sites. *Information & Management*, 47(3), 150–157. DOI: 10.1016/j.im.2010.01.003

Luo, X., Zheng, Y., Xie, J., & Ngai, E. W. T. (2020). Customer churn prediction using deep learning in telecommunication networks. *Neurocomputing*, 408, 125–139.

Lupton, D. (2022). From human-centric digital health to digital One Health: Crucial new directions for mutual flourishing. *Digital Health*, 8. Advance online publication. DOI: 10.1177/20552076221129103 PMID: 36171960

Lusch, R.-F., & Vargo, S.-L. (2006). Service-Dominant Logic: Reactions, Reflections and Refinements. *Marketing Theory*, 6(3), 281–288. DOI: 10.1177/1470593106066781

Lv, H., Shi, S., & Gursoy, D. (2022). A look back and a leap forward: A review and synthesis of big data and artificial intelligence literature in hospitality and tourism. *Journal of Hospitality Marketing & Management*, 31(2), 145–175. DOI: 10.1080/19368623.2021.1937434

MacCannell, D. (2013). *The tourist: A new theory of the leisure class*. Univ of California Press. DOI: 10.1525/9780520354050

Mahavidyalya, S. V. M. (2024). *The ethics of artificial intelligence in wildlife conservation*. College Sidekick. https://www.collegesidekick.com/study-docs/14694957

Malik, A., & Jain, P. (2022). Understanding Travel Consumer Behaviour in India: A Study of Hyper-personalization and its Impact on Decision-Making. *International Journal of Hospitality Management*, 109, 104033.

Mangold, W. G., & Faulds, D. J. (2009). Social media: The new hybrid element of the promotion mix. *Business Horizons*, 52(4), 357–365. DOI: 10.1016/j.bushor.2009.03.002

Manosso, F. C., & Domareski Ruiz, T. C. (2021, October 18). *Using Sentiment Analysis in Tourism Research: A Systematic, Bibliometric, and Integrative Review*. Social Science Research Network. https://papers.ssrn.com/sol3/papers.cfm?abstract_id=3938896

Manthiou, A., & Klaus, P. (2022). The interplaying factors of the robotic tourism experience : The customer journey's touchpoints, context, and qualities. *Technological Forecasting and Social Change*, 177, 121552. DOI: 10.1016/j.techfore.2022.121552

Mao, Y., Liu, Q., & Zhang, Y. (2024). Sentiment analysis methods, applications, and challenges: A systematic literature review. Journal of King Saud University. Computer and Information Sciences/Ma ala am'a Al-Malīk Saud: Ùlm Al- asib Wa Al-Ma'lumat, 36(4), 102048–102048. DOI: 10.1016/j.jksuci.2024.102048

Marasco, A., Buonincontri, P., Van Niekerk, M., Orlowski, M., & Okumus, F. (2018). Exploring the role of next-generation virtual technologies in destination marketing. *Journal of Destination Marketing & Management*, 9, 138–148. DOI: 10.1016/j.jdmm.2017.12.002

Mariani, M., & Borghi, M. (2021). Customers' evaluation of mechanical artificial intelligence in hospitality services: A study using online reviews analytics. *International Journal of Contemporary Hospitality Management*, 33(11), 3956–3976. DOI: 10.1108/IJCHM-06-2020-0622

Marion, G. (2016). *Le consommateur coproducteur de valeur. L'axiologie de la consommation*. Cormelles-le-Royal, Editions EMS. DOI: 10.3917/ems.mario.2016.01

Markauskaite, L., Marrone, R., Poquet, O., Knight, S., Martinez-Maldonado, R., Howard, S., Tondeur, J., De Laat, M., Buckingham Shum, S., Gašević, D., & Siemens, G. (2022). Rethinking the entwinement between artificial intelligence and human learning: What capabilities do learners need for a world with AI? *Computers and Education: Artificial Intelligence*, 3, 100056. DOI: 10.1016/j.caeai.2022.100056

Markets and Markets. (n.d.). Online travel booking platform market - global forecast to 2030. [Online]., from https://www.marketsandmarkets.com/Market-Reports/online-travel-booking-platform-market-115208171.html

Martella, F., & Enia, M. (2021). Towards an Urban Domesticity. Contemporary Architecture and the Blurring Boundaries between the House and the City. *Housing. Theory and Society*, 38(4), 402–418. DOI: 10.1080/14036096.2020.1789211

Masteriarsa, M. F., & Riyanto, R. (2023). Tourism Destination Mapping Based on Tourism Characteristics and Carrying Capacity of Province in Indonesia. *Jurnal Perencanaan Pembangunan: The Indonesian Journal of Development Planning*, 7(3), 344–361. Advance online publication. DOI: 10.36574/jpp.v7i3.460

Mateo, S. (2020). Procédure pour conduire avec succès une revue de littérature selon la méthode PRISMA. *Kinésithérapie, la Revue*, 20(226), 29–37. DOI: 10.1016/j.kine.2020.05.019

McKinsey & Company. (2020). Artificial Intelligence in Travel & Hospitality. https://www.mckinsey.com/industries/travel-logistics-and-infrastructure/our-insights/the-promise-of-travel-in-the-age-of-ai

McLean, G., & Barhorst, J. B. (2022). Living the Experience Before You Go . . . but Did It Meet Expectations? The Role of Virtual Reality during Hotel Bookings. *Journal of Travel Research*, 61(6), 1233–1251. DOI: 10.1177/00472875211028313

Mercan, S., Cain, L., Akkaya, K., Cebe, M., Uluagac, S., Alonso, M., & Cobanoglu, C. (2021). Improving the service industry with hyper-connectivity: IoT in hospitality. *International Journal of Contemporary Hospitality Management*, 33(1), 243–262. DOI: 10.1108/IJCHM-06-2020-0621

Meyer, L., Apps, K., Bryars, S., Clarke, T., Hayden, B., Pelton, G., Simes, B., Vaughan, L. M., Whitmarsh, S. K., & Huveneers, C. (2021). A multidisciplinary framework to assess the sustainability and acceptability of wildlife tourism operations. *A Journal of the Society for Conservations Biology, 14*(3). DOI: 10.1111/conl.12788

Milton. (2024). Artificial Intelligence Transforming Hotel Gastronomy: An In-depth Review of AI-driven Innovations in Menu Design, Food Preparation, and Customer Interaction, with a Focus on Sustainability and Future Trends in the Hospitality Industry. *International Journal for Multidimensional Study Perspectives, 2*(3), 47–61. DOI: 10.61877/ijmrp.v2i3.126

Mingotto, E., Montaguti, F., & Tamma, M. (2021). Challenges in re-designing operations and jobs to embody AI and robotics in services. Findings from a case in the hospitality industry. *Electronic Markets*, 31(3), 493–510. DOI: 10.1007/s12525-020-00439-y

Mishra, A. K. (2023). Artificial intelligence in wildlife conservation. *International Journal of Avian and Wildlife Biology*, 7(2), 67. DOI: 10.15406/ijawb.2023.07.00192

Mittal, N., Chaudhary, M., & Alavi, S. (2017). Learning management through mobile apps-a new buzzword. *International Journal of Business Innovation and Research*, 13(3), 271–287. DOI: 10.1504/IJBIR.2017.084419

Mittal, R., & Khan, M. A. (2020). The Role of Hyper-personalization in Enhancing Customer Experience in the Indian Travel and Tourism Industry. *Journal of Internet Commerce*, 23(3), 351–374.

Mohammad Badruddoza Talukder, Firoj Kabir, K. M., & Das, I. R. (2023). Emerging Concepts of Artificial Intelligence in the Hotel Industry: A Conceptual Paper. *International Journal of Research Publication and Reviews, 4,* 1765-1769. DOI: 10.55248/gengpi.4.923.92451

Mohammad Badruddoza Talukder, Kumar, & Das. (2024a). Implications of Blockchain Technology- Based Cryptocurrency in the cloud for the Hospitality Industry. In *Emerging Trends in Cloud Computing Analytics, Scalability, and Service Models* (p. 19). DOI: 10.4018/979-8-3693-0900-1.ch018

Mohammad Badruddoza Talukder, Kumar, & Das. (2024b). Perspectives of Digital Marketing for the Restaurant Industry. In *Advancements in Socialized and Digital Media Communications* (p. 17). DOI: 10.4018/979-8-3693-0855-4.ch009

Mohammad. B. Talukder, & Kumar, (2024). Revisiting intention in food service outlet of five-star hotels:A quantitative approach based on food service quality. Sport i Turystyka. Środkowoeuropejskie Czasopismo Naukowe, 7(1), 137–156. DOI: 10.16926/sit.2024.01.08

Moher, D., Liberati, A., Tetzlaff, J., & Altman, D. G.The PRISMA Group. (2009). Preferred Reporting Items for Systematic Reviews and Meta-Analyses : The PRISMA Statement. *PLoS Medicine*, 6(7), e1000097. DOI: 10.1371/journal.pmed.1000097 PMID: 19621072

Moher, D., Shamseer, L., Clarke, M., Ghersi, D., Liberati, A., Petticrew, M., Shekelle, P., & Stewart, L. A.PRISMA-P Group. (2015). Preferred reporting items for systematic review and meta-analysis protocols (PRISMA-P) 2015 statement. *Systematic Reviews*, 4(1), 1. DOI: 10.1186/2046-4053-4-1 PMID: 25554246

Molitor, D., Spann, M., Ghose, A., & Reichhart, P. (2020). Effectiveness of Location-Based Advertising and the Impact of Interface Design. *Journal of Management Information Systems*, 37(2), 431–456. Advance online publication. DOI: 10.1080/07421222.2020.1759922

Montero, A. A., Sales, L. H., Idrissi, M. Y., & López-Sánchez, J. A. (2023). Web accessibility and inclusivity of tourist destinations at social media management. An intercultural analysis of Andalusia and Northern Morocco. *Universal Access in the Information Society*, •••, 1–17. DOI: 10.1007/s10209-023-01020-y

Moore, K., Buchmann, A., Månsson, M., & Fisher, D. (2021). Authenticity in tourism theory and experience. Practically indispensable and theoretically mischievous? *Annals of Tourism Research*, 89, 103208. DOI: 10.1016/j.annals.2021.103208

Moradi, M., Roche, S., & Mostafavi, M. A. (2022). Exploring five indicators for the quality of OpenStreetMap road networks: A case study of Québec, Canada. *Geomatica*, 75(4), 178–208. Advance online publication. DOI: 10.1139/geomat-2021-0012

Morais, G. M., Santos, V. F., & Gonçalves, C. A. (2020). Netnography: Origins, Foundations, Evolution and Axiological and Methodological Developments and Trends. *The Qualitative Report*, 25(1), 441–455. DOI: 10.46743/2160-3715/2020.4227

Mordor Intelligence. (2024, February). India online travel market size, share & industry analysis. [Online]. https://www.mordorintelligence.com/industry-reports/online-travel-market-in-india/market-trends

Munar, A. M., & Jacobsen, J. K. S. (2014). Motivations for sharing tourism experiences through social media. *Tourism Management*, 43, 46–54. DOI: 10.1016/j.tourman.2014.01.012

Muniz, E. C. L., Dandolini, G. A., Biz, A. A., & Ribeiro, A. C. (2021). Customer knowledge management and smart tourism destinations: A framework for the smart management of the tourist experience–SMARTUR. *Journal of Knowledge Management*, 25(5), 1336–1361. DOI: 10.1108/JKM-07-2020-0529

Naik, G., Wani, S., Pawar, R., & Randhir, R. (2022). Tourist Place Reviews Sentiment Classification Using Machine Learning Techniques. *International Journal for Research in Engineering Application & Management*, 08, 2454–9150. DOI: 10.35291/2454-9150.2022.0161

Nakamura, S., Sakaoka, A., Ikuno, E., Asou, R., Shimizu, D., & Hagiwara, H. (2019). Optimal implantation site of transponders for identification of experimental swine. *Experimental Animals*, 68(1), 13–23. DOI: 10.1538/expanim.18-0052 PMID: 30078789

Nam, K., Dutt, C. S., Chathoth, P., Daghfous, A., & Sajid Khan, M. (2021). The adoption of artificial intelligence and robotics in the hotel industry: Prospects and challenges. *Electronic Markets*, 31(3), 553–574. DOI: 10.1007/s12525-020-00442-3

Nandutu, I., Atemkeng, M., & Okouma, P. (2021). Integrating AI ethics in wildlife conservation AI systems in South Africa: A review, challenges, and future research agenda. *AI & Society*, 38(1), 245–257. DOI: 10.1007/s00146-021-01285-y

Nandutu, I., Atemkeng, M., & Okouma, P. (2022). Intelligent systems using sensors and/or machine learning to mitigate wildlife–vehicle collisions: A review, challenges, and new perspectives. *Sensors (Basel)*, 22(7), 2478. Advance online publication. DOI: 10.3390/s22072478 PMID: 35408093

Nandwani, P., & Verma, R. (2021). A review on sentiment analysis and emotion detection from text. *Social Network Analysis and Mining*, 11(1), 81. Advance online publication. DOI: 10.1007/s13278-021-00776-6 PMID: 34484462

Nannelli, M., Capone, F., & Lazzeretti, L. (2023). Artificial intelligence in hospitality and tourism. State of the art and future research avenues. *European Planning Studies*, 31(7), 1325–1344. DOI: 10.1080/09654313.2023.2180321

Narasimha, I. D. V., Moses, I. S., & Balaji, H. (2023). Automated animal identification and detection of species. *International Journal of Advanced Research in Science. Tongxin Jishu*, 3(2), 29–33. https://ijarsct.co.in/Paper11305.pdf

Nazarian, A., Atkinson, P., & Foroudi, P. (2017). Influence of national culture and balanced organizational culture on the hotel industry's performance. *International Journal of Hospitality Management*, 63, 22–32. DOI: 10.1016/j.ijhm.2017.01.003

Needham, C., Allen, K., & Hall, K. (2016). Enacting personalisation on a micro scale. In *Micro-Enterprise and Personalisation* (pp. 111–128). Policy Press. DOI: 10.2307/j.ctt1t890w5.12

Neuhofer, B. (2016). Value co-creation and co-destruction in connected tourist experiences. In Information and Communication Technologies in Tourism 2016: Proceedings of the International Conference in Bilbao, Spain, February 2-5, 2016 (pp. 779-792). Springer International Publishing. DOI: 10.1007/978-3-319-28231-2_56

Neuhofer, B., Buhalis, D., & Ladkin, A. (2013), Experiences, co-creation and technology: a conceptual approach to enhance tourism experiences, Tourism and Global Change: On the Edge of Something Big, *Conference Proceeding*.

Ng, P. (2020). Platform Urbanism: Planning towards Hyper-Personalisation. *International Journal of Urban and Civil Engineering*, 14(7), 189–192.

Ni, W., Sumartini, S., Ketut, I., Putra, G. D., Sudarma, M., & Sukarsa, I. M. (2024). Enhance sentiment analysis in big data tourism using hybrid lexicon and active learning support vector machine. *Bulletin of Electrical Engineering and Informatics*. DOI: 10.11591/eei.v13i5.7807

Nikitas, A., Njoya, E. T., & Dani, S. (2019). Examining the myths of connected and autonomous vehicles: Analysing the pathway to a driverless mobility paradigm. *International Journal of Automotive Technology and Management*, 19(1-2), 10–30. DOI: 10.1504/IJATM.2019.098513

Nur, Malik, & Nur. (2023). Sentiment classification from reviews for tourism analytics. *IJAIN (International Journal of Advances in Intelligent Informatics)*, 9(1), 108–108. https://doi.org/DOI: 10.26555/ijain.v9i1.1077

O'Donoghue, P., & Rutz, C. (2016). Real-time anti-poaching tags could help prevent imminent species extinctions. *Journal of Applied Ecology*, 53(1), 5–10. DOI: 10.1111/1365-2664.12452 PMID: 27478204

Obura, D. O., Aeby, G., Amornthammarong, N., Appeltans, W., Bax, N., Bishop, J., Brainard, R. E., Chan, S., Fletcher, P., Gordon, T. A. C., Gramer, L., Gudka, M., Halas, J., Hendee, J., Hodgson, G., Huang, D., Jankulak, M., Jones, A., Kimura, T., & Wongbusarakum, S. (2019). Coral reef monitoring, reef assessment technologies, and ecosystem-based management. *Frontiers in Marine Science*, 6, 580. Advance online publication. DOI: 10.3389/fmars.2019.00580

Oliveira, E., & Panyik, E. (2015). Content, context and co-creation: Digital challenges in destination branding with references to Portugal as a tourist destination. *Journal of Vacation Marketing*, 21(1), 53–74. DOI: 10.1177/1356766714544235

Orduña-Malea, E., & Costas, R. (2021). Link-based approach to study scientific software usage: The case of VOSviewer. *Scientometrics*, 126(9), 8153–8186. DOI: 10.1007/s11192-021-04082-y

Osgood, C. E. (1975). *Cross-Cultural Universals of Affective Meaning*. University of Illinois Press.

Ostwald, M. J., & Waller, S. T. (2024). Rehearsing Emergency Scenarios: Using Space Syntax and Intelligent Mobility Modelling for Scenario Visualisation and Disaster Preparedness. *Climate Disaster Preparedness: Reimagining Extreme Events through Art and Technology*, 151–165.

Pai, C.-K., Liu, Y., Kang, S., & Dai, A. (2020). The Role of Perceived Smart Tourism Technology Experience for Tourist Satisfaction, Happiness and Revisit Intention. *Sustainability (Basel)*, 12(16), 16. Advance online publication. DOI: 10.3390/su12166592

Pang, B., Lee, L., & Vaithyanathan, S. (2002). Thumbs up?: Sentiment classification using machine learning techniques. *Proceedings of the ACL-02 Conference on Empirical Methods in Natural Language Processing*, 10, 79-86. DOI: 10.3115/1118693.1118704

Panhale, T., Bryce, D., & Tsougkou, E. (2023). Augmented reality and experience co-creation in heritage settings. *Journal of Marketing Management*, 39(5-6), 470–497. DOI: 10.1080/0267257X.2022.2120061

Park, D. H., Lee, J., & Han, I. (2007). The effect of on-line consumer reviews on consumer purchasing intention: The moderating role of involvement. *International Journal of Electronic Commerce*, 11(4), 125–148. DOI: 10.2753/JEC1086-4415110405

Pelánek, R., Effenberger, T., & Jarušek, P. (2024). Personalized recommendations for learning activities in online environments: A modular rule-based approach. *User Modeling and User-Adapted Interaction*, 34(4), 1–32. DOI: 10.1007/s11257-024-09396-z

Pérez Enríquez, M., Mencía, J., & Segura-Bedmar, I. (2022). *Transformers Approach for Sentiment Analysis: Classification of Mexican Tourists Reviews from TripAdvisor*. https://ceur-ws.org/Vol-3202/restmex-paper11.pdf

Perry, G. L., Seidl, R., Bellvé, A. M., & Rammer, W. (2022). An outlook for deep learning in ecosystem science. *Ecosystems (New York, N.Y.)*, 25(8), 1700–1718. DOI: 10.1007/s10021-022-00789-y

Phutela, N. (2022). Drivers of Customer Experience (CX) in Smart Tourism-A Qualitative Study. *Journal of Positive School Psychology*, 6(2), 871–881.

Pillmayer, M., Karl, M., & Hansen, M. (Eds.). (2024). *Tourism Destination Development: A Geographic Perspective on Destination Management and Tourist Demand* (Vol. 11). Walter de Gruyter GmbH & Co KG. DOI: 10.1515/9783110794090

Pine, B. J., II. & Gilmore, J. H. 1999. The Experience Economy. Work is Theatre and Every Business a Stage. Harvard Business School Press. Boston

Pine, J. B., & Gilmore, J. H. (1999). The Experience Economy.

Pine, B. J., & Gilmore, J. H. (1998). *Welcome to the experience economy* (Vol. 76). Harvard Business Review Press Cambridge. https://enlillebid.dk/mmd/wp-content/uploads/2012/03/Welcome-to-the-Experience-Economy-Pine-and-Gilmore.pdf

Ponte, E. B., Carvajal-Trujillo, E., & Escobar-Rodríguez, T. (2015). Influence of trust and perceived value on the intention to purchase travel online: Integrating the effects of assurance on trust antecedents. *Tourism Management*, 47, 286–302. DOI: 10.1016/j.tourman.2014.10.009

Prahadeeswaran, R. (2023). A Comprehensive Review : The Convergence of Artificial Intelligence and Tourism. *International Journal for Multidimensional Research Perspectives*, 1(2), 2.

Prahadeeswaran, R. (2023). A Comprehensive Review: The Convergence of Artificial Intelligence and Tourism. *International Journal for Multidimensional Research Perspectives*, 1(2), 12–24.

Prevéraud, J.-F. (2016), Réseaux sociaux: quels sont les risques pour les entreprises? https://www.industrie-techno.com/reseaux-sociaux-quels-sont-les-risques-pour-les-entreprises.9703

Puh, K., & Bagić Babac, M. (2022). Predicting sentiment and rating of tourist reviews using machine learning. *Journal of Hospitality and Tourism Insights*, 6(3), 1188–1204. DOI: 10.1108/JHTI-02-2022-0078

Puntoni, S., Reczek, R. W., Giesler, M., & Botti, S. (2021). Consumers and Artificial Intelligence: An Experiential Perspective. *Journal of Marketing*, 85(1), 131–151. DOI: 10.1177/0022242920953847

Qumsieh-Mussalam, G., & Tajeddini, K. (2019). Innovation in tourism destination marketing. In *Tourism, hospitality and digital transformation* (pp. 165–174). Routledge. DOI: 10.4324/9780429054396-10

Rafiyya, A., Kraiwanit, T., & Charoenphandhu, N. (2024). Boosting global tourist brand recognition in the digital era: A case study of Maldives. *Journal Of Economy, Tourism And Service*, 3(5), 66–75.

Rahman, E. Z. (2024). *The Effect of the Regenerative Tourism Movement on the Global Industry and the Role of Artificial Intelligence. The Role of Artificial Intelligence in Regenerative Tourism and Green Destinations*. Emerald Publishing Limited.

Räikkönen, J., & Honkanen, A. (2013). Does satisfaction with package tours lead to successful vacation experiences? *Journal of Destination Marketing & Management*, 2(2), 108–117. DOI: 10.1016/j.jdmm.2013.03.002

Raji, M. A., Olodo, H. B., Oke, T. T., Addy, W. A., Ofodile, O. C., & Oyewole, A. T. (2024). Digital marketing in tourism: A review of practices in the USA and Africa. *International Journal of Applied Research in Social Sciences*, 6(3), 393–408. DOI: 10.51594/ijarss.v6i3.896

Rane, N., Choudhary, S., & Rane, J. (2023). Hyper-personalization for enhancing customer loyalty and satisfaction in Customer Relationship Management (CRM) systems. SSRN *Electronic Journal*. DOI: 10.2139/ssrn.4641044

Rane, N., Choudhary, S., & Rane, J. (2023). Sustainable tourism development using leading-edge Artificial Intelligence (AI), Blockchain, Internet of Things (IoT), Augmented Reality (AR) and Virtual Reality (VR) technologies. *Blockchain, Internet of Things (IoT), Augmented Reality (AR) and Virtual Reality (VR) technologies.*

Rane, N., Choudhary, S., & Rane, J. (2023). *Sustainable tourism development using leading-edge artificial intelligence (AI), blockchain, internet of things (IoT), augmented reality (AR) and virtual reality (VR) technologies.* SSRN. http://dx.doi.org/DOI: 10.2139/ssrn.4642605

Rashid, B. (2013). *The Role of Affective Dimensions on Tourist Visit Experience.* https://www.academia.edu/download/86273203/78487609.pdf

Rasool, H., Maqbool, S., & Tarique, M. (2021). The relationship between tourism and economic growth among BRICS countries: A panel cointegration analysis. *Future Business Journal*, 7(1), 1. Advance online publication. DOI: 10.1186/s43093-020-00048-3

Rayhan, A. (2023). *AI and the environment: Toward sustainable development and conservation.* ResearchGate. DOI: 10.13140/RG.2.2.12024.42245

Reed, M. S., & Fazey, I. (2021). Impact Culture : Transforming How Universities Tackle Twenty First Century Challenges. *Frontiers in Sustainability*, 2, 662296. DOI: 10.3389/frsus.2021.662296

Reichenberger, I. (2017). C2C value co-creation through social interactions in tourism. *International Journal of Tourism Research*, 19(6), 629–638. DOI: 10.1002/jtr.2135

Renganathan, V., & Upadhya, A. (2021). Dubai Restaurants: A Sentiment Analysis of Tourist Reviews. *ProQuest*. https://www.proquest.com/docview/2627538050?sourcetype=Scholarly%20Journals

Rezapour, M. (2024). Emotion Detection with Transformers: A Comparative Study. ArXiv.org. https://arxiv.org/abs/2403.15454

Rickly, J. M., & McCabe, S. (2017). Authenticity for tourism design and experience. *Design Science in tourism: Foundations of destination management*, 55-68.

Robinson, R. N., Martins, A., Solnet, D., & Baum, T. (2019). Sustaining precarity: Critically examining tourism and employment. *Journal of Sustainable Tourism*, 27(7), 1008–1025. DOI: 10.1080/09669582.2018.1538230

Rodriguez, A., Negro, J. J., Mulero, M., Rodriguez, C., Hermandez-Pliego, J., & Bustamante, J. (2012). The eye in the sky: Combined use of unmanned aerial systems and GPS data loggers for ecological research and conservation of small birds. *PLoS One*, 7(12), e50336. Advance online publication. DOI: 10.1371/journal.pone.0050336 PMID: 23239979

Rokade, P. P., & D, A. K. (2019). Business intelligence analytics using sentiment analysis-a survey. *International Journal of Electrical and Computer Engineering (IJECE)*, 9(1), 613–620. https://ijece.iaescore.com/index.php/IJECE/article/view/10540/11092

Rosa-Jiménez, C., Reyes-Corredera, S., & Nogueira-Bernárdez, B. (2016). New possibilities of GIS for mapping a mature destination: A case in Benalmádena, Spain. *Anatolia*, 27(1), 82–90. Advance online publication. DOI: 10.1080/13032917.2015.1083211

Rosni, N. A., & Zainol, R. (2022). Transformative impact of covid 19 pandemic on the urban public spaces. *Planning Malaysia*, 20. Advance online publication. DOI: 10.21837/pm.v20i24.1205

Ruan, L., Long, Y., Zhang, L., & Lv, G. (2021). A platform and its applied modes for geography fieldwork in higher education based on location services. *ISPRS International Journal of Geo-Information*, 10(4), 225. Advance online publication. DOI: 10.3390/ijgi10040225

Ruel, H., & Njoku, E. (2021). AI redefining the hospitality industry. *Journal of Tourism Futures*, 7(1), 53–66. DOI: 10.1108/JTF-03-2020-0032

Sachan, P., Yadav, K. A., Pandey, S., Agrawal, S., & Singh, V. (2023). The role of artificial intelligence in environmental monitoring and conservation. *International Journal of Advanced Research in Science. Tongxin Jishu*, 3(2), 106–112. https://ijarsct.co.in/A13017.pdf

Sahar, S. N., & Dar, H. (2024). Artificial Intelligence-Enhanced Global Healthcare: The Future of Medical Tourism. In *Impact of AI and Robotics on the Medical Tourism Industry* (pp. 194-216). IGI Global.

Saiwa. (2023, December 10). *AI in wildlife conservation: A comprehensive overview*. https://saiwa.ai/blog/ai-in-wildlife-conservation/

Saleem, M., Shah, M. J., Wajid, M., Akhter, M., & Malik, J. A. (2024). A Comprehensive Study of AI and IoT's Impact on Smart Tourism Destinations. *Journal of Computing & Biomedical Informatics*.

Samala, N., Katkam, B. S., Bellamkonda, R. S., & Rodriguez, R. V. (2020). Impact of AI and robotics in the tourism sector : A critical insight. *Journal of Tourism Futures*, 8(1), 73–87. DOI: 10.1108/JTF-07-2019-0065

Samancioglu, N. (2022). *Smart Building and Campus Framework: A Determination of Smart Campus Parameters to Predict Potential Smartness of University Campuses* [PhD Thesis, Universidad Politécnica de Madrid]. DOI: 10.20868/UPM.thesis.70353

Šandor, D., & Bagić Babac, M. (2024). Sarcasm detection in online comments using machine learning. *Information Discovery and Delivery*, 52(2), 213–226. DOI: 10.1108/IDD-01-2023-0002

Saraswathi, N., Sasi Rooba, T., & Chakaravarthi, S. (2023). Improving the accuracy of sentiment analysis using a linguistic rule-based feature selection method in tourism reviews. *Measurement. Sensors*, 29, 100888. DOI: 10.1016/j.measen.2023.100888

Sarial-Abi, G., Merdin-Uygur, E., & Gürhan-Canli, Z. (2020). Responses to replica (vs. genuine) touristic experiences. *Annals of Tourism Research*, 83, 102927. DOI: 10.1016/j.annals.2020.102927

Sarkar, D., & Anderson, J. T. (2022). Corporate editors in OpenStreetMap: Investigating co-editing patterns. *Transactions in GIS*, 26(4), 1879–1897. Advance online publication. DOI: 10.1111/tgis.12910

Saydam, M. B., Arici, H. E., & Koseoglu, M. A. (2022). How does the tourism and hospitality industry use artificial intelligence? A review of empirical studies and future research agenda. *Journal of Hospitality Marketing & Management*, 31(8), 908–936. DOI: 10.1080/19368623.2022.2118923

Schäfer & Kaya. (2024). Sailing Through Themes: A Cruise Tourist's Perspective: A Qualitative Study on the Impact of Themed Cruisescapes on Tourist Experiences. *Springer Texts in Business and Economics*.

Schein, E. H. (2010). *Organizational Culture and Leadership*. John Wiley & Sons.

Scheyvens, R., & Biddulph, R. (2018). Inclusive tourism development. *Tourism Geographies*, 20(4), 589–609. DOI: 10.1080/14616688.2017.1381985

Schmitt, B. (1999). Experiential Marketing. *Journal of Marketing Management*, 15(1-3), 53–67. DOI: 10.1362/026725799784870496

Schneider, J., Abraham, R., Meske, C., & Vom Brocke, J. (2023). Artificial Intelligence Governance For Businesses. *Information Systems Management*, 40(3), 229–249. DOI: 10.1080/10580530.2022.2085825

Schuster, R., Buxton, R., Hanson, J. O., Binley, A. D., Pittman, J., Tulloch, V., La Sorte, F. A., Roehrdanz, P. R., Verburg, P. H., Rodewald, A. D., Wilson, S., Possingham, H. P., & Bennett, J. R. (2023). Protected area planning to conserve biodiversity in an uncertain future. *Conservation Biology*, 37(3), e14048. DOI: 10.1111/cobi.14048 PMID: 36661081

Sebo, J. (2022). *Saving animals, saving ourselves: Why animals matter for pandemics, climate change, and other catastrophes*. Oxford University Press. DOI: 10.1093/oso/9780190861018.001.0001

Senecal, S., & Nantel, J. (2004). The influence of online product recommendations on consumers' online choices. *Journal of Retailing*, 80(2), 159–169. DOI: 10.1016/j.jretai.2004.04.001

Serhat, G., & Uzuncan, B. (2021). Impossibility of authentic experience? The existential estrangement which turns to performance. *Journal of Tourism and Cultural Change*, 19(5), 681–695. DOI: 10.1080/14766825.2020.1748637

Shah, D., & Murthi, B. P. S. (2021). Marketing in a data-driven digital world : Implications for the role and scope of marketing. *Journal of Business Research*, 125, 772–779. DOI: 10.1016/j.jbusres.2020.06.062

Shamseer, L., Moher, D., Clarke, M., Ghersi, D., Liberati, A., Petticrew, M., Shekelle, P., Stewart, L. A., & the PRISMA-P Group. (2015). Preferred reporting items for systematic review and meta-analysis protocols (PRISMA-P) 2015 : Elaboration and explanation. *BMJ*, 349(1), g7647-g7647. DOI: 10.1136/bmj.g7647

Sharma, A., Sharma, S., & Chaudhary, M. (2020). Are small travel agencies ready for digital marketing? Views of travel agency managers. *Tourism Management*, 79, 104078. DOI: 10.1016/j.tourman.2020.104078

Sharp, J. (2023, November 11). *The role of AI in wildlife conservation*. West Tech Fest Blog. https://westtechfest.com/the-role-of-ai-in-wildlife-conservation/

Shin, H. H., Jeong, M., So, K. K. F., & DiPietro, R. (2022). Consumers' experience with hospitality and tourism technologies : Measurement development and validation. *International Journal of Hospitality Management*, 106, 103297. DOI: 10.1016/j.ijhm.2022.103297

Shin, H. H., Shin, S., & Gim, J. (2023). Looking back three decades of hospitality and tourism technology research: A bibliometric approach. *International Journal of Contemporary Hospitality Management*, 35(2), 563–588. DOI: 10.1108/IJCHM-03-2022-0376

Shivaprakash, K. N., Swami, N., Mysorekar, S., Arora, R., Gangadharan, A., Vohra, K., Jadeyegowda, M., & Kiesecker, J. M. (2022). Potential for artificial intelligence (AI) and machine learning (ML) applications in biodiversity conservation, managing forests, and related services in India. *Sustainability (Basel)*, 14(12), 715. Advance online publication. DOI: 10.3390/su14127154

Shmarkov, M. S., Shmarkova, L. I., & Shmarkova, E. A. (2019, May). Digital technologies in the organization and management of tourist organizations. In *1st International Scientific Conference" Modern Management Trends and the Digital Economy: from Regional Development to Global Economic Growth"(MTDE 2019)* (pp. 98-101). Atlantis Press. DOI: 10.2991/mtde-19.2019.18

Simonis, L. (2023). *Customer experiences for senior guests: Challenges and opportunities for the hospitality industry*. DOI: 10.21256/ZHAW-30196

Singh, S., & Singh, J. (2020). Location Driven Edge Assisted Device and Solutions for Intelligent Transportation. In *Fog*. Edge, and Pervasive Computing in Intelligent IoT Driven Applications., DOI: 10.1002/9781119670087.ch7

Singla, S. (2020). AI and IoT in healthcare. *Internet of things use cases for the healthcare industry*, 1-23.

Sinha, R., Hassan, A., & Ghosh, R. K. (2020). Changes in tourism destination promotion with the technological innovation. In *The Emerald handbook of ICT in tourism and hospitality* (pp. 213–228). Emerald Publishing Limited. DOI: 10.1108/978-1-83982-688-720201014

Sirgy, M. J., & Su, C. (2000). Destination image, self-congruity, and travel behavior: Toward an integrative model. *Journal of Travel Research*, 38(4), 340–352. DOI: 10.1177/004728750003800402

Sivasankaran, E. S. (2016). *Impact of culture in human resource management—ProQuest*. https://www.proquest.com/openview/32a26afa2a906de973f07d725586ab43/1?pq-origsite=gscholar&cbl=2030322

Skandrani, H., Touzani, L., & Touzani, M. (2009). *Identification des perceptions et des déterminants de l'image d'une destination touristique: une application de l'approche netnographique*. Revue Marocaine de Recherche en Management et Marketing.

Skift. (2023, September 27). How AI can personalize the travel experience for every guest. [Online], from https://skift.com/insight/new-report-personalizing-the-travel-experience-using-data-and-ai/

Smirnov, A., Kashevnik, A., Mikhailov, S., Shilov, N., Orlova, D., Gusikhin, O., & Martinez, H. (2020). Context-Driven Tourist Trip Planning Support System: An Approach and OpenStreetMap-Based Attraction Database Formation. *Advances in Geographic Information Science*, 1, 139–154. Advance online publication. DOI: 10.1007/978-3-030-31608-2_10

Smith M. K. (2009). Issues in Cultural Tourism Studies. Routledge.

Socher, R., Perelygin, A., Wu, J., Chuang, J., Manning, C. D., Ng, A. Y., & Potts, C. (2013). Recursive deep models for semantic compositionality over a sentiment treebank. *Proceedings of the 2013 Conference on Empirical Methods in Natural Language Processing*, 1631-1642.

Solakis, K., Katsoni, V., Mahmoud, A. B., & Grigoriou, N. (2024). Factors affecting value co-creation through artificial intelligence in tourism: A general literature review. *Journal of Tourism Futures*, 10(1), 116–130. DOI: 10.1108/JTF-06-2021-0157

Sorokina, E., Wang, Y., Fyall, A., Lugosi, P., Torres, E., & Jung, T. (2022). Constructing a smart destination framework: A destination marketing organization perspective. *Journal of Destination Marketing & Management*, 23, 100688. DOI: 10.1016/j.jdmm.2021.100688

Sousa, B. B., Magalhães, F. C., & Soares, D. B. (2021). The Role of Relational Marketing in Specific Contexts of Tourism: A Luxury Hotel Management Perspective. In Rodrigues, P., & Borges, A. P. (Eds.), (pp. 223–243). Advances in Marketing, Customer Relationship Management, and E-Services. IGI Global. DOI: 10.4018/978-1-7998-4369-6.ch011

Souza, V. S., Marques, S. R. B. D. V., & Veríssimo, M. (2020). How can gamification contribute to achieve SDGs? Exploring the opportunities and challenges of ecogamification for tourism. *Journal of Hospitality and Tourism Technology*, 11(2), 255–276. DOI: 10.1108/JHTT-05-2019-0081

Spalević, Ž., Milosavljević, B., & Marković, S. (2024). Legal Basis of Educational Processes of Artificial Intelligence Algorithms in E-tourism. *International Journal of Cognitive Research in Science. Engineering and Education*, 12(1), 209–217.

Sparks, B., Bradley, G., & Jennings, G. (2011). Consumer value and self-image congruency at different stages of timeshare ownership. *Tourism Management*, 32(5), 1176–1185. DOI: 10.1016/j.tourman.2010.10.009

SPER Market Research. (2023, February 15). Online travel booking platform market size to reach usd 1745.94 billion by 2033 at a cagr of 10.01%, from https://www.linkedin.com/pulse/online-travel-booking-platform-market-igraf

Sthapit, E., Björk, P., Coudounaris, D. N., & Stone, M. J. (2022). A new conceptual framework for memorable Airbnb experiences: Guests' perspectives. *International Journal of Culture. International Journal of Culture, Tourism and Hospitality Research*, 16(1), 75–86. DOI: 10.1108/IJCTHR-01-2021-0002

Sthapit, E., Coudounaris, D. N., & Björk, P. (2019). Extending the memorable tourism experience construct: An investigation of memories of local food experiences. *Scandinavian Journal of Hospitality and Tourism*, 19(4-5), 333–353. DOI: 10.1080/15022250.2019.1689530

Štilić, A., Nicić, M., & Puška, A. (2023). Check-in to the future: Exploring the impact of contemporary information technologies and artificial intelligence on the hotel industry. *Turisticko Poslovanje*, 31(31), 5–17. DOI: 10.5937/turpos0-43739

Stone, M., Aravopoulou, E., Ekinci, Y., Evans, G., Hobbs, M., Labib, A., Laughlin, P., Machtynger, J., & Machtynger, L. (2020). Artificial intelligence (AI) in strategic marketing decision-making : A research agenda. *The Bottom Line (New York, N.Y.)*, 33(2), 183–200. DOI: 10.1108/BL-03-2020-0022

Strasser, T., de Kraker, J., & Kemp, R. (2019). Developing the Transformative Capacity of Social Innovation through Learning : A Conceptual Framework and Research Agenda for the Roles of Network Leadership. *Sustainability (Basel)*, 11(5), 5. Advance online publication. DOI: 10.3390/su11051304

Strasser, T., de Kraker, J., & Kemp, R. (2020). Three Dimensions of Transformative Impact and Capacity : A Conceptual Framework Applied in Social Innovation Practice. *Sustainability (Basel)*, 12(11), 11. Advance online publication. DOI: 10.3390/su12114742

Stylos, N., Zwiegelaar, J., & Buhalis, D. (2021). Big data empowered agility for dynamic, volatile, and time-sensitive service industries: The case of tourism sector. *International Journal of Contemporary Hospitality Management*, 33(3), 1015–1036. DOI: 10.1108/IJCHM-07-2020-0644

Sugai, L. S. M., Silva, T. S. F., Ribeiro, J. W.Jr, & Llusia, D. (2019). Terrestrial passive acoustic monitoring: Review and perspectives. *Bioscience*, 69(1), 15–25. DOI: 10.1093/biosci/biy147

Su, H.-N., & Lee, P.-C. (2010). Mapping knowledge structure by keyword co-occurrence: A first look at journal papers in Technology Foresight. *Scientometrics*, 85(1), 65–79. DOI: 10.1007/s11192-010-0259-8

Sunny, S., Patrick, L., & Rob, L. (2019). Impact of cultural values on technology acceptance and technology readiness. *International Journal of Hospitality Management*, 77, 89–96. DOI: 10.1016/j.ijhm.2018.06.017

Sustacha, I., Banos-Pino, J. F., & Del Valle, E. (2023). The role of technology in enhancing the tourism experience in smart destinations: A meta-analysis. *Journal of Destination Marketing & Management*, 30, 100817. DOI: 10.1016/j.jdmm.2023.100817

Talukder, M. B. (2024). Implementing Artificial Intelligence and Virtual Experiences in Hospitality. In *Innovative Technologies for Increasing Service Productivity* (pp. 145–160). IGI Global. DOI: 10.4018/979-8-3693-2019-8.ch009

Talukder, M. B., & Das, I. R. (2024). The Technology Impacts and AI Solutions in Hospitality. I-manager's Journal on Artificial Intelligence &. *Machine Learning*, 2(1), 56–72. DOI: 10.26634/jaim.2.1.20291

Talukder, M. B., & Hossain, M. M. (2021). Prospects of Future Tourism in Bangladesh: An Evaluative Study. I-Manager's. *Journal of Management*, 15(4), 1–8. DOI: 10.26634/jmgt.15.4.17495

Talukder, M. B., & Kumar, S. (2024). The Development of ChatGPT and Its Implications for the Future of Customer Service in the Hospitality Industry. In Derbali, A. (Ed.), *Blockchain Applications for Smart Contract Technologies* (pp. 100–126). IGI Global. DOI: 10.4018/979-8-3693-1511-8.ch005

Talukder, M. B., Kumar, S., & Das, I. R. (2024). Mindful Consumers and New Marketing Strategies for the Restaurant Business: Evidence of Bangladesh. In Ramos, C., Costa, T., Severino, F., & Calisto, M. (Eds.), *Social Media Strategies for Tourism Interactivity* (pp. 240–260). IGI Global. DOI: 10.4018/979-8-3693-0960-5.ch010

Talukder, M. B., & Muhsina, K. (2024). Prospect of Smart Tourism Destination in Bangladesh. In Correia, R., Martins, M., & Fontes, R. (Eds.), *AI Innovations for Travel and Tourism* (pp. 163–179). IGI Global. DOI: 10.4018/979-8-3693-2137-9.ch009

Tang, J. (2016), *Comment définir sa stratégie digitale?* http://www.jacques-tang.fr/comment-mettre-en-place-sa-strategie-digitale

Taylor, P., Davies, L. E., Wells, P., Gilbertson, J., & Tayleur, W. (2015). *A review of the Social Impacts of Culture and Sport*.

Technavio. (2023, November 16). Indian travel and tourism market 2024-2028: growth, trends, covid-19 impact, and forecasts.

Teemu, M., & Elisa, L. (2024). Navigating new horizons—How AI will transform the tourism industry. *Global Journal of Tourism, Leisure and Hospitality Management, 1*(4), 1–3. https://juniperpublishers.com/gjtlh/pdf/GJTLH.MS.ID.555570.pdf

Tham, A., Croy, G., & Mair, J. (2013). Social media in destination choice: Distinctive electronic word-of-mouth dimensions. *Journal of Travel & Tourism Marketing, 30*(1-2), 144–155. DOI: 10.1080/10548408.2013.751272

Theofanous, G., Thrassou, A., & Uzunboylu, N. (2024). Digital Inclusivity: Advancing Accessible Tourism via Sustainable E-Commerce and Marketing Strategies. *Sustainability (Basel), 16*(4), 1680. DOI: 10.3390/su16041680

Tiberghien, G., Bremner, H., & Milne, S. (2017). Performance and visitors' perception of authenticity in eco-cultural tourism. *Tourism Geographies, 19*(2), 287–300. DOI: 10.1080/14616688.2017.1285958

Tiberghien, G., Bremner, H., & Milne, S. (2020). Authenticity and disorientation in the tourism experience. *Journal of Outdoor Recreation and Tourism, 30*, 100283. DOI: 10.1016/j.jort.2020.100283

Tlili, A., Altinay, F., Altinay, Z., & Zhang, Y. (2021). Envisioning the future of technology integration for accessible hospitality and tourism. *International Journal of Contemporary Hospitality Management, 33*(12), 4460–4482. DOI: 10.1108/IJCHM-03-2021-0321

Tong, S., Luo, X., & Xu, B. (2020). Personalized mobile marketing strategies. *Journal of the Academy of Marketing Science, 48*(2), 64–78. DOI: 10.1007/s11747-019-00693-3

Torabi, Z. A., Shalbafian, A. A., Allam, Z., Ghaderi, Z., Murgante, B., & Khavarian-Garmsir, A. R. (2022). Enhancing memorable experiences, tourist satisfaction, and revisit intention through smart tourism technologies. *Sustainability (Basel), 14*(5), 2721. DOI: 10.3390/su14052721

Tracey, B., & Swart, M. P. (2020). Training and development research in tourism and hospitality: A perspective paper. *Tourism Review, 75*(1), 256–259. DOI: 10.1108/TR-06-2019-0206

Trave, C., Brunnschweiler, J., Sheaves, M., Diedrich, A., & Barnett, A. (2017). Are we killing them with kindness? Evaluation of sustainable marine wildlife tourism. *Biological Conservation, 209*, 211–222. DOI: 10.1016/j.biocon.2017.02.020

Travel + Leisure. (2023, August 11). How AI is transforming travel personalization. [Online], from https://blog.operasolutions.com/ai-is-reimagining-travel-personalisation

Troisi, O., Visvizi, A., & Grimaldi, M. (2023). Digitalizing business models in hospitality ecosystems: Toward data-driven innovation. *European Journal of Innovation Management*, 26(7), 242–277. DOI: 10.1108/EJIM-09-2022-0540

Tuia, D., Kellenberger, B., Beery, S., Costelloe, B. R., Zuffi, S., Risse, B., Mathis, A., Mathis, M. W., van Langevelde, F., Burghardt, T., Kays, R., Klinck, H., Wikelski, M., Couzin, I. D., van Horn, G., Crofoot, M. C., Stewart, C. V., & Berger-Wolf, T. (2022). Perspectives in machine learning for wildlife conservation. *Nature Communications*, 13(1), 792. Advance online publication. DOI: 10.1038/s41467-022-27980-y PMID: 35140206

Tung, V. W. S., & Law, R. (2017). The potential for tourism and hospitality experience research in human-robot interactions. *International Journal of Contemporary Hospitality Management*, 29(10), 2498–2513. DOI: 10.1108/IJCHM-09-2016-0520

Turney, P. D. (2002). Thumbs up or thumbs down?: Semantic orientation applied to unsupervised classification of reviews. *Proceedings of the 40th Annual Meeting of the Association for Computational Linguistics*, 417-424. DOI: 10.3115/1073083.1073153

Tussyadiah, I., & Zach, F. (2013). Social media strategy and capacity for consumer co-creation among destination marketing organizations. In Information and Communication Technologies in Tourism 2013: Proceedings of the International Conference in Innsbruck, Austria, January 22-25, 2013 (pp. 242-253). Springer Berlin Heidelberg. DOI: 10.1007/978-3-642-36309-2_21

Tussyadiah, I., Li, S., & Miller, G. (2019). Privacy protection in tourism: Where we are and where we should be heading for. In *Information and Communication Technologies in Tourism 2019: Proceedings of the International Conference in Nicosia, Cyprus, January 30–February 1, 2019* (pp. 278-290). Springer International Publishing.

Tussyadiah, I. (2020). A review of research into automation in tourism : Launching the Annals of Tourism Research Curated Collection on Artificial Intelligence and Robotics in Tourism. *Annals of Tourism Research*, 81, 102883. DOI: 10.1016/j.annals.2020.102883

Tussyadiah, I. P., Zach, F. J., & Wang, J. (2020). Do travelers trust intelligent service robots? *Annals of Tourism Research*, 81, 102886. Advance online publication. DOI: 10.1016/j.annals.2020.102886

U.S. Centers for Disease Control and Prevention. (n.d.). *One Health*. https://www.cdc.gov/one-health/index.html

Ullah, S. (2024). A multimodal approach to cross-lingual sentiment analysis with ensemble of transformer and LLM. *Scientific Reports*, 14(1), 9603. Advance online publication. DOI: 10.1038/s41598-024-60210-7 PMID: 38671064

UNWTO & UNEP. (2020). *Making tourism green: A guide for public policy makers*. World Tourism Organization and United Nations Environment Programme.

Urry, J., & Larsen, J. (2011). The tourist gaze 3.0.

van Esch, P., Cui, Y., Das, G., Jain, S. P., & Wirtz, J. (2022). Tourists and AI: A political ideology perspective. *Annals of Tourism Research*, 97, 103471. DOI: 10.1016/j.annals.2022.103471

Vargo, S. L., & Lusch, R. F. (2004). Evolving to a new dominant logic for marketing. *Journal of Marketing*, 68(1), 1–17. DOI: 10.1509/jmkg.68.1.1.24036

Verhoef, P. C., Hoekstra, R. J., & Bruinsma, M. (2019). Artificial intelligence: An engine for customer experience transformation in travel and hospitality. *Journal of Travel Research*, 58(8), 1478–1489.

Verma, S., Warrier, L., Bolia, B., & Mehta, S. (2022). Past, present, and future of virtual tourism-a literature review. *International Journal of Information Management Data Insights*, 2(2), 100085. DOI: 10.1016/j.jjimei.2022.100085

Vetrivel, S. C., Sowmiya, K. C., Gomathi, T., & Arun, V. P. (2024b). Engaging Online Classes Through Gamification: Leveraging Innovative Tools and Technologies. In R. Bansal, A. Chakir, A. HafazNgah, F. Rabby, & A. Jain (Eds.), AI Algorithms and ChatGPT for Student Engagement in Online Learning (pp. 171-191). IGI Global. DOI: 10.4018/979-8-3693-4268-8.ch012

Vetrivel, S. C., Sowmiya, K. C., & Sabareeshwari, V. (2024a). Digital Twins: Revolutionizing Business in the Age of AI. In Ponnusamy, S., Assaf, M., Antari, J., Singh, S., & Kalyanaraman, S. (Eds.), *Harnessing AI and Digital Twin Technologies in Businesses* (pp. 111–131). IGI Global. DOI: 10.4018/979-8-3693-3234-4.ch009

Vlami, A. (2023). Correction to: Developments and Challenges in the Greek Hospitality Sector for Economic Tourism Growth: The Case of Boutique Hotels. In Balsalobre-Lorente, D., Driha, O. M., & Shahbaz, M. (Eds.), *Strategies in Sustainable Tourism, Economic Growth and Clean Energy* (pp. C1–C1). Springer International Publishing. DOI: 10.1007/978-3-030-59675-0_15

Von Durckheim, K. E. M. (2017). *The use of mobile technologies in the South African private wildlife sector* [Master's thesis, Stellenbosch University]. ResearchGate. https://www.researchgate.net/profile/Katharina-Em-Von-Durckheim/publication/364657841_THE_USE_OF_MOBILE_TECHNOLOGIES_IN_THE_SOUTH_AFRICAN_PRIVATE_WILDLIFE_SECTOR/links/6356431612cbac6a3eee3a84/THE-USE-OF-MOBILE-TECHNOLOGIES-IN-THE-SOUTH-AFRICAN-PRIVATE-WILDLIFE-SECTOR.pdf

Von Gönner, J., Herrmann, T. M., Bruckermann, T., Eichinger, M., Hecker, S., Klan, F., Lorke, J., Richter, A., Sturm, U., Voigt-Heucke, S., Brink, W., Liedtke, C., Premke-Kraus, M., Altmann, C., Bauhus, W., Bengtsson, L., Büermann, A., Dietrich, P., Dörler, D., & Bonn, A. (2023). Citizen science's transformative impact on science, citizen empowerment and socio-political processes. *Socio-Ecological Practice Research*, 5(1), 11–33. DOI: 10.1007/s42532-022-00136-4

Vu, H. Q., Law, R., & Li, G. (2019). Breach of traveller privacy in location-based social media. *Current Issues in Tourism*, 22(15), 1825–1840. DOI: 10.1080/13683500.2018.1553151

Vuscan, S., & Muntean, R. (2023). Multifunctional Homes: A Sustainable Answer to the Challenges of the Future. *Sustainability (Basel)*, 15(7), 5624. DOI: 10.3390/su15075624

Waddell, S., Waddock, S., Cornell, S., Dentoni, D., McLachlan, M., & Meszoely, G. (2015). Large Systems Change : An Emerging Field of Transformation and Transitions. *Journal of Corporate Citizenship*, 2015(58), 5–30. DOI: 10.9774/GLEAF.4700.2015.ju.00003

Wahyuningtyas, N., Yaniafari, R. P., Ratnawati, N., Megasari, R., Aini, D. N., Dewi, K., & Rosita, F. A. D. (2022). Development e-tourism as an effort to support tourism charm programme in Indonesia. *Geo Journal of Tourism and Geosites*, 42(2 supplement), 759–766. Advance online publication. DOI: 10.30892/gtg.422spl15-886

Walther, J. B. (1996). Computer-mediated communication: Impersonal, interpersonal, and hyperpersonal interaction. *Communication Research*, 23(1), 3–43. DOI: 10.1177/009365096023001001

Wang, M.-R., & Chen, C.-L. (2024). Exploring the Value Co-Creation of Cultural Creative Hotels: From the Perspective of Social Innovation. *Sustainability (Basel)*, 16(11), 4510. DOI: 10.3390/su16114510

Wang, X. (2022). Artificial Intelligence in the Protection and Inheritance of Cultural Landscape Heritage in Traditional Village. *Scientific Programming*, 2022, 1–11. Advance online publication. DOI: 10.1155/2022/9117981

Wang, X., Li, X., Zhen, F., & Zhang, J. H. (2016). How smart is your tourist attraction?: Measuring tourist preferences of smart tourism attractions via a FCEM-AHP and IPA approach. *Tourism Management*, 54, 309–320. DOI: 10.1016/j.tourman.2015.12.003

Wang, Y., Li, J., & Wang, Y. (2020). A framework for privacy protection in AI-powered tourism. *Sustainability (Switzerland)*, 12(13), 5458.

Wang, Y., So, K. K. F., & Sparks, B. A. (2016). Technology Readiness and Customer Satisfaction with Travel Technologies : A Cross-Country Investigation. *Journal of Travel Research*, 56(5), 563–577. DOI: 10.1177/0047287516657891

Wankhade, M., Rao, A. C. S., & Kulkarni, C. (2022). A survey on sentiment analysis methods, applications, and challenges. *Artificial Intelligence Review*, 55(55), 5731–5780. Advance online publication. DOI: 10.1007/s10462-022-10144-1

Weiss, A. M., Lurie, N. H., & MacInnis, D. J. (2008). Listening to strangers: Whose responses are valuable, how valuable are they, and why? *JMR, Journal of Marketing Research*, 45(4), 425–436. DOI: 10.1509/jmkr.45.4.425

Wider, W., Gao, Y., Chan, C. K., Lin, J., Li, J., Tanucan, J. C. M., & Fauzi, M. A. (2023). Unveiling trends in digital tourism research: A bibliometric analysis of co-citation and co- word analysis. *Environmental and Sustainability Indicators*, 20, 100308. DOI: 10.1016/j.indic.2023.100308

Wigboldus, S., Brouwers, J., & Snel, H. (2020). How a Strategic Scoping Canvas Can Facilitate Collaboration between Partners in Sustainability Transitions. *Sustainability (Basel)*, 12(1), 1. Advance online publication. DOI: 10.3390/su12010168

Wilson, T., Wiebe, J., & Hoffmann, P. (2009). Recognizing Contextual Polarity: An Exploration of Features for Phrase-Level Sentiment Analysis. *Computational Linguistics*, 35(3), 399–433. DOI: 10.1162/coli.08-012-R1-06-90

Winter, C. (2020). A review of research into animal ethics in tourism: Launching the annals of tourism research curated collection on animal ethics in tourism. *Annals of Tourism Research*, 84, 102989. Advance online publication. DOI: 10.1016/j.annals.2020.102989

Witell, L., Kowalkowski, C., Perks, H., Raddats, C., Schwabe, M., Benedettini, O., & Burton, J. (2020). Characterizing customer experience management in business markets. *Journal of Business Research*, 116, 420–430. DOI: 10.1016/j.jbusres.2019.08.050

Witmer, G. W. (2005). Wildlife population monitoring: Some practical considerations. *Wildlife Research*, 32(3), 259–263. DOI: 10.1071/WR04003

Wohlin, C. (2014). Guidelines for snowballing in systematic literature studies and a replication in software engineering. *Proceedings of the 18th International Conference on Evaluation and Assessment in Software Engineering*, 1-10. DOI: 10.1145/2601248.2601268

World Tourism Organisation. (1998). *Guide for local authorities on developing sustainable tourism*. World Tourism Organisation.

Wozniak, T., Schaffner, D., Stanoevska-Slabeva, K., & Lenz-Kesekamp, V. (2018). Psychological antecedents of mobile consumer behaviour and implications for customer journeys in tourism. *Information Technology & Tourism*, 18(1-4), 85–112. DOI: 10.1007/s40558-017-0101-8

Wu, D., Song, Z., & Guo, H. (2022). Artificial Intelligence Algorithms in Ice and Snow Tourism Promotion from Digital Technology. *Wireless Communications and Mobile Computing*, 2022, 1–9. Advance online publication. DOI: 10.1155/2022/1806611

Wu, Z., Zhang, C., Gu, X., Duporge, I., Hughey, L. F., Stabach, J. A., Skidmore, A. K., Hopcraft, J. G. C., Lee, S. J., Atkinson, P. M., McCauley, D. J., Lamprey, R., Ngene, S., & Wang, T. (2023). Deep learning enables satellite-based monitoring of large populations of terrestrial mammals across heterogeneous landscape. *Nature Communications*, 14(1), 3072. Advance online publication. DOI: 10.1038/s41467-023-38901-y PMID: 37244940

Xiang, Z., Gong, S., & Xu, Y. (2022). A survey of tourism recommendation systems. *Journal of Computational Science*, 18(3), 547–569.

Xiang, Z., & Gretzel, U. (2010). Role of social media in online travel information search. *Tourism Management*, 31(2), 179–188. DOI: 10.1016/j.tourman.2009.02.016

Xiang, Z., Gretzel, U., Gong, S., & Li, J. (2019). Understanding the dark side of personalization in tourism e-commerce: A conceptual framework and research agenda. *Journal of Hospitality and Tourism Technology*, 10(2), 434–452.

Xiao, L., & Li, J. (2020). Artificial intelligence for tourism marketing: A review of the literature and future directions. *Journal of Travel Research*, 59(7), 1459–1480.

Xu, Y., Li, J., Zhao, Y., & Fu, Y. (2023). How can AI benefit tourism: A review and research agenda for responsible development. *Journal of Sustainable Tourism*, 31(2), 437–458.

Yaacoub, J.-P., Noura, H., Salman, O., & Chehab, A. (2020). Security analysis of drones systems: Attacks, limitations, and recommendations. *Internet of Things : Engineering Cyber Physical Human Systems*, 11, 100218. Advance online publication. DOI: 10.1016/j.iot.2020.100218 PMID: 38620271

Yacoub, L., & ElHajjar, S. (2021). How do hotels in developing countries manage the impact of COVID-19? The case of Lebanese hotels. *International Journal of Contemporary Hospitality Management*, 33(3), 929–948. DOI: 10.1108/IJCHM-08-2020-0814

Yamashita, J., Seto, T., Nishimura, Y., & Iwasaki, N. (2019). VGI contributors' awareness of geographic information quality and its effect on data quality: a case study from Japan. *International Journal of Cartography*. DOI: 10.1080/23729333.2019.1613086

Yang, F. X., & Wang, Y. (2023). Rethinking metaverse tourism: A taxonomy and an agenda for future research. *Journal of Hospitality & Tourism Research (Washington, D.C.)*. DOI: 10.1177/10963480231163509

Yang, L., Driscol, J., Sarigai, S., Wu, Q., Chen, H., & Lippitt, C. D. (2022). Google Earth engine and artificial intelligence (AI): A comprehensive review. *Remote Sensing (Basel)*, 14(14), 3253. Advance online publication. DOI: 10.3390/rs14143253

Yin, D., Li, M., & Qiu, H. (2023). Do customers exhibit engagement behaviors in AI environments? The role of psychological benefits and technology readiness. *Tourism Management*, 97, 104745. DOI: 10.1016/j.tourman.2023.104745

Yoo, K. H., Lee, Y., Gretzel, U., & Fesenmaier, D. R. (2009). Trust in travel-related consumer generated media. In *Information and communication technologies in tourism 2009* (pp. 49–59). Springer. DOI: 10.1007/978-3-211-93971-0_5

Zacharopoulou, D., Skopeliti, A., & Nakos, B. (2021). Assessment and visualization of osm consistency for european cities. *ISPRS International Journal of Geo-Information*, 10(6), 361. Advance online publication. DOI: 10.3390/ijgi10060361

Zammar, N. (2012), Réseaux Sociaux numériques: essai de catégorisation et cartographie des controverses. Thèse de doctorat en Sociologie. Université Européenne de Bretagne, Rennes 2, France.

Zarezadeh, Z. Z., Rastegar, R., & Xiang, Z. (2022). Big data analytics and hotel guest experience: A critical analysis of the literature. *International Journal of Contemporary Hospitality Management*, 34(6), 2320–2336. DOI: 10.1108/IJCHM-10-2021-1293

Zelenka, J., Azubuike, T., & Pásková, M. (2021). Trust Model for Online Reviews of Tourism Services and Evaluation of Destinations. *Administrative Sciences*, 11(2), 34. DOI: 10.3390/admsci11020034

Zhang, L., & Sun, Z. (2019). The application of artificial intelligence technology in the tourism industry of Jinan. *Journal of Physics: Conference Series*, 1302(3), 032005. Advance online publication. DOI: 10.1088/1742-6596/1302/3/032005

Zhang, X., Ding, X., & Ma, L. (2022). The influences of information overload and social overload on intention to switch in social media. *Behaviour & Information Technology*, 41(2), 228–241. DOI: 10.1080/0144929X.2020.1800820

Zhang, X., Tavitiyaman, P., & Tsang, W. Y. (2023). Preferences of Technology Amenities, Satisfaction and Behavioral Intention: The Perspective of Hotel Guests in Hong Kong. *Journal of Quality Assurance in Hospitality & Tourism*, 24(5), 545–575. DOI: 10.1080/1528008X.2022.2070817

Zhang, Y., Diao, W., Nie, Y., & Wang, Q. (2024). Design of signage guidance system for tourist attractions based on computer vision technology. *Journal of Computational Methods in Sciences and Engineering*, 24(1), 413–426. DOI: 10.3233/JCM-237032

Zhang, Y., Sotiriadis, M., & Shen, S. (2022). Investigating the impact of smart tourism technologies on tourists' experiences. *Sustainability (Basel)*, 14(5), 3048. DOI: 10.3390/su14053048

Zhao, J., Guo, L., & Li, Y. (2022). Application of Digital Twin Combined with Artificial Intelligence and 5G Technology in the Art Design of Digital Museums. *Wireless Communications and Mobile Computing*, 2022, 1–12. Advance online publication. DOI: 10.1155/2022/8214514

Zheng, Y., & Wu, Y. (2023). An investigation of how perceived smart tourism technologies affect tourists' well-being in marine tourism. *PLoS One*, 18(8), e0290539. DOI: 10.1371/journal.pone.0290539 PMID: 37624780

Zhou, G., Liu, Y., Hu, J., & Cao, X. (2023). The effect of tourist-to-tourist interaction on tourists' behavior : The mediating effects of positive emotions and memorable tourism experiences. *Journal of Hospitality and Tourism Management*, 55, 161–168. DOI: 10.1016/j.jhtm.2023.03.005

Zhou, Q., Wang, S., & Liu, Y. (2022). Exploring the accuracy and completeness patterns of global land-cover/land-use data in OpenStreetMap. *Applied Geography (Sevenoaks, England)*, 145, 102742. Advance online publication. DOI: 10.1016/j.apgeog.2022.102742

Zhou, Q., Zhang, Y., Chang, K., & Brovelli, M. A. (2022). Assessing OSM building completeness for almost 13,000 cities globally. *International Journal of Digital Earth*, 15(1), 2400–2421. Advance online publication. DOI: 10.1080/17538947.2022.2159550

Zhou, T., & Lu, Y. (2011). The effect of interactivity on the flow experience of mobile commerce user. *International Journal of Mobile Communications*, 9(3), 225–242. DOI: 10.1504/IJMC.2011.040604

Zlatanov, S., & Popesku, J. (2019). Current Applications of Artificial Intelligence in Tourism and Hospitality. Proceedings of the International Scientific Conference - Sinteza 2019. DOI: 10.15308/Sinteza-2019-84-90

Zsarnoczky, M. (2017). How does artificial intelligence affect the tourism industry? *Journal of Management*, 31(2), 85–90. https://www.ceeol.com/search/article-detail?id=583144

Zuniga, R. B. (2019). Developing community-based ecotourism in Minalungao National Park. *African Journal of Hospitality, Tourism and Leisure*, 5, 1–10. https://www.ajhtl.com/uploads/7/1/6/3/7163688/article_13_se_gbcss_2019.pdf

Zupic, I., & Čater, T. (2015). Bibliometric methods in management and organization. *Organizational Research Methods*, 18(3), 429–472. DOI: 10.1177/1094428114562629

About the Contributors

Reason Masengu is a highly experienced Senior Lecturer of Business Management at Middle East College in Muscat, Oman, with over 7 years of experience in higher education. He specializes in Global Marketing, Marketing Management, Digital Marketing, and related courses. Dr. Masengu holds a Ph.D. in Business Management (Marketing strategy), North West University, South Africa, a Master of Commerce in Marketing Strategy, Midlands State University, Zimbabwe, and a Bachelor of Technology Hons in International Marketing, Chinhoyi University of Technology, Zimbabwe. He has obtained certifications in marketing, brand strategy, and data analytics from prestigious institutions such as the Chartered Institute of Marketing and Google. Dr. Masengu is a Fellow of the Chartered Institute of Marketing, Certified Practicing Marketer, Australia Marketing Institute and Senior Manager Member -Marketers Association of Zimbabwe. He holds various positions including International Faculty Advisor, reviewer for the IEOM Society, and other international accredited journals. His research interests include digital marketing, financial inclusion, marketing research, business management, sustainable marketing, and technology adoption, logistics and supply chain management. With international exposure in administering research grants, he contributes significantly to the fields of marketing, logistics, and supply management through his dedicated research endeavours in Oman.

* * *

Mourad Aarabe is a PhD student at the National School of Business and Management of Fez, Sidi Mohamed de Ben Abdellah University. His research focuses on tourism, marketing, digital marketing, and management.

Munir Ahmad is a seasoned professional in the realm of Spatial Data Infrastructure (SDI), Geo-Information Productions, Information Systems, and

Information Governance, boasting over 25 years of dedicated experience in the field. With a PhD in Computer Science, Dr. Ahmad's expertise spans Spatial Data Production, Management, Processing, Analysis, Visualization, and Quality Control. Throughout his career, Dr. Ahmad has been deeply involved in the development and deployment of SDI systems specially in the context of Pakistan, leveraging his proficiency in Spatial Database Design, Web, Mobile & Desktop GIS, and Geo Web Services Architecture. His contributions to Volunteered Geographic Information (VGI) and Open Source Geoportal & Metadata Portal have significantly enriched the geospatial community. As a trainer and researcher, Dr. Ahmad has authored over 50 publications, advancing the industry's knowledge base and fostering innovation in Geo-Tech, Data Governance, and Information Infrastructure, and Emerging Technologies. His commitment to Research and Development (R&D) is evident in his role as a dedicated educator and mentor in the field.

Lhoussaine Alla, professor in management sciences at the National School of Applied Sciences, researcher at the LAREMEF laboratory, Sidi Mohamed Ben Abdellah University, Fez, Morocco. Prof. Lhoussaine ALLA has invested more in scientific research in various themes inherent in marketing, finance, entrepreneurship, tourism, logistics. He is also editor of the journal "Management et Alternatives Economiques - AME" (https://revues.imist.ma/index.php/AME). Prof. Lhoussaine ALLA has accumulated as many educational and scientific experiences, which he constantly mobilizes to catalyze a large team of researchers and experts in analysis, reflexivity and application of innovative and intelligent solutions from Data Engineering and AI in various management dimensions. Prof. Lhoussaine ALLA is a co-editor of collective works published by IGI Global: InteIntegrating Intelligence and Sustainability in Supply Chains; Applying Qualitative Research Methods to Science and Management; Using Technology to Manage Territories.

Y. Suresh Babu is working as a Professor in Dept of Computer Science, JKC College, Guntur. He holds a Doctorate in Computer Science & Engineering, Image processing as specialization with a combined experience of 26 years in Academics & Administration. He has published nearly 45 research papers in various National and International Journals of reputed.

Nouhaila Ben Khizzou is a PhD student at the National School of Business and Management of Fez, Sidi Mohamed de Ben Abdellah University. His research focuses on tourism, marketing, digital marketing, and management.

Ahmed Benjelloun is a teacher-researcher at the National School of Business and Management of Fez, Sidi Mohamed de Ben Abdellah University.

Badr Bentalha teaches Supply Chain and Operations Management at National School Of Business and Management – Fez, Sidi Mohamed Ben Abdellah University – Morocco. Dr. Bentalha investigates the structural dynamics and control of complex networks, applying his findings to supply chain management, Industry 4.0, risk analysis, and digital supply chains. His work emphasizes the intersection of supply chain management, operations research, industrial engineering, and digital technology. As a professor, he teaches undergraduate, graduate, and, doctoral courses in operations management, supply chain management, logistics, management information systems, and strategic management. Through guest lectures, webinars, and scholarly presentations, he engages students and fosters an active learning environment. Professor Bentalha specializes in supply chain and operations management, operations research, and service management. He is passionate about integrating knowledge across disciplines to solve real-world problems. He has delivered numerous invited plenary talks, keynotes, and panel discussions at conferences and global webinars.

Meryem Bouizgar is a PhD student at the National School of Business and Management, Sidi Mohamed Ben Abdellah University, Fez, Morocco.

Monica Chaudhary is an Associate Professor and Deputy Head of Business School, Melbourne Institute of Technology, Australia. She has PhD in Management (Marketing) and double Masters in Management and Economics with rich experience in Academics, Research, Consulting and Industry. She has authored several refereed research papers in reputed research journals (SSCI, SCOPUS indexed, ABDC listed) with academic citations. She is also Editorial Board Member and Reviewer for leading peer reviewed research journals and conferences. She has chaired many conferences sessions, delivered talks, conducted workshops and is an active researcher. She can be contacted at monicarana@gmail.com.

Mudasir Ahmad Dar is bakery chef by profession. Currently, he is working with Vivanta by Taj hotel, Kashmir-India. He has obtained post graduate degree in hotel management. Besides, keeping he academic passion alive, he is pursuing post graduate degree in tourism management. He is actively involved in research activities for impactful practical research implications.

Uma N. Dulhare is working as a Professor, Department of Computer Science & Engg, MJCET, Banjara Hills, Hyderabad. She has more than 20 years teaching experience. She has published more than 30 research papers in reputed National & International Journals & as a book chapter. She is member of Editorial Board and reviewer of International Journals like IJACEA, ICDIWC and ICEOE, IIE, IJERTREW, IJDMKD, Elsevier Procedia. She was Keynote & Chair Person of

International Congress on Multimedia 2014 [ICMM2014], Bangkok, Kingdom of Thailand & also 5th National Conference on National "Computer Network & Information Security" NCCNIS-2016 Vasavi College, Hyderabad . She is also the member of various professional societies like ISTE, CSTA of ACM,ASDF,IAENG & Fellow member of ISRD. She has also received a Best research paper Award in 2010, ASDF Global Award for Best Computer Science Faculty of the Year 2013 by the Lt. Governor of Pondicherry & also Best Academic Researcher of the year 2015. She honored with Outstanding Educator & Scholar Award 2016 by NEFD. Her area of interest is Networking, Database, Data Mining, Information Retrieval and Neural Networks & Big Data Analytics.

Ushaa Eswaran is an esteemed author, distinguished researcher, and seasoned educator with a remarkable journey spanning over 34 years, dedicated to advancing academia and nurturing the potential of young minds. Currently serving as a Principal and Professor in Andhra Pradesh, India, her vision extends beyond imparting cutting-edge technical expertise to encompass the nurturing of universal human values. With a foundation in Electronics Engineering, Dr. Eswaran delved into the realm of biosensors, carving a pioneering path in nanosensor models, a remarkable achievement that earned her a well-deserved Doctorate. Her insights have been encapsulated in her acclaimed book, "Internet of Things: Future Connected Devices," offering profound insights into the evolving IoT landscape. Her expertise also finds its place in upcoming publications centered around computer vision and IoT technologies. Dr. Eswaran's commitment to literature is rooted in her unwavering passion to equip the younger generation with the latest knowledge fortified by ethical principles. Her book stands as a beacon of practical wisdom, providing a roadmap through the intricate IoT terrain while shedding light on its future societal impacts. Her forthcoming contributions unveil her interdisciplinary perspective, seamlessly integrating electronics, nanotechnology, and computing. Bolstering her scholarly contributions.

Vishal Eswaran is an accomplished Senior Big Data Engineer with an impressive career spanning over 6 years. His fervor for constructing robust data pipelines, unearthing insights from intricate datasets, identifying trends, and predicting future trajectories has fueled his journey. Throughout his tenure, Vishal has lent his expertise to empower numerous prominent US healthcare clients, including CVS Health, Aetna, and Blue Cross and Blue Shield of North Carolina, with informed business decisions drawn from expansive datasets. Vishal's ability to distill intricate data into comprehensive documents and reports stands as a testament to his proficiency in managing multifaceted internal and external data analysis responsibilities. His aptitude for synthesizing complex information ensures that insights are both accessible and impactful for strategic decision-making. Moreover, Vishal's distinction extends to his role as a co-author of the book "Internet of Things - Future Connected Devices." This book not only underscores his prowess in the field but also showcases his visionary leadership in the realm of Internet of Things (IoT). His insights resonate with a forward-looking perspective, emphasizing the convergence of technology and human life. As the author of "Secure Connections: Safeguarding the Internet of Things (IoT) with Cybersecurity," Vishal Eswaran's reputation as a thought leader is further solidified. His work is a manifestation of his commitment to ensuring the security of interconnected devices within the IoT landscape, a vital consideration in our digitally driven world. Vishal's dedication to enhancing the safety and integrity of IoT ecosystems shines through in his work.

Vivek Eswaran, with 8 years of experience as a Senior Software Engineer specializing in front-end development, brings a vital perspective to securing the Internet of Things (IoT). At Medallia, Vivek played an instrumental role in crafting engaging user interfaces and optimized digital experiences. This profound expertise in front-end engineering equips them to illuminate the crucial synergy between usability and cybersecurity as IoT adoption accelerates. In the new book "Secure Connections: Safeguarding the Internet of Things with Cybersecurity," Vivek combines their real-world experiences building intuitive and secure software systems with cutting-edge insights into strengthening IoT ecosystems. Drawing parallels between front-end best practices and security imperatives, they offer readers an invaluable guide for fortifying IoT without compromising usability. As businesses and consumers continue rapidly connecting people, processes, and devices, Vivek's contribution provides timely insights. Blending user empathy with security proficiency, Vivek empowers audiences to realize the potential of IoT through resilient and human-centered systems designed for safety without friction.

Suhail Ghouse is an Associate Professor of Marketing and Entrepreneurship at Dhofar University with an experience of more than 15 years in academics, research & industry. His teaching and research interests pertain to consumer behavior and entrepreneurship. Has published in reputed outlets like Int. Journal of Entrepreneurial Behaviour and Research, Journal of Entrepreneurship in Emerging Economies, Young Consumers, Journal of Islamic Marketing, and Int. Journal of Small Business and Entrepreneurship, etc.

Firoj Kabir is a researcher, Lecturer and coordinator of the Department of "Tourism and Hospitality Management" at the Daffodil Institute of IT (DIIT), Dhaka, Bangladesh, with a solid academic background in BBA and MBA majoring in Tourism and Hospitality Management from the University of Dhaka. His passion lies in exploring the intersection of travel and culture. His diverse areas of interest include archaeological tourism, sustainable tourism, and the unique characteristics of Generation Z travelers. Through extensive research and insightful writing, he sheds light on the intricate connections between historical sites, responsible tourism, and the evolving preferences of the next generation of travelers. His work not only enriches the field of tourism but also inspires readers to engage with the world around them in meaningful and responsible ways.

Saifullah Khalid stands as a beacon of innovation and excellence in the domains of Electrical Engineering and Aviation Technology. With a distinguished career that spans over two decades, his contributions have been instrumental in shaping the future of air traffic management and engineering research. His impressive credentials include serving as a Visiting Researcher at Nanyang Technological University, Singapore, and holding a pivotal role as a Senior Manager (ATM) at SGRDJI Airport Amritsar, in addition to his association with the Civil Aviation Research Organization (CARO) in India. Dr. Khalid's academic prowess is underlined by a Doctorate of Philosophy in Electrical Engineering from Dr. APJ Abdul Kalam Technical University, India. His commitment to education and research is further evidenced by his role in nurturing the next generation of engineers and researchers, evidenced by his mentorship of PhD students focusing on cutting-edge technologies in aviation. A testament to his inventive genius, Dr. Khalid has secured 58 patents, showcasing groundbreaking technologies that range from AI-enhanced fault detection systems to innovative solutions in renewable energy.

A. V. Senthil Kumar has industrial experience for five years and teaching experience of 27 years. He has also received his Doctor of Science (D.Sc in Computer Science). He has to his credit 33 Book Chapters, 220 papers in International and National Journals 60 papers in International Conferences in International and National Conferences, and edited 12 books (IGI Global, USA). He is as Associate Editor of IEEE Access. He is an Editor-in-Chief for many journals and Key Member for India, Machine Intelligence Research Lab (MIR Labs). He is an Editorial Board Member and Reviewer for various International Journals. He is also a Committee member for various International Conferences. He is a Life member of International Association of Engineers (IAENG), Systems Society of India (SSI), member of The Indian Science Congress Association, member of Internet Society (ISOC), International Association of Computer Science and Information Technology (IACSIT), Indian Association for Research in Computing Science (IARCS), and committee member for various International Conferences.

Kudzai Masvingise is a dedicated and accomplished PhD candidate in Agricultural Economics with a stellar academic record. With a passion for exploring the intersection of economics and agriculture, Kudzai has demonstrated exceptional academic prowess throughout their studies. Graduating with cum laude for her Honours degree, Kudzai has consistently displayed a strong work ethic, analytical skills, and a commitment to excellence in her research. Her pursuit of a PhD in Agricultural Economics reflects her ambition to contribute valuable insights to the field and make a positive impact on agricultural practices and policies. Kudzai Masvingise is a rising scholar poised to make significant contributions to the academic community and beyond.

Kashif Mehmood Khan earned his B.S. degree in Computer Science from Hamdard University, Karachi, in 2016, and completed his M.S. in Computer Science from Shaheed Zulfikar Ali Bhutto Institute of Science and Technology, Karachi, where he achieved the Chancellor's Honor Roll for highest CGPA. His research interests encompass Computer Vision, Digital Image Processing, Artificial Intelligence, Data Mining, Natural Language Processing, Deep Learning, Machine Learning, Expert Systems and GEO-AI, focusing on digital twins of computer vision, GEO-AI and deep learning real time world problems and applications . Kashif specializes in face detection for security and surveillance systems, crowd counting and density estimation in real-time scenarios such as Hajj and pilgrimages. His undergraduate work in Image Processing, specifically on URDU OCR, stands as a significant contribution to Urdu literature, demonstrating strong technical skills and a solid understanding of these domains. Kashif is motivated by a mission to apply his skills and expertise towards driving digital transformation and growth in society with Next Generation AI.

Nyarai Margaret Mujuru is an esteemed academic and scholar specializing in the fields of Economics and Agricultural Economics. With a strong publication record, Nyarai has established herself as a leading voice in her areas of expertise. Currently serving as a lecturer at the University of Fort Hare, she is dedicated to shaping the minds of future professionals in the field. Nyarai's research focuses on critical areas such as smallholder development, entrepreneurship, food security, and agribusiness, contributing valuable insights to these important fields. Her work is instrumental in advancing knowledge and understanding in the fields of Economics and Agriculture.

VidhyaPriya P. is a dedicated academician with a strong foundation in both computer science and business management. She holds an MBA from Avinashilingam Deemed University, Coimbatore, and earned her Ph.D. from Bharathiar University,

Coimbatore, in 2010. Before transitioning to academia, she gained valuable industry experience working with a textile firm for over three years. In 2000, she joined Kongu Engineering College, where she has since built an illustrious career in research and teaching. With over 24 years of academic experience, Dr. VidhyaPriya's research interests lie in corporate finance, corporate governance, and behavioral finance. She has published 57 research papers in reputed national and international journals, including Scopus-indexed publications. Throughout her career, she has actively engaged with the academic community by attending numerous Faculty Development Programs (FDPs) at leading B-Schools, including IIM Bangalore, IIT Madras, Pondicherry University, and Mangalore University. Dr. VidhyaPriya has also presented papers at 30 national and international conferences and has organized multiple conferences, seminars, FDPs, workshops, and training programs. She has successfully completed two ICSSR-sponsored projects focused on start-up entrepreneurship and the Stand-Up India Scheme for entrepreneurs.

Garima Sahani is a scholar studying at S P Jain School of Global Management, Australia.

Vetrivel S. C. is a faculty member in the Department of Management Studies, Kongu Engineering College (Autonomous), Perundurai, Erode Dt. Having experience in Industry 20 years and Teaching 16 years. Awarded with Doctoral Degree in Management Sciences in Anna University, Chennai. He has organized various workshops and Faculty Development Programmes. He is actively involved in research and consultancy works. He acted as a resource person to FDPs & MDPs to various industries like, SPB ltd, Tamilnadu Police, DIET, Rotary school and many. His areas of interest include Entrepreneurship, Business Law, Marketing and Case writing. Articles published more than 100 International and National Journals. Presented papers in more than 30 National and International conferences including IIM Bangalore, IIM Kozhikode, IIM Kashipur and IIM Indore. He was a Chief Co-ordinator of Entrepreneurship and Management Development Centre (EMDC) of Kongu Engineering College, he was instrumental in organizing various Awareness Camps, FDP, and TEDPs to aspiring entrepreneurs which was funded by NSTEDB – DST/GoI.

Mohammad Badruddoza Talukder is an Associate Professor, College of Tourism and Hospitality Management, IUBAT - International University of Business Agriculture and Technology, Dhaka-1230, Bangladesh. He holds PhD in Hotel Management from Lovely Professional University, India. He has been teaching various courses in the Department of Tourism and Hospitality at various universities in Bangladesh since 2008. His research areas include tourism management, hotel management, hospitality management, food & beverage management, and accommodation management, where he has published research papers in well-known journals in Bangladesh and abroad. Mr. Talukder is one of the executive members of the Tourism Educators Association of Bangladesh. He has led training and consulting for a wide range of hospitality organizations in Bangladesh. He just became an honorary facilitator at the Bangladesh Tourism Board's Bangabandhu international tourism and hospitality training institution.

Arun V. P. is a driven and accomplished professional with a diverse educational background and extensive hands-on experience across various industries. Graduating with honors, Arun earned his Master of Business Administration (M.B.A) with a specialization in Human Resources and Marketing from the renowned Sona School of Management in Salem in 2018, where he excelled academically with an impressive 8.3 Cumulative Grade Point Average (CGPA). Throughout his academic journey, Arun displayed an unwavering commitment to learning and personal growth, actively seeking opportunities to expand his knowledge and skills beyond the confines of traditional education. He sought practical experiences to complement his theoretical understanding, such as a 45-day summer internship focused on conducting a feasibility study for R-Doc Sustainability in the market. Additionally, Arun broadened his horizons through a 7-day industrial visit to Malaysia and Singapore, immersing himself in diverse cultural and professional environments. Arun's academic pursuits were further enriched by his involvement in hands-on projects, including a comprehensive study on Employee Job Satisfaction at Roots Cast Private Limited. His professional trajectory includes serving as a Growth Officer at Parle Agro Private Limited, where he played a crucial role in driving sales growth and market expansion. Arun is a dedicated professional, currently employed at JKKN Engineering College in the Management Studies Department. He holds expertise in his field and has contributed significantly to academia through the publication of two journal articles. Arun's work focuses on advancing knowledge and understanding in management studies, making valuable contributions to the academic community.

Index

A

Accessible Tourism 212, 214
AI 1, 2, 3, 4, 5, 6, 7, 8, 9, 10, 11, 12, 13, 14, 15, 16, 17, 18, 19, 20, 21, 22, 23, 24, 25, 26, 27, 28, 29, 31, 32, 33, 34, 35, 36, 37, 38, 39, 40, 41, 42, 43, 44, 45, 46, 47, 48, 49, 50, 51, 52, 53, 54, 56, 57, 59, 60, 61, 62, 63, 64, 65, 66, 68, 69, 70, 71, 72, 73, 74, 75, 76, 77, 78, 79, 81, 83, 85, 86, 90, 91, 92, 93, 94, 95, 96, 97, 98, 99, 100, 101, 102, 103, 104, 105, 106, 107, 108, 109, 110, 111, 112, 113, 114, 115, 116, 117, 118, 121, 122, 123, 124, 125, 126, 127, 128, 129, 130, 131, 132, 133, 134, 135, 136, 137, 138, 139, 141, 142, 144, 145, 146, 147, 148, 149, 150, 151, 152, 153, 154, 160, 162, 166, 167, 168, 169, 170, 171, 174, 175, 176, 178, 179, 196, 206, 208, 213, 220, 235, 251, 278, 279, 280, 285, 286, 289, 291, 292, 293, 294, 295, 296, 297, 298, 299, 300, 301, 302, 304, 305, 306, 307, 308, 309
Animals 114, 115, 116, 117, 119, 122, 126, 127, 129, 134, 137, 139, 143, 144, 146, 148
Apps 33, 34, 36, 43, 47, 52, 86, 88, 97, 101, 102, 108, 142, 144, 153, 154, 176, 187, 190, 194, 202, 203, 204, 205, 209, 217, 219, 234, 263, 265, 302
Artificial Intelligence 1, 2, 4, 5, 29, 30, 32, 33, 34, 35, 39, 41, 42, 43, 44, 46, 56, 57, 60, 61, 63, 64, 65, 66, 68, 69, 70, 71, 72, 74, 76, 77, 78, 79, 80, 81, 83, 84, 85, 91, 92, 94, 95, 96, 97, 100, 106, 110, 111, 112, 118, 122, 123, 124, 138, 139, 141, 142, 143, 144, 145, 146, 147, 148, 149, 150, 151, 153, 162, 170, 174, 175, 176, 196, 206, 210, 211, 212, 213, 217, 246, 251, 263, 277, 278, 279, 280, 282, 285, 286, 287, 290, 291, 292, 293, 294, 295, 296, 297, 298, 299, 300, 301, 302, 303, 304, 305, 306, 307, 308, 309

B

Behavioral Analysis 295
Bibliometric 4, 118, 121, 135, 138, 139, 148, 210, 213, 214, 249, 303
Brand Loyalty 39, 45, 85, 149, 150, 151, 156, 167, 168, 169, 172

C

Chatbots 1, 3, 5, 6, 14, 18, 20, 29, 32, 33, 34, 35, 38, 39, 42, 45, 46, 50, 51, 52, 61, 69, 73, 85, 86, 91, 97, 102, 128, 132, 153, 167, 170, 280, 286, 291, 292, 293, 294
Co-Creation 5, 30, 81, 138, 211, 253, 255, 257, 259, 260, 261, 262, 263, 264, 265, 266, 269, 270, 271, 272, 273, 274, 275, 291, 309
Co-Creation of Value 211, 255
Crowd Management 10, 14, 27, 83, 85, 86, 87, 88, 89, 90, 91, 92, 93, 94, 95, 96, 97, 100, 102, 103, 104, 105, 106, 107, 108, 109
Customer Experience 3, 39, 40, 43, 44, 56, 57, 60, 64, 84, 85, 98, 152, 176, 202, 203, 204, 212, 217, 218, 256, 259, 272, 278, 280, 281, 291, 295, 301, 307
Customer Satisfaction 6, 26, 62, 85, 93, 99, 149, 150, 151, 166, 169, 170, 218, 280, 294, 295, 296, 307

D

Digital Age 44, 75, 153, 157, 202, 203, 209, 273
Digital Transformation 60, 74, 76, 155, 212, 259, 261, 300

E

Emerging Technologies 3, 28, 33, 60, 173, 278, 282, 291, 297

Engagement 3, 7, 8, 11, 13, 15, 17, 20, 39, 49, 54, 85, 100, 112, 150, 151, 153, 162, 166, 168, 169, 175, 185, 186, 191, 192, 193, 202, 203, 204, 206, 207, 209, 218, 260, 262, 264, 266, 267, 269, 270, 280, 291, 292, 293, 294, 295, 297, 308

Environmental Awareness 138

G

Guest Experience 66, 69, 72, 73, 76, 82, 97, 204

H

Hospitality Industry 59, 60, 62, 63, 68, 69, 73, 74, 77, 79, 80, 81, 98, 111, 150, 151, 174, 279, 291, 293, 294, 295, 305

I

India 1, 31, 60, 83, 119, 135, 142, 146, 149, 150, 151, 154, 164, 169, 174, 175, 176, 181, 201, 303, 309

M

Machine Learning 2, 3, 4, 7, 10, 15, 60, 61, 71, 72, 81, 83, 91, 92, 93, 95, 96, 99, 102, 109, 114, 121, 141, 144, 146, 153, 206, 215, 216, 217, 218, 219, 221, 222, 224, 228, 230, 231, 233, 234, 235, 236, 238, 244, 245, 246, 247, 248, 249, 250, 251, 280, 285

Mapping 113, 117, 118, 120, 138, 140, 144, 146, 181, 182, 183, 184, 185, 186, 187, 189, 191, 192, 194, 195, 197, 198, 199, 300

Marketing 2, 8, 12, 14, 29, 30, 37, 39, 43, 44, 45, 57, 66, 76, 77, 78, 79, 80, 81, 98, 100, 153, 156, 160, 162, 165, 166, 167, 168, 169, 170, 171, 173, 174, 175, 177, 178, 179, 183, 184, 196, 197, 199, 201, 202, 203, 206, 209, 210, 211, 212, 213, 214, 216, 218, 223, 224, 254, 256, 259, 263, 267, 270, 271, 272, 273, 274, 275, 278, 279, 280, 281, 285, 288, 289, 291, 292, 298, 299, 300, 302, 303, 304, 305, 306, 308

O

OpenStreetMap 181, 182, 183, 185, 186, 187, 188, 189, 190, 191, 193, 194, 195, 196, 197, 198, 199

OSM 181, 182, 185, 186, 187, 188, 189, 190, 191, 192, 193, 194, 196, 198, 199

Overtourism 4, 7, 10, 14, 18, 20, 27, 33, 36, 50, 88, 89, 206, 207, 208, 301

P

Personalization 2, 3, 4, 5, 6, 8, 14, 15, 17, 19, 20, 26, 27, 28, 31, 32, 33, 35, 36, 37, 39, 41, 42, 44, 45, 46, 47, 48, 50, 51, 52, 53, 57, 70, 71, 72, 73, 80, 85, 95, 99, 107, 149, 150, 151, 152, 153, 157, 162, 165, 166, 168, 169, 170, 173, 174, 175, 176, 179, 180, 201, 208, 281, 291, 292, 293, 295, 296

Personalized Experiences 23, 26, 28, 32, 35, 39, 45, 52, 70, 150, 151, 154, 166, 168, 208, 263, 265, 269

Personalized Room Management 59, 60, 69, 73, 74

Personalized Travel 3, 6, 26, 33, 34, 35, 46, 98, 159, 280

Predictive Analytics 1, 5, 14, 18, 28, 32, 39, 71, 72, 88, 90, 92, 93, 101, 102, 106, 109, 129, 130, 154

R

Real-Time Data 3, 6, 10, 18, 24, 62, 73, 83, 85, 93, 95, 100, 102, 106, 107, 108, 129, 162, 181, 182, 188, 189, 194

Recommendation Systems 1, 3, 5, 13, 27, 32, 43, 46, 50, 57, 128, 218

Research Trends 115, 118, 222

Responsible Travel 2, 10, 44, 54, 116, 139, 208

Revenue Management 14, 64, 69, 74, 76

S

Satisfaction 1, 3, 6, 7, 8, 9, 10, 11, 12, 13, 14, 15, 17, 18, 23, 26, 27, 59, 61, 62, 66, 69, 73, 76, 80, 82, 85, 91, 93, 95, 98, 99, 100, 101, 107, 117, 128, 149, 150, 151, 153, 155, 156, 162, 165, 166, 167, 168, 169, 170, 172, 173, 176, 177, 191, 214, 217, 218, 223, 224, 245, 256, 258, 259, 266, 271, 280, 282, 286, 291, 293, 294, 295, 296, 305, 307

Science Mapping 113, 117, 118, 140, 144

Sentiment Analysis 14, 23, 215, 216, 217, 218, 219, 220, 221, 222, 223, 224, 225, 226, 228, 229, 230, 231, 232, 233, 234, 235, 236, 237, 245, 246, 247, 248, 249, 250, 251, 252

Serengeti National Park 129

Smart Destination 1, 4, 5, 181, 182, 187, 208, 213

Smart Destinations 4, 175, 181, 182, 187, 189, 191, 194, 211, 214, 265, 306

Smart Tourism 6, 12, 24, 29, 56, 81, 101, 110, 160, 175, 200, 201, 204, 210, 211, 212, 213, 214, 253, 263, 264, 272, 273, 278, 279, 281, 282, 285, 286, 291, 298, 299, 300, 301, 303, 304, 305, 307, 308

Social Media 4, 7, 8, 10, 12, 17, 24, 35, 36, 39, 41, 43, 45, 46, 48, 68, 81, 86, 88, 91, 92, 93, 98, 100, 106, 107, 108, 154, 157, 158, 160, 174, 176, 179, 180, 201, 202, 203, 209, 210, 212, 217, 218, 220, 222, 223, 226, 233, 254, 256, 264, 269, 272, 274, 275, 281, 286, 291

Social Networks 199, 253, 254, 255, 256, 260, 261, 262, 263, 265, 267, 270, 271

South Africa 13, 113, 126, 144

Spatial Data 200

Sub-Saharan Africa 129

Sustainable Tourism 1, 2, 3, 4, 5, 6, 7, 10, 11, 13, 20, 24, 27, 32, 34, 37, 38, 47, 48, 49, 50, 52, 54, 56, 57, 77, 81, 88, 91, 95, 96, 113, 114, 116, 117, 118, 121, 122, 123, 128, 130, 131, 135, 136, 138, 140, 143, 145, 147, 148, 162, 171, 177, 184, 185, 202, 207, 209, 212, 213, 289, 292, 295, 302

T

Technological Advancements 2, 33, 34, 38, 42, 56, 71, 123, 151, 169, 170, 201, 202, 221, 280, 281, 297

Technological Perspectives 253

Tourism 1, 2, 3, 4, 5, 6, 7, 8, 10, 11, 12, 13, 14, 15, 16, 17, 18, 19, 20, 21, 22, 23, 24, 25, 26, 27, 28, 29, 30, 31, 32, 33, 34, 35, 36, 37, 38, 40, 41, 42, 43, 44, 45, 46, 47, 48, 49, 50, 51, 52, 53, 54, 56, 57, 60, 66, 74, 76, 77, 78, 80, 81, 82, 83, 84, 85, 86, 87, 88, 89, 90, 91, 94, 95, 96, 97, 100, 101, 102, 103, 104, 105, 106, 107, 108, 109, 110, 111, 112, 113, 114, 115, 116, 117, 118, 121, 122, 123, 124, 128, 129, 130, 131, 132, 133, 135, 136, 137, 138, 139, 140, 141, 142, 143, 144, 145, 146, 147, 148, 149, 150, 151, 152, 154, 158, 159, 160, 161, 162, 170, 171, 173, 174, 175, 176, 177, 178, 179, 180, 183, 184, 185, 186, 187, 195, 196, 197, 198, 199, 200, 201, 202, 203, 204, 205, 206, 207, 208, 209, 210, 211, 212, 213, 214, 215, 216, 217, 218, 219, 220, 222, 223, 224, 226, 228, 231, 232, 233, 234, 235, 236, 245, 246, 247, 248, 249, 250, 251, 253, 254, 255, 256, 257, 259, 260, 261, 262, 263, 264, 265, 266, 267, 269, 270, 271, 272, 273, 274, 275, 277, 278, 279, 280, 281, 282, 283, 285, 286, 287, 288, 289, 290, 291, 292, 293, 294, 295, 296, 297, 298, 299, 300, 301, 302, 303, 304, 305, 306, 307, 308, 309

Tourism Development 108, 121, 138, 145, 203, 213

Tourism Success 201

Tourism Technology 43, 76, 173, 174, 175, 180, 203, 208, 211, 213, 214, 288, 289, 299, 305

Tourist 1, 2, 3, 4, 7, 8, 10, 12, 13, 14, 18, 27, 28, 30, 33, 34, 35, 36, 37, 42, 43, 47, 54, 76, 77, 85, 86, 87, 88, 89, 90, 91, 95, 96, 100, 101, 102, 103, 104, 105, 108, 109, 117, 131, 132, 155, 156, 158, 161, 162, 173, 176, 179, 183, 184, 188, 191, 198, 199, 200, 204, 205, 206, 207, 208, 209, 210, 211, 212, 213, 214, 216, 218, 219, 222, 223, 224, 225, 230, 231, 232, 233, 234, 235, 242, 245, 246, 247, 249, 250, 251, 253, 257, 258, 260, 261, 263, 264, 265, 268, 270, 273, 274, 275, 278, 279, 280, 281, 282, 285, 286, 287, 289, 290, 292, 294, 295, 297, 302, 304, 305, 307, 308

Tourist Experience 3, 4, 7, 13, 27, 37, 77, 95, 184, 210, 211, 212, 245, 253, 261, 265, 270, 273, 279, 286, 287, 294, 304

Transformation 2, 28, 46, 57, 60, 74, 76, 143, 149, 151, 154, 155, 201, 211, 212, 254, 255, 259, 261, 270, 272, 283, 284, 300, 307

Transformer Based Models 231

Travel 1, 2, 3, 6, 7, 8, 9, 10, 12, 13, 14, 15, 16, 17, 20, 21, 22, 23, 24, 25, 26, 27, 28, 29, 32, 33, 34, 35, 36, 37, 38, 39, 40, 41, 42, 43, 44, 45, 46, 47, 48, 49, 50, 51, 52, 53, 54, 56, 57, 60, 68, 79, 81, 84, 85, 87, 88, 95, 97, 98, 99, 100, 110, 111, 114, 115, 116, 123, 133, 139, 143, 148, 149, 150, 151, 152, 153, 154, 155, 156, 157, 158, 159, 160, 161, 162, 163, 164, 165, 166, 167, 168, 169, 170, 171, 172, 173, 174, 175, 176, 177, 178, 179, 180, 188, 190, 191, 194, 197, 202, 203, 205, 206, 207, 208, 209, 216, 217, 219, 220, 223, 225, 226, 232, 241, 247, 249, 254, 262, 265, 270, 274, 280, 282, 292, 294, 295, 296, 297, 307, 308, 309

V

VGI 198
Vosviewer 113, 118, 122, 145

W

Wildlife Monitoring 115, 116, 124, 125